ALYCE MAHON

Surrealism and the Politics of Eros, 1938–1968

With 180 illustrations in colour and black and white

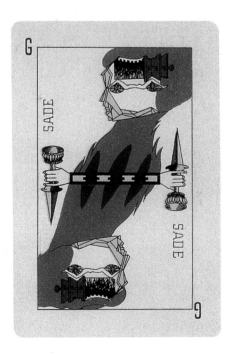

Thames & Hudson

First published in the United Kingdom in 2005 by Thames & Hudson Ltd, 181A High Holborn, London WC1V 7QX

www.thamesandhudson.com

© 2005 Alyce Mahon

British Library Cataloguing-in-Publication Data A catalogue record for this book is available from the British Library

ISBN-13: 978-0-500-23821-9
ISBN-10: 0-500-23821-9

Printed and bound in Singapore by C.S. Graphics

Supported by

Arts & Humanities Research Council

To my parents, Evelyn and Joseph

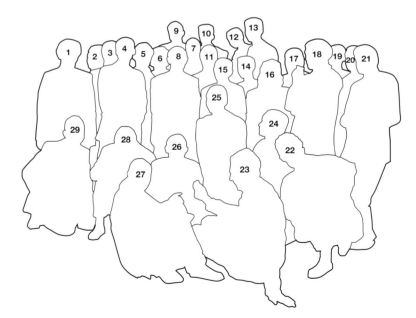

Page 1 **Jean Benoît in costume for *Execution of the Testament of the Marquis de Sade*, Paris, 1959. Photo by Gilles Ehrmann.**

Page 2 **Photograph by Denise Bellon of the organizers of the 'Surrealism in 1947' exhibition at the Galerie Maeght, Paris, 1947. Bellon (1902–99) played a vital role as photographer of the Surrealist group and their international exhibitions from the 1930s until the 1960s. Alongside her Surrealist activities she was also a leading figure in photojournalism as a member of the Alliance photo agency, founded in 1934, and was a contributor to many publications, including *Arts et métiers graphiques, Lilliput, Paris-Magazine, Plaisirs de France* and *Match*.**

Frontispiece key
1 **Maurice Baskine**
2 **Pierre Demarne**
3 **Maurice Henry**
4 **Jerzy Kujawski**
5 **Claude Tarnaud**
6 **Francis Bouvet**
7 **Marcel Jean**
8 **Victor Brauner**
9 **Enrico Donati**
10 **Jacques Kober**
11 **Sarane Alexandrian**
12 **Stanislas Rodanski**
13 **Gaston Criel**
14 **Madame Seigle**
15 **Toyen**
16 **Nora Mitrani**
17 **Hans Bellmer**
18 **André Breton**
19 **Henri Seigle**
20 **Henri Pastoureau**
21 **Gheerbrandt**
22 **Unknown**
23 **Aimé Maeght**
24 **Henri Goetz**
25 **Jacques Hérold**
26 **Jindrich Heisler**
27 **Frederick Kiesler**
28 **Robert Matta**
29 **Frédéric Delanglade**

Page 3 **'Sade' playing card, from the Surrealist *Jeu de Marseille/Marseilles Deck of Cards*, 1940, published in *VVV*, New York, nos 2–3, 1943. The Marquis de Sade was a key figure of sexual and moral revolt for the Surrealists.**

CONTENTS

ACKNOWLEDGMENTS

I am indebted to the many people who have supported and assisted me in my research for this book and in its writing. The book has its origins in my doctoral thesis, awarded by the Courtauld Institute of Art, University of London in 1999, where Sarah Wilson was a wonderfully energetic and sponsoring supervisor, her passion for post-war French art a constant source of inspiration. At Cambridge University I would like to express my appreciation to my colleagues, especially Deborah Howard and Jean Michel Massing, who have been a constant source of support and scholarly advice. I would also to thank David Lomas, Robert Short and Brandon Taylor who have supported my research, and Michèle C. Cone who provided me with insightful feedback and suggestions on the manuscript.

I owe a particular and warmly felt debt of gratitude to those individuals who shared with me their first-hand recollections and/or their personal archives relating to Surrealism and post-war Paris and who welcomed me into their homes: Sarane Alexandrian, Jean Benoît, Christian Descamps, Paul Destribat, Gilles Ehrmann, Ruth Henry, Muguette Hérold, Radovan Ivsic, Pierre and Denise Klossowski, Annie le Brun, Adrian Maeght, Jean-Luc Mercié, Mimi Parent, Jean-Jacques Pauvert, José Pierre, Jean-François Rabain and André Thirion. A very special thanks goes to Jean-Jacques Lebel with whom I have enjoyed many spirited discussions on art and politics since we first met in 1995 and who has been exceptionally generous in sharing his extensive archive and knowledge of Surrealism with me.

In France and in the United States, I have been assisted by many individuals, galleries and institutes in my archival and picture research. At the Musée National d'Art Moderne in Paris, I was assisted by Didier Semin, who directed me to the Victor Brauner archive, and Vivienne Tarenne to the Daniel Cordier archive. I am grateful to Marcel Fleiss of the Galerie 1900–2000 who introduced me to many people when I first began this project, and to Aube Breton Elleouët, Marie-François Lely and Claire Paulhan who kindly authorized my consultation of archival documents at the Bibliothèque Littéraire Jacques Doucet and the Institut Mémoires de l'Edition Contemporaine. In Los Angeles, I thank Marcia Reed and the reference librarians who helped me source archives and photographs at the Getty Research Institute, and I thank Paul Martineau in the Department of Photographs at the J. Paul Getty Museum. Thank you also to Adam Boxer of the Ubu Gallery, New York for his expert help when I was researching Hans Bellmer.

Those institutions who have given financial support to this project must also be sincerely thanked. A Chevening scholarship from the British Council and a British Academy scholarship funded my doctoral research, for which I am most grateful. I thank the Senate House Central Research Fund, the University of Southampton and the British Institute in Paris for awards in support of my primary research in France. I also gratefully acknowledge the generous financial support of the Master and Fellows of Trinity College, Cambridge and of the Arts and Humanities Research Council towards my research in France and the United States and towards the cost of illustrations.

I am grateful to all the team at Thames & Hudson, including Julia MacKenzie for her skilful editing, Katie Morgan for deftly handling the picture research, and Keith Lovegrove for his design expertise.

Finally, I owe a great debt to my family and all my friends for their unstinting support of this project at every stage. Thanks to the Shiel family for their warm support, and to my brother and sister, James and Amy, for providing encouragement and good humour when I needed it most. I thank my parents, Evelyn and Joseph, for showing me the value of art and politics, for their love of intellectual debate, and their moral support throughout. Last but certainly not least thanks to my husband, Mark Shiel for his love and critical opinions, and for keeping it fun.

1 The central grotto of the 'International Surrealist Exhibition', Galerie Beaux-Arts, 140 rue du Faubourg Saint-Honoré, Paris, 17 January– 24 February 1938. Some of the 1200 coal sacks by Marcel Duchamp can be seen suspended from the ceiling as well as an artificial pool, dead leaves, and one of four large beds – intended as a symbol of love. Photo by Denise Bellon.

2 La Main à Plume's *The Conquest of the World by the Image* (*La Conquête du monde par l'image*), incorporating Pablo Picasso's *Head of a Bull* (1942), an object ingeniously fashioned from a bicycle seat and handlebars.

The Politics of Eros: Surrealism in France 1938–1968

'Of Eros and the struggle against Eros!' In its enigmatic form, this
exclamation by Freud happens to obsess me on certain days as only
some poetry can.

André Breton, *L'Amour fou*, 1937[1]

The Surrealist movement in France began with the first Surrealist manifesto of
1924 and its official end was announced by Jean Schuster in *Le Monde* in 1969.[2]
In the intervening forty-five years three key phases in the history of Surrealism
may be identified. Firstly, Surrealism from 1924 to 1938, when a group of young,
anti-bourgeois thinkers radicalized art and literature in their exploration of
automatism, paranoia, hysteria, *amour fou* (mad love) and taboo. Secondly,
Surrealism in exile from 1939 to 1946 when themes of myth, magic and occultism
were pursued, especially in the works of artists such as Jacques Hérold, Wifredo
Lam and Roberto Matta, and when André Breton attempted to retain a group
sensibility in the United States, while a few Surrealists and the neo-Surrealist group
La Main à Plume continued to promote Surrealism in war-torn France [2]. Thirdly,
post-war Surrealism from 1946 to 1969, during which time the Surrealist group
was reinvigorated by a new generation of artists and writers such as Jean Schuster,
Mimi Parent and Jean Benoît [3], organized three major international exhibitions in

Paris devoted to the myth of 'Great Transparent Ones', Eros, and 'Absolute Deviation' (L'Ecart absolu), respectively, and issued thirty-three tracts, many of which directly engaged in national and international politics.

The history of Surrealism has typically been presented in terms of a neat cycle, with the movement emerging out of the ashes of World War I, taking a key role in French culture by the mid-1930s, suffering a gradual decline with the outbreak of World War II, and ultimately dying after the war as new art movements arose, such as Abstract Expressionism in the United States and *Art Informel* in Paris. Indeed, the dominant tendency has been to dismiss Surrealism as an active movement in post-World War II French culture. This dismissal was begun by Maurice Nadeau in his *Histoire du surréalisme*, first published in 1945.[3] To a considerable degree it is an account that has remained uncontested since then, as evidenced by numerous publications, exhibitions and catalogues in English and French. For example, the most recent exhibition devoted specifically to Surrealism, held in the Musée National d'Art Moderne, Paris, entitled 'La Révolution surréaliste' (2002) and curated by Werner Spies, ended Surrealism in 1945.[4] The history of Surrealism still tends to be confined to its canonical inter-war years.

The history of the movement has also been affected by the predominant reading of post-war French culture in general as either promoting a moral, stabilizing art which had no time for the decadent, individualism of Surrealism, or as suffering from what Serge Guilbaut has termed a 'self-satisfied do-nothingism' as it faced the onslaught of American culture and the takeover of modern art from Paris by New York.[5] These readings first arose in the immediate aftermath of the war when many French authors relegated Surrealism to the margins of European culture due to its self-imposed exile from France during the war and the new role of Socialist Realist and Existentialist art in post-war Paris. The cosmopolitan and inclusive nature of Surrealist art (embracing international artists, including young American artists) ostracized it from Communist and Existentialist circles, both of which supported the Soviet Union and rebuked America during these years. René Huyghe's *Les Contemporains* of 1949 argued that Surrealism's place was on the shores of America, not France, stating that the war had simply removed Surrealism from the French artistic scene.[6] Jean Bazaine's *Notes sur la peinture d'aujourd'hui* of 1953 claimed that post-war artistic sensibilities lay in the real, not the 'unreal' (i.e. sur-real) or decadent.[7]

Yet the Surrealists not only contributed to the rise of New York as a cultural centre through exhibiting there in the 1930s and spending the war years there in exile, but the majority of them also chose to return to France after the war and to play a key role in the reconstruction of cultural life in Europe. Post-war, the Surrealists remained key figures in cultural debate and took stands over a number of political events, including the wars in Indochina and Algeria and the revolt of May 1968. Far from signalling the end of Surrealism, World War II led to a philosophical renaissance for Surrealism as it fortified pre-war interests and embraced myth, occultism and Sadean transgression in new ways. Surrealism also attracted a new generation of male and female artists and writers after the war including Jean Benoît, Jean Schuster, Mimi Parent and José Pierre. These younger artists and writers rallied round André Breton and contributed to a number of collective activities – notably the international exhibitions of 1947, 1959 and 1965 and tracts addressing the political situations of Indochina, Hungary, Algeria and Cuba – which demonstrated a renewed aesthetic and political fervour. Accordingly,

3 **The Surrealists at the Désert de Retz, near Saint-Nom-la-Bretéche, April 1960, including, standing, Aube and Elisa Breton (2nd and 4th from left), Georges Goldfayn (6th from left), Toyen (7th from left), Mimi Parent (8th from left), André Breton (9th from left), Edouard Jaguer (3rd from right); sitting, Gérard Legrand (2nd from left), Nicole Espagnol (3rd from left), Alain Joubert (4th from left), Robert Benayoun (6th from left), José Pierre (3rd from right) and Jean Benoît (extreme right). Photo by Denise Bellon.**

4 *Le Pavé* (The Paving Stone), the broadsheet of the Mouvement du 22 mars, which was widely distributed in Paris in May 1968. Its title referred to the paving stones which were used by student protestors as projectiles against the police. Graffiti slogans evoked a sense of the *pavé* as revolutionary symbol, e.g 'Sous les Pavés la Plage' (Under the paving stones, the beach). The cartoon depicts Charles de Gaulle drowning in excrement.

5 Mimi Parent, *Français, Me Voila!* (Frenchman, here I am!), poster, Paris, May 1968. Parent joined the Surrealist movement in 1959 and was among those Surrealists who took part in the events of May 1968. Her poster challenged de Gaulle's military intervention against the students (tanks appeared on the Paris ring roads on 30 May).

it is a major thesis of this book that to neglect the years after the displacement of Surrealism from Paris in 1939 is to deny Surrealism its full history and cultural impact. I contend that it is only by examining the movement's response to the war itself and the post-war world that we may appreciate the evolution of the movement's philosophical and political motivations and aspirations.

For this reason, my analysis focuses on the period of the Surrealists' activities that was for a long time neglected by cultural historians and has only very recently begun to attract significant attention: that is, from 1938, as war loomed, to the events of May 1968, when a different kind of social and political crisis shattered the French and indeed international status quo. I defend Surrealism against the dominant reading of its obsolescence in these years and demonstrate that its artistic practice remained cutting edge while its understanding of art and Eros remained richly philosophical and political. I argue that this was manifest in their major international exhibitions in Paris, held in 1938, 1947, 1959 and 1965 respectively, and that it reached an apotheosis in May 1968 when Eros became a key aspect of the revolt in the streets of Paris. From the 1938 exhibition, when the Surrealists created a microcosm of a Surrealist world of desire where moral and political rhetoric were subverted on a scale never before witnessed in a Surrealist show, to the 1965 exhibition when they continued to marry poetics and politics in a radical fusion of art and theatrical *mise-en-scène*, the Surrealists staged their revolt through erotic desire and an erotic exhibition environment. In 1968, the Surrealists' battle for revolutionary desire was recognized by those students who painted graffiti on the walls of the Sorbonne which echoed Surrealist manifestos: 'The more I make love the more I desire to make a revolution/The more I make a revolution the more I desire to make love.' Situationist and Happening artists seized Breton's appreciation of the city as a locus for the marvellous chance encounter and went further again with that idea by making the city a locus for political *détournement*, appropriating art, words, or mass culture in general, to challenge the status quo and present an oppositional message. The subversive intent of many involved in the events of May 1968 and their graffiti, posters and publications, such as the broadsheet *Le Pavé*, were indebted to the Surrealists' radical fusion of poetry and politics, text and image, to counter-cultural effect [4].

My intention here is not simply to write the history of the second half of the Surrealist movement, but to demonstrate its agency during those years as a cultural weapon of resistance. Surrealism, as a philosophical stance, entailed the rejection of Enlightenment rationalism and its reification of the artist as individual genius, in favour of a universal sensibility. From the start, the Surrealists saw art as a weapon for social and political revolt and voiced their position through it. In addition, their oppositional stance never wavered throughout the history of the movement: in 1924, the Surrealists supported the young anarchist Germaine Berton who had killed an activist of the extreme right nationalist party, L'Action Française [6], while forty-four years later, several Surrealists, including Roberto Matta, Jacques Hérold, Jean Benoît, Mimi Parent and Jean Schuster, participated in the events of May 1968 [5]. The prominent role of dream, myth, primitive cultures, occultism and the concept of dialecticized love and desire in Surrealism all stemmed from this vision of art and faith in its collective potential. Yet it was the attempt to synthesize political activism with the unconscious which alienated Surrealism from party politics, as evidenced by Breton's failed liaison with the Parti Communiste Français (PCF) in 1927 and his allegiance instead to Léon Trotsky.[8] As Breton stated in the pre-war 'Manifesto for

6 *La Révolution surréaliste*, no.1, 1 December 1924. This arrangement of portrait photographs in the first edition of the Surrealist review demonstrated the Surrealists solidarity with Germaine Berton, the young anarchist who, on 22 January 1923, had walked into the office of the extreme right nationalist party L'Action Française and shot Marius Plateau, the head of the Camelots du Roi. The police mug shot of Berton (centre) is counterpointed by the citation of Baudelaire (bottom): 'Woman is the being who projects the greatest shadow or the greatest light into our dreams' (La femme est l'être qui projette la plus grande ombre ou la plus grande lumière dans nos rêves').

La femme est l'être qui projette la plus grande ombre ou la plus grande lumière dans nos rêves.
Ch. B.

an Independent Revolutionary Art', which he drew up with Trotsky (though officially signing it with Diego Rivera) in Mexico in July 1938 on behalf of the Fédération Internationale de l'Art Révolutionnaire Indépendant (FIARI):

> True art is unable not to be revolutionary, not to aspire to a complete and radical reconstruction of society[…]the artist cannot serve the struggle for freedom unless he subjectively assimilates its social content, unless he feels in his very nerves its meaning and dream and freely seeks to give his own inner world incarnation in his art.[9]

In sum, the Surrealists' political stance adhered to the principle of proletarian revolution but insisted that art and literature should be free to adopt an individualized revolutionary poetic in their pursuit of a collective revolt. In so doing, Surrealism remained true to a historical understanding of avant-gardism where art is not subsumed by political propaganda but is part of political action, with the power to transfigure the object world and alter the nature of perception itself.[10] This stance was typical of Western Marxist critical theory and the contemporary writings of authors such as Walter Benjamin, who recognized Surrealism's important role in combating the bourgeois regime on the cultural plane. In a 1929 essay entitled 'Surrealism: The Last Snapshot of the European Intelligentsia', Benjamin wrote that Surrealism's model for praxis was one of translating the experience of 'profane illumination' into political action.[11] He described this strategy of profane illumination as central to Breton's novel *Nadja* (1928), set in Paris, and to Surrealism's general project to 'win the energies of intoxication for the revolution' in all its writings and enterprises.[12] Benjamin explains Surrealism as the energizing of the public in a manner comparable to the experiences of other types of 'illuminati', from the thinker to the opium eater to the dreamer.

As I argue throughout this book, the recourse to 'profane illumination', to borrow Benjamin's words, was a central part of Surrealism's collective psychology and stemmed from a deep interest in, and debt to, psychoanalysis, specifically the writings of Sigmund Freud. Freud offered a whole new visual and theoretical vocabulary to artists. As Lionel Trilling put it:

> Freud discovered in the very organization of the mind those mechanisms by which art makes its effects, such devices as the condensations of meanings and the displacement of accent.[13]

French translations of Freud's writings emerged in the early 1920s and the Surrealists were one of the first groups of writers and artists to recognize the potential of his ideas and to put them into use in their art.[14] Their conception of art itself was indebted to psychoanalysis as evidenced in the first Surrealist manifesto of 1924, where Surrealism was defined in terms of 'psychic automatism in its pure state', based on a belief in the 'omnipotence of dream'.[15]

The Surrealists took up Freud's connection between dream and repressed desire, and his understanding of art as an activity liberated from the reality-principle. Freud recognized that art could make the unconscious conscious, it could liberate repressed instincts and, in the process, it could challenge reason and repression – the pillars of civilization. The Surrealists seized upon this concept of art as a mode of instinctual liberation. In their writing, art, collective games and exhibitions, they pursued the possibility of dream and desire, believing that contact between artists and spectators could lead to the establishment of a collective consciousness. They saw art as 'a developed play' within which the dialectic relationship between art and society, the artist and the spectator could all be teased out.[16] Most importantly, they recognized that this 'play' could lead to the liberation of inhibitions – sexual, social and political. Sexuality was key to Freud's psychoanalytic theory: his investment of dream, hysteria, taboo and neuroses with erotic significance, and his recognition of society's need to curb sexual desire for the sake of 'civilization', fascinated the Surrealists.[17] As Louis Aragon proclaimed in 1930, Freud focused 'the scandalous eyes of sexuality on the incomprehensible'.[18] Accordingly, Freud's understanding of sexuality and eroticism informed the Surrealists' understanding of Eros, the life force, as a philosophical concept concerned with the profound human drive towards creativity and social fulfilment. Eros is also inevitably bound to its counterpart, Thanatos, the destructive, death drive, and to society and its repressive codes of behaviour. At the same time, the Surrealists broke with Freud's insistence on the need to control Eros and instead claimed that it should be deliberately unleashed for subversive, political ends.[19]

In both classical Greek and Christian terms, Eros is understood as a bodily demand akin to enjoyment and at the same time as an excessive desire which goes beyond the sensory and economic aspects of bodily pleasure.[20] However, Freud took these understandings of Eros further, and it is his analysis of Eros that informs Surrealist art. Freud saw Eros as the life drive but also as the force of the pleasure-principle itself. As he explained in his 1923 essay 'The Ego and the Id' (which was translated into French in 1927), the id is the source of Eros and is guided by the pleasure-principle. In Freud's account, the Self is made up of the id, ego and the superego: the id is the source of instinctual sexual impulses and demands the satisfaction of primitive needs, the superego is the conscience and counteracts the id, and the ego stands between the id and the superego, balancing primitive, instinctual needs and moral beliefs and taboos. Freudian Eros is about union between the human ego and the object world, and Freud defends the need to control the id for the good of society and morality. André Breton drew on this essay in the programme issued by the Surrealists in support of Salvador Dalí and Luis Buñuel's film *L'Age d'or* (1930) for its screening at Studio 28 in Paris, and again in his book *L'Amour fou* (1937) in which he admitted to being intrigued by Freud's concept of Eros and 'the struggle against Eros'.[21] He also paraphrased a section of 'The Ego and the Id' in a lecture entitled 'Political Position of Today's Art', which he delivered in Prague on 1 April 1935. Here Breton stated that Surrealism was concerned with 'the id, meaning thereby all the psychic elements in which the ego (which is conscious by definition) is prolonged' and 'the arena of the struggle that brings Eros and the death instinct to grips.'[22] He described the id in feminine, spatial terms: 'the immense and almost virgin territory of the id in all directions.'[23] Three years later, in the 'Manifesto for an Independent Revolutionary Art' (1938), Breton discusses art's role in political revolution in terms of the 'powers of the interior world, the id, which are common to all men' and which, it is asserted, need to be emancipated.[24] Breton's stance on Eros never wavered while he was in exile in the United States during World War II. In an interview in *View* magazine in 1941 he stated that 'we must all learn to read with and look through the eyes of Eros.'[25] And in 1959 he and Marcel Duchamp organized an international Surrealist exhibition at the Galerie Daniel Cordier in Paris specifically dedicated to Eros, as we shall see in Chapter 4 [7].

However, it is my contention in this book that Surrealist art must not only be viewed in terms of Freud's concept of Eros, as the Surrealists rejected society's need to 'civilize' Eros, and that their radical 'politics of Eros', which embraced the power of the id, is the best route to understanding post-war Surrealism, its subversive

7 **The interior of the 1959 EROS exhibition, Galerie Daniel Cordier, 8 rue de Miromesnil, Paris, 15 December 1959 – 29 February 1960. The organization and décor of the gallery space evoked an uncanny and uterine passageway. Photo by Denise Bellon.**

intent and vital role in the culture of that period. I argue that the Surrealist project radicalized the individualism at the heart of Freud's psychoanalysis and his dualism of Eros and Thanatos, to its own political end.[26] The Surrealists seized upon Eros as the pursuit of the pleasure-principle in all its pre-rational, child-like force and as a means of initiating the spectator into a world liberated from the reality-principle. Accordingly, Surrealism is understood in this book as adopting a dialectical approach to man as choosing between internal (life versus death/Eros versus Thanatos) and external (individual versus culture) forces in which the repressive reality-principle can be overthrown by the libertarian pleasure-principle.[27] The book intends not only to account for the Surrealists' obsessive interest in desire and all things erotic, but also to uncover the motivation behind the renewal of that obsession in the post-war years. Therefore, I attempt to show how the Surrealists recognized the potential of Eros as one of man's primary means of unsettling and interrogating reality, of recovering collective psychic forces, and of launching socio-political revolt. The politics of Eros is thus a term I use to express the conjunction of eroticism and politics in Surrealism, specifically the Surrealists' adoption of a Freudian understanding of Eros for a revolutionary end.

In the chapters that follow, I demonstrate how they expressed this politics of Eros through a focus on the sexual, erotic body and its uncanny power in their art and exhibitions. This body takes on many guises or roles: it is 'polymorphously perverse', as Freud describes infantile sexuality; it explores the dangerous slippage between desire and destruction, Sadism and masochism, in keeping with the battle between Eros and Thanatos; it involves a sense of black humour akin to Freud's notion of 'wit' in its attempt to regain 'lost infantile laughter'; and it engages with collective psychology in its exploration of myth, occultism and ritual.[28] Throughout Surrealist art, the represented erotic body provokes self-consciousness on the part of the spectator, often with the aim of inciting instinctual liberation and socio-political subversion. Michel Foucault's analysis of the body as politically and culturally inscribed sheds light on the represented erotic body: 'The body is the inscribed surface of events (traced by language and dissolved by ideas), the locus of a disassociated Self (adopting the illusion of a substantial unity), and a volume in perpetual disintegration.'[29] When faced with the erotic body and corporeal-erotic spaces we are, in effect, faced with a representation of the *body politic.*

In their recourse to Eros and the erotic body the Surrealists exploited the disturbing potential of the *uncanny.* As Freud explained in his 1919 essay 'Das Unheimliche' (The Uncanny), it is a psychic state where reality is made strange through the process of repression and is triggered by something that should have remained hidden but instead is revealed.[30] In spatial terms, the uncanny is often triggered by a sense of fear and alienation in a dwelling or a crowd; it is linked to a fear of castration and the death drive, and by extension to the impossible desire/fear to return to the mother, to the womb, described by Freud as 'a certain lasciviousness – the phantasy, I mean, of intra-uterine existence'.[31] In this way it defies boundaries, signifying at once the familiar and the strange, the maternal (the homeliness of the mother) and the threatening (castration), life (the womb) and death (the tomb). Similarly, Freud explains, while the *heimlich* of *unheimlich* may connote home and the mother, it also evokes their opposites – the notion of the strange and of concealment and the fact that the mother's sex is hidden from sight. There is an element of repression as this homeliness takes on an unfamiliar edge and the mother's sex acts as a brutal reminder of the threat of castration, which is staged in the '*un*', so that the link between the mother and the home is ruptured and she becomes a threat.[32]

Freud also notes in his essay that uncanny has shades of meaning when the German is compared to other languages. In Latin it denotes an uncanny place/locus, in Greek something foreign, and in English something gloomy, dismal, repulsive or haunted. In Spanish and French it conveys a feeling of immense unease – *mal à l'aise*.[33] Clearly the uncanny is not just about the individual subject and his/her experience of the 'return of the repressed', it is also about the collective and historical repressed: how we determine a place, person or thing is different, foreign, a threat to us. As Julia Kristeva words it, Freud 'teaches us to detect foreignness in ourselves'.[34] The uncanny threatens 'the tranquillity of reason itself' and forces us to confront our/the *Other*.[35] I adopt Kristeva's understanding of the Other in this book – the Other is the non-linear, the disruptive, the carnivalesque and the foreign. It is abject, for abjection 'disturbs identity, system, order' and 'does not respect borders, positions, rules'.[36] This sense of Otherness threatens the boundaries of 'normal' existence, psychical dynamics and a person's sense of selfhood.

It is this double-edged nature of the uncanny and its disturbing power that I take in my reading of the Surrealist uncanny. Specifically, the key aspect of Freud's conceptualization of the uncanny that I ask the reader to keep in mind as we follow the history of Surrealism from 1938 to 1968 might be summarized as follows: it challenges the homely, familiar and the sense of security they instil; it evokes the cycle of life (womb to tomb; female sex to threat of castration), especially through the fragmented, castrated or abject body; it is spatially labyrinthine and often disorientating; it is often dark and ghostly; and finally that there is an element of surprise, revelation or exposure in the uncanny, as Freud cites Schelling: 'everything is *unheimlich* that ought to have remained secret and hidden but has come to light.'[37] When we proceed with this concept of the uncanny – as the familiar made strange, as corporeal and feminized, as labyrinthine, as the pleasant, cosy, walled space become gloomy, dismal or even haunted and as the secret revealed – we begin to appreciate the potential of the uncanny for Surrealist expression and socio-political subversion. We also note the spatial, theatrical and sensorial nature of the uncanny.

While the Surrealists did not specifically refer to Freud's essay in their written work, their appreciation of uncanny spaces and the illuminating power of the uncanny permeate their writings, art and philosophical outlook. Breton defines the uncanny in his own style: in *Nadja* he writes of a sense of the uncanny in certain locations in Paris ('In Paris the statue of Etienne Dolet, place Maubert, has always simultaneously attracted me and caused me unbearable discomfort'); in the second manifesto of 1930 he writes of the Surrealist aim to illuminate 'hidden places' and 'forbidden territory'.[38]

Of course, others have already considered the uncanny nature of Surrealist texts and art works: Anthony Vidler has written of the uncanny nature of Surrealist conceptions of architectural space; Margaret Cohen of Breton's fascination with the uncanny effects of Parisian places; Hal Foster of the uncanny nature of Surrealist automatism, and individual Surrealists' fascination with the automaton and erotic masochism; Rosalind Krauss of the uncanny optical unconscious in Surrealist photography.[39] However, the *political* potential and ramifications of the uncanny have yet to be fully addressed.

Both the erotic body and the uncanny are integral to the main focus of my study: the international Surrealist exhibitions in Paris of 1938, 1947, 1959 and 1965. I draw

8 *La Révolution surréaliste*, no.1, 1 December 1924. The front cover of the first edition of the Surrealists' review demonstrates their affinity with the erotic body, especially the female body. Three photographs by Man Ray of members of the 'Bureau de Recherches Surréaliste' are arranged so as to suggest a truncated female form with legs apart. Between the 'legs' of the form the caption reads, 'We must arrive at a new declaration of the rights of man' ('If faut aboutir à une nouvelle déclaration des droits de l'homme').

eroticism and the uncanny together in my assessment of the role of the feminine in Surrealist exhibition practice. Since the Surrealists primarily explored Eros in terms of the female body and uncanny spatial play which exploited the association between the mother/womb and a fear of castration/death, gender politics is central to my argument. For Freud, woman was a 'dark continent', unexplorable and threatening. In his essay on 'Femininity' he asserted that she was a 'riddle' and a 'problem'.[40] Like Eros and the pleasure-principle, woman had to be controlled and repressed for the good of civilization. For the Surrealists, this 'dark continent' had to be explored further: woman was a key agent in defying and subverting civilization. She was the path to the marvellous, the object of desire, the *femme-enfant* (child-woman), and the mythological heroine who could redeem man since she was 'a creature of grace and promise close in her sensibility and behaviour to the two sacred worlds of childhood and madness'.[41] She could bring the redemptive power of Eros into the real world, a move the Surrealists supported through their art. With her infantile, perverse power and her sex that reminded man of life and death simultaneously, she was effectively the embodiment of Eros; her Otherness could confront 'the masculine' world of the ego and thus begin the process of subjective and then collective political consciousness.

The Surrealists' elevation and objectification of woman has often been viewed as romantic or, worse, misogynistic.[42] However, the Surrealists aligned themselves with the feminine from the outset – the cover of the first edition of *La Révolution surréaliste* (1 December 1924) even juxtaposed three photographs of the Surrealists in such a way as to take on the form of a truncated female form with legs apart [8]. At the very 'entrance' to the female sex, that dark labyrinthine world problematized by Freud, we read in capitals: 'We must end up at a new declaration of the rights of man.' The feminine was the path and the space for revolt. Or, as Breton asserted in his wartime novel, *Arcane 17* (1944): 'it rests with the artist to make visible everything that is part of the feminine, as opposed to the masculine, system of the world.'[43] Accordingly, the feminine is not to be understood in this book in essentialist terms, as a characteristic assigned to biological identity, but as the opposite of traditional, masculine characteristics and ideals (patriotism, rationalism, order, etc.). Hence when male Surrealist artists focus on the female body in their paintings or installations, they celebrate the erotic power of the female body and the uncanny power of the feminine in us all.

I bring these ideas together in the chapters that follow through close analysis of each of the four international exhibitions of 1938, 1947, 1959 and 1965 – their design, content and reception. These major exhibitions have yet to receive detailed historical attention, nor have they been extensively politically contextualized. I show how the Surrealists used the exhibition space to symbolic and psychoanalytic affect to create an environment of hostility and surprise through physical discomfort, lighting, sound, smell and a playing with perceptual constants (e.g. the gallery walls). I present the Surrealist exhibition as a space that attacks the safe and the familiar and, to use James Clifford's understanding of Surrealism, provokes 'the irruption of otherness – the unexpected'.[44] The Surrealist exhibition demanded a self-conscious participation from the spectator and, through erotic reference, its corporeal architecture and feminine abjectivity evoked spaces of Otherness as a means of challenging not just bourgeois expectations but bourgeois political passivity too. The exhibition space offered a means of affecting human practice. As Henri Lefebvre acknowledges in *The Production of Space* (1974):

> The leading Surrealists sought to decode inner space and illuminate
> the nature of the transition from this subjective space to the material
> realm of the body and the outside world, and thence to social life.[45]

These exhibitions brought the politics of Eros into the third dimension.

In the first chapter, I focus on the 1938 'International Surrealist Exhibition' (Exposition Internationale du Surréalisme) at the Galerie Beaux-Arts in Paris. I argue that the Surrealists' appreciation of the political potential of the public exhibition was heightened by the use of the public exhibition for nationalist propaganda the previous year, on the occasion of the 'Degenerate Art' (Entartete Kunst) exhibition in Munich and the 'International Exhibition of Arts and Technology applied to Modern Life' (Exposition Internationale des Arts et Techniques dans la Vie Moderne) in Paris. The chapter demonstrates how the 1938 exhibition began the Surrealists' radical appropriation of the public exhibition to expose repressed, national desires and fears through an uncanny manipulation of the gallery space. It introduces Surrealism's politics of Eros as mapped out in the international exhibition, through the staging of the 'underbelly' of Paris with a parade of erotic mannequins and brothel-like beds, hysterical performance and an overall induction of the spectator into a profane, Surrealist world-view through the overhaul of the modernist 'white cube' gallery into a dark, warm, moist space that reeked of feminine abjectivity.

In the second chapter, I assess the role of Eros in Surrealist texts produced during World War II, beginning with Breton's writings in exile in the United States and ending with the collective publications of the neo-Surrealist group La Main à Plume in occupied Paris. I argue that Breton in New York, and artists such as Hans Bellmer and Jacques Hérold in occupied France, never wavered from their faith in the power of Eros to effect, disrupt, and initiate the public into a radically new way of seeing the world. Looking at the 1942 'First Papers of Surrealism' exhibition and

9 **Young students outside the 'Sciences-Po' (National Institute for Political Sciences), Paris, May 1968. Behind them is an example of the graffiti which became a hallmark of the moment, 'LA POLITIQUE A TOUS' ('Politics for everyone'). Photo Bruno Barbey.**

Peggy Guggenheim's Art of this Century gallery in New York, I show how the Surrealists continued to investigate the potential of the exhibition and how Frederick Kiesler was a key influence on their conceptualization of the gallery space on their return to Paris after the war.

In the third chapter, I analyse the first post-war international Surrealist exhibition, entitled 'Surrealism in 1947' (Le Surréalisme en 1947), which was held at the Galerie Maeght in Paris in that year. Dedicated to the myth of the 'Great Transparent Ones' (Les Grands Transparents), Kiesler and Duchamp designed the gallery space to evoke a sense of initiation and superstition. I present the exhibition's thematic exploration of myth and the uncanny nature of 'magical powers' as key to the Surrealists' vision of Eros as reconstructive and, by extension, as an aesthetic engagement with the dominant moral and cultural debates in post-war France. I also show how contemporary critiques of Surrealism, including those made by the Communist poet and essayist Tristan Tzara and the Existentialist philosopher Jean-Paul Sartre, testify to the continuing critical and artistic relevance of Surrealism in its ideological role in post-war French culture.

The fourth chapter examines the 1959 EROS exhibition (Exposition InteRnatiOnale du Surréalisme). I read the exhibition's fantastic architectural scheme with its sandy floor, breathing, sighing walls covered in velvet, and celebration of the Marquis de Sade, fetishism and the carnivalesque, as a renewed appreciation of the political potential of Eros at a time when the Surrealists were condemning de Gaulle's new Fifth Republic's colonial war in Algeria. I argue that the provocative, intra-uterine nature of the exhibition space, and the celebration of the Sadean, the primitive and the sexually explicit throughout the show may be read as a subversion of imperialist mentality and its fear of the foreign Other, and ultimately as an anti-colonial demonstration.

In the final chapter, I focus on the last major international Surrealist exhibition in Paris in the post-war era: the 'Absolute Deviation' (L'Ecart absolu) exhibition of 1965 where the Surrealists took a polemical stand once more against de Gaulle's France and its consumer culture, and called for the kind of revolt advocated by the French utopian socialist Charles Fourier in the early nineteenth century. I then show how this exhibition linked the Surrealists to the generation of 1968 and younger avant-garde groups. Jean-Jacques Lebel's Happening of 1966, entitled *120 Minutes dedicated to the Divine Marquis*, is compared to the deployment of Sadean Eros by the Surrealists and seen as a vital indication of Surrealism's influence on 1960s counter-culture.

The book concludes with an analysis of the influence of Surrealism on the events of May 1968 in Paris [9]. I propose that these events should be viewed as the apotheosis of Surrealism as well as a new beginning.

10 André Masson, *Mannequin with Bird Cage*, 'International Surrealist Exhibition', Galerie Beaux-Arts, Paris, 17 January – 24 February 1938. Masson's mannequin was the most sado-masochistic: naked except for her plumed g-string, her head was encased in a bird cage, her mouth muted by a green gag with a purple pansy, and her waist 'gashed' with a red ribbon. Goldfish also 'swam' through her cage, birds nested in her armpits and she stood on a base of course salt decorated with little traps holding red, 'phallic', pimentos. Photo by Denise Bellon.

11 The cover of the catalogue to the 'Degenerate Art' (Entartete Kunst) exhibition, Munich, 19 July – 30 November 1937. The exhibition travelled to Berlin and eleven other cities in Germany and Austria during 1938. Otto Freundlich's sculpture *The New Man* (1912) was selected for the cover as it was thought to exemplify what the Nazis deemed to be an endemic 'degeneracy' in modern art.

CHAPTER ONE

Profane Illumination: the 1938 Surrealist Exhibition

We can say without any exaggeration that never has human
civilization been menaced so seriously as today. The Vandals, with
instruments which were barbarous and comparatively ineffective,
blotted out the culture of antiquity in one corner of Europe. But
today we see world civilization, united in its historical destiny, reeling
under the blows of reactionary forces armed with the entire arsenal of
modern technology. We are by no means thinking only of the world
war that draws near. Even in times of 'peace' the position of art and
science has become absolutely intolerable.

André Breton and Diego Rivera, 'Manifesto for an Independent
Revolutionary Art', 25 July 1938[1]

The Surrealists' radical approach to the exhibition as a means of initiating the
public into a Surrealist world view by enacting the politics of Eros in the gallery
space is first evident in the 'International Surrealist Exhibition' (Exposition
Internationale du Surréalisme) of 1938.[2] This occurred at a significant moment in
French and European history, when political positions were being played out in the
cultural arena and when the ideology of Fascism was gaining considerable support
across Europe. As a reaction to the assault on so-called 'degenerate' art in Germany

12 **Photograph of the grounds, looking from the Palais de Chaillot, of the 'International Exhibition of Arts and Technology applied to Modern Life', Paris, 4 May – 25 November 1937. On the left of the Eiffel Tower stands the German pavilion, designed by Albert Speer, adorned by a monumental sculpture of a naked Teutonic couple at ground level and topped by a German eagle, a swastika in its claws. On the right stands the Soviet pavilion, designed by Boris Iofan and bearing a heroic peasant couple with hammer and sickle.**

and to the promotion of a nostalgic modernism in France at the time, the Surrealists subverted the exhibition as a temple-like, cultural arena.[3] Two exhibitions dominated the public imagination in Germany and France in 1937: the 'Degenerate Art' (Entartete Kunst) exhibition of contemporary art, held in Munich in the arcaded Hofgarten wing of the Residenz at Galeriestrasse 4 from July to November 1937 [11], and the 'International Exhibition of Arts and Technology applied to Modern Life' (Exposition Internationale des Arts et Techniques dans la Vie Moderne) held at the Palais de Chaillot in Paris from May to November 1937 [12].

The 'Degenerate Art' exhibition intended to berate 'Bolshevik art' and was set up to act as the antithesis of 'true German art' which was being simultaneously exhibited in the 'Great German Art Exhibition' (Grosse deutsche Kunstausstellung) held in the nearby House of German Art (Haus der Deutschen Kunst).[4] The 'Degenerate Art' exhibition attracted over two million people and was intended to demonstrate Nazi cultural and racial superiority through a dramatic display of paintings and texts, contemporary and primitive art.[5] As Hitler had announced in his 'Address on Art and Politics' at the Nuremberg Parteitag on 11 September 1935, German art had to be rid of 'degeneracy which is utterly corrupt and diseased'.[6] The exhibition was intended to re-educate the public through shock tactics with its display scheme and use of prescriptive captions and interpretative texts. Adolf Ziegler, a key figure in the selection of works on show and a painter himself, whose style was emphatically neoclassical, announced at the opening of the exhibition:

> You see around you the products of madness, or impudence, of ineptitude and decadence. This show produces in us feelings of shock and repugnance.[7]

The exhibition instilled a sense of fear in the public between the degeneracy that threatened to disease the German state and Hitler's insistence that it, and anyone who supported it, should be wiped out. Over 650 works of art were shown in the exhibition, including paintings by Alexander Archipenko, André Derain, Giorgio de Chirico, Marc Chagall, Max Ernst, Paul Gauguin, Vincent van Gogh, Henri Matisse, Piet Mondrian, Wassily Kandinsky and Pablo Picasso. Even the paintings of Emil Nolde, who sympathized with Nazi anti-Semitism and whose work was a favourite of propaganda minister Joseph Goebbels, was deemed 'degenerate'. His paintings of *The Life of Christ* were discredited as 'mockery of the Divine'.

Dummheit oder Frechheit — oder beides — auf die Spitze getrieben!

Ein wertvolles Geständnis:

„Wir können bluffen wie die abgesottensten Pokerspieler. Wir tun so, als ob wir Maler, Dichter oder sonst was wären, aber wir sind nur und nichts als mit Wollust frech. Wir setzen aus Frechheit einen riesigen Schwindel in die Welt und züchten Snobs, die uns die Stiefel abschlecken, parce que c'est notre plaisir. Windmacher, Sturmmacher sind wir mit unserer Frechheit."

Aus dem Manifest von A. Undo
in „Die Aktion" 1915.

14 **Page from the catalogue for the 'Degenerate Art' exhibition, Munich, 19 July – 30 November 1937, in which certain works are singled for their 'stupidity or impudence': Max Ernst, *The Beautiful Gardener* (also known as *Creation of Eve*), 1923; Willi Baumeister, *Figure with Pink Stripe III*, 1920; and Johannes Molzahn, *Twins*, c.1930.**

The equation of Bolshevism with degeneracy and the general assault on the avant-garde evident in the exhibition could not but have outraged the Surrealists. Chagall, who would exhibit with many of the Surrealists in New York in an exhibition entitled 'Artists in Exile' held at the Pierre Matisse Gallery in March 1942, was denounced with his painting *Rabbi* (*c*.1912) in the second gallery of the exhibition devoted to mocking the Jew. Dada art, exhibited in the third gallery alongside abstract art, was mocked with offensive condemnations and the ironic use of Dada slogans – such as 'Take Dada seriously! It's worth it!' [13]. Images by Dadaist Otto Dix, including his *War Cripples* (1920), were marked 'Insult to the German Heroes of the Great War'. The collection of the art of the insane belonging to the psychiatrist and art historian Hans Prinzhorn (whose *Artistry of the Mentally Ill* of 1922 was a source of inspiration for Breton), was also used as visual proof that the work of Paul Klee and others was an art of 'the idiot, the cretin, and the cripple'.[8] Finally, Max Ernst's *The Beautiful Gardener* of 1923 was used as a visual example of 'insults to German womanhood' and was categorized in the exhibition catalogue as an example of 'the ultimate in stupidity or impertinence – or both – pushed to the limit' [14].[9] In his painting, since lost, Ernst had painted a beautiful female gardener whose sex was partially covered by a dove.[10]

Jimmy Ernst, Max's son, saw the 'Degenerate Art' exhibition when it toured to Hamburg, where it was shown in trailers which acted as a temporary gallery. The layout of the show was similar to the exhibition in Munich, but the narrow spaces inside the trailers meant that people could not stand in front of any one painting for long and were encouraged to keep moving by officials. Indeed, he noted that people were scared to spend too long at the exhibition as 'nobody wanted to run the risk of being called a lover of this *Kultur Bolschewismus*'.[11] Significantly, Ernst elaborates on the nature of the display as being not only dogmatic but 'staged in the manner of a side-show of freaks at a tawdry carnival'.[12] He was proud to see his father's *The Beautiful Gardener* hanging between paintings by Ernst Ludwig Kirchner and Otto Dix, and noted that it was one of the paintings that caused 'periodical jam-ups' of spectators, who seemed to peer at the image 'as if in hope of seeing what the bird was hiding'.[13] However, the young Ernst also noted that as he was viewing his father's art a recording of Hitler's speech at the opening of the officially approved German art exhibition at the House of German Art was being played from loudspeakers in each room, a speech which promised to 'make short shrift of this degeneracy'. He was also questioned by a stranger about the show, which led him to wonder if this was an undercover Nazi – one of 'them'.[14]

Unsurprisingly, the 'Degenerate Art' exhibition attracted a lot of international press attention. For example, the Parisian weekly dedicated to the arts, *Beaux-Arts*, ran a headline asking, 'Will Van Gogh, Matthias Grünewald and Rembrandt be expelled from German Museums?'[15] *Beaux-Arts* was published by Georges Wildenstein, who would host the international Surrealist exhibition just a few weeks after the end of the Nazi show. While the Surrealists in Paris did not refer publicly to the 'Degenerate Art' exhibition at the time, they were obviously aware of it through the media, personal accounts (such as that of Jimmy Ernst), and the reaction of the British Surrealist group to it, since the latter held a counter-exhibition in London.[16] The Surrealists represented everything that Nazism detested: they were a movement of intellectuals, writers and artists who stood against nationalism, imperialism and political and cultural repression; they celebrated the art of primitive peoples, naives and the insane; their art was indebted to the avant-gardism of Dada and Weimar art;

Hans Bellmer, *The Doll* (*Die Puppe*), photograph taken 1934, printed 1936. Bellmer created this 1.2m (4 ft) high doll sculpture in papier mâché and plaster over an armature of wood and metal in 1933, the year that Adolf Hitler became Chancellor of Germany. The mechanism of the doll is apparent in her stomach and right leg, and the *mise-en-scène* disturbingly confronts the viewer with the image of a battered *femme-enfant* and Bellmer's ghost-like male figure ominously staring at the camera.

and their political sympathies lay with Communism. In Paris, the Surrealists had braved Fascism before 1937. They had countered a Fascist assault on Salvador Dalí and Luis Buñuel's film, *L'Age d'or*, in 1930, when its screening at Studio 28 in Paris was sabotaged by right-wing protesters, the Camelots du Roi and the Jeunesses Patriotiques, who stampeded the cinema, threw ink at the screen, fired guns and slashed the Surrealist canvases that hung in the foyer.[17] In 1935, Breton, Benjamin Péret, Paul Eluard and Maurice Heine had joined Georges Bataille's Contre-Attaque: Union de lutte des intellectuels révolutionnaires. This was a non-party group of 'revolutionary intellectuals' who met from 1935 to 1936, who challenged the PCF and for whom the psychology of Fascism was a priority topic. As Breton explained in 'The Political Position of Surrealism' (1935), his reasons for joining the collective were fuelled by 'the impossibility of any longer believing in any improvement in this sense of ideology on the parties of the left'.[18] Dedicated to 'revolutionary violence', other members included the atomic physicist Georges Ambrosino and the writer Pierre Klossowski, and key authors discussed included Nietzsche and the Marquis de Sade.[19] However, Breton and Bataille's collaboration was short-lived, due to Breton's discomfort with what he saw as Bataille's over-fascination with the psychological structure of Fascism.[20] As a result, Breton began to dissociate from Contre-Attaque and by May 1936 labelled it '*sur-fasciste*'; later Bataille would himself admit that it may have displayed 'a paradoxical fascist tendency'.[21]

Breton's unease over discussions on the psychology of Fascism was no doubt affected by the rise of Fascism in Spain and by fellow Surrealists' first-hand information on the state of the avant-garde in Nazi Germany. With the outbreak of the Spanish Civil War in July 1936, Buñuel, Roland Penrose and David Gascoyne went to Spain to help the Republicans (Spain's Popular Front government) against Franco and his German allies.[22] The Surrealists in Paris showed their allegiance by issuing a tract in August 1936 criticizing Blum's Popular Front government's refusal to aid the Spanish Republicans in the conflict with Franco. New members of the Surrealist group brought their political anxieties with them and strategies for using the erotic to political ends. In 1933, when National Socialism replaced Weimar democracy, Hans Bellmer, who was working as a commercial artist in Berlin, quit his job in protest against the new regime. He despised his father, who joined the National Socialist Party, and, as Peter Webb and Robert Short have documented, he came under pressure to conform, often finding 'messages stuck to his door asking if he had joined the Nazi Party [yet]'.[23] In this environment Bellmer created *Die Puppe*, his first doll sculpture, a disturbing object about 1.2m (4 ft) in height with moveable limbs, made of papier mâché and plaster over an armature of wood and metal. The doll was the subject of a series of ominous photographs by the artist published as *Die Puppe* in 1934. In one photograph, the artist appears as a semi-transparent, ghost-like Jack the Ripper, his presence adding to the disturbing import of the fragmented body of his created *femme-enfant*.[24] [15]

Bellmer's second doll, *La Poupée* (usually titled in French to distinguish it from the first), soon followed in 1935. This doll was made of glue and tissue paper and was more voluptuous in form and flesh-like in colour. It was structured around a central ball-joint which allowed for greater articulation of the doll's limbs and more provocative erotic gymnastics, and was photographed indoors and out, with Mary-Jane shoes, ribbons in its hair, and other props. The doll's libidinal potential was celebrated by the Surrealists and explored by Paul Eluard in *Les Jeux de la poupée* (Games of the Doll), a collaborative publication Eluard produced with Bellmer, for

16 The cover of the weekly paper *Vu et Lu* devoted to 'L'Accueil de Paris aux visiteurs de l'exposition' (Paris's welcome to visitors to the exhibition), no.492, 18 August 1937. Richly illustrated with photographs and emphasizing the international appeal of the event, the paper included several feature articles on the 'International Exhibition of Arts and Technology applied to Modern Life', Paris, 1937.

17 A photograph of the 'International Exhibition of Arts and Technology applied to Modern Life' Paris, 1937, looking north from the Italian pavilion on the Quai Branly to the Soviet (left) and German (right) pavilions across the Seine.

which the poet wrote prose-poems about the doll accompanied by a frontispiece and fourteen hand-coloured photographs by Bellmer.[25]

Bellmer's dolls may be interpreted on sexual and political levels – as symbols of a subversive, Sadistic eroticism, an adolescent, anti-Oedipal rebellion; but also, in more historically specific terms, they can be seen as an anti-Nazi statement. Created for the first time in 1933, the year that Hitler became Chancellor, the uncontrolled 'degenerate' sexuality of Bellmer's dolls acted as an allegorical statement against all that Nazism represented, as both Hal Foster and Therese Lichtenstein have persuasively argued.[26] If Nazi iconography emphasized the comfort of the maternal, moral, natural feminine (enforcing the Third Reich *Kinder, Kirche, Küche* dictat for women), Bellmer's doll emphasized the uncanny power and the *threat* of the feminine. Bellmer's explanation of the doll spoke to the relationship between the erotic body and the body politic. Through his erotic art Bellmer hoped to lead people to look at the world with new eyes:

> I tried to rearrange the sexual elements of a girl's body like a sort of plastic anagram. I remember describing it thus: the body is like a sentence that invites us to rearrange it, so that its real meaning becomes clear through a series of endless anagrams. I wanted to reveal what is usually kept hidden – it was no game – *I tried to open people's eyes to new realities.*[27]

Bellmer's photographs of his second doll would be included in the 1938 Surrealist exhibition. However, he would find that in Paris people were not necessarily more welcoming of 'new realities' in art. The populist nature of the 'Degenerate Art' exhibition was shared by the 'International Exhibition of Arts and Technology applied to Modern Life' in Paris. The last major international exhibition in Paris before World War II, it attracted over thirty-one million visitors [16]. As Eric Hobsbawm has noted, such major international exhibitions were 'perhaps the most characteristic form in which art and power collaborated during the era of bourgeois liberalism', celebrating not only the state and political power but also civil society, economic, technical and cultural achievement, and the supposedly happy coexistence of nations.[28]

Involving displays from thirty-eight nation states, the international exhibition was an attempt to heal cultural and political wounds in France and Europe in 1937. The chief commissioner of the exhibition, Edmond Labbé, hoped that 'Art would confer an irresistible lustre' not only on France but on Europe and in the process enact 'a power of seduction to forget all the present difficulties'.[29] This was an exhibition that lent France an air of civility and optimism and that belied the horror of the Spanish Civil War and the imminent threat of war in the rest of Europe.

The exhibition was perceived as the triumphant product of the French Left – Léon Blum's Popular Front government – over the Right.[30] Yet the Exposition was emphatically conservative in tone and scheme as evidenced in the neoclassical design of the new modern art museum at the Palais de Tokyo, and in the privileging of the Soviet Union and Germany. Their imposing pavilions, built by Boris Iofan and Albert Speer respectively, dominated the show physically from the Palais de Chaillot on the right bank of the Seine and metaphorically, through the rhetorical power of art and architecture. The German pavilion had a monumental sculpture of a naked Teutonic couple at ground level and was topped by a German eagle, a swastika in its claws. The Russian pavilion bore a heroic peasant couple brandishing a hammer and sickle. These pavilions faced each other, powerfully demonstrating the glory

and triumph of power itself in their unabashed propagandistic architectural styles which revealed aesthetic similarity despite their opposing political regimes [17].

Labbé described the exhibition in the official guide (*Livre d'or officiel*) in optimistc terms:

> In a world on which the menace of the future weighs heavily, it has seemed for some time that civilization had begun to lost faith in itself, in its values, energies and duties. A kind of discouragement and lassitude has overrun people's spirits, undermining the very basis of hope. And now here is the Exhibition, springing up suddenly, with a supreme will and momentum, rising to the sky like a great cry of confidence and ardour from the whole of humanity.[31]

The only art to threaten this monolithic cry of confidence was in the Spanish pavilion. Here Pablo Picasso's mural *Guernica* [18] took pride of place on the ground floor, opposite Alexander Calder's *Mercury Fountain*, exposing the horrors experienced by the Spanish Republic. Joan Miró's mural *The Reaper* [19] continued the theme and provided a dramatic focal point too as it was strategically positioned on the flight of stairs that joined the second floor back to the ground floor and exit, so that all visitors had to pass by it.[32] It is no coincidence that Picasso, Calder and Miró had all been involved in Surrealist activities and/or exhibitions prior to this and took the opportunity here to voice their political dissent; but, as James Herbert has pointed out in his analysis of the exhibition, the Spanish pavilion and its relatively disturbing art works were largely ignored in the official guide and press reviews.[33]

The Surrealists were not given any space in the exhibition, not even in the French pavilion. Instead painters Robert and Sonia Delaunay, Fernand Léger and Albert Gleizes, and sculptors Henri Bouchard and Alfred Janniot were awarded government commissions. The Surrealists' contribution to France's cultural programme was only represented in literary terms. Eluard spoke about

18 **Pablo Picasso, *Guernica*, 1937.** Picasso's mural response to the bombing of the Basque village of Guernica on 27 April 1937 by Franco's forces and the German Condor Legion was the centrepiece of the Spanish pavilion at the 'International Exhibition of Arts and Technology applied to Modern Life'. The mural then toured Europe and North America to raise public awareness of the threat of fascism.

19 **Joan Miró, *The Reaper*, 1937.** Miró's mural in the Spanish pavilion depicted a Catalan peasant wearing the traditional Catalan *barretina*, a statement of revolt against Franco. After the 'International Exhibition', the mural was dismantled and subsequently lost or destroyed.

'The Future of Poetry', Breton gave a lecture on black humour, and Sylvain Itkine directed two plays by Alfred Jarry with the assistance of a number of the Surrealists.[34] However, an aspect of the 'International Exhibition of Arts and Technology applied to Modern Life' that must have attracted the attention of the Surrealists was the Fashion pavilion. It was designed by Emile Aillaud, who employed the young sculptor Robert Couturier to create the mannequins for the pavilion. Couturier's vision and staging [20] undoubtedly influenced the Surrealists' display of fashion mannequins in their own 1938 exhibition, as we shall see below. Even Couturier's description of his plans for the pavilion seems to harbour a Surrealist influence as it evokes a labyrinthine city, fantastic women and a romantic nostalgia for ruins:

> I imagined a long, winding tunnel with the atmosphere of an ochre-toned Mediterranean town. Scattered here and there, in complete harmony with the decor, fantastic giants of terracotta – but in fact a mixture of plaster and oakum – more than six feet tall, presented the public with a new silhouette: a slim waist and powerful muscles. I wanted tragic silhouettes that were intentionally devoid of any of the pleasantness, the gentleness, that usually go with elegance. Their defensive, frightened gestures, their featureless faces, their badly balanced bodies, recalled the inhabitants of Pompeii surprised by a cloud of ashes rather than the *habitués* of the Faubourg Saint-Honoré or Avenue Montaigne. I didn't expect such violent reactions. There was an enormous scandal and a public demonstration.[35]

The press certainly saw Surrealism in Couturier's actual design and his theatrical arrangement of a series of faceless mannequins. As Dominique Autié has documented, the magazine *Femina* reported: 'We like the fact that the world of fashion looks like a cavern full of treasures, and that these tall, thin statues with tiny breasts have no faces, because the sculptor wanted each of us to give them the face of our dreams.'[36] The *London Bystander* saw the mannequins as 'the crystallization of Surrealism'; while in the French press, *Le Temps* explained that in the Fashion pavilion 'perspectives open up mysteriously like fragments of architecture à la Chirico'.[37] In these responses the characteristics of Surrealism were recognized – its fascination with the female, the city and the fantastic – but on a superficial level as a popular style rather than as a subversive agenda. This is not surprising given the 'International Exhibition of Arts and Technology applied to Modern Life' demonstrated a burgeoning nationalism and cultural conservatism in mainstream French culture under Blum's socialist government. Blum's cultural programme marginalized avant-gardes in favour of a history of great modern masters.

The Surrealists were not represented in the 'International Exhibition of Arts and Technology applied to Modern Life', nor in two ancillary exhibitions which were organized alongside it: the 'Chefs d'oeuvre de l'art français' [21], devoted to French masterpieces, at the Palais de Tokyo and 'Les Maîtres de l'art indépendant', a municipal exhibition dedicated to modern art at the Petit Palais. The former exhibited French art from the fourteenth to the nineteenth century, ending on a nostalgic note with the art of Monet and Cézanne, and representing 'a census of our national artistic wealth' according to Jean Zay, Minister of National Education and Fine Arts.[38] The latter exhibited some 1,500 works but emphasized a select few, namely Braque, Matisse, Picasso and Rouault in order to present the 'most audacious tendencies of French art' according to Raymond Escholier, Head of the Municipal Curatorial Staff.[39] The staging of a third, smaller exhibition entitled

20 **Robert Couturier mannequins wearing Lanvin gowns in the Fashion pavilion of the 'International Exhibition of Arts and Technology applied to Modern Life', Paris, 1937. Photo by Denise Bellon.**

21 **Installation view of Hall 4 of the 'Chefs d'oeuvre de l'art français' exhibition, Paris 1937.**

'Origines et développement de l'art international indépendant', at the Musée du Jeu de Paume, was meant to promote the avant-garde. It displayed Futurist, Dada, Constructivist, Abstract and Surrealist art. Surrealism was represented most notably by eight paintings by Salvador Dalí, though this show too emphasized the precursors of modernism (Paul Cézanne, Paul Gauguin, Odilon Redon, Pierre-Auguste Renoir, Henri Rousseau, Georges Seurat), thereby down-playing the radical break with the French tradition which avant-garde movements had made. Indeed, the Surrealists were critical of the biased selection of works in the exhibition and had forbidden Dalí to submit his paintings.[40] Breton was one of the signatories to an open letter in August 1937 to cabinet ministers Jean Zay and Camille Chautemps (President of the Council of Ministers), and exhibition director Georges Huisman (Director General of Fine Arts), in which writers and artists protested against the exhibition's insular selection of contemporary art.[41]

Like the 'Degenerate Art' exhibition, these exhibitions in Paris in 1937 influenced the Surrealists and their own international exhibition the following year. While the Surrealists had always adopted a strategy of 'profane illumination' in their art and writings, as recognized by Benjamin, their approach to the exhibition now took a radical new direction. Seeing the exhibition as the perfect space for manipulating the public's desires and fears, and for initiating them into the Surrealist world view, the Surrealists went much further than any previous group exhibition they had organized. The 1938 exhibition may be seen as an assault on these official exhibitions in Germany and France in which art had been put at the service of the nation state. It opposed Nazi triumphalism and intolerance through its celebration of avant-garde sexual and moral 'degeneracy' and it mocked French bourgeois liberalism's inadequacies in stemming Fascist expansion. It was to be expected that Surrealism would be deemed 'degenerate' by the Nazis, but for Surrealism to be overlooked in major exhibitions in Paris only added insult to injury.

The 1938 international Surrealist exhibition was designed as the uncanny opposite of these streamlined, official 1937 exhibitions. As Breton later stated, the 1938 exhibition and the stir it caused was 'fairly expressive of the mental climate prevailing in 1938' and specific 'aspects of its structure intended to open to everyone that zone of agitation that lies on the borders of the poetic and of the real'.[42] Breton, Paul Eluard and Marcel Duchamp were the main organizers of the exhibition and, according to Breton, 'concentrated their efforts on creating an atmosphere as remote as possible from that of an "art" gallery'.[43] Breton's recent venture in the gallery business, his Galerie Gradiva on rue de Seine, had already indicated his desire to break the gallery mould. The very name he chose for the gallery indicated this, standing for 'She who moves forward': a homage to Wilhelm Jensen's 1903 novel *Gradiva: A Pompeiian Fantasy* and Freud's 1907 analysis of it ('Delusions and Dreams in Jensen's Gradiva'), and also to the women Surrealists whose names were written under each letter of the name on the façade: Gisèle (Prassinos), Rosine, Alice (Paalen), Dora (Maar), Inès, Violette (Nozières), and Alice again. The entrance door was designed by Duchamp in the shape of a silhouette of a couple, a large man and slim woman, and was a dramatic and romantic invitation to enter. The interior presented Breton's break from the clichéd art gallery: it had a combination of paintings, artworks and curiosities on show, and a designated reading corner with a library of books chosen for their illuminating power, from children's picture books to poetry books. In his essay 'Gradiva', published that year, Breton wrote of the power of the muse to instil a new wakefulness, to stand 'On the border of utopia and truth'.[44] Breton's vision of the muse speaks to his conception of a dramatically new gallery experience. Thus while the Gradiva gallery may have failed as a business, it too paved the way for the international exhibition a year later.

Duchamp was again called up for the 1938 exhibition – he was, in his own words, 'borrowed from the ordinary world by the Surrealists' to act as 'Generator-Arbiter'.[45] Salvador Dalí and Max Ernst assisted as 'Special Advisers', Wolfgang Paalen with the placement of 'water and underbrush', and Man Ray with the lighting.[46] The exhibition was a collective effort on the part of the Surrealists, presenting the work of artists from fourteen countries – for example, Eileen Agar, Humphrey Jennings and Henry Moore from England, Paul Delvaux and René Magritte from Belgium, Roberto Matta's wife Ann Clark and Joseph Cornell from the United States, and Toyen (Marie Čerminová) and Jindřich Štyrský from Czechoslovakia.

The show broke the art exhibition mould, won the attention of the international press and outraged much of the public. As Marcel Jean, who was involved in the exhibition, wrote in his history of Surrealism:

> [T]he entire press spoke of the event. With very few exceptions, it
> was an outcry of indignated [*sic*] sneers, insults, recriminations,
> expressions of disgust. Naturally the general public packed the
> Galerie Beaux-Arts throughout the run of the exhibition.[47]

The fashionable Galerie Beaux-Arts was located at 140 rue du Faubourg Saint-Honoré and run by Georges Wildenstein. While the typical exhibitions this gallery held were far from avant-garde – the show prior to the Surrealist one was devoted to El Greco – Wildenstein was generous in his budget for the exhibition and gave the Surrealists free rein with his space.[48] The gallery's regular clientele may have suspected that something unusual was afoot when they received their invitations, which listed a performance by Hélène Vanel, a field of clover and a chained rooster

22 Salvador Dalí, *Rainy Taxi* installation, 'International Surrealist Exhibition', Paris, 17 January – 24 February 1938. Here we see Dalí's mockery of what he called 'snobbish Surrealist ladies', a chauffeur-driven blonde covered with chicory leaves and live snails in a car drenched in rain. Photo by Denise Bellon.

INVITATION
pour le
17 Janvier 1938
TENUE DE SOIRÉE

EXPOSITION INTERNATIONALE
DU
SURRÉALISME

A 22 heures
signal d'ouverture
par André BRETON

APPARITIONS
D'ÊTRES-OBJETS

L'HYSTÉRIE

LE TRÈFLE
INCARNAT

L'ACTE MANQUÉ

PAR

Hélène
VANEL

COQS ATTACHÉS

CLIPS
FLUORESCENTS

DESCENTE
DE LIT
EN FLANCS D'
HYDROPHILES

LES
PLUS BELLES
RUES DE PARIS

TAXI PLUVIEUX

CIEL DE
ROUSSETTES

Le descendant authentique de Frankenstein, l'automate "Enigmarelle", construit
en 1900 par l'ingénieur américain Ireland, traversera, à minuit et demi, en fausse
chair et en faux os, la salle de l'Exposition Surréaliste.

GALERIE BEAUX-ARTS, 140, RUE DU FAUBOURG SAINT-HONORÉ — PARIS

as some of the attractions of the exhibition. The invitation was also illustrated by a photograph of an automaton by the name of Enigmarelle (taken when it was first exhibited in London in 1905) [23] and promised that the automaton would appear at midnight in 'false flesh and false blood'.[49] But while the invitation may have hinted at the shocking and pseudo-scientific tone of the exhibition, the public would not have been prepared for the outrageous Surrealist enterprise that lay behind the bourgeois façade of the Galerie Beaux-Arts on the evening of the opening on 17 January.

That night, invitees clad in evening dress stepped out of their cars to be greeted by a parody of their bourgeois selves – Salvador Dalí's *Rainy Taxi* installation, an automobile with headlights on, driven by a goggle-wearing mannequin whose head was helmeted in shark-teeth, behind whom sat a glamorous blonde mannequin-lady, with an omelette on her lap and a sewing machine by her side, surrounded by lettuce and chicory heads [22 & 24].[50] In Dalí's words, the taxi was for 'snobbish Surrealist ladies'.[51] To make the spectacle even more disarming, the taxi interior was drenched with 'rain' (thanks to perforated pipes of water on the car ceiling), and infested with 200 live Burgundy snails. A taxi, usually a safe haven from the rain and pests, here served as a Surrealist 'found object' *par excellence*. In addition, through his installation's inversion of function and 'assault' on this elegant lady, Dalí hinted at the shocking delirium to come in the exhibition. Dalí's *Rainy Taxi* was one of a number of equally intriguing and erotically suggestive Surrealist objects on show in the exhibition. These included Oscar Domínguez's *Never* (1937), a Victrola with horn that the artist painted white and adapted to biomorphic effect: a pair of high-heeled legs jutted out of the horn and the arm/record needle was a lady's hand which 'caressed' a breasted turntable [25]. Kurt Seligmann continued the erotic-corporeal play with the animate and inanimate in his *Ultra Furniture* (1938), a stool whose legs consisted of four high-heeled, pink-stockinged, ladies

23 **Invitation to the 'International Surrealist Exhibition' (Exposition internationale du surréalisme), Galerie Beaux-Arts, Paris, 17 January – 24 February 1938. The invitation advertised a number of bizarre attractions, including a field of clover, a performance of** *L'Acte manqué* **(Unconsummated Act) by Hélène Vanel, 'chained roosters', and 'the most beautiful streets of Paris'. The photograph is of the automaton Enigmarelle taken during its first exhibition at the London Hippodrome in 1905.**

24 **Salvador Dalí's** *Rainy Taxi* **installation in front of the Galerie Beaux-Arts during the 'International Surrealist Exhibition', Paris, 1938. Photo by Josef Breitenbach.**

25 Photograph of Oscar Dominguez's *Never*, 1937, at the 'International Surrealist Exhibition', Galerie Beaux-Arts, Paris, 1938. This 'assisted ready made', a Victrola horn with a pair of mannequin legs jutting out of it and a mannequin arm for a record needle hovering over a breast-like turntable, exemplifies the Surrealists' use of the object as fetish. Salvador Dalí's *Sleep* (1937) and Marcel Duchamp's suspended coal sacks and a lighted iron brazier are visible in the background. Photo by Denise Bellon.

26 **Photograph of the 'International Surrealist Exhibition', Galerie Beaux-Arts, Paris, 1938. In the corner of the room is André Breton's *Object Chest* (1938), in which female mannequin legs and hands are used fetishistically to represent the desired whole woman, demonstrating the latent erotic potential of seemingly banal objects. Photo by Josef Breitenbach.**

27 **Photograph of Kurt Seligmann's *Ultra Furniture*, 1938, at the 'International Surrealist Exhibition', Galerie Beaux-Arts, Paris, 1938. Seligmann's humorous and metamorphic stool with four female legs incorporates classic fetishes such as high heels and stockings but, in its cutting-off of the full figure, also suggests the fear of castration.**

legs [27]. In a similar vein, Breton's *Object Chest* (1938) [26], with its disembodied hands on top and mannequin legs below, offered a clever exploration of the fetishist's fascination with the body part and the Surrealists' continued fascination with the *exquisite corpse*, specifically the exquisite corpse game.[52]

Equally, Meret Oppenheim's *Object (Le Déjeuner en fourrure)* (1936) (a cup, spoon and saucer covered in gazelle fur) [28], which had been exhibited at the 1936 'Exhibition of Surrealist Objects' (Exposition surréaliste d'objets) at the Galerie Charles Ratton in Paris [29 & 30], explored the desire/repulsion paradox of fetishism. It played on a series of patriarchal fetishizations of the female body: Freud's equation of the spoon and vessel with the nourishing breast, Edouard Manet's painting *Le Déjeuner sur l'herbe* (1863), which set up a nature-culture divide between the female and male sexes, and Leopold von Sacher-Masoch's novel *Venus in Furs* (1869), in which the male protagonist indulges his fur fetish.[53] In covering functional, mass-produced objects in fur, Oppenheim inverted the everyday to produce an uncanny art object, but she specifically exploited the taboo of female genitals, rather than the more conventional erotic icon of breasts or legs, in order to play on Freud and the association between the maternal and the oral, and the female sex and castration complex.[54] The shape of the cup as a cavity or receptacle covered in tactile fur evokes the female sex and epitomized the open-ended nature of desire-repulsion apparent in many of the art works on show. Oppenheim's work offers an interesting comparison to the uncanny art works of her male colleagues. These included Wolfgang Paalen's humorous, visual conundrum *Articulated Cloud* (1938), an umbrella made of sponges [31], and two original Dada works: Man Ray's *The Gift* (1921), an iron adorned with tacks, and a 1925 rotary demisphere by Duchamp which consisted of a spinning disc on which was inscribed the tongue-tying title: *Rrose Sélavy et moi nous esquivons les ecchymoses des esquimaux aux mots exquis* (Rrose Sélavy and me let us dodge the bruises of the Eskimos to exquisite words).

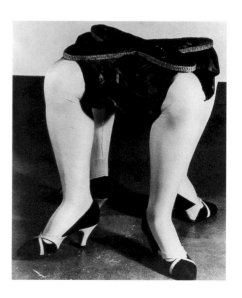

28 **Meret Oppenheim's** *Object (Le Déjeuner en fourrure)*, **1936, turns everyday objects into erotic objects through a fetishistic play on the association between fur, the vessel, and a woman's sex. André Breton gave the work its title, punning on Edouard Manet's** *Le Déjeuner sur l'herbe* **(1863) and Sacher-Masoch's erotic novel** *Venus in Furs* **(1869). The work was inspired one day when Pablo Picasso and Dora Maar admired her fur-covered bracelet in a Paris café, leading Oppenheim to wittily ask the waiter for a little more 'fur' for her coffee. It was first exhibited at the 'Exhibition of Surrealist Objects' (Exposition surréaliste d'objets) at the Galerie Charles Ratton, 14 rue Marignan, Paris, 22–29 May 1936, and subsequently purchased by Alfred H. Barr, Jr, for the Museum of Modern Art, New York.**

29, 30 **Photographs of the 'Exhibition of Surrealist Objects' at the Galerie Charles Ratton, Paris, May 1936.** The week-long exhibition included mathematical models, natural objects, primitive objects, found objects, irrational objects, ready-made objects, interpreted objects, incorporated objects and mobile objects, as well as Surrealist art works. In his 1936 essay on the exhibition, Breton explained the objects were chosen for 'their sheer power of evocation, overwhelming us with the conviction that they constitute the repositories, in art, of that miraculous charm which we long to capture.'

31 **Wolfgang Paalen, *Articulated Cloud*, 1938. An umbrella made of sponges, Paalen's object continued the Surrealist play with the rational expectations of the spectator in subverting the umbrella's original function. Born in Vienna in 1905, Paalen joined the Surrealists in 1935 and in 1938 invented a new automatic painting process called 'fumage' (creating images on canvas through the use of a burning candle, smoke and soot).**

32 **A spectator looking at paintings with a flashlight at the 'International Surrealist Exhibition', Galerie Beaux-Arts, Paris, 1938. Photo by Josef Breitenbach.**

Inside the Galerie Beaux-Arts the invitees were provided with flashlights [32], and they groped their way from object to object in semi-darkness. The exhibition space thus recalled Freud's description of the uncanny space as one in which 'one may wander about in a dark, strange room, looking for the door or the electric switch, and collide time after time with the same piece of furniture'.[55] The spectator could only move hesitantly through the dimly lit series of spaces, becoming in him/herself a sort of object to be seen rather than a seer in control. Indeed, Simone de Beauvoir almost echoes Freud's description of the uncanny in describing the exhibition as remarkable with 'various objects looming up out of the carefully contrived semi-darkness: a fur-lined dish, an occasional table with the legs of a woman'.[56] Photographs of the exhibition taken by Raoul Ubac and Denise Bellon at the time indicate the bemusement of the public as they make their way through the exhibition and alongside such objects, with one even showing a pretty young female spectator sitting on Seligmann's stool. Clearly, the Surrealists wanted the viewer to engage directly with the art, but also to experience a sense of confrontation and dislocation as familiar objects were made strange through bizarre juxtaposition. The art exhibition demanded an active theatrical role of the spectator, as emphasized by the inclusion in a small room adjacent to the main gallery space of a chandelier made of gargantuan women's bloomers under which paintings were hung on revolving doors. Even in looking up at the ceiling, the spectator – perhaps going round and round and catching glimpses of an imaginary monumental female sex – could not but take on the role of Peeping Tom, unable to escape the monstrous feminine.[57]

This participatory role continued in the two main exhibition rooms. Firstly, the spectator passed along a *rue surréaliste*, a long corridor with street signs which took on the appearance of a red-light promenade as photographs of Bellmer's doll and sixteen mannequin ladies-of-the-night traded their wares, each fetishistically attired

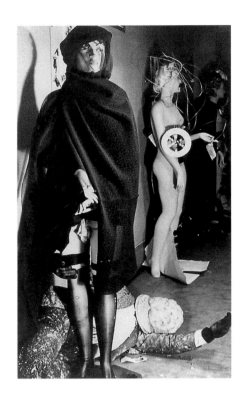

33 **A mannequin by Joan Miró (background) and Max Ernst's** *Widow Mannequin* **(foreground), at the 'International Surrealist Exhibition', Galerie Beaux-Arts, Paris, 1938. As part of Ernst's work, we see on the floor the only male mannequin in the exhibition – a 'dead' one. Raoul Ubac's photograph clearly shows the widow mannequin's strategically parted cape, revealing stockings and hands and drawing the spectator's eye to her sex.**

by a Surrealist artist [33]. As Lewis Kachur has documented, the Surrealists put on a fantastic parade of sexual costuming, one that catered to every possible fetishistic desire.[58] The first mannequin was by Jean Arp and was smothered in a black bag with 'Papapillon' (papa butterfly) printed on it, then Yves Tanguy's mannequin wearing very little apart from a bulb, lit up, on her head as if she were leading the way. Then came Sonia Mossé's mannequin, veiled in green tulle with a green beetle at her mouth [34]. Following these were more mannequins by Marcel Duchamp, André Masson, Kurt Seligmann, Max Ernst, Joan Miró, Augustín Espinoza, Wolfgang Paalen, Salvador Dalí, Maurice Henry, Man Ray, Oscar Dominguez, Léo Malet and Marcel Jean.

According to Georges Hugnet, the Surrealists were most particular about the mannequins they used: they rejected the first lot that were delivered to them and chose a different model which they felt better embodied the 'Eternal Feminine'. These ones had svelte bodies, fashionable hairstyles, long eyelashes and slim breasts.[59] The Surrealists then turned the female fashion mannequin – typically a sexless, passive object – into an animate object of desire through erotic or bizarre dress, accessories, posture and lighting. As an object used to display consumer culture, the mannequin offered a symbolic means of addressing the trappings of commodity fetishism with her slim body, perfect face and dainty hands and feet. In using lifeless mannequins to evoke sexual titillation, the Surrealists paradoxically defied sexual desire, for it is the nature of the female mannequin that despite the perfect face, breasts, hands and feet she is ultimately sexless, having only a flattened pubic mound.

The mannequins on exhibit explored modern woman as surface and the iconography of consumer and modern sexual culture. The charged signification of the mannequin was noted by Walter Benjamin in his analyses of the aesthetics of mass culture. Writing about Paris in *The Arcades Project* (1927–40), Benjamin explained:

> The wax figure is in fact the scene where the appearance of
> humanity capsizes. That is to say, human surface, complexion
> and colour are expressed in her so completely and unsurpassably
> that this reproduction of its appearance outdoes itself, so that now
> the mannequin represents nothing but a dreadful, artful mediation
> between entrails and costume.[60]

Man Ray's mannequin seemed to stand in a state of metamorphosis between objectivity and subjectivity, between waxen clinical perfection and real flesh. She had glass tears on her face and under her armpits, glass bubble pipes in her hair, and ribbon around her waist inscribed with the words 'adieu foulard' (goodbye scarf). Her feet were encased in a cylindrical container, suggesting she was a shop mannequin, just arrived from her manufacturer and awaiting clothing for her perfect body.[61] She is an inanimate object but caters to the fantasy of a living doll, her ingeniously life-like face looking as if she could cry real tears.

Marcel Duchamp's mannequin contributed to the Surrealists' 'troubling' of traditional gender roles and their embrace of the feminine. She was *Rrose Sélavy*, a pun on 'Eros c'est la vie' (Eros, that's life), his alter ego and the subject of a series of images of Duchamp himself in transvestite dress which were taken by Man Ray in 1921 and 1924 [35]. Duchamp continued the cross-dressing theme in his mannequin, presenting Rrose in a waistcoat, jacket (with a red bulb in the breast pocket), tie and hat, her lower body naked to the male gaze apart from

34 Sonia Mossé's mannequin, veiled in green
tulle with a green beetle at her mouth, others in
her hair, and water lilies on her nubile body, at
the 'International Surrealist Exhibition', Galerie
Beaux-Arts, Paris, 1938. Photo by Gaston Paris.

35 **Man Ray, *Rrose Sélavy*, c.1921. In 1921
and 1924, Man Ray took portraits of Duchamp
cross-dressed as his female alter-ego, Rrose
Sélavy (a pun on 'Eros, c'est la vie', or 'Eros,
that's life'). Duchamp achieves a credible feminine
appearance by wearing a distinctly fashionable
and luxurious hat, stoal and coat. His hands
are actually those of Germaine Everling, Francis
Picabia's partner, who is hidden from view.**

her sensible men's brogues [36]. Where the male gaze might linger – across her exposed but sexless pubic mound – Duchamp had scrawled her name, as if Rrose had autographed her own sex. Here, gender roles were reversed through the simple inversion of dress codes and through a clever use of a word for visual effect. The potential for unselfconscious visual pleasure was disturbed and the mannequin, the object of desire and the male gaze, had become subject in mastering her own sex and returning the gaze.

André Masson's *Mannequin with Bird Cage* [10] also retaliated against the male gaze while playing on the power of the female as erotic Other. His mannequin's mouth was muted by a green velvet gag and a purple pansy, her head was trapped in an open-door birdcage through which celluloid goldfish swam, birds nested under her armpits, and her genitals were covered by a g-string and a plume, rising out of her bare pubic mound like fallopian tubes. Masson also placed a red ribbon around her waist, a detail that seemed to suggest a gash, or the separation of lower body and upper mind. This is like his contemporary mythological paintings, such as *Gradiva* (1939) [38], where a monstrous gaping vagina is juxtaposed with a raw steak.[62] In both the mannequin and painting, Masson explores the taboo of sexual violence. Woman's sex is presented as the gate to a labyrinth, the marvellous, a subterranean world of unleashed desire. For the mannequin's sex is richly adorned: eight tiger-eye gemstones decorate her g-string, which is made of mirror glass. Catching and reflecting the light, the tiger-eye naturally draws the spectator to it, while as an 'eye' it, and the mirror glass, reflect the spectator's gaze. Masson here reinforces the Surrealists' erotic eye but also plays on the traditional Cartesian mind-body dualism: his work juxtaposes the mystical power of the tiger-eye to concentrate the mind with the peculiar ability of the female sex to distract it. The spectator is encouraged to 'penetrate' a Surrealist world whose lighting, adornment and optical challenges speak not to an orderly, masculine rationalism but a disorderly, abject femininity. It is not surprising that Breton singled out Masson's mannequin and its 'veiled erotic' qualities for praise.[63]

The erotic potential of the mannequin had already been explored by Hans Bellmer in the the first and second doll, and in the Surrealist street six photographs of the second doll, *La Poupée*, hung between the mannequins of Hans Arp and Sonia Mossé, and another six between the mannequins of Léo Malet and Marcel Jean [37]. The photographs of the ball-jointed doll offered an interesting contrast in scale to the life-size mannequins, while the doll's contorted limbs and graphically exposed genital areas tied in perfectly with the Surrealists' aim to disorientate the spectator [40]. They generated a sense of the uncanny in depicting a polymorphously perverse object of desire.[64] They injected a note of death and sinister violence – the doll's grotesque imperfection contrasting starkly with the mass-produced beauty of the mannequins.

The various representations of mannequins at the Surrealist exhibition mixed appreciation of the erotic female form as harbouring a sense of life and death, attraction and repulsion. This was magnified by the use of evocative street signs which were displayed on the wall behind the mannequins and which alternated real street signs for the 'Rue Vivienne' or 'Porte de Lilas' with made-up signs for the 'Street of Lips', 'All Devils Street', 'Weak Street' and 'Blood Transfusion Street' [39]. Between the mannequins and the street signs, the *rue surréaliste* subverted the role of the street in the city as a space of commerce and social order, and staged instead an uncanny city of marvellous encounters and commotion.

36 **Marcel Duchamp, Rrose Sélavy mannequin, 'International Surrealist Exhibition', Galerie Beaux-Arts, Paris, 1938. Photo by Raoul Ubac.**

37 **Mannequins by Oscar Dominguez (left), Léo Malet (centre) and Marcel Jean (right), with photographs of Hans Bellmer's *La Poupée* in between, in the street of mannequins at the 'International Surrealist Exhibition', Galerie Beaux-Arts, Paris, 1938. Photo by Josef Breitenbach.**

38 **André Masson, *Gradiva*, 1939.** Influenced by Sigmund Freud's 1907 analysis of Wilhelm Jensen's *Gradiva: A Pompeian Fantasy* (1903), and Giorgio de Chirico's paintings of *Ariadne* from 1913, Masson shows Gradiva in the midst of metamorphosis: stone turns to flesh, honey bees swarm at her breast and Vesuvius erupts in the background. Gradiva's right foot casts a dagger-like shadow which penetrates her monstrously dilated sex which is in turn juxtaposed with a large fleshy steak. Masson's variation on the myth of Pygmalion reflects his fascination with the Marquis de Sade and sexual violence, played out on woman as erotic terrain.

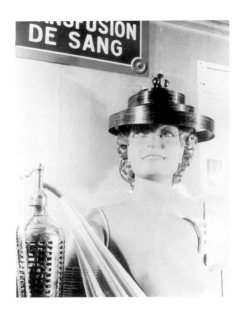

39 Oscar Dominguez's mannequin under the street sign 'Blood Transfusion Street' at the 'International Surrealist Exhibition', Galerie Beaux-Arts, Paris, 1938. Photo by Raoul Ubac.

It evoked Surrealist *amour fou* (mad love), the glamorous decadence of brothels, and the 'Secret Paris' of the 1930s, with its half-dressed prostitutes, seedy couples in cafés, tramps and opium dens made famous by the contemporary photographer Brassaï.[65] The 'Surrealist city' was mapped out in the dictionary-cum-catalogue produced for the exhibition, *Le Dictionnaire abrégé du surréalisme* (Concise Dictionary of Surrealism).[66] This city drew on the familiar aspects of Paris while insisting on a peculiarly Surrealist vision of it. It evoked the Paris of Breton's *Nadja* or Louis Aragon's *Paysan de Paris* (1926): a city full of potential for the unforeseen erotic encounter. The exhibition brought the outmoded spaces of Paris into the limelight, and made the unwitting spectator feel a sense of un-homeliness in his/her own city as a result.

This unveiling of the unknown also operated on another level which drew its charge from the conservative sexual mores of inter-war bourgeois French society and in particular the taboo which surrounded imagery and discussion of sex. The Surrealists were well aware that no single image carried more power than that of the female sex – an image which, as we have seen, they frequently deployed in their painting, photography and objects. However, it can be argued that the very layout of the 1938 Surrealist exhibition was itself a representation of the female sex in spatial terms. In Breton and Eluard's collaborative, automatic text *The Immaculate Conception* (1930) a section on 'intra-uterine life' revels in the utopian vision of a world where the conventional separation of private and public, inner and outer experience, rational and automatic thought, day and night are done away with.[67]

The intra-uterine theme was also continued in the Surrealist review *Minotaure*, notably in articles by Tristan Tzara and Roberto Matta. As Anthony Vidler has pointed out, the Surrealists antipathy to modernist, functionalist architecture and fascination with architecture's 'unconscious' was made evident in Tzara and Matta's essays, where primitive, maternal, intra-uterine constructions were promoted.[68] In his 1933 essay on taste in *Minotaure*, Tzara contrasts modern architecture, which is 'hygienic and lacking in ornaments' and so 'has no chance of living', to primitive architecture, which is imbued with life and has an inherently maternal, vaginal nature:

> Ever since the cave, for man inhabits the earth, 'the mother', through
> to the yurt of the Eskimo, the intermediary form between the grotto
> and the tent, remarkable example of uterine construction which one
> enters through cavities with vaginal forms, to the conical or half-
> spherical hut fitted at its entrance with a post of sacred character,
> the dwelling symbolizes prenatal comfort.[69]

For Tzara the architecture of the future will be 'intra-uterine...if it renounces its interpretor-servant role for the bourgeoisie'.[70]

Tzara's appreciation of the maternal, intra-uterine space was further explored by Matta in an article in 1938 in which he outlined his design for an apartment [41]. It would be vertiginous with 'different levels, a stairs without a handrail to overcome the void' and had such details as 'Ionic psychological columns' and 'supple pneumatic armchairs'.[71] This was an emphatically soft, tactile maternal space: 'Man misses the dark thrusts of his origin which enveloped him in damp walls where the blood beat close to the eye with the noise of the mother'.[72] Matta's essay evokes an architecture that resonates with the feminine and the power of the mother, ending with an evocative call: 'We ask our mothers to give birth to an apartment with warm lips'.[73]

40 Hans Bellmer, *The Doll* (*La Poupée*), 1935.
Bellmer's second doll, with her ball joints and
multiple limbs, allowed for greater physical,
and by extension greater erotic, manipulation.
Her four-legged, headless, naked form, staged in
nature, presents the spectator with a disturbing
image of illicit desire.

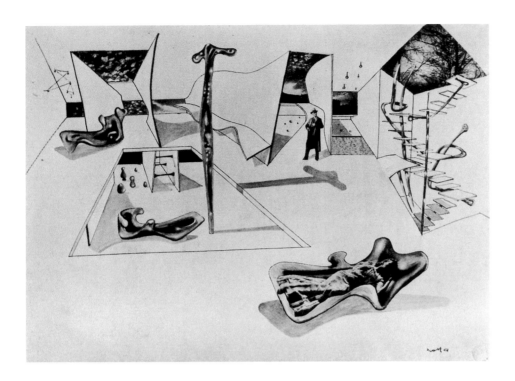

41 **Roberto Matta, illustration for 'Mathématique sensible – Architecture du temps',** *Minotaure,* **no.11, Spring 1938, p.43. Matta's vision of an intra-uterine architecture in his essay is reflected in his drawing with its organic, curvaceous forms. His furniture design (right foreground) bears striking similarities with the furniture Frederick Kiesler designed for Peggy Guggenheim's Art of this Century gallery in New York in 1942.**

These two essays offer a useful corporeal description for the architectural design of the 1938 exhibition. The *rue surréaliste* led to the main room of the exhibition, a round central gallery space which took the form of a dark, warm and wet grotto. It was designed by Duchamp and described by Marcel Jean as 'one of the most remarkable object-pictures – on the architectural scale – which Surrealism has ever known'.[74] In it 1,200 coal sacks (filled with newspaper) were suspended from the ceiling, over a grate which was the only source of light.[75] Like Dalí's *Rainy Taxi*, Duchamp's grotto inverted the entire gallery experience, negating the room's classical interior. The denial of the traditional, supposedly 'neutral' viewing experience continued in other elements of the grotto's design: there were dead leaves on the floor and installations each with their own symbolic significance, such as an artificial pool (symbolic of the synthesis of the inner and outer world), an iron brazier burning coals (symbolic of friendship), and four immense beds (symbolic of love) [1 & 43]. In addition, the smell of brewing Brazilian coffee ('odeurs du Brésil' as the catalogue described it) and the sound of hysterical laughter filled the room.[76] This laughter had been recorded at an insane asylum and was played on a hidden phonograph. It lent an uncanny, macabre tone to the spectator's experience for, as Man Ray stated, it was intended to dissuade 'any desire on the part of visitors to laugh and joke'.[77] The sound of German marching music also filled the air. The space contradicted the 'Degenerate Art' exhibition where Hitler's voice had been broadcast over a public-address system and the work of the avant-garde and the insane had been conflated.

The exhibition also involved a performance by the dancer Hélène Vanel which took the taboo and fear of hysteria even further. Wearing nothing but a torn white costume, she performed her erotic *L'Acte manqué* (Unconsummated Act) on the beds offering an autonomous invocation of uninhibited movement [42].[78] Spectators saw Vanel gyrating, wailing and wrestling with a live rooster as well as splashing in

42 **Hélène Vanel performing** *L'Acte manqué*
(Unconsummated Act*)* **at the 'International
Surrealist Exhibition', Galerie Beaux-Arts, Paris,
17 January 1938. Vanel is described in the
1938** *Dictionnaire abrégé du surréalisme* **as
a 'Surrealist dancer' and 'The Iris of Mists'.**

43 **The main grotto, leading from the street of
mannequins, at the 'International Surrealist
Exhibition', Galerie Beaux-Arts, Paris, 1938.
Photo by Josef Breitenbach.**

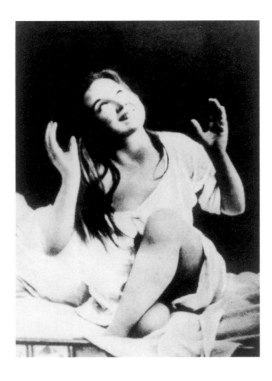

44 Photograph of 'Augustine', a patient of Jean-Martin Charcot at the Salpêtrière Hospital in Paris in the 1870s and 1880s, from the André Breton and Louis Aragon article on 'Les Attitudes Passionelles en 1878' in *La Révolution surréaliste*, no.11, 15 March 1928.

the pool. This 'proto-Happening' was described by Dalí as having a 'Dionysiac fervour' which 'carried the whole audience into demential delirium'.[79] Indeed, the performance was reminiscent of the hysteria documented by Jean-Martin Charcot at Salpêtrière Hospital in Paris in the 1870s and 1880s, especially those women suffering from 'hystero-epilepsy' where the patient's attack had three stages: the epileptoid phase where the woman lost consciousness and foamed at the mouth; the clownish phase where she contorted her body; and the 'attitudes passionnelles' phase, where she mimed incidents and emotions from her life. This last phase was often sexual and photographs of patients engaged in it were given such labels as 'ecstasy', 'eroticism' and 'amorous supplication' by Charcot in his records. Charcot claimed that parts of the body could trigger these convulsions when pressed – the ovarian region was particularly sensitive, he found.[80] The Surrealists celebrated Charcot's studies and the phenomenon of ecstatic 'hysteria' in an issue of their review *La Révolution surréaliste* in 1928 [44].[81] Vanel's performance, while *staged*, unleashed the disturbing power not just of uncontrolled eroticism but insanity too, exploiting the 'uncanny effect of epileptic fits, and of manifestations of insanity' in Freud's words.[82] Not only was the central grotto reminiscent of a brothel with its beds, it now took on the chaos of an asylum. Indeed, it might be seen as a celebration of what Julia Kristeva would later describe as the abject power of *jouissance* – 'a time of oblivion and thunder…where the subject is swallowed up'.[83] This orgiastic mood was compounded by the works on exhibit such as Joan Miró's *Le Corps de ma brune* (1925) where text caresses image [45] and Roland Penrose's 1937 collage *Real Woman* [46], which hung beside one of the beds. In this collage a fragmented female torso (without head, arms or legs) and a bird's head are linked by decalcomania detail and cut-out touristique postcard images to a bright orange trail that leads from the bird to a tropical image strategically positioned to cover her sex.

As if this were not enough lascivious drama for one evening, visitors also nervously awaited the appearance of the 'authentic descendant of Frankenstein, the automaton Enigmarelle' due, as it was stated on the invitation, to cross the main hall at midnight 'in false flesh and false blood'. The public must have been relieved when the *Nosferatu*-like creature did not materialize within this microcosmic Surrealist city, and yet one suspects the Surrealists realized that Enigmarelle's absence lent it greater presence, the unseen object of horror often being more frightening than the seen. The exhibition attempted to capture the city in all its uncanny Gothic aspects, in addition to invoking a sense of erotic temptation and fear (that doubled-edged power of the uncanny) in its citizens. Given the architectural design of the exhibition, the orchestration and lighting of the gallery space, the erotic installations, the special effects (noise, smells) that punctuated the spectator's experience, and Vanel's performance, this was an exhibition that revelled in the uncanny and all its hysterical, abject, feminine power.

The exhibition created a space which was at once tactile and interactive as well as emphatically feminine. It was staged so as to invoke a sense of dislocation, of subjective intuition and emotional outbursts as the spectator was 'liberated' from the repressive day-to-day masculine environment. The space exposed repressed psychological anxiety and abandoned rationality (a male characteristic according to the western metaphysical tradition), and replaced it with irrationality and its feminine qualities (the insane, the primitive, subjective intuition, emotion and passion according to the same tradition).[84]

But there was also a political subversion and resistance behind this uncanny exhibition, its intra-uterine forms, passionate celebration of hysteria and general assault on the spectator. In its evocation and celebration of the feminine Other, the exhibition may be viewed as an allegorical assault on contemporary Fascism and French pacifism towards Hitler. As witnessed in the 'Degenerate Art' exhibition of 1937, Hitler's propaganda machine pronounced anyone who did not conform to the Aryan ideal to be weak and beneath contempt. Jews, Communists, homosexuals, Negroes, the insane, Freemasons, Dadaists and the avant-garde were all depicted in terms of the despicable Other – an Other which was frequently depicted in feminized or sexually deviant terms. Despite the burgeoning threat of Hitler in Germany, in 1937 the French government gave pride of place to the German pavilion at the 'International Exhibition of Arts and Technology applied to Modern Life'.[85] The 1938 Surrealist exhibition retaliated with everything the Nazis despised – exhibiting degenerate artists and sexually provocative art that evoked hysteria and the contamination of blood (and so of race). Vanel's performance mocked the patriotic masculinity of the French state. In wrestling with a rooster, an emblem of bravery in France, her hysterically erotic performance may be seen as mocking French *patrimoine* and bourgeois passivity.

The reaction of the French press to the exhibition compounded the political tension at the time. The exhibition was criticized for its assault on French taste and its 'foreignness'. In a review of 20 January in the Catholic daily, *La Croix*, the critic Louis Brunet described it as 'amusing' but accused Surrealism of having a brain incapable of appreciating beauty, lacking talent, and intending simply to 'shock the bourgeois'. Brunet dismissed Surrealism as 'no more French than a Hottentot', a derogatory and colonialist reference to South African native peoples, stereotyped by Imperial French culture for their supposed primitive sexual lasciviousness.[86]

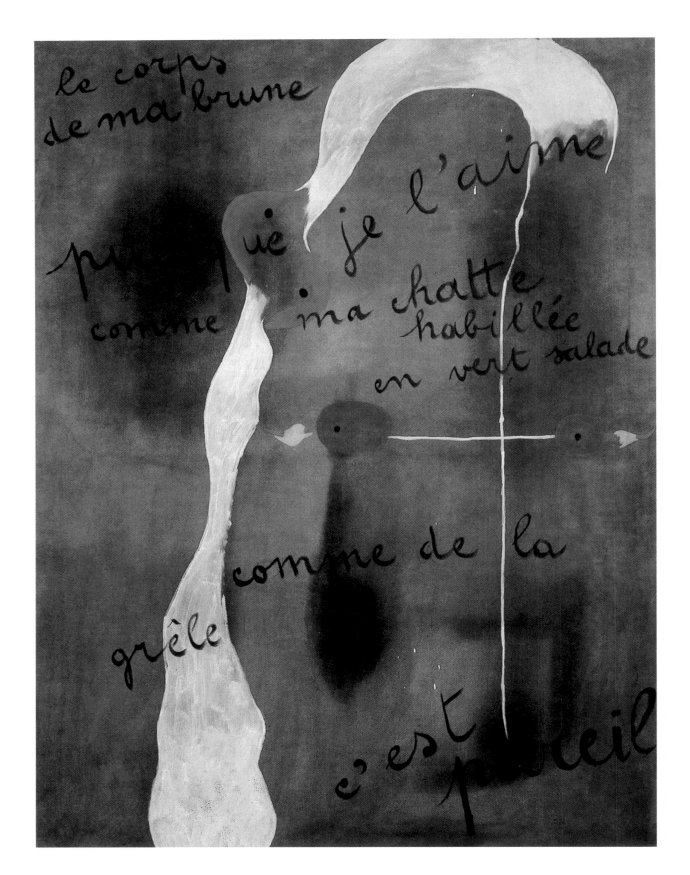

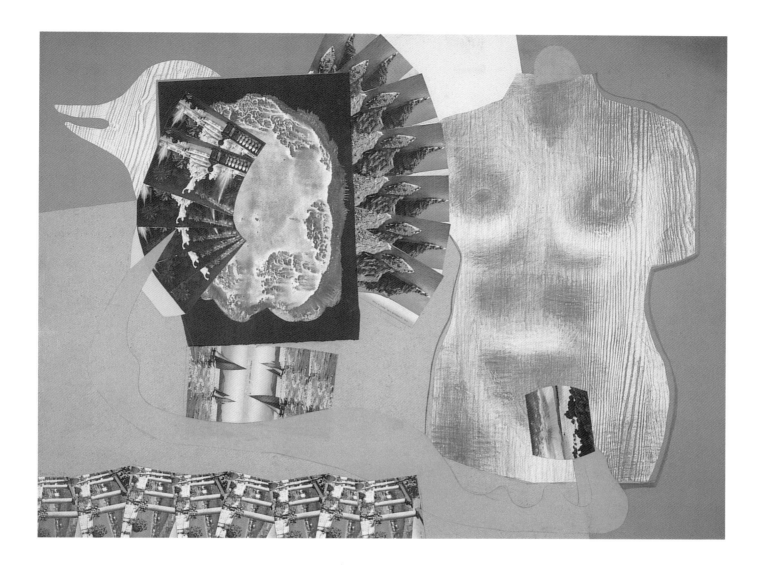

45 Joan Miró, *Le Corps de ma brune*, 1925. In this poem-painting, woman is traced with the words 'Le corps de ma brune puisque je l'aime comme ma chatte habillée en vert salade comme de la grêle c'est pareil' which translates as 'The body of my dark-haired woman because I love her like my cat dressed in salad green like hail it's all the same.' She appears frontally, with blue breasts on a bare skeletal cross and in profile, swooning with enflamed red breasts. Words and image fluctuate to create a sense of pulsating desire.

46 Roland Penrose, *Real Woman*, collage, 1937. Penrose plays with Freudian displacement and encourages the spectator to find images within images, most notably associating woman with an exotic bird of prey, and her sex with a vibrant sunset.

The magazine *Marianne* produced a more sophisticated response, giving lengthy, illustrated accounts of the exhibition in two articles. Maurice Henry's 'Le Surréalisme dans le décor' spoke directly to the exhibition's fantastic design and was illustrated with photographs of six mannequins (the heads of the mannequins by Jean, Dalí, Seligmann, Paalen, Ernst and Masson), and three of the paintings on show – Dalí's *Sleep* (1937) [47], Magritte's *The Healer* (1937) [48] and Penrose's *Seeing is Believing* (1937) [49]. Henry, a writer and cartoonist and member of the Surrealist group since 1933, wrote that Surrealist exhibitions inspire a variety of responses from the public: 'curiosity, sympathy or reprobation.' The 1938 exhibition, he explained, was intended as 'an honest expression of the current state of the movement.' It was staged so that the visitor had to 'abandon him/herself to an adventure', and that the mannequins of 'very beautiful women' were intended to 'invite [the spectator] to dream'.[87] The call to sensory and sexual abandon, he wrote, was augmented by paintings by Ernst, Masson, Picasso and Tanguy.

Yet if Henry's article revels in the tension between dream and nightmare in the exhibition, then René Guetta's review, 'L'Expo du rêve', two pages later in *Marianne*, gives us an even greater appreciation of the erotic nature of this tension and its uncanny effect on the viewing public. Guetta effectively re-enacts the experience of the exhibition space for his readers, as a 'poor little boy', a sexual innocent, who finds the whole experience renders him sexually 'limp'. Guetta evokes the sense of excitement and chaos at the opening night of the show; indeed, it was the sight of cars and crowds of elegantly clad couples excited and agitated and battling to enter the gallery that intrigued him and led him to want to see the show for himself on the opening night. He emphasizes the sheer horror of seeing so many mutilated, erotic bodies on show. He describes Dalí's semi-nude mannequin in the *Rainy Taxi* as cadaverous and the mannequins as 'mute, haughty' and 'delicious'. Guetta praises the round grotto room whose beds remind him of a brothel ('lits d'hôtel de passe') and which engenders 'A creepy, gnawing sensation of sickness, but real in my throat', an experience he finds 'sinisterly erotic'.[88] Every object leads him to think of torture, especially Dominguez's *Never* whose turning wheel allows a disembodied hand to caress disembodied breasts. Hugnet's gargantuan bloomers and later Miró's painting *Le Corps de ma brune* seem to overwhelm Guetta with an excess of the feminine erotic.

Aspects of the exhibition's *Concise Dictionary of Surrealism* suggest Guetta's experience was the very one the Surrealists hoped for. Several of the definitions allude to the uncanny and its feminine qualities in spatial terms. 'Eroticism' is defined as 'a sumptuous ceremony in an underground passage' and 'Woman' in Charles Baudelaire's terms as 'the being who casts the greatest shadow or light in our dreams'.[89] The erotic, brothel-cum-asylum atmosphere of the exhibition, staged in an emphatically 'nocturnal' light, seems to have been best described by Breton's own definition of 'night': 'Dirty night, night of flowers, night of groans, intoxicating night, deaf night whose hand is an abject kite held back by strings on all sides, black strings, ashamed strings!'[90]

Meanwhile, the *Concise Dictionary of Surrealism* and the exhibition may be seen as having made several references to the 'International Exhibition of Arts and Technology applied to Modern Life'. In a parody of that exhibition, the Surrealist exhibition pamphlet had a list of 'participating artists' and below a list of 'countries represented' but it refused to link specific names to specific nations. For the Surrealists, international meant without nation, united through Surrealism.

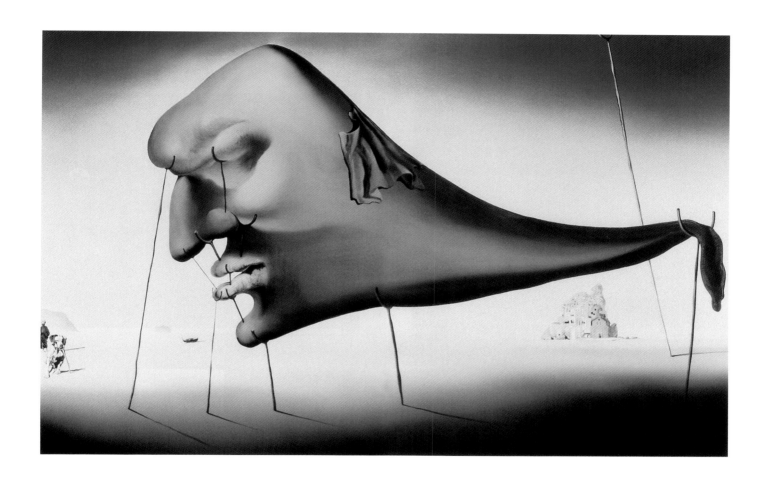

47 **Salvador Dalí,** *Sleep*, **1937. The sleeping face in profile may be that of Dalí or an allusion to the 'Sleeping Rock' of his beloved Cap Creus. The crutch symbolizes sexual anxiety, while the cape on the creature's neck may allude to the little cape which billows on the back of the cyclist in Dalí and Buñuel's 1928 film,** *Un Chien andalou*. **In** *Minotaure*, **no.10, Winter 1937, Dalí claimed Michelangelo and Gaudí saw sleep in similar terms, and linked the town to the right with 'the well-known summering town that appears in the boring dream of Piero della Francesca'.**

48 René Magritte, *The Healer*, 1937. The subject of several works by Magritte, *The Healer* has no face but could be an image of the artist as shaman or a self-portrait. The latter reading is fortified by the fact that in 1937 Magritte was photographed in the same pose with a blanket over his head and a canvas where the bird cage is.

49 Roland Penrose, *Seeing is Believing (I'lle Invisible)*, 1937. Michel Remy, in *Surrealism in Britain*, suggests this is the town of Ys which, in Breton mythology, was covered by the tide when the King's daughter drowned and metamorphosed into a mermaid, 'Morgane'. Certainly, André Breton favoured this enchantress, also known as Fata Morgana and Morgan le Fay. She is often represented by a castle half on land, half on sea, as she is a creature who would lure unsuspecting sailors to their death with the mirage of a safe harbour.

50 **André Breton, Diego Rivera and Léon Trotsky, Mexico, July 1938.**

Where the 'International Exhibition of Arts and Technology applied to Modern Life' attempted to unite opposites and to reassure the public of French power in Europe, the 1938 Surrealist exhibition did the very opposite. It celebrated difference, disorientated the spectator, mocked the search for knowledge and truth in art and exhibitions, and erased the cult of nationalism. The 1938 exhibition was not a neutral space but an uncanny one and, by extension, a *contested* terrain which exposed society's desires and fears, vulnerable Self and abject Other. It was a prophetic indicator of the dark days to come. As Breton acknowledged in 1947:

> [That the exhibition] proved to be, alas, only too premonitory, too portentous, has only been borne out in terms of gloom, suffocation, and shadiness. To those who, so vehemently at the time, accused us of having wallowed in that atmosphere, it will be all too easy to point out that we had stopped well short of the darkness and of the underhanded cruelty of the coming days. We did not deliberately create that atmosphere: it merely conveyed the acute sense of foreboding with which we anticipated the coming decade.[91]

Soon after the exhibition was shown at the Galerie Beaux-Arts a selection of the works went on display in Amsterdam (3 June – 1 August at the Robert Gallery) and then in The Hague (10–30 September at the Koninklijke Kunstzaal Kleykamp), both shows organized by Georges Hugnet as Breton was in Mexico. It was there, in the summer of 1938, that Breton formulated his resistance to totalitarianism, in Germany and the Soviet Union, in a tract he wrote with Trotsky [50]. The tract, published by the Fédération Internationale de l'Art Révolutionnaire Indépendant (FIARI) in their review *Clé*, called for an 'independent art', free from political constraints and propaganda.[92] This was a clear stand against Fascism, and was warmly welcomed by the neo-Surrealist *Réverbères* review in November 1938.[93] The tracts 'N'imitez pas Hitler!', published in *Clé* in February 1939, and 'Le Nationalisme dans l'art', published in May 1939 in the last number of *Minotaure*, further indicate the Surrealists' resistance to Fascism and their disillusionment with the French government.

On 10 April 1938, Léon Blum had fallen from power as Prime Minister of France, largely due to the failure of his government to resist Franco in the Spanish Civil War. He was replaced by Edouard Daladier who joined with Adolf Hitler, Neville Chamberlain and Benito Mussolini in signing the Munich Agreement, which transferred the Sudetenland of Czechoslovakia to Germany, on 30 September 1938. This strategy of appeasement was in vain, however: Hitler violated the agreement by invading the rest of Czechoslovakia in March 1939, and invaded Poland on 1 September 1939, which provoked France and Britain to declare war on Germany on 3 September. Raul Reynaud became France's new Prime Minister in March 1940 and Daladier the Minister of War. In May 1940, the worst fears of Surrealists and non-Surrealists alike were realized when Germany invaded France. On 3 June the Germans bombed Paris and ten days later marched on the capital to begin a four-year occupation of the city which would end the first phase of Surrealism and would have severe repercussions for the direction of the movement and the lives of its members. [51].

51 **Albert Speer, Adolf Hitler and Arno Breker on the esplanade of the Palais de Chaillot, Paris, 23 June 1940.**

52 Leonora Carrington and Max Ernst at St Martin d'Ardèche, Summer 1939. Carrington met Max Ernst in London in 1937 and was living with him at St Martin d'Ardèche until the outbreak of World War II when he was interned as an enemy alien. Photo by Lee Miller.

53 Max Ernst, *The Robing of the Bride*, 1940. This painting may be seen as a portrait of war and of Leonora Carrington, whom Ernst called 'The Bride of the Wind'. Ernst's own imprisonment is suggested by the heron-like green creature that captures the 'Bride', a magnificent woman, mirrored in a decalcomania painting (the chance 'finding' of pictorial form in wet, sometimes sponged/blotted, paint) on the wall behind. Her magical powers are revealed in her plumed robe, the engorged throat (which may symbolize the expulsion of demons) of her female ally with wild (decalcomania) hair, the grotesque creature of fertility in the lower right, and her owl-like face which identifies her with magic, superstition and the night. Amidst this struggle, the Bride calmly looks out at the spectator, reminding us that the owl was the bird sacred to Pallas Athene, the Greek goddess of wisdom.

CHAPTER TWO

Surrealism and World War II

A new spirit will be born from the present war…The new intellectual
'frissons' are all that count. As always in such periods when socially
human life is almost worthless, I think we must learn to read with
and look through the eyes of Eros – Eros, who, in time to come, will
have the task of re-establishing that equilibrium briefly broken for
the benefit of death.

André Breton, *View*, 1941[1]

By the time Hitler marched on Paris, most of the Surrealists had fled the city. André
Breton, who had been demobilized from the army medical corps in Poitiers, was *en
route* to Martigues, near Marseilles, where his wife Jacqueline Lamba and daughter
Aube were staying with Pierre Mabille. André Masson was in Fréluc in the Auvergne
with his wife Rose (who was Jewish) and his two sons. Max Ernst, who had been
imprisoned at internment camps – first at Largentière and then at Camp des Milles
near Aix-en-Provence – was *en route* to Marseilles. His lover, the painter Leonora
Carrington, had fled from their home in St Martin d'Ardèche to Spain when Ernst
was first interned [52 & 53]. There she suffered a mental breakdown and was
briefly committed to Dr Morales's Psychiatric Clinic in Santander by her family, an
experience she would document in 'Down Below' (1944).[2] Like Ernst, Hans Bellmer

54 **Vichy police on patrol in Marseilles, 1940.**

55 **Varian Fry, Marseilles, Autumn 1940. Fry (1907–66), a young editor from New York, courageously committed himself to a mission to rescue endangered prominent persons, including André Breton, from Marseilles in 1940–1. He was posthumously honoured by the United States Holocaust Memorial Council with the Eisenhower Liberation Medal in 1991 and by Yad VaShem, the Holocaust Martyrs' and Heroes' Remembrance Authority, Jerusalem as the first American 'Righteous Among the Nations' in 1996.**

was also interned in Milles in September 1939 and when he was released in June 1940 he travelled to Marseilles. By then René Magritte and Raoul Ubac were also in the south, staying in Carcassonne with Joë Bousquet. Victor Brauner, Jacques Hérold and Oscar Dominguez were staying with the poet Robert Rius in Perpignan.[3] Benjamin Péret, who had been mobilized at Nantes and then imprisoned at Rennes for 'threatening State security', would move south to Marseilles in the autumn, and then, to escape what he called 'l'enfer de Pétain', he fled to Mexico via Casablanca with the painter Remedios Varo in the winter of 1941–2.[4] Wolfgang Paalen had moved to Mexico in 1939, where he was to launch the review *Dyn* in 1942. Joan Miró had made his way to Varengeville in Normandy and then on to Palma de Majorca. Yves Tanguy fled to New York when war was declared and went on to settle in Reno, Nevada with the artist Kay Sage. Other Surrealists to leave France for the United States in 1939 were Kurt Seligmann and Roberto Matta. Man Ray and Gordon Onslow Ford followed them in 1940, as did the now ex-member Dalí (who had been ousted from the movement in 1939 for being enamoured with Fascism, and who was nicknamed *Avida Dollars* by Breton for his love of money).[5] Dalí sailed from Lisbon with Gala; Duchamp also sailed from Marseilles to the United States via Casablanca and Lisbon in May 1942.

The mass exodus to the south of France was not peculiar to the Surrealist group. In May 1940, the month before the armistice between Vichy France and Germany, 406 boats carrying 135,000 passengers sailed from Marseilles.[6] The city was still relatively safe for political refugees, as well as the first step to the United States or Cuba via North Africa or Spain, because it was under the control of Marshal Pétain's Vichy regime until the Nazis occupied the whole of France in 1942 [54]. As a result, Marseilles was an important transit point for artists, writers and philosophers, especially those whose work was deemed undesirable on political or artistic grounds by Vichy French and German officials. Parisian exiles grouped together in Marseilles: Jean Ballard's review *Les Cahiers du sud* offered a voice to artists and writers; Sylvain Itkine directed a number of plays including André Roussin's *Les Barbes nobles* (for which Jacques Hérold designed the sets and costumes); and Léo Sauvage, who set up Les Compagnons de la Basoche in 1940, gathered refugee comedians who performed at the Salle de l'Ecran and the Salle Mazenod.[7]

The Surrealists also regrouped in Marseilles and were organized by Breton from a villa in which he was staying called Air Bel. The villa was run by the Emergency Rescue Committee, set up by American patrons to rescue German refugees and Jewish and Communist intellectuals from the Nazis.[8] The man charged with organizing this rescue project in France was Varian Fry [55]: a young American Quaker and ex-Harvard scholar in classics, who had travelled to Germany in 1935 and witnessed the Hitler regime first-hand and who was determined to save its victims.[9] When Fry arrived in Marseilles on 14 August 1940 it was full of demobilized soldiers and refugees. Amidst the chaos he proceeded to put his rescue campaign into action, setting up a Centre Américain de Secours (American Relief Centre) on the rue Grignan and then the boulevard Garibaldi, and renting the villa Air Bel from an old man by the name of Dr Thumin as a safe house half an hour from Marseilles. Between August 1940 and September 1941, with the aid of legitimate and forged passports and visas, the committee organized the successful escape of some 2,000 refugees from Pétainist France, including writers Hannah Arendt and Wilhelm Herzog, film theorist Siegfried Kracauer, novelist Franz Werfel,

painter Marc Chagall, sculptor Jacques Lipchitz, photographer Hans Namuth and Breton's friend the Trotskyite writer Victor Segre. Some refugees on Fry's list were less fortunate. Some took their own lives – for example, Fry noted in his memoir that 'Ernst Weiss, the Czech novelist had taken poison in his room in Paris when the Germans entered the city', and that Carl Einstein, 'the art critic who specialized in Negro art had hanged himself at the Spanish frontier when he found he could not get across.'[10]

André Breton was also on the list and he and his family were given a large room in the villa, an imposing building described by Fry as: 'closed as tight as a fortress, the walls and garden overrun with weeds...but the view across the valley to the Mediterranean was enchanting.' It was 'solid nineteenth-century bourgeois from top to bottom.'[11] The Surrealists congregated here around Breton [56 & 57]. According to Fry, Breton 'talked magnificently about everything and everybody, and held Surrealist reunions on Sunday afternoons, attended by the entire Deux Magots crowd, as mad as ever.'[12] His wife, Jacqueline Lamba, was described by Fry in equally colourful terms as 'blonde and beautiful and savage, with painted toenails, necklaces of tiger's teeth, and bits of mirror in her hair.'[13] A contemporary drawing by Masson [58], who was one of the Surrealists who spent a lot of time with Breton at the villa, captures Breton and Lamba in a manner that echoes Fry's vision of them. Done in February 1941, it shows Lamba, muse-like with sparkling hair and long eyelashes, beside a leonine Breton who bears a stern stare and who is shielded by her breast on one side and the sea on the other. Masson's art at the outbreak of war had been more aggressive in tone. In 1939 in his *Anatomy of My Universe*, he

56 **Wifredo Lam, Jacques Hérold, André Breton and Oscar Dominguez in front of Villa Air Bel, Marseilles, 1941.**

57 **Varian Fry (right foreground), André Breton (centre) and friends at Villa Air Bel, Marseilles, Winter 1940–1.**

58 André Masson, *Portrait of André Breton and Jacqueline Lamba*, 1941. Masson's ink drawing portrays Breton as defiantly leonine and his second wife, the artist Jacqueline Lamba, as 'blonde and beautiful and savage', in Varian Fry's words.

revealed his obsession with attraction and repulsion, masochism and Sadism. He depicted a 'Sadean constellation', which he defined as a 'primordial instinct' and embodied in ink as a half-beast and half-man wielding a phallic knife, which he has just used to wound a contorted female victim.[14] In Masson's work in the first year of the war bodily trauma seemed to echo national trauma. However, his images of 1940–1, produced during this period in Marseilles, are much more pensive and often naive in style. In his pastel drawing, *The Roughneck Soldier* [59], we see a cartoon-like image of a soldier with a menacing mouth with teeth, machine-like head and plumed helmet. A more sophisticated style is evident in his charcoal and gouache painting *Study for the Voyage* (1941–2), where we find the French landscape nostalgically evoked through feminine curves and brilliant Mediterranean colours, so that Marseilles harbour is like a face, a clump of flora like a breast, and *la belle France* portrayed almost as a lover whom Masson is forced to leave.

This is certainly the nostalgic mood of the art and life at Air Bel where food was scarce but conversation plentiful. As well as Masson, Oscar Dominguez, Wifredo Lam, Jacques Hérold and Victor Brauner were among the regular visitors to the Bretons at the villa. During the first year of the war other Surrealists came too: Hans Bellmer, Benjamin Péret, René Char, Max Ernst (with Peggy Guggenheim whom he would marry in New York on 30 December 1941), Gilbert Lely, Raoul Ubac as well as Marcel Duchamp, Marc Chagall and Tristan Tzara. As a result of such numbers, collective activities were plentiful. Breton organized collective drawings (notably with Brauner, Dominguez, Lam, Hérold, Jacqueline Lamba), communicated drawings (where a participant was shown an image quickly and then had to draw it from memory), collective collages (Dominguez, Lam, Breton), and a collective book (as a birthday gift for Wifredo Lam's wife, Helena Holzer).[15] The group even staged a mock art auction led by Sylvain Itkine.[16] These activities, though ludic, were poignantly political. For example, a collective drawing of 1940 displayed caricatures of Adolf Hitler and the Vichy Prime Minister Pétain [60]. Beside the comic Pétain are cut-out letters that spell *l'âne* (donkey). In another frame he is again caricatured with graffiti-eyebrows and two cartoon kings mock his status. In a third frame a dove is depicted. Such collective works of art served to keep spirits up and, as Masson explained, to 'ward off the anxiety'.[17]

Breton planned to hold an exhibition of works by the Surrealists in Marseilles in January 1941, with the assistance of Jean Ballard, but his plans fell through. Instead, he devised a game that resulted in what might be seen as a miniature, portable exhibition of works – *Le Jeu de Marseille/Marseilles Deck of Cards* [61]. This was a Surrealist deck of cards based on the Tarot of Marseilles, a deck that dated back to the Renaissance and was famously engraved by Nicolas Conver in 1760. The Surrealists modification of the deck of cards was not just artistic, it was political. Breton noted that their design reflected the Surrealists 'sensibility' at the time and that 'Historiographers of the playing card are agreed that the modifications it has undergone over the centuries have always been linked with great military setbacks'.[18] The Surrealists replaced the King and Queen – symbols of authority and tyranny – with their own totemic figures, namely the Genius and the Mermaid; while the Joker was replaced with the Magus in the person of Alfred Jarry's *Ubu*. Four new suits of cards were devised to complement these new figures: the flame (signifying love), the black star (signifying dream), the wheel (signifying revolution), and the lock (signifying knowledge). The face cards were replaced by

59 André Masson, *The Roughneck Soldier*, 1940–1.

60 *Collective Drawing*, 1940. Made of ink, colour pencils and collage on paper, this collective drawing demonstrates the Surrealists' black sense of humour in their political subversion as they mock Pétain and Hitler. Breton organized many creative sessions, notably involving Victor Brauner, Oscar Dominguez, Wifredo Lam, Jacques Hérold, Jacqueline Lamba and Breton himself, where collective drawings, communicated drawings (where a participant was shown an image quickly and then had to draw it from memory), and collective collages were made.

61 **Victor Brauner, André Breton, Oscar Dominguez, Max Ernst, Jacques Hérold, Wifredo Lam, Jacqueline Lamba and André Masson**, selection of cards from *Le Jeu de Marseille/Marseilles Deck of Cards*, 1940, reproduced in *VVV*, New York, nos 2–3, 1943.

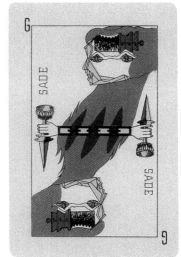

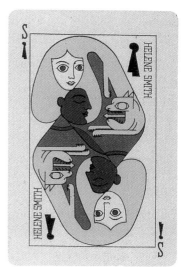

62 **Wifredo Lam, 'Alice' card, *Le Jeu de Marseille/Marseilles Deck of Cards*, 1940.** Lewis Carroll's *Alice's Adventures in Wonderland* (1865) was one of the books favoured by the Surrealists and Alice was selected for the deck as a 'siren of dream'.

a number of Surrealist forefathers, including Freud, Sade, Lautréamont, the German romantic poet Novalis, the sixteenth-century occultist Paracelsus, Baudelaire, Hegel, the Mexican revolutionary Pancho Villa, the seventeenth-century romantic writer known as 'the Portuguese nun', and the late nineteenth-century medium and Outsider artist (Catherine Elise Müller) known as Hélène Smith, whose paintings Breton had used to illustrate his article on 'Le Message automatique' in *Minotaure*, nos 3–4, 1933. There were also literary characters, namely Stendhal's female heroine Lamiel, and Lewis Carroll's Alice in Wonderland. Lots were drawn to decide on who would design which card and, with some exchanging between individuals, a new deck of cards devised accordingly: Hérold designed the Sade and Lamiel, Masson the Portuguese nun and Novalis, Brauner the Hegel and Hélène Smith, Dominguez the Freud, Lam the Lautréamont and Alice [62], and Breton the Paracelsus.[19]

As a portable work by several artists, which could be packed into a suitcase, the *Marseilles Deck of Cards* may be seen as a symbol of this period of disruption and exile. According to Breton, in an interview given in New York in the autumn of 1941, the deck of cards came to signify 'the *unity* of aspiration between Surrealism here [United States] and over there [France]', since it involved artists who left France and others who did not.[20] Furthermore, as Breton explained in a later article of 1943, it also emphasized that the Surrealists were reinstating the importance of collective activity, and secondly that the strength of art lies in the fact that signs (unlike symbols) are arbitrary and signification is unfixed – or as Breton put it, 'in matters of faith, ideals and honour, from every corner we can observe the survival of the sign over the thing signified.'[21] The Surrealists continued to subvert bourgeois expectations and academic art even at a time of immense despair and anxiety. As Masson noted, 'our games always had a moral value, or more precisely a value of exploration, in every field.'[22]

Breton's organization of collective games at a time of war demonstrated his faith in art as a weapon of resistance. He also saw his individual writings as retaliation against the Vichy regime. Prior to the outbreak of the war, he wrote *Anthologie de l'humour noir*. It was published on 10 June 1940, the day Paris fell to the Nazis, and the following year it was banned on the grounds that it was 'the negation of the spirit of the national revolution'.[23] His anthology's list of black humorists included Sade, Fourier, Swift, Poe, Baudelaire, Nietzsche. Their talent lay in their status as *agents provocateurs* who satirized or otherwise attacked social mores and urged readers to break with them. Breton's preference for controversial writers may have been the main reason his work was seen as a threat to the political status quo. For example, he acknowledged the seminal work of the German Marxist philosopher Ernst Bloch (who fled Nazi Germany for the United States in 1938) and the poet, critic and Surrealist mentor Guillaume Apollinaire (who had championed Cubism and coined the term '*surréalisme*' in 1917). Breton also praised Sade's literary evocation of human perversion and he included two extracts from Sade's writings that exemplified his revolutionary role.[24] The first extract was Sade's will in which he asked to be buried at Lacoste without any religious ceremony or cross. The second was from *Juliette*, the story of a convent girl turned libertine who revels in sexual debauchery, vice and murder; Apollinaire saw her as the 'new woman', and Theodor Adorno and Max Horkheimer as a debauched product of the Enlightenment, Catholicism and civilization as a whole.[25] These two excerpts chosen by Breton could be interpreted as rallying calls against the power of the

63 Wifredo Lam, illustration in André Breton's *Fata Morgana*, 1942. Lam's illustrations and preparatory drawings for Breton's text are dominated by the *'femme cheval'*, the horse-headed female seen here. This figure has the strong facial features of Lam's second wife, Helena Holzer and while reminiscent of Picasso's *Minatouramachy* suite of 1935, draws specifically on the Afro-Cuban religion of Lucumí where the *femme-cheval* represents a possessed devotee.

Church and patriarchal society. The *Anthologie*, written on the brink of war, celebrated revolutionary thought and individualism at a time when Fascism was repressing both.

While in Marseilles Breton wrote his poem *Fata Morgana*, and Wifredo Lam illustrated it before leaving France for Cuba [63].[26] It was also censored for its anti-nationalism, though printed by Editions des Lettres Françaises in Buenos Aires in 1942. Ostensibly, it is a love poem to Jacqueline, to whom it is dedicated, but it may also be seen as an affirmation of the power of Eros, the life drive, and as a cry of resistance to the bleak political masochism which Breton saw in France. In November 1940, Breton referred to *Fata Morgana* in an interview in *Le Figaro* in contemptuous political terms, describing it as a demonstration of 'just how sympathetic I am to the Marshal's [Pétain] racist concepts'.[27] In his illustrations, Lam presents woman as symbol of the occult (with stylized stars and flowers in her hair), and as a figure of stoic strength even when depicted with nightmarish creatures surrounding her. Lam's totemic approach to the figure and use of occultist signs undoubtedly influenced Breton, who would soon talk in occultist terms of a 'New Myth'. In a 1941 interview with Charles Henri Ford in New York, Breton reiterated his political view of the work:

> [T]his poem states my resistance, which is more intransigent than ever, to the masochistic enterprises in France that tended to restrict poetic freedom or to immolate it on the same altar as other freedoms.[28]

Considering Breton's residence in Air Bel, his writings, and his political non-conformism at a time of burgeoning political repression, it is not surprising that on 3 December 1940, the day before Pétain made a state visit to Marseilles, Air Bel was raided by the police and Breton and members of the Rescue Committee were arrested. The house was suspected of Communist activity, though the only example of Surrealist art that the police confiscated was a recently made drawing of a rooster

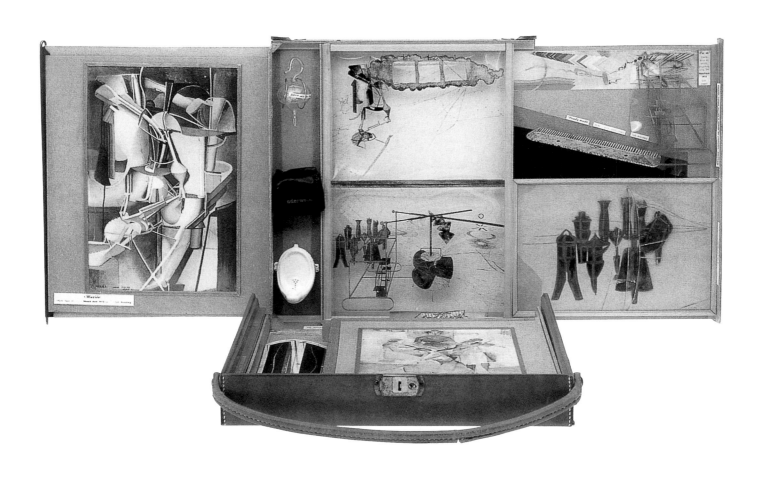

64 Marcel Duchamp, *La Boîte-en-valise*, *c.*1935–41. Duchamp's 'portable museum' questions the value placed on the unique work of art and the role of the museum in preserving art as knowledge. The multiple box assemblage contains reproductions of his art works (e.g. *The Bride Stripped Bare by her Bachelors Even/Large Glass*, 1915–23) and miniature replicas of his ready-mades (e.g. *Paris Air*, 1919, *Traveller's Folding Item*, 1916, and *Fountain*, 1917).

with the words 'Le terrible crétin de Pétain' written on it. Breton argued to the police that the word was not Pétain but *'putain'* (whore) but since it appeared alongside the symbol of French force, the French rooster, it was deemed revolutionary propaganda.[29] After four days of detention on the docked liner, the *Sinaïa*, Fry, Breton and the others were released. Even during their imprisonment Breton encouraged his companions to play Surrealist games, demonstrating, as Breton's friend the historian Sarane Alexandrian put it, the Surrealists' 'manner of testifying that life was fascinating, despite the bad forces that were striving to degrade it'.[30] That said, immediately on his release, Breton wrote to Robert Rius and Jean-François Chabrun of the Réverbères group, asking them to clear his rue Fontaine studio of anything which might prove politically compromising.[31] While his defiance of the police over the Pétain drawing was brave, he was now very eager to leave France. The defeat of France, the Vichy regime, the threat of further arrest, the assassination of Trotsky in Mexico on 21 August 1940, and the publication of the 'Liste Otto' by German ambassador Otto Abetz, forbidding the publication or sale of works by Jews, Communists and anti-Fascists, all led Breton to realize that the situation was 'extremely sober'.[32]

In early March 1941, Breton left France on the SS *Capitaine Paul Lemerle*, bound for New York via the French colony of Martinique. He was accompanied by Jacqueline and their daughter Aube. Also on board was the anthropologist Claude Lévi-Strauss. Others sailed too. Max Ernst escaped as Peggy Guggenheim's companion, meeting her in Lisbon and travelling with her and others (her children, Pegeen and Sinbad, her former husband Laurence Vail and his former wife and her four children) to New York. Ernst's ex-wife Louise Straus-Ernst was not so fortunate. While Jimmy Ernst sent her visa and affidavits to Marseilles she was unable to secure a French exit visa in time and was arrested by the Gestapo. She was interned at Drancy and she died at Auschwitz. Duchamp left Marseilles in May 1942, having safely journeyed from Paris using false papers which identified him as a cheese merchant. He set sail for America with a portable museum of miniatures of his own art in hand ready to be assembled into his *Boîte-en-valise* when he arrived in New York on 25 June [64].[33]

While Breton would be surrounded by many friends in New York he quit France reluctantly, having told his friend Maud Bonneaud before his departure that 'America has become necessary...only in the most negative sense: I don't like exile and I have my doubts about exiles'.[34] However, his journey immediately opened new doors. He not only befriended Lévi-Strauss, he also had the opportunity to meet Aimé Césaire, the poet and editor of the review *Tropiques*, at Fort-de-France when the ship stopped in Martinique. This journey inspired Breton's later publication, illustrated by André Masson, *Martinique charmeuse de serpents* (1948) [65]. He and his family made the rest of their journey to the United States on the SS *Presidente Trujillo*, accompanied by the Massons who had joined them in Martinique, stopping in Guadeloupe and Santo Domingo on the way. The combination of new friends, the exposure to Caribbean poetry and art and non-western lands that Breton experienced during his voyage, all contributed to his renewed interest in the primitive, myth and occultism during and after the war. In 1942, Breton issued the 'Prolegomena to a Third Surrealist Manifesto or Not', in which he spoke of Aimé Césaire as his 'black and magnetic' friend whose poetry was the type needed at a time of war. He also outlined his idea of 'Great Transparent Ones', which would be the subject of the 1947 exhibition, as we shall see in the next chapter.[35] In this

65 André Masson, illustration in André Breton's *Martinique charmeuse de serpents*, Paris, Sagittaire, 1948.

66 Salvador Dalí, *Dream of Venus* pavilion, New York World's Fair, 1939–40. Dalí's fantastic façade with its classical beauties and entrance framed by female legs led inside to bare-breasted swimming girls in a wet tank and a flower-strewn sleeping Venus in a dry tank. Described by *Time* magazine as a shrewd combination of 'Surrealism and sex', his pavilion drew on the 1938 Surrealist exhibition in many of its ideas, but lacked the political dimension which was so vital to the Surrealist cause.

manifesto, Breton was acutely aware of the threat war posed for Surrealist activity: he writes that the recent death of Freud would lead to an assault on psychoanalysis, an 'exemplary instrument of liberation', which might now be portrayed as one of repression. Such 'evils', he adds, 'lie in wait even for Surrealism'.[36]

Elsewhere, one finds subtle attempts at self-justification for exile: on 10 December 1942, Breton spoke to French students at Yale University and promised to continue to campaign for 'the pure state' of liberty. He insisted on the continuing relevance of Surrealism to war-torn society and claimed that after the war there would be liberty for those who deserve it, but not 'for those who are the enemies of liberty'.[37] He restated the Surrealists' philosophy and aesthetic agenda in terms of five central characteristics: the exploration of the unconscious; the unification of the supposedly disparate (dream and action, the irrational and rational); faith in chance which unveils the veiled in society; humour, which refuses to allow man to wallow in tragedy; knowledge of oneself and one's desires. This was a reiteration of his vision of a 'new spirit' where people 'read with and look through the eyes of Eros' as stated in his interview in *View* magazine on his arrival in New York.[38]

The Surrealists' renewed philosophical and aesthetic agenda was demonstrated to an extent by their collective activities while in exile in America, though it is clear that Breton did not try to adapt to American art circles. It must be remembered that Breton arrived in New York 'past middle age, a cultural hero and also a hero of anti-culture', as Lionel Abel put it.[39] He did not need to court American audiences or artists; rather, he simply continued in New York the Surrealist rituals he had set up in Paris. So the group met regularly at a coffee shop on 57th Street, browsed in second-hand shops on the look out for 'found' objects, and visited antique stores, especially those that sold Oceanic and Native American art. Young New York-based artists such as Joseph Cornell, David Hare, Jackson Pollock, Adolph Gottlieb, Peter Busa, Robert Motherwell, William Baziotes and Arshile Gorky took part in these gatherings, most of them having been introduced through Matta.[40] Of course, New Yorkers were relatively familiar with Surrealist art. Surrealism's presence had been felt in New York since the 1930s when Julien Levy, following his visit to Paris in 1927, promoted it in his gallery on Madison Avenue. Organizing solo exhibitions for many Surrealists (Dalí, Ernst, Man Ray, Cornell, Magritte, Frida Kahlo, Matta), a major group show in 1932 and publishing a Surrealist anthology, *Surrealism*, in 1936, Levy was a vital link between Paris and New York.[41] It was also Levy who co-ordinated Dalí's *Dream of Venus* pavilion [66] at the New York 1939 World's Fair (after unsuccessfully proposing his own pavilion for the fair, a fun house in the form of a huge eyeball and eyebrow).[42] Alfred H. Barr, Jr's major exhibition 'Fantastic Art, Dada and Surrealism' at the Museum of Modern Art in 1936 was also a landmark exhibition for the introduction of Surrealism to American audiences.

The Surrealists in exile were perhaps most indebted to Peggy Guggenheim, however. She had come to know the Surrealists in London and Paris in the summer of 1937 when she first began to collect art for her Guggenheim Jeune gallery at Cork Street, London.[43] She had funded the passage of the Bretons and Max Ernst from Marseilles to New York, and her Art of this Century gallery, which opened at 30 West 57th Street in New York on 20 October 1942 with a benefit for the Red Cross was inaugurated with '127 Objects, Drawings, Photographs, Paintings, Sculptures and Collages from 1910 to 1942', an exhibition on which Guggenheim was advised by Breton, Duchamp and Ernst and in which there were many Surrealist works of

67 **Photograph by Berenice Abbott of Frederick Kiesler sitting on the furniture he designed in the Surrealist Gallery, Art of this Century gallery, 30 West 57th Street, New York, 1942.** Abbott (1898–1991) was introduced to Surrealism through Man Ray in Paris in the mid-1920s. She returned to the United States in 1929 and became known for her images of New York and her portraits of intellectuals, writers and artists.

art. The catalogue of the collection also included the first English translation of Breton's 1942 essay 'Genesis and Perspective of Surrealism in the Plastic Arts'.

The gallery itself was a homage to Surrealism with its curved walls, paintings hung at odd angles, and a lighting scheme that alternately lit up each side of the room so that it all pulsated 'like your blood', according to the design of the young Austrian-born architect Frederick Kiesler [67].[44] He was a Jewish emigré who had been a member of the De Stijl group and came to international attention with his utopian design for a future 'City in Space' for the Austrian theatre section at the 'Exposition Internationale des Arts Décoratifs et Industriels Modernes' in Paris in 1925, and when he was invited to New York in 1926 to exhibit at the 'International Theater Exhibition' held in Steinway Hall from 27 February to 15 March 1926. Kielser was an established architect by the 1940s having designed the Film Guild Cinema, his first built project in America, on West 8th Street in 1929. It had a Bauhaus-De Stijl façade and, more famously, an eye-shaped projection screen (where the iris 'unfolded' to reveal the screen) – the latter indicating a Surrealist-like fascination with the eye, and the desire to blur the distinction between vision and reality, art and life. In 1930 he published *Contemporary Art Applied to the Store and Its Display* in which he aligned himself clearly to French Modernism, writing on the influence of Constantin Brancusi, Paul Klee, Henri Matisse and Pablo Picasso on the modernist canvas *par excellence* – the shop window. In 1936 he was included in Alfred H. Barr, Jr's 'Cubism and Abstract Art' exhibition at MOMA. He was working as Director of the Laboratory of the School of Architecture at Columbia University and Scenic Director at the Juilliard School of Music when Guggenheim wrote to him to ask for his help 'remodelling two tailor shops into an Art Gallery' in February 1942.[45]

In Guggenheim's Art of this Century gallery, Kiesler created a fantastic environment where architecture, art and installation became one, described as having:

> [M]ovable walls made of stretched deep-blue canvas, laced to the floors and ceiling...The floors were painted turquoise, Peggy's favourite colour. Unframed pictures 'swaying in space' at eye level were actually mounted on triangular floor-to-ceiling rope pulleys resembling cat's cradles.[46]

In the first Abstract Gallery, paintings were suspended in such a way that the spectator meandered through floating art and free-standing sculpture as Kiesler defied the modernist cube and did away with the wall itself. The Daylight Gallery, in contrast, was a bright, white-walled space for Guggenheim's large collection, but Kiesler again challenged the usually passive stance of the spectator by including a library of works of art which spectators could sit down with and look through. In the third room, the Surrealist Gallery, Guggenheim's vast collection of Surrealist works was revealed to the American public, but the design of the space was Surrealist in itself too.[47] The walls and ceiling of the gallery were painted black: the painter Charles Selliger remembers how the 'concave tunnel-like walls, darkened except for individual lighting on the paintings, created a mysterious, dreamlike atmosphere'.[48] Selliger's description evokes the uncanny qualities of the 1938 Surrealist exhibition: the sense of darkness, labyrinthine space and dream-like disorientation, though he does not seem to have felt the anxiety caused by these effects in the earlier Surrealist exhibition. No doubt the general member of the public, as opposed to a young artist, might have been more upset by the darkness

and other details he does not mention: the lighting was timed to go off every two minutes and to light one side of the gallery, then the other in a rhythm, and the alarming sound of a train that could only make the spectator self-conscious filled the room. Amid these special effects, the hanging was intimate, again echoing that of 1938 [68]. The public was free to adjust the angles at which they viewed the paintings since they were mounted on cantilevered wooden arms that protruded from the curved panels attached to the walls. The works seemed to defy gravity. Kiesler explained this system as allowing the painting to be 'separated from the wall and brought closer to the spectator. The picture seems to float freely. It ceases to be a decoration on the wall and becomes a small solid island in space.'[49] Miró-like, biomorphic props or 'correalist tools' acted as supports for sculptures and paintings, including Alberto Giacometti's disturbing bronze sculpture, *Woman with her Throat Cut* (1932, cast 1940). Others were left vacant for the public to sit on. This unorthodox treatment of the gallery led many critics to associate it with Surrealism, and Robert Coates of the *New Yorker* claimed 'the Surrealist section seemed to me to be the most integrated and the most inclusive', noting that it has 'everyone of consequence' from de Chirico's *The Rose Tower* (1913) to works by Ernst and Masson.[50]

Leading from the Surrealist room to the last exhibition space, the Kinetic Gallery, was a 'vision machine': fourteen reproductions from Duchamp's *Boîte-en-valise* (1941) arranged behind a peep hole [69]. To see them the spectator had to turn a wheel. In a similar vein, the spectator pulled a lever to see Breton's *Portrait of the Actor A.B. in his memorable Role in the Year of Our Lord 1713* (1942). Another vision machine was used to show paintings by Paul Klee: a paternoster, moved by an invisible light beam, which allowed the paintings to be shown in quick succession, under a spotlight, unless the automatic rotation was halted by the spectator, who could do so by pressing a button. The artist John Cage described the gallery as 'a kind of fun house…you couldn't just walk through it you had to become part of it.'[51] The space anticipated Kiesler's work with Duchamp on the 1947 international Surrealist exhibition: both were concerned for the spectator to recognize that he/she was, as Kiesler said, 'a participant in the creative process no less essential and direct than the artist's own'.[52] Duchamp recognized that 'As an architect, [Kiesler] was far more qualified than I to organize a Surrealist exhibition.'[53]

While New York became fascinated with Surrealism through such exciting displays of Surrealist art, the Surrealists in turn became fascinated by indigenous American art. This was helped by their exposure to exhibitions such as the Museum of Modern Art's 'Indian Art of the United States' in 1941 and also by individual pilgrimages. Max Ernst made a tour of Arizona, New Mexico and California in 1941, and when he lived in Sedona, Arizona in the years 1946 to 1956, he regularly visited Hopi, Zuñi and Navajo Indians [70]. André Masson, who settled on the territory of the Iroquois in New Preston, Connecticut in the autumn of 1941, felt their spirit affected his series of mythological landscapes.[54] The Surrealists regularly went to see the art of Northwest Coast American Indians at the American Museum of Natural History. Furthermore, they spent a lot of time collecting Native American, Oceanic and Japanese art from dealers in New York. They bought indigenous artefacts from Julius Carlebach, the Third Avenue dealer who always had an impressive stock of Pacific Northwest, Melanesian and Eskimo pieces. They also purchased masks and objects from the Bronx warehouse of the Museum of the

68 **Hans Richter and unknown lady in front of Joan Miró's** *Seated Woman II* **(1939), in the Surrealist Gallery, Art of this Century gallery, New York, 1942. Photo by Berenice Abbott.**

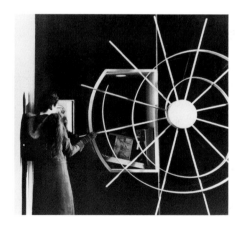

69 **Photograph of** *Vision Machine* **for Marcel Duchamp's** *Boîte-en-valise* **in the Kinetic Gallery, Art of this Century gallery, New York, 1942. Photo by Berenice Abbott.**

70 **Max Ernst and his collection of Hopi and Zuñi Kachina dolls, 1941, published in** *View*, **Max Ernst special issue, Spring 1942. Ernst bought his collection of dolls for $5 to $7 each at a tourist trading post in the Grand Canyon on a visit to Arizona in 1941 with Peggy Guggenheim, her daughter Pegeen, and his son Jimmy. Photo by James Thrall Soby.**

American Indian. Indeed, they amassed so substantial a collection that Max Ernst, Barnett Newman and others were able to mount an exhibition of Northwest Coast Indian painting at the Betty Parsons Gallery in 1946.

The Surrealists links with home were not lost however. Breton was heard in Europe thanks to his new post as announcer for Voice of America radio broadcasts. He began reading the 'Commentary Show' in March 1942, having been recommended to Pierre Lazareff, a newspaper magnate who was the head of French broadcasts, by the American art historian Patrick Waldberg. At the station Breton worked two-and-a-half hour shifts in the early morning, with Lévi-Strauss, Nicolas Calas, Edouard Roditi, Georges Duthuit, Denis de Rougemont, Robert Lebel and others for a salary of $250 a month.[55] Denis de Rougemont recollected that Breton 'would appear at 5 a.m. at the end of a large room, supremely courteous and with the patient air of a lion who had decided to ignore the bars of his cage. He lent us his noble voice but kept for himself his tinge of irony and solemn carriage.'[56] Roditi, Breton's former editor in Paris at Editions du Sagittaire, echoes Rougemont's analysis, opining that Breton 'believed he refrained from committing himself [politically] by only "renting" his voice'.[57] However, in a later radio interview with André Parinaud, Breton stated that he prided himself in 'not having betrayed the spirit of the resistance' in accepting this job.[58] André Thirion, an ex-Surrealist and a member of the French Resistance, supported this view. He described Breton's voice on Voice of America as both 'easily recognizable' and uplifting for those who heard it back in occupied France. Indeed, according to Thirion, Breton's broadcasts 'resounded like an encouraging call'.[59]

Two periodicals, *View* and *VVV*, gave the Surrealists an artistic and political mouthpiece on American shores. *View* was founded and edited by Charles Henri Ford and launched in September 1940 as a small review of six pages with the subtitle 'Through the Eyes of Poets'. By the time it devoted a whole issue to Surrealism in the October–November edition of 1941, it had developed into a substantial periodical. In that issue, Breton gave his only interview during his five-year exile and dealt directly with the topics of Hitler, artistic resistance and the need to look to Eros for spiritual and artistic reconstruction.[60] *View*'s special edition devoted to Marcel Duchamp in March 1945 was equally important as a collaborative venture between Ford and Breton, and signalled the Surrealists' creative friendship with Kiesler. The cover was designed by Duchamp who described it as 'a smoking bottle bearing, in the form of a label, a page from my military papers' [71].[61] The photographed bottle was also floating up into a starry sky and so it was quite ambiguous: alluding to the war and to the future. As Calvin Tomkins has observed: 'It could be taken as an ironic comment on his own genie-like reputation, as ephemeral as smoke; it might also refer to the *Large Glass* [on view at the Museum of Modern Art in New York at the time] or to the war...or to the notion of "infra-thin"'. The latter theme was evoked by Duchamp's words on the back cover of the edition: 'Quand la fumée de tabac sent aussi de la bouche qui l'exhale, les deux odeurs s'épousent par infra-mince' (When the tobacco smoke also smells of the mouth which exhales it, the two odours are married by infra-thin).[62] The issue reprinted Breton's 1935 article on Duchamp, 'Lighthouse of the Bride', which acknowledged the importance of Duchamp's ready-mades, the most 'dazzling' of his works for Breton.[63] Kiesler contributed a centrepiece triptych entitled *Les Larves d'Imagie d'Henri Robert Marcel Duchamp*. The triptych, according to Ford, 'nearly broke the magazine it cost so much to print and cut out', but it did demonstrate Kiesler's friendship with Duchamp and his exciting approach to architectural space and time.[64] It also signalled the importance Kiesler would have for Surrealism in this period of exile. By 1945 Kiesler was discussing plans for a major Surrealist show back in Paris, which resulted in the 1947 exhibition.

Where *View* acted as a forum for a number of avant-garde ideas, artists and writers, the magazine *VVV* was a peculiarly Surrealist venture, spearheaded by Breton himself, and edited by the young sculptor and photographer David Hare.[65] It was the Surrealists' true voice of resistance on American shores, publishing three issues from 1942 to 1944. *VVV* was launched in June 1942 with a cover designed by Max Ernst [72], and an editorial explaining the fighting moral and political purpose its title was supposed to imply:

> V + V + V...V as a vow – and energy – to return to a habitable and
> conceivable world, Victory [a reference to Churchill's famous hand
> gesture] over the forces of regression and of death unloosed at present
> on the earth....V again over all that is opposed to the emancipation of
> the spirit, of which the first indispensable condition is the liberation
> of man....[66]

The first edition included Breton's 'Prolegomena to a Third Surrealist Manifesto or Not' (in French and English). This manifesto itself demonstrated the Surrealists sense of being political refugees because it drew on the virulence of the revolutionary *sans-culottes* journal *Père Duchesne* and attacked the Nazis and Pétainists back home: 'Father Duchesne is in damn fine spirits! Whichever way he turns, mentally or physically, skunks are queens of the walk! These gentlemen in uniforms of old garbage peelings on the terraces of Paris cafés, the triumphant return of Cistercians and Trappists...with money you can keep on stuffing your face at Lapérouse without a ration card, the Republic having been sent to the smelter.'[67] In its embrace of anthropology, sociology and psychology, *VVV* indicated

71 **Cover of *View*, Marcel Duchamp special issue, March 1945. *View* was edited by Charles Henri Ford though Breton collaborated with him for this special edition.**

72 **Cover of *VVV*, no.1, June 1942, designed by Max Ernst. *VVV* was edited by David Hare with André Breton and Max Ernst as advisers. This first edition included articles by Claude Lévi-Strauss, Roger Caillois, Robert Motherwell, Lionel Abel, William Carlos Williams and Breton's 'Prolegomena to a Third Surrealist Manifesto or Not'.**

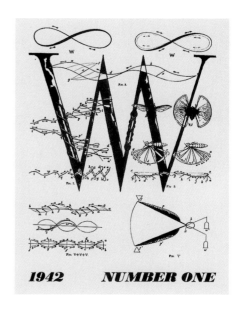

Surrealism's poetic path of resistance during and after the war, away from Western civilization and towards indigenous, primitive, occultist cultures and their faith in alchemy and collective myth. In addition, Breton saw his role in *VVV* as comparable to his role on Voice of America in its element of resistance to the Nazi machine. He stated in a post-war interview that both roles were acts against Nazism: 'Emancipation from the Nazi yoke took precedence in both cases.'[68]

The final issue of *VVV* indicates that Breton's mind was on his homeland, not on his American audience, as nearly all the essays in the last edition are in French, even the photo captions. Of course he also published in French in poetry journals. His essay on Aimé Césaire entitled 'Un Grand Poète Noir' (A Great Black Poet) came out in the Fall/Winter 1943/4 edition of *Hemispheres*, the French-American quarterly of poetry published by Yvan Goll in New York, and was published again in 1944 in *Fontaine*, the monthly poetry review of Max-Pol Fouchet published in Algiers, and, in May 1944, in Césaire's own journal in Martinique, *Tropiques*.[69] In recognizing 'The word of Césaire, as beautiful as oxygen being born' Breton insisted on the affinity between Surrealism and what he termed 'peoples of colour', a sensitivity no doubt enhanced by his own experience of forced exile, a foreigner without English in the United States. This reading is also the context for Breton's vocal support of Benjamin Péret's research and planned book on Latin American culture in Mexico at the time.

In 1943, Breton, Duchamp, Ernst, Matta, Tanguy and Charles Duits were responsible for the publication of *La Parole est à Péret* (Péret has the Floor). This pamphlet consisted of Péret's preface for a planned study of myths, folklore and legends from the Americas in which he aligns poetry, myth and liberation; claims that magic is the very blood and soil of poetry; decries religion and science's ruination of the magical interpretation of the world; and insists that the marvellous is everywhere.[70] In their introductory note, Breton and the other editors lauded Péret's uncompromising stance on total liberty. Their introduction was accompanied by a list of co-signatories from nine different countries whose presence, as Gérard Durozoi points out, reinforced the international nature and allegiance of the Surrealists: England (Jacques Brunius, Valentine Penrose), Belgium (Magritte, Nougé, Ubac), Chile (Braulio Arenas, Jorge Caceres), Cuba (Lam), Egypt (Hénein), France (Brauner, Dominguez, Hérold), Haiti (Mabille), Martinique (Aimé and Suzanne Césaire, René Ménil), and Mexico (Carrington and Francès).[71] Péret's sense of revolution undoubtedly reminds us of the Surrealists' radical view of art as a weapon of liberation not just at this moment of crisis in world history but throughout its long history – poetry and revolution were indivisible.

The Surrealists' 'First Papers of Surrealism' exhibition in New York also brought the group, locally and internationally together. It was the first major collective Surrealist exhibition put on during this period of exile. Opening a week before Guggenheim's Art of this Century gallery, the exhibition was organized by Breton with the aid of Marcel Duchamp and was on show from 14 October to 7 November 1942 in the former Whitelaw Reid Mansion on Madison Avenue, which then housed the Co-ordinating Council of French Relief Societies [73].[72] The exhibition involved those Surrealist artists exiled in New York – Carrington, Ernst, Masson, Matta, Paalen, Seligmann and Tanguy. A small fee was charged to visitors, a catalogue was designed, and the Surrealists contributed drawings to the Council's 1943 fund-raising calendar, *France in America*. However, from the outset, the exhibition was viewed as a fund-raising activity and never as part of the Surrealists' project

73 **Photograph of Marcel Duchamp and Frederick
Kiesler's installation,** *Sixteen Miles of String,* **for
'First Papers of Surrealism' exhibition, Whitelaw
Reid Mansion, 451 Madison Avenue, New York,
14 October – 7 November 1942. Access to
paintings in the gallery space was impeded
by sixteen miles of criss-crossing string which
created a dramatic contrast to the classical
interior of the mansion. On the opening night,
at the invitation of Duchamp, children played
ball in the gallery space.**

of major international exhibitions. In a letter to Man Ray in early October 1942, Duchamp refers to it only briefly: 'I'm taking care of the Surrealist Show which will be nothing like the Paris one.'[73] Breton also only mentioned it in passing when asked about his wartime activity in a series of radio interviews carried out on his return to Paris, in which he stated that it was organized to raise funds for war relief.[74] The opening night was a relatively simple affair compared to the 1938 exhibition in Paris. The only performance was poignant rather than shocking as Duchamp organized it so that Sidney Janis's son, Carroll, and his friends, played ball in the gallery, and a group of girls played jacks and hopscotch. Here, like the Surrealists' playful activities at Air Bel, defiance was voiced though the spirit of the child. This was despite the fact that certain aspects of the opening – the tricolour-themed invitations and the display of a bust of Pétain – jarred with the Surrealists antipathy towards all forms of nationalism.

Aspects of the 'First Papers' show demonstrated the Surrealists' recognition of the exhibition as a vehicle for subversion in the active interface between art and politics within the gallery space. In deciding to call it 'First Papers', they drew attention to the fact that they were refugees from a war in which citizenship and identity papers determined one's fate. The catalogue, designed by Duchamp, showed a photograph of a wall with five bullet holes (actual holes were punched into the paper) on the front [74].[75] The photograph on the back cover (though it bore the catalogue title) was of Swiss cheese. It too evoked the war (Duchamp's false papers which allowed him to travel as a cheese merchant; hardship and starvation). Inside the cover was a statement by Breton, in French and English, which clearly indicated the Surrealists' continued faith in art as political weapon. It read:

> The Surrealist cause, in art as in life, is the cause of freedom itself.
> Today more than ever to speak abstractly in the name of freedom or to praise it in empty terms is to serve it ill. To light the world freedom must become flesh and to this end must always be reflected and recreated in the *word*.[76]

The catalogue indicated Breton's current concern – mythology. This theme was explored via visual and verbal references to fifteen myths from *L'Age d'or* (illustrated by a reproduction of a Bosch painting and a still from Dalí and Buñuel's film) to *Les Grands Transparents* (illustrated by a medieval woodcut, a quote from Guy de Maupassant and a photographic work by David Hare).[77] It included extracts from letters 'written to our friends Pierre Matisse and J.R. by their fathers in France', along with a series of substitute portraits of Surrealists and other artists. These were the idea of Breton and Duchamp, partly necessitated by the fact that some of those depicted were still in Europe (Arp, Bellmer, Dominguez, Picasso are listed). Masson was represented by a photograph of an Eskimo, Matta by a little boy in a sailor suit, Duchamp by a haggard woman photographed by Ben Shahn during the Depression, and Leonora Carrington by Walker Evans's 1936 photographic portrait of Allie Mae Burroughs, a sharecropper's wife.

The hanging of the art in the space was also politically evocative. The main gallery was designed by Duchamp and created by Kiesler so that the spectator's access to the paintings was impeded by a web of string (some sixteen miles of it according to the press release for the exhibition), which criss-crossed the gallery, linking the temporary partitions on which the paintings were hung. In this way, the exhibition space became dysfunctional and the viewing experience frustrated, the tangle of string no doubt evoking the difficulties and anxieties of wartime.

 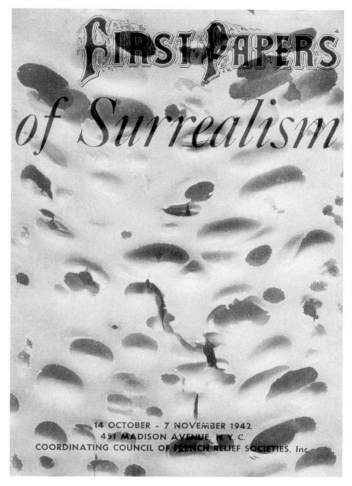

74 Marcel Duchamp, cover of exhibition catalogue
for 'First Papers of Surrealism', Whitelaw Reid
Mansion, 451 Madison Avenue, New York, 1942.
The front of the catalogue showed five bullet holes
in a wall, the back (with the title) showed the
surface of Swiss cheese, alluding to Duchamp's
false identity papers which named him as a
cheese merchant.

The 'First Papers' exhibition allowed American artists such as William Baziotes, Robert Motherwell, David Hare, Hedda Sterne, Morris Hirschfield and Kay Sage to exhibit alongside established Surrealist names. It also confirmed that Roberto Matta, whom we recall had written of a psychological, feminine architecture in *Minotaure* in 1938, had become a key figure for Surrealism. His painting *The Earth is a Man* (1942) won the praise of critics [75].[78] In this work, as in his other drawings and paintings produced during the war, Matta sought 'new images of man', believing that man had to be depicted as a social and historical victim of politics and war. As he stated in an interview in 1965, he tried to create a 'social morphology' to reflect the horror of society itself:

> [W]hen I realized what the war was, and the concentration camps, and I went one step further in my understanding, I tried to use, not my personal psychic morphology, but a social morphology. Using the totemic images involved in a situation which was more historical: the torture chambers and so on...cultures confronting each other. Battlegrounds of feelings and ideas, fighting to see if something would come out of these clashes.[79]

Matta's morphology was inspired by the pre-war Surrealist technique of automatism, Masson's and Tanguy's biomorphism, and Duchamp's spatial play. He abandoned his earlier *paysages* (landscapes) of the mind, and developed *personnages* (personalities) – nightmarish images of body-machines impaling each other – where the very real horrors of war were expressed in images of emotional trauma and victimization. Matta's oil painting *The Vertigo of Eros* (1944) [76] exemplifies this new direction with its hallucenogenic molecular structures, floating planets and abstracted human forms in an eerie landscape. The title of this work has always been interpreted as a reference to Freud's description of Eros as comparable to the sense of vertigo as one gazes down at Thanatos-Death. But once again Matta penetrates space with, as Alain Jouffroy puts it, 'feminine intelligence', building on his faith in compartmentalized architecture and form that is moulded according to our psychological fears and needs.[80] In his art, he binds man to architecture through a time-space continuum. Matta's own analysis of Eros typifies that of the Surrealists in general at this traumatic moment in history. He expresses the belief that man's hatred is directly linked to his quest for love – a sense of the Self through the quest for the loved Other – just as the microcosmic relationship-battle between two people was, he believed, directly linked to the social macrocosm and the emergence of a Nietzschean ethos based on survival rather than salvation in the twentieth century. Matta explained that '[p]ropaganda of love is the subject of art', but he lamented the fact that 'sophistication has created a climate of being ashamed of love. What is called modern man is the builder of cathedrals to hate.'[81] The figures in Matta's canvases are never isolated, but are always in combat with each other, and people become unidentifiable bodies objectified for the sake of 'advance' in a techno-scientific, rationalist society.

Considering his stance on Eros, it is unsurprising then that Matta also illustrated one of Breton's key wartime texts, *Arcane 17*, which was written in the latter half of 1944 and published by Brentanos, New York. Where Breton's *Anthologie de l'humour noir* had focused on revolutionary men, this publication was concerned with the revolutionary potential of Eros and myth, and demonstrated Breton's increased interest in occultism during the war. The title, *Arcane 17*, refers to the

75 Roberto Matta, *The Earth is a Man*, 1942. Matta
trained as an architect at the Academia de Bellas
Artes in Santiago, went to Paris to study under
Le Corbusier in 1934, and by 1938 was part of
the Surrealist group. In the summer of 1941 he
made a trip to Mexico and began to paint *The
Earth is a Man* whose spectacular forms reveal
his fascination with non-Euclidian geometry.

76 Roberto Matta, *The Vertigo of Eros*, 1944.
Matta gives visual form to Freud's description
of Eros as vertiginous by rejecting traditional
perspective, based on a single vanishing point,
and instead using concentric circles, floating
forms and colours to lead the eye in every
direction, successfully creating a sense of
movement and receding space.

seventeenth card in the Hebraic-Bohemian-Egyptian tarot pack: it is the card of the morning star, which follows the devil (the fifteenth card), and darkness (the sixteenth card).[82] The choice of card evokes Breton's hope for mythical renewal after the war. In *Arcane 17* Breton uses Melusina as his mythological redemptress who will lead society out of spiritual ruin: 'she's the one I invoke, she's the only one I can see who could redeem this savage epoch.'[83] Melusina, a figure from fifteenth-century French folklore, who was part woman, part serpent, guarded the Château of Luignan. As Anna Balakian has pointed out, Melusina may be seen as the symbol of the dispossessed because she guards over France.[84] In *Arcane 17*, Breton recognizes the power of myth both to unify modern society and to teach it not to despair at the 'trails of spilled blood' scattered across war-torn Europe.[85] He states that 'allegorical truth' lies in myth, especially in this moment of psychological and moral turmoil, and that this crisis creates a gap for a new myth.[86] In addition, *Arcane 17* reclaims myth for the development and renewal of France. Of course, myth had always been a central concern in Surrealist manifestos and writings, but in *Arcane 17* it is presented in terms of objective, political history. Breton heard of the liberation of Paris while writing *Arcane 17* and, as Balakian has suggested, he may have been warning French society that liberation did not necessarily mean true freedom – to attain *that* the French would need to renew their faith in the power of myth.[87] The celebration of love, poetry and liberation in *Arcane 17* may be seen as the culmination of Breton's wartime resistance and continued faith in Eros. However, by this time resistance in France had developed into a fully-fledged armed activity and it fell to a few Surrealists there, and to the Main à Plume group with whom they joined forces, to prove the spirit of Surrealist resistance in a different way.

It will be recalled that while most Surrealists had made it to Marseilles, they did not all manage to leave France. Hans Bellmer, who had been interned in the camp at Milles with his compatriot Max Ernst when war began, and had subsequently managed to make his way to Marseilles, never left France, though he had hoped to according to Breton.[88] He spent the war years in Castres in the southeast of France, and in May 1942 married Marcelle Céline Sutter, a woman from Colmar. This union resulted in twin daughters, Doriane and Béatrice, but only lasted two years, leading to separation in the summer of 1944 and divorce in 1947. Bellmer continued to produce art during the war. Even when he was interned over seven months in 1940, he sketched a number of portraits of Max Ernst and the artist Ferdinand Springer. He was surrounded by a variety of internees, including German refugees, Austrian victims of the *Anschluss* and former soldiers of the French Foreign Legion, but he was permitted to draw. As Springer reported, 'None of us artists had to work. The officers knew our pictures were worth money so they left us alone and granted us privileges.'[89] Bellmer produced portraits of the officers, as did Ernst and Springer, as well as his own fantastic sketches. Ernst noted in his autobiography: 'Hans and I drew all the time, in order to overcome our anger and our hunger.'[90] The camp was a converted brickworks and in a number of his drawings we find Bellmer constructing faces and scenes out of bricks. In one portrait in gouache of Ernst he depicts the artist's physical and mental repression at the camp by constructing his forlorn-looking face out of bricks [77]. This portrait bears a striking resemblance to Man Ray's 1936 drawing of Sade where his face is built up in bricks, which was published in his 1937 collaboration with Paul Eluard, *Les Mains libres*, and which Man Ray developed into an *Imaginary Portrait of the Marquis de Sade* in 1938

77 Hans Bellmer, *Portrait of Max Ernst*, 1941–2. Bellmer produced a number of portraits at the Camp des Milles, including this one of Max Ernst. In building up Ernst's face in bricks Bellmer alludes to Man Ray's 1938 and 1940 portraits of the Marquis de Sade where the libertine's face is built up from bricks too.

78 Man Ray, *Imaginary Portrait of the Marquis de Sade*, 1938. Hailed as 'Surrealist in Sadism' in the first Surrealist manifesto, the Marquis de Sade remained a constant source of inspiration for the Surrealists. Here Man Ray cites Sade's Last Will and Testament and portrays the corpulent libertine as a bastion of liberty against the burning Bastille.

and 1940 (two versions exist) [78], and much later into a bronze sculpture. Bellmer is undoubtedly paying homage to Ernst as an artist by comparing him to Sade.[91]

Bellmer continued to do portraits during the war years which demonstrated his technical skill, such as his pencil portrait of the *Fuchs Family at Mazamet* (1943–4), but the doll, and the theme of erotic metamorphosis, was still ever present. Indeed, cephalism abounds in his war-time work in the combining of forms, usually for heightened, and uncanny, erotic ends. In a series of works produced from 1939 to 1943, and entitled Cephalopod (or variations on that title), Bellmer depicts erotic women whose buttocks morph into breasts and female limbs. All of these have a sense of violent metamorphosis about them, working and reworking motifs of orgasm, the eye, the female sex and the anus. Indeed, these were motifs which Bellmer extended in his *Céphalopode à la rose* (1946) [79]. This in turn became the basis for Bellmer's treatise *Petite Anatomie de l'inconscient physique ou l'anatomie de l'image* (1957), a text divided into three sections: images of the self, the anatomy of love, and the exterior world, and concerned throughout with the 'anagrammatic' possibilities of the female body. In this work Bellmer not only refers to the nineteenth-century physician Cesare Lombroso and his analysis of female hysteria, he also draws on Freud's essay 'The Interpretation of Dreams' in his exploration of the distinction between the 'real' and the 'virtual' and in his view of 'The Anatomy of Love' as the merger of the subject and object, Self and Other. The anagram-poem 'Rose au coeur violet', also published in *L'Anatomie de l'image*, sheds further light on Bellmer's war-time art. Written in 1947–8 with his then-lover Nora Mitrani, a Jewish woman from Bulgaria and an important Surrealist poet, the poem cuts up a line from Nerval – 'Rose au coeur violet' (rose with the violet heart) – and rearranges it to explore the theme of the violation (*violé*) of the female sex (*rose*) and the easy slippage between desire and destruction, love and violence, Eros and Thanatos so that it ends with the phrase 'O rire sous le couteau' (to laugh beneath the knife).[92]

When one views these cephalopods in the light of Bellmer's thoughts on the anatomy and violence of desire, it comes as no surprise that in a letter to Robert Valançay in March 1946 he listed the eight works by or about Sade that he owned and asked Valançay to look out for *Justine* and *Philosophy in the Boudoir*. He was obviously devouring Sade's writings at this time. Indeed he would begin illustrations for both books the following month, although these were never actually published (apart from one which was used as the frontispiece for an edition of *Justine* in 1950). In a letter dated 21 November 1946, he explained to Robert Valançay how he was working on this Sadean project:

> For two months I have devoted my work exclusively to the work of de Sade. This is an important project for me, but with great risks, taking into account the surveillance of my ex-wife, and the vigour with which the state, in these days (cf. Henry Miller's *Tropic of Capricorn*) keeps watch on such creations. That is why I ask you to observe absolute discretion about this work of mine.[93]

One drawing, *Subterranean* (1946) [80] depicts an interior with dungeon-like ante-chambers and phallic alcoves. A vagina-like entrance acts as a horizon line while the indentation of the body of a gargantuan bottle and erect penis (almost hung up like a cadavre) dominate the right plane, a splayed female made up of four legs the middle plane, and a kind of ejaculate mass the left plane. The bricks of the camp at Milles, the cephalopod, the fear of castration and the sense of an uncanny,

afin que... les traces de ma tombe disparaissent de dessus de la surface de la terre, comme je me flatte que ma mémoire s'effacera de l'esprit des hommes... D.A.F. SADE.

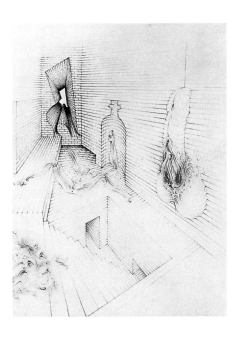

79 **Hans Bellmer, *Céphalopode à la rose*, 1946.**
Bellmer's cephalopod female mirrors the unlimited
power of desire and metamorphosis in the dream
state. Produced in the same year he illustrated
Georges Bataille's erotic novel *Histoire de l'oeil*
(1928), Bellmer shared with Bastille a fascination
with the adolescent woman. The *rose* of the title
suggests the expression *perdu votre rose*, to
loose one's virginity, as well as the *rosette* (the
anus), and *rosée* (sperm).

80 **Hans Bellmer, *Subterranean*, 1946.** The bricks
of the Camp des Milles (a former brick factory) are
evoked in this nightmarish interior, as is the prison
cell of the Marquis de Sade. From *c.*1939 to 1948
Bellmer repeatedly turns to the brick motif as a
means of exposing the anatomy of desire and
power of the erotic imagination through the
'flayed' architectural or anatomical form.

81 **Victor Brauner, *Self-Portrait*, 1931.** Seven
years after painting this self-portrait Brauner
actually lost his eye when acting as peacemaker
between two brawling friends, Oscar Dominguez
and Esteban Frances. Pierre Mabille wrote of
this strange premonition in his essay 'L'Oeil du
peintre', published in *Minotaure*, nos 12–13, 1939.

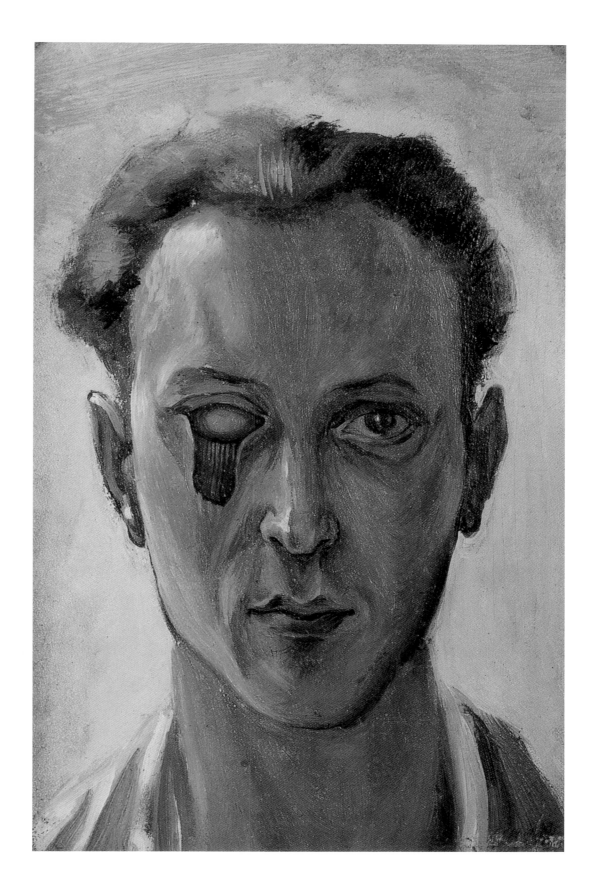

cavernous space with pockets of shadow, and that lascivious fantasy of the intra-uterine experience that Freud wrote of in 1919, are all staged here. Bellmer's fascination with displacement, dismemberment and erotic metamorphosis shows that he remained true to the Surrealist theme of Eros (and its darker side, Thanatos). However, the prison-like nature of this uncanny space, the allusions to a camp cell, the descending steps and vagina-window or exit speak to the trauma of the war through the erotic, Freudian motif too. In historical and political terms we have already noted how Bellmer's doll was produced alongside the rise of Nazi power in Germany. Given his concern with the reality and psychology of Fascism in his art before the war, one must appreciate his fascination with Sade in socio-political terms too. Joë Bousquet read Bellmer's drawings in 1947 as using beauty to instil revulsion and as demonstrative of the scandalous nature of reality itself.[94]

Bellmer's drawings undoubtedly continue his concern to open people's eyes to the reality of living in and surviving a war. Indeed, Bellmer was actively involved in the Resistance and fought for three years with the *maquis* of Sidobre.[95] He and his friend Jean Brun managed to organize his first post-war exhibition in Toulouse at a small bookshop, the Librairie Silvio Trentin, just two months after the town's liberation.[96] He exhibited his drawings, illustrations for Georges Hugnet's *Oeillades ciselées en branche* (1939), his 1936 photographs of his *Doll*, and his dossier for *Les Jeux de la poupée.* Soon after, he wrote a limited edition essay which was published in December 1944: '3 tableaux, 7 dessins, 1 texte.' Significantly, it was dedicated to Breton.

Victor Brauner was another Surrealist who stayed in the south of France for the duration of the war. He too tried to get a visa to the United States from Marseilles but failed. However, he did manage to get false identity papers so that he could pass as an Alsatian and a *permis de secours* so that he could undergo an operation on a stomach ulcer in 1941. From 1942 until the end of the war, he lived at Celliers de Rousset. Like Bellmer, he continued with pre-war themes, adapting them to his new-found conditions. Brauner had always been interested in the occult, and famously predicted his own future in a self-portrait of 1931. He depicted himself with an eye gouged out, the same eye that he was to lose when separating a fight between Oscar Dominguez and Esteban Frances in Paris in late August 1938 [81]. By the outbreak of war, his art had become more mystical, with themes of magic and alchemy emerging in his imagery. In his notebooks, Brauner wrote of the need to push the possibilities of 'le flou' – the vague chance that occurs between objects, and an interest underpinning the theme of metamorphosis in his drawings.[97] During the war, this interest became all the more pronounced and his art became dominated by the concept of spell and counter-spell. For example, in his *Portrait of Dina Vierny* (1942), done in ink and pastel on board, we see elements of occultism – the sun, a sunflower – interwoven with a portrait of a Vierny, Aristide Maillol's last muse and model, who was staying with the sculptor at Banyuls-sur-Mer at the time. She seems to stand as a symbol of hope amid political despair [82]. Below her, Brauner's handwritten inscription reads 'en souvenir de cette époque inéffasable [*sic*]' (in memory of this ineffaceable time).

Like many artists faced with a materials shortage during the war, Brauner also invented new artistic techniques. He began to use candle wax, sometimes mixing it with colour pigment, a practice he continued until his death in 1966. His wax images might be described as primitive or child-like in their simple forms and totemic expression. These works may be linked to the indigenous art of Africa,

83 **Victor Brauner,** *Object of Counter-Bewitchment,* **1943. In using cabalistic signs and texts, and an amulet-like piece of lead (for the head), Brauner evokes primitive rituals and the use of talismans for protection against evil at time of war.**

America and Oceania – a homage to primitive art that would have been deemed degenerate by the Nazis. In *Object of Counter-Bewitchment* (1943) Brauner creates an object that embodies his mythical hope and political despair simultaneously [83]. The head is made of wax, clay, lead and paper, the bound male body of clay, and the whole object is set into a wooden box-frame. On the figure's forehead, Brauner has inscribed the sign of Saturn and it appears again to the figure's left, interwoven with the sign of a demon. Intertwined, the two signs form a totemic figurine with a raised right hand within which are cryptic letters, denoting the following words: 'I evoke your power in this ambiance that weaves the correspondences in your strength.' To the bottom right of the object Brauner has marked Hebrew letters; beneath the figure is parchment on which code is used again, followed by the two signs of Saturn – his demonic and intelligent signs.[98] In using cabalistic signs and texts, and an amulet-like piece of lead for the head, Brauner evokes primitive rituals and the use of talismans for protection against evil. He turns to magic, specifically to Saturn, the angel of solitude according to the nineteenth-century occultist Eliphas Lévi, as a means of addressing his own isolation and fear at the height of the war.

Like Bellmer, Brauner also seems to conflate the sexual instinct and the death instinct in these works which combine ritualistic and magical potency with an element of destruction or even torture. We see this too in his images of women who seem half magical, half demonic and in his *Conglomeros* creatures, where the forms of women, cats, fish and other creatures are fused. Examples include his ink drawing *Air Bel, Marseille* (1941), in which we see a woman-bird, the crayon drawing *Banyuls* (1942), in which we see a naked woman with a fish on her head holding two flower-like forms in each hand (a sun and in the other a moon), and in an untitled ink drawing, dated 9 October 1942, in which he presents a naked female form very similar to an exquisite corpse with a plumed bird head, bird-beak hand, eagle's feet and the emerging form of a fox.

Brauner stayed in contact with Oscar Dominguez and Jacques Hérold during the war and was involved with them in the activities of the Main à Plume, a neo-Surrealist group based largely in occupied Paris from 1943. Dominguez had spent a brief spell in Marseilles, but returned to Paris where he managed to spend the war years eking out a living – often through the forging of fellow Surrealists' works which he sold to the art dealer Augustinci under the pretence that they had been given to him by his Surrealist comrades in the United States.[99] Jacques Hérold was slower to return to Paris. Like Brauner, he was constantly evading the attention of both the French and German police, and his friendship with Brauner grew all the more once Breton quit Marseilles and Brauner moved into Air Bel in Breton's place.[100]

Hérold was arrested four times during his stay in Marseilles; once he was held for eight days of questioning. He made false identification papers, taking the name Herald and faking the signatures of Gaston Leroux (the deceased author of detective novels starring the reporter Rouletabille) and the writer, actor and artist Antonin Artaud (who was interned at Rodez at the time) as witnesses. Hérold continued to paint, and decorated a new bar called Eden in Marseilles designed by the Jewish French architect Bernard Zehrfuss and the sculptor Etienne Martin.[101] However, by the autumn of 1941 those Surrealists who had been in Air Bel had left. Dominguez, having returned to Paris, wrote to Hérold in November advising him to return too.[102] But Hérold stayed on in Marseilles, renting a flat with his wife Violette and exhibiting in a group exhibition entitled 'Le Mot d'Ordre' at the Galeries Barbès (19 December 1941–10 January 1942), and another in May at the Galeries de Rome. In April 1942, he went to visit Zehrfuss in his country house at Oppède in the Luberon; from here he made a trip to the Marquis de Sade's chateau at Lacoste, where he found inspiration for a number of Sadean works.[103]

Hérold's interest in Sade had been rekindled when he designed the Sade card for the *Marseilles Deck of Cards*. As far back as 1930 Hérold had done a drawing entitled *Homage to Sade*, but it was his friendship with Gilbert Lely, who would publish a biography of Sade in 1952, which developed his interest at this time.[104] He made his trip to Lacoste with Lely and René Char. Char had visited Lacoste with Paul Eluard and Jean and Valentine Hugo in 1931. Then it had been a journey of celebration, but when he brought Hérold back there a decade later it was as an ex-Surrealist (as he had left the group in 1935), as a Resistance fighter, but also still a poet who believed in the power of words to fight.[105] The pilgrimage resulted in Hérold's *The Eagle Reader* (1942), a painting of an eagle soaring out from the lap of a female who is reading [84]. Like Brauner, Hérold plays on the theme of magical metamorphosis here, fusing the female with the winged creature that symbolizes freedom of mind and spirit. While it might be tempting to see the eagle as an emblem of Fascism morphing out of *la belle France*, Hérold explained this image in more banal terms in an interview with Michel Butor published in 1964. It seems Hérold simply noticed a peculiar number of eagles in the Lacoste region, specifically in the Luberon grottoes, and that as he made his journey to Sade's chateau, one seemed to lead the way. Yet Sade remained a constant in his art from this point.[106]

Another aspect of Hérold's wartime art that emerged at this time was his technique of 'crystallization': creating crystalline figures which were intended to represent the mutilated form of society itself.[107] Hérold's *Flayed Figures* (1943) exemplifies this crystallizing process as we see the flayed bodies of a man and a woman, their sinewy limbs appearing like traces of flesh [85]. The artist's use of

gouache formally reinforces the tension between line and mass, trace and volume, as well as reminding us of the technical and economic effect of war, since more and more artists turned to gouache as a relatively inexpensive, quick-drying medium suitable for small-scale, portable works.[108] In his text of 1957, *Maltraité de peinture*, Hérold elaborated on his crystallization of figures, stating that the role of the painter was to 'to give to reality a profundity which the human, in general, refuses for want of liberty'.[109] Of course, this thematic emphasis in his work was also closely related to the practical fight for liberty which would increasingly occupy him, once he was back in Paris.

Hérold had decided to leave Marseilles in the autumn of 1942 since it was becoming particularly dangerous to live there with German soldiers filling the city in response to the arrival of English and American troops in North Africa. He had been stopped by the police on numerous occasions, but when, on 29 December, he was ordered by the Commissariat Général aux Questions Juives de Marseille to report with his civic and religious identity cards, he recognized that the time had come to leave. As a Romanian Jewish artist he was in great danger. He travelled by foot, dressed as a ragman, towards Annemasse in the hope of crossing the border into Switzerland. When this plan failed he made his way to Annecy, where he stayed for a few months before joining up with Adolphe Acker, a doctor, ex-member of the Surrealist group and now member of the Main à Plume group, who was hiding out with his wife in Allevard-les-Bains.[110] Acker taught him how to forge military documents so that he could present himself at Grenoble and get legal papers to return to Paris.[111] It was through this arduous and brave journey that Hérold found himself back in Paris in June 1943, where he joined Main à Plume.

Formed in the summer of 1941 by Noël Arnaud, Main à Plume was a group of writers and artists many of whom had been members of the Réverbères group (such as Jean-François Chabrun, Adolphe Acker and Robert Rius).[112] They continued to promote Surrealism from Paris up until the end of 1943. The group included ex-Surrealists (Paul Eluard, Georges Hugnet, Maurice Henry and Jean Ferry), Surrealists who had spent time with Breton in Air Bel (Dominguez, Hérold, Brauner), and a group of young men who would be involved in post-war Surrealism and its legacy in new avant-garde groups such as CoBrA – including Gérard de Sède, Christian Dotremont, Marc Patin, Gérard Vulliamy, Marco Ménegoz, André Still and Edouard Jaguer.

The group took its name from Rimbaud's phrase in *Une saison en enfer* (1873): 'La main à plume vaut la main à charrue' (The hand with a pen is worth as much as the hand with a plough).[113] Their intention was to keep the Surrealist flame burning in occupied France. Sarane Alexandrian has described them as 'surréalistes résistants' but, of course, their resistance was poetic *and* militant, involving the continued publication of Surrealist literature as well as contributing to official acts of resistance.[114] They published twelve issues under the imprint Editions de la Main à Plume from May 1941 to May 1944, printing poems, articles and drawings, all anonymously.[115] In addition to anonymity, the design and layout of each issue varied so that it did not appear to be a periodical, thus evading the official ban on such publications. The review was in keeping with those of the Surrealists in the 1930s: it included collective poems, analyses of dreams, articles on the German Romantics and on the revolutionary potential of desire.[116] Its aesthetic stance was largely based on the first and second Surrealist manifestos, closer to Breton's Marxism than his later occultism.

85 **Jacques Hérold, *Flayed Figures*, 1943.**

84 **Jacques Hérold, *The Eagle Reader*, 1942. Hérold saw a splendid eagle hovering over the ruined walls of the château of the Marquis de Sade in Lacoste when he first visited it in 1942 and would subsequently paint this image as homage to Sadean liberty.**

One event they organized also paid homage to the Surrealists' radical approach to the exhibition as a space within which to disorientate and re-educate the public. In July 1941, the group staged an exhibition of 'Poésie-Peinture' (paintings, drawings, poems and sculptures) at the Galerie Matières et Formes on 70 rue Bonaparte, near Saint-Germain-des-Prés. On the opening night of the exhibition, at seven o'clock, they staged a series of manifestations: Olga Luchaire sang the music of Erik Satie and Claude Dubosq, accompanied by the composer Henri Sauguet on piano; Geneviève La Haye and Jean Lucas interpreted a mime poem by Arnaud, while Arnaud, Jean Hoyaux and Marc Patin presented the public (many of whom were seated on the floor) with three paintings – one of which was a blank canvas with a patch smeared with cigarette ash – while reciting poems in honour of Clément Pansaers, the Belgian Dadaist who died in 1922. Then, to disrupt this ceremony and end it with a neo-Dada assault, several of the artists grabbed dried fruits from a large basket which had been passed around during the mimed poem and began to throw them at the audience from behind a curtain that separated the main gallery space from another room. This was the first such spectacle since the occupation of Paris and since the group knew that their exhibition was attended by three representatives of the *Propagandastaffel*, their bold tactics demonstrated their resistance to the Germans and their knowing political defiance through poetic expression.[117]

Their political engagement sometimes countered previous exclusions from Breton's Surrealist group. While Eluard had been excluded from the Surrealist group for giving his poem 'Les Vainqueurs d'hier périront' to the Communist periodical edited by Aragon, *Commune*, he was recognized by the Main à Plume group as a Surrealist nonetheless and they invited him to collaborate with them.[118] Eluard's pre-war poem 'Les Raisons de rêver' (an extract from his collection *Marines*, dedicated to Alberto Giacometti) was published in the third review, entitled *Transfusion du verbe*, in December 1941.[119] This was the first edition of the group's review to include illustrations by Surrealist artists Oscar Dominguez and Raoul Ubac. The fourth edition of their review, published in June 1942, included many Surrealists. It was entitled *La Conquête du monde par l'image* and had Picasso's *Head of a Bull*, fashioned from a bicycle seat and handlebars, on the cover, and a cartoon by Maurice Henry inside the cover [2]. Reproductions of works by Paul Delvaux, René Magritte, Valentine Hugo, Oscar Dominguez, Maurice Henry and Picasso illustrated the edition and Christian Dotremont's 'Notes techniques sur l'image dite Surréaliste' and Raoul Ubac's 'Note sur le mouvement et l'oeil', spoke to Surrealist concerns. The article that gave the edition its title, written by J.-V. Manuel, explained the force of Surrealism and the responsibility of the poet:

> The surrealist picture, a most direct demonstration of desire in the face of the immobile conspiracy of a congealed reality, is at once the emotional and scientific arm that must serve the conquest of a world where the last border will be erased. Limits will no longer exist between the visible and the invisible, the real and the imaginary, reason and the spirit....In this conquest, the poet representing the public imagination, must be the first to the attack and, should the need arise, the last to retreat.[120]

In October of the following year, the group also published Eluard's *Poésie et vérité 1942*, which included his resistance poem 'Liberté' in which freedom's name is never spoken but the 'power of the word' asserted.[121] As the war went on, the Main à Plume's clandestine activities became increasingly dangerous. The round up of Jews in Paris on 16 and 17 July 1942 led to the arrest of 13,000 people, including 4,000 children, and one of the Main à Plume group, a Jewish artist by the name of Tita, was arrested by the Germans and never seen again. Soon other members of the group were under suspicion and Noël Arnaud and his wife Cécile, as well as Chabrun, Acker and others, fled Paris for the south. Further publications by the group were printed under the auspices of a review published in Lyons, *La Vie vivante*.

Despite the distance that separated them, Main à Plume did maintain a relationship with Breton. The fifth of their issues published his poem 'Pleine Marge'. In July 1943, members of the group drafted a letter to Breton in America.[122] In this they outlined their decision to unite all Surrealists and ex-Surrealists at a time of extreme hardship and in the name of Surrealism, and declared their mission to continue the cause of Surrealism in occupied France. They stated that they regretted Breton's absence but were still proud to be a Surrealist movement. However, the letter never reached Breton; its courier was arrested en route to Switzerland from where the letter was to be sent to New York. With the enforcement of Obligatory Work Service in February 1943, when over 100,000 people were forced to leave France and work in Germany, many members of the group decided to join the Communist Party, and so to break with Breton's refusal to partake of party politics. Understandably, all members of Main à Plume became more active in the Resistance as the political situation worsened. Hérold, with the help of a young man by the name of Boris Rybak, made false French and German identity papers for those escaping Obligatory Work Service, for the *maquis* who were fighting with Chabrun, who was now a Resistance leader and a captain in the Forces Françaises de l'Intérieur, and for the poet Maurice Blanchard, who was responsible for the combat network, Réseau Brutus.

Other acts of resistance were more in keeping with pre-war Surrealism. From 28 June to 2 July 1943, the group printed up hundreds of multicoloured cards with Surrealist slogans inscribed on them, such as 'Si vous aimez l'AMOUR, vous aimerez le SURRÉALISME' (If you love LOVE, you will love Surrealism) which they distributed.[123] This activity indicated that they still saw language itself as a valid weapon in a time of war. Their faith in the political power of the word was all the more evident in their August 1943 review publication entitled *Le Surréalisme encore et toujours*. This was a luxury publication, including an original drawing by Tanguy, an unpublished drawing by Breton and another by Péret, as well as illustrations by Ernst, Hérold, Masson, Lam, Rémedios Varo, Picasso and even Dalí.[124] It also included an illustrated essay by Hérold on his representation of the fragmented, crystallized body and how it reflected the angst of society and the dire need for humanism during a time of horror. *Le Surréalisme encore et toujour*s insisted on the revolutionary power of poetry and art and on the right to have the freedom to create at a time when liberty was constantly being denied.

Other projects were more politically absurdist, such as the idea mooted in November 1943 to produce a collective *plaquette* on 'Notes sur la fonction psychologique et poétique de la moustache'. Here Chabrun, Rybak, Gérard de Sède and others were to write up their analyses of the moustache and Hérold was to provide an image of one. This idea was not just another example of Surrealist humour however; it was also a coded means of attacking Hitler, since he was the moustached figure that haunted everyone's lives at the time.

Even at the height of the war, in May 1944, the Main à Plume published *Informations surréalistes*, still insisting on the power of the pen as a weapon of war. The cover was designed by Hérold and depicted a head bound in chains in flame. The group's final act before the end of the war was to assist in the liberation of Paris in 1944. Hérold fought as one of the 'milices patriotiques' and helped seize the *mairie* of the 14th *arrondissement* on 19 August; until 25 August he fought the Germans at the porte d'Orléans, place Denfert-Rochereau and the Cité Universitaire. Indeed, he was awarded a certificate of bravery for his courageous involvement in the liberation of Paris.[125]

The Main à Plume had fought on behalf of Surrealism to promote poetry as a weapon of revolution. This was their revolt: to keep poetry alive in occupied France. In total, the group lost eight members to the war, killed in battle or exterminated in camps, and, as Chabrun noted in his memoirs, as such they witnessed the bitter truth of the Surrealist term 'exquisite corpse'.[126] While in the villa Air Bel, many had played at this game; in exile in the United States, others, like Ernst, had explored the terror of war through abstract imagery and frottage technique; but those who stayed in France had experienced the war first-hand. Robert Rius was shot by the Germans in July 1944 while fighting with the *maquis* in the forest of Fontainbleau; Marco Ménegoz, a seventeen-year-old poet who had two poems in *L'Avenir du surréalisme*, was shot in the Arbonne forest. Other members of the Surrealist milieu who had remained in France and been killed included Itkine, who returned to Paris at the end of 1942, was captured and tortured by the Gestapo, and died in a concentration camp; and Benjamin Fondane, who was sent to Auschwitz in 1944 and gassed in Birkenau.[127] Their sacrifice and their continued faith in Surrealism despite the very real horrors of war stand as testimony to the power of art as an act of resistance.

Pablo Picasso recognized the importance of the Main à Plume during the war. He assisted them financially and gave them a signed and dated photo of his *Head of a Bull* sculpture for the 1942 review issue *La Conquête du monde par l'image* [2]. Of course, Picasso's affiliation with Surrealism had begun before the war – for example, one of his *Glass of Absinthe* (1914) sculptures was included in the 1936 exhibition of Surrealist objects at the Galerie Charles Ratton in Paris, and he had a relationship with Dora Maar who was one of the women listed on Breton's Gradiva gallery sign when it opened on the rue de Seine in Paris in 1937. During the war, Picasso became particularly close to Paul Eluard and his wife Nusch, such that Eluard dedicated the second volume of his *Livre ouvert*, published in January 1942 by *Cahiers d'art*, to him.[128] Picasso also collaborated with Robert Desnos, who had been a member of the Surrealist group from 1924 to 1929. Desnos wrote a text for Picasso's 1943 exhibition 'Picasso: Seize peintures 1939–1943'. Picasso, in turn, provided an etching for Desnos's collection of poems *Contrée* (1944). This was published three months after Desnos was arrested by the Gestapo for acts of resistance. In it he demonstrates a Surrealist faith in desire and love, notably in 'The Landscape', where he writes 'I had dreamed of loving, I still love but love/Is no longer that bouquet of lilacs and roses/…It is the spark of flint under my footsteps at night'.[129] Furthermore, Picasso's play *Desire Caught by the Tail* (begun on 14 January 1941 and written in three days) also demonstrated a fusion of political reality, Alfred Jarry-like humour and Surrealist word play. It used absurdity, puns, eroticism and Surrealist-like metaphors to evoke Nazi atrocity and the hardship that the French were suffering under the Occupation.[130] A reading of the play was organized in March 1944, directed by Albert Camus, and held at the apartment of Michel and

Louise Leiris who acted in the play alongside Jean-Paul Sartre, Simone de Beauvoir, Germaine Hugnet, Zanie and Jean Aubier, Raymond Queneau, Jacques-Laurent Bost and Dora Maar. Georges Hugnet provided the musical accompaniment, and those who heard the reading included Paul Eluard, Valentine Hugo, Jacques Lacan, Georges and Sylvie Bataille, Henri Michaux, Georges Braque and Brassaï.[131]

However, while Picasso's activities during the war bore some relationship to those of the Main à Plume group, the latter have never been recognized to the same extent despite Picasso's admiration of them. Christian Zervos, a friend of Picasso who had fought in the Resistance, recognized that artistic practice – *in and of itself* – was an act of political resistance, though he acknowledged that Picasso's actions never went beyond painting. As Zervos stated in March 1945:

> Picasso simply kept his dignity during the Occupation the way millions of people did here. But he never got involved in the Resistance. Realize that his work itself is the greatest form of resistance, not only against an enemy but against millions of pretentious imbeciles.[132]

Yet neither Main à Plume, nor the Surrealists in America, have been properly credited for their resistance. The Surrealists who fled to America were deemed to have sold out, even by ex-Surrealists such as Georges Hugnet, who argued that in leaving France Breton had 'dishonoured Surrealism', or André Thirion who, despite his praise of Breton in his memoirs, suggests that Benjamin Péret took the 'safe path' in fleeing to Mexico.[133]

It is little wonder that a negative view of Surrealism's conduct during the war became widespread in later years. Maurice Nadeau in his massively influential *Histoire du surréalisme* suggested that Surrealism had not only abandoned France but had *died* during the war. Nadeau claimed the Surrealist project no longer had a place on French soil, especially as 'the bonds imposed by family, morality, religion' had been effectively destroyed by the Occupation and by the undeclared civil war which followed between *Resistants* and collaborators.[134] It is this critical reception and traumatized political landscape which faced Breton when he returned to France on 26 May 1946 and which the Surrealists had to try to come to terms with in their first post-war international exhibition in 1947.

86 Pablo Picasso, *The Charnel House*, 1945.
Recalling the palette, form and tone of *Guernica*,
this powerful image of death coincided with
the horrific discovery and documentation in
photographs and newsreel footage of the Nazi death
camps. It was exhibited at the major exhibition
'Art et Resistance' held at the Musée National d'Art
Moderne in Paris in February–March 1946.

CHAPTER THREE

Post-War Paris and 'Surrealism in 1947'

Since his return André Breton has been content to observe. Now he
is preparing, in close secrecy, his re-entry and that of the Surrealist
group, a sensational exhibit to be held in the month of May. The
director of one of the most luxurious Paris galleries has agreed and
it is said that he is even underwriting the cost. It will be a 'grand plat
Surréaliste' with Duchamp as the great producer – one counts on him
not simply to repeat the exhibition of 1938.

Combat, February 1947[1]

Maurice Nadeau's 1945 *Histoire du surréalisme* claimed that Surrealism had died
with the war but events belie this. Ernst, Masson, Tanguy and Miró all exhibited in
the Surrealist room at the Salon d'Automne in Paris in 1944; solo exhibitions of Ernst,
Lam and Miró were held in private Paris galleries in 1945; Breton's *Surrealism
and Painting* and collected *Surrealist Manifestoes* were reprinted in 1945–6; and his
Ode à Charles Fourier, written in exile in 1945, was published in 1947. In Mexico in
1945, Benjamin Péret's *Le Déshonneur des poètes*, an assault on *L'Honneur des poètes*
(the 1943 anthology of French poets of the Resistance), was also published. It was a
polemical reminder of Surrealism's unwavering stance against the use of poetry for
religious, political or nationalist propaganda and for the total liberation of the mind.

Quite a number of intellectuals and artists criticized Surrealism's absence from France during the war, and tended to dismiss its continued faith in desire and the unconscious – rather than real-life experience and socio-political action – as escapist and/or nihilistic. By extension, they deemed it defunct. The discrepancy between the actual activities of the Surrealists and their reported demise according to certain French writers and intellectuals was fuelled by the polarization of post-war French intellectual life into two camps, neither of whom had any time for Surrealism: the Communists around Louis Aragon and the Existentialists around Jean-Paul Sartre. In addition, post-war intellectuals were obsessed with the need to purge France of its political and intellectual collaborators, and post-war art, by extension, was largely dominated by recourse to social realism or abstraction. Breton and the Surrealists obviously never resorted to either of these styles and they were concerned with very different things, notably myth and magic. Furthermore, Breton, in contrast to the dominant discourse of terror and purge, claimed in his *Ode à Charles Fourier* that societal reconstruction and psychic healing could occur only when Fourier's harmonious system based on the laws of 'passionate attraction' was adopted.[2]

The passions were a key element of Fourier's utopian plans for a 'phalanstere', a phalanx of 1,620 people (twice the 810 different psychological types he identified, as it was a two-sex community, male and female), where the twelve key passions – five of the senses (hearing, sight, smell, touch, taste), four of the soul (love, friendship, ambition and parenthood), and three 'distributive' passions (*la Papillone*, love of variety, *la Cabaliste*, competition/conspiracy, and *la Composite*, a combination of all the passions leading to a kind of orgasmic, overwhelming passion) – were given free rein. It was a community in which manual labour would be made pleasurable and where the total freedom of sexual activity was allowed (heterosexual and same-sex relationships and freedom to pursue any sexual preference, including Sadism and bestiality, provided no force was used). As a result it would be a community of harmony and satisfaction.

Breton's faith in Fourier's socialist, utopian ideas, as expressed in Fourier's *Traité de l'association domestique-agricole* (1822), later republished as *Theorie de l'unité universelle*, and other writings, became even keener during the war and was in keeping with the Surrealists' faith in the politics of Eros in insisting on the powerful force of desire and the erotic to lead the individual to pursue a common good. In 1945 Breton had procured the five-volume 1846 edition of Fourier's complete works in New York and took them on his journey west from New York to Nevada, Arizona and New Mexico, writing his homage, *Ode à Charles Fourier*, en route. Breton's turn towards myth at this time, his embrace of Native American and Haitian culture, and total confidence in the power of love, the imagination and magic to guide man out of wartime despair and into a new era, were part of this same Fourierist, integral humanist direction. Yet Breton's embrace of Fourier was evidently a far cry from the concerns, ideas and language of those intellectuals, writers and artists who dominated the cultural arena in post-war Paris and seemed far too utopian a direction for those who had stayed in France and lived through the horrors of the war.

However, the Surrealists' recourse to myth, magic and Fourierist desire *was* an attempt to address the horrors of the war: they responded to the profanity of war with renewed faith in the power of art (free expression) and the 'sacred' to heal. This was indicated by Breton himself in 'A Tribute to Antonin Artaud', his first post-war public lecture in Paris, given at the Théâtre Sarah Bernhardt on 7 June 1946. He began the lecture by admitting that he was feeling somewhat unsure of himself, a little out of touch, as he inevitably was, given his long absence. But he was no less sure of the continuing relevance of Surrealism: 'Especially in view of the events of these past few years, let me add that I find laughable any kind of so-called engagement that falls short of this indivisible threefold objective: to transform the world, to change life, to reshape the human mind.'[3]

Breton alludes to his 1935 'Speech to the Congress of Writers' here, which ended on a rallying cry that seemed even more pertinent now given what he saw as post-war political and cultural dogmatism: '"Transform the world", Marx said; "change life", Rimbaud said. These two watchwords are one for us.'[4] His words demonstrate a continued trust in total freedom of artistic expression, a trust he had voiced in the FIARI manifesto, and indicate his belief that this total liberty – the reshaping of the human mind – could still be achieved by a fusion of Marxism and Rimbaud. Fourier offered a possible route and would remain at the forefront of Breton's thoughts in the post-war period, culminating in the Fourier-inspired 'Absolute Deviation' (L'Ecart absolu) exhibition in 1965, as we shall see in Chapter 5.

The exhibition 'Surrealism in 1947' (Le Surréalisme en 1947), held the following year, is best appreciated in the light of Breton's comments. In it the Surrealists retaliated against political prescription in art and the burgeoning call for 'authentic' subject-matter in post-war France. They responded to the horrors of the war by bringing together an international field of artists, the art of the insane and non-western art, to insist upon the need for creative rebirth. Through display and installation, a thematic focus on myth and magic, and lengthy essays in the accompanying catalogue, the exhibition reflected Breton's determination, explained in 1941, to turn to Eros as a means of 're-establishing that equilibrium' broken by the war.[5] The 1947 exhibition marked Surrealism's re-entry to French culture and its belief that art and the exhibition should act as a forum within which the spectator could be initiated into a new world vision.

French society and culture remained in a state of trauma in 1947. Three years earlier, following the Allied landings of 6 June 1944 and the subsequent liberation of Paris in August, French culture had begun the slow process of reconstruction. After four years of occupation, France had been left, in the words of Charles de Gaulle, 'exposed, from one end to another', and was a 'mutilated' nation.[6] France had lost one and a half million people, a quarter of its buildings had been destroyed and a million families were homeless. The economy was shattered by the war and the country was left with a ruined transport system, depleted coalmines and severe food shortages. Amid this economic hardship, often accompanied by deep psychological suffering, French artists and intellectuals attempted to make ends meet and to come to terms with the war, especially with Vichy France's collaboration with the Germans. The trauma of this 'Vichy syndrome' as explained by historian Henry Rousso, was a result of the 'internal divisions within France' revealed 'in political, social and cultural life'.[7] Vichy France became a mnemonic site within post-war French intellectual writing, and philosophers, writers and artists turned to terror and trauma as subjects of immediate and historical significance which tested man in new, existential and ethical ways. As Tony Judt has documented, terror was repeatedly invoked as a means of addressing this trauma and its aftermath: 'Terror as an ideal, terror as a method, terror as a regrettable necessity, terror as a metaphor, terror in every shape and form permeated intellectual consciousness.'[8]

This terror was literal and began with the purging of collaborators (the *épuration*) when some 9,000 summary executions were carried out.[9] The philosopher Albert Camus described this process in frightening terms in 1945:

> The hatred of the killers forged in response a hatred on the part of the victims....The killers once gone, the French were left with a hatred partially shorn of its object. They still look at one another with a residue of anger.[10]

The trial of Robert Brasillach was particularly high profile. Brasillach was tried under Article 75 of the French Penal Code for his wartime collaboration, specifically for his anti-Semitic articles in *Je suis partout*, his attendance at the International Congress of Writers in Germany in 1941, and for 'rapports intellectuels' with the Nazis. He was found guilty of treason and sentenced to death on 19 January 1945.[11] His case, like so many others, was dominated by a discourse loaded with Manichaean terms – Good/Evil, Resistant/Collaborator, Communist/Capitalist.

The subject of national and individual sovereignty, and its attendant issues of responsibility, punishment and redemption, was at the forefront of critical debate in post-war Paris. In this debate the body was a key political metaphor. The rhetoric of the Resistance and post-war *Resistantialisme* was emphatically corporeal: the political language of the French Left and Right repeatedly referred to the nation in terms of the body, both in their damnation of collaborators and in their aspirations for a new France. In post-war French art, the body, which allowed exploration of the themes of trauma, terror and political engagement, was depicted in the prevailing realist or abstract styles. The former direction was found in the work of Pablo Picasso, Boris Taslitzky and Francis Gruber and was evident in the Communist-sponsored exhibition dedicated to 'Art et Resistance' held at the Musée National d'Art Moderne in February–March 1946.[12] Here Picasso's *The Charnel House* (1945), with its evocation of death, sacrifice and rebirth was deemed to epitomize good, politically engaged art [86]. Picasso in turn donated the painting to a Communist-run charity for former Resistance fighters. Although his artistic style was hardly socialist realist, the style favoured by the Party, Picasso's value to the Party lay not so much in his style but in his prestige as a painter with a special ability to make great art accessible to the masses, as Gertje R. Utley has argued.[13] That said, *Charnel House* was undoubtedly a politically loaded work that set out to confront the public with contemporary reality, much as his *Guernica* had in 1937.[14] In its content and mood it emphasized the suffering of individuals, of a mother and child, and in its restricted palette of blacks and greys it evoked contemporary newsreel and press reports of death camps. Yet it also looked forward to the rebirth of liberty in the guise of the militant male who reaches up in a salute even in death.

The paintings of Boris Taslitzky, who had been imprisoned in Buchenwald and sketched during his incarceration, offered a more brutal realism to the public, a more monumental approach to death and sacrifice which was more in keeping with Soviet socialist realism. His *The Small Camp at Buchenwald* (1945) was bought for the French nation and depicts the disturbing world of the camp where emaciated bodies are thrown aside like cigarette butts and soldiers and their dogs attack those who are barely alive [87]. Taslitzky said that he 'spat out the deportation in my canvases'.[15] In his imagery and use of clashing colours, he used art to insist that the political obscenity of the recent past should not be forgotten by the French people. Francis Gruber also confronted the public with the horror of the war in his bleak

87 Boris Taslitzky, *The Small Camp at Buchenwald*,
1945. The Jewish painter Taslitzky fought in the
Resistance, was captured and imprisoned in
Clermont-Ferrand, Riom and Saint-Sulpice-la-
Pointe, and then deported to Buchenwald in August
1944. The quarantine camp was known as the
'Small Camp' and in 1945 it became increasingly
overcrowded with Jewish prisoners, moved there
from abandoned camps in Poland. Disease was
rampant (a typhus epidemic killed half of all the
prisoners who died at Buchenwald).

paintings. Gruber was an active member of the Resistance during the war; he joined the Communist Party in 1944, and died at the young age of thirty in 1948. His images of unnamed, wretched and emaciated individuals in dishevelled settings, as in his 1942 painting *The Poet*, offered little hope and evoked the psychic angst of the French nation.

The second direction taken by the artistic representation of the body in post-war Paris was towards the abstract and gestural: this was not the 'tricolour abstraction' that the painter Jean Bazaine had endorsed during the Occupation, but rather a new crude emphasis on surface texture.[16] Artists such as Jean Dubuffet and Jean Fautrier exemplify this shift, their recourse to muddy, gestural, formlessness seeming to reflect the traumatized psyche of the French people. Before the Occupation the soil and the feminine were synonymous symbols of nationalistic nostalgia in French art; now, in post-war paintings, the soil and the feminine became synonymous with despair and/or corruption.[17] Dubuffet literally smeared the surface of the canvas with earth and grit as if to capture moral rot and the end of fine art as it had been prior to the Final Solution, as well as demonstrating his 'anti-cultural positions' and preference for the primitive over the Occidental.[18] His 1944 *Matière et Mémoire* (Matter and Memory) series was almost carnivalesque in its attempt to address the horror of the war. He attacked the surface of the canvas as if to scratch out existence itself. His *Murs* (Walls) series of lithographs of 1945, which illustrated poems by his friend Eugène Guillevic (a civil servant and Communist who had fought in the Resistance and became celebrated as a Resistance poet), can be read on a human or political level: each documents the real dilapidation of walls and the traces of man left on them (wear and tear, graffiti, stains), as well as mnemonically evoking that area of the Parisian periphery known as the 'zone' where executions were carried out and victims buried during the Occupation.[19] Jean Fautrier's wartime series of paintings and sculptures of *Hostages* was equally emotive. Exhibited at the Galerie René Drouin in 1945, these paintings were reminiscent of primitive cave art in their crudeness, indicating a rejection of the 'civilization' that led to the war in the first place, but also evoking the literal traces of war in the city of Paris (the bullet holes, ruins and blood stains). The series, including paintings such as *Hostage no. 22* (1944), were small and intimate in scale [88]. Their anonymous protagonists were described by the writer Francis Ponge in 1946 as Christ-like, but here the 'anonymous man replaces the painted Christs'.[20] Through his representation of the wretched face or the violated form, Fautrier portrays the human – and, by extension, France herself – as crushed and mutilated.

In the Fourth Republic (1946–58) such corporeal metaphors were ubiquitous, and often fuelled by those who had fought in the Resistance and did not want France's corruption to be forgotten. Many Resistants were members and supporters of the Communist Party, which gained 25 per cent of the vote in 1945, secured the position of Deputy Prime Minister for Maurice Thorez in 1946–7 and maintained the support of many intellectuals until the mid-1950s. The party was a force to be reckoned with by any Surrealist who returned to Paris. The ex-Surrealist Paul Eluard persuaded his friend Picasso to join the Communist Party and praised Louis Aragon as the poet who was 'most right...he has shown me the way', despite what some saw as Aragon's hard-line socialist realist aesthetics.[21] Aragon edited the newspaper *Ce Soir* until 1953 when he began to edit the arts and literature weekly *Les Lettres françaises*, and he served on the Central Committee of the French Communist Party from 1950 to 1960. Surrealism had to battle for its place in post-war Paris given the power and influence of Aragon and his Communist comrades. This power and influence was a great concern for Breton:

> The Stalinists, the only ones who had a strong organization during the clandestine period, had managed to fill almost all the key positions in publishing, the press, the radio, the art galleries, etc....On an intellectual level, it goes without saying that it was vital to neutralize and silence those who were in a position to denounce such an operation...[22]

Tristan Tzara had also turned his back on Dada and Surrealism and converted to Communism. On 17 March 1947, Breton had a public run-in with his old Dada colleague when he attended his lecture at the Sorbonne on Surrealism and the post-war period. Here Tzara attacked Surrealism for its impotence during the war, and its absence 'from our hearts and our action during the Occupation'.[23] He stated that the war had profoundly affected people's understanding of reality, implying that the Surrealists' traditional concern to heighten reality was now beside the point. Tzara levelled a number of criticisms against the movement which may be read as indicative of the political and cultural power of the Communist Party in post-war Paris, and its distrust of Breton's avant-gardist internationalism, his artistic libertarianism, and what they saw as his seduction by America. Firstly, Tzara traced the beginning of the end of Surrealism all the way back to Aragon's departure from the Surrealist group for Communism in 1930–2.[24] Secondly, he stated that Benjamin Péret's *Le Déshonneur des poètes* (1945) was an insult to the poets who stayed, fought and sometimes died during the Occupation.[25] Thirdly, he argued that Surrealism's ideas were no longer effective and that they had lost touch with France. This 'distance' was typified, in his view, by *VVV* which he said had nothing to do with the reality of the Nazi occupation and was at best inoffensive.[26] Finally, Tzara claimed that La Main à Plume's activity in Paris was 'secondary', demonstrated by the fact that its participants abandoned it to join the Resistance in 1943. Ultimately, Tzara deemed poetry and art to be relevant to the revolutionary process, giving it a face and an iconography, but rejected those Surrealists who judged the Occupation 'from high atop the Statue of Liberty' without ever dirtying their hands in combat.[27] On hearing this, Breton was enraged: he stood and shouted at Tzara, criticized him for speaking in the old Richelieu amphitheatre (the antithesis of all Dada stood for), jumped up on stage and drank Tzara's glass of water (with Dada flair) before stomping away.

A second level of assault on Surrealism came from the ranks of the Existentialists. Jean-Paul Sartre – who also embraced Communism at this time, though he never joined the Party – claimed that Surrealism was nothing more than an outmoded, parasitic movement. Although he admired Alberto Giacometti, who was a Surrealist in the 1930s and wrote an essay for an exhibition of David Hare's sculptures at the Galerie Maeght in 1947, his essay 'What is Literature?' (1947) claimed that Surrealism was too distant from the pertinent moral questions that needed to be posed in a post-war society which had been face to face with evil. He accused Surrealism of not being proletarian enough and only affecting the bourgeoisie.[28] Sartre defined the Surrealist enterprise as a nihilistic one, involving the 'destruction of painting by painting and of literature by literature', which resulted in what he called 'nothingness':

> a Nothingness which is only the endless fluttering of contradictions....It is neither Hegelian Negativity, nor hypostasized

88 Jean Fautrier, *Hostage no.22*, 1944. Fautrier was arrested by the Gestapo in January 1943, on his release – thanks to the intervention of Arno Breker – he retreated to the grounds of the medical clinic of Dr Henry le Savoureux in the Vallée-aux-Loups near Paris, and produced his *Hostages*. In his preface to the catalogue of Fautrier's 1945 exhibition at the Galerie René Drouin, André Malraux described them as 'the first attempt to dissect contemporary pain, down to its tragic ideograms, and force it into the world of eternity'.

Liberté est un mot vietnamien

Y a-t-il une guerre en Indochine ? On s'en douterait à peine : les journaux de la France « libre », soumis plus que jamais à la consigne, font le silence. Ils publient timidement des résumés militaires victorieux mais embarrassés. Pour réconforter les familles, on assure que les soldats sont « économisés » (des banquiers se trahissent par le style des communiqués). Pas un mot de la féroce répression exercée là-bas au nom de la Démocratie. Tout est fait pour cacher aux Français un scandale dont le monde entier s'émeut.

Car il y a la guerre en Indochine, une guerre impérialiste entreprise, au nom d'un peuple qui lui même vient d'être libéré de cinq ans d'oppression, contre un autre peuple unanime à vouloir sa liberté.

Cette agression revêt une signification grave :

d'une part, elle prouve que rien n'est changé : comme en 1919 le capitalisme, après avoir exploité tant le patriotisme que les plus nobles mots d'ordre de liberté, entend reprendre un pouvoir entier, réinstaller la puissance de sa bourgeoisie financière, de son armée et de son clergé, il continue sa politique impérialiste traditionnelle :

d'autre part, elle prouve que les élus de la classe ouvrière, au mépris de la tradition anti-colonialiste qui fut un des plus fermes vecteurs du mouvement ouvrier, en flagrante violation du droit maintes fois proclamé des peuples à disposer d'eux-mêmes, acceptent — les uns par corruption, les autres par soumission aveugle à une stratégie imposée de haut et dont les exigences, dès maintenant illimitées, tendent à dérober ou à invertir les véritables mobiles de lutte — d'assumer la responsabilité de l'oppression ou de s'en faire, en dépit d'une certaine ambivalence de comportement, les complices.

Aux hommes qui gardent quelque lucidité et quelque sens de l'honnêteté nous disons : il est faux que l'on puisse défendre la liberté *ici* en imposant la servitude *ailleurs*.

Il est faux que l'on puisse mener au nom du peuple français un combat si odieux sans que des conséquences dramatiques en découlent rapidement.

La tuerie agencée adroitement par un moine amiral ne tend qu'à défendre l'oppression féroce des capitalistes, des bureaucrates et des prêtres. Et ici, n'est-ce pas, trêve de plaisanterie : il ne saurait être question d'empêcher le Vietnam de tomber entre les mains d'un impérialisme concurrent car où voit-on que l'impérialisme français ait conservé quelque indépendance; où voit-on qu'il ait fait autre chose depuis un quart de siècle que céder et se vendre ? Quelle protection se flatte-t-il d'assurer à tels ou tels de ses esclaves ?

Les surréalistes, pour qui la revendication principale a été et demeure la libération de l'homme, ne peuvent garder le silence devant un crime aussi stupide que révoltant. Le surréalisme n'a de sens que *contre* un régime dont tous les membres *solidaires* n'ont trouvé comme don de joyeux avènement que cette ignominie sanglante, régime qui à peine né s'écroule dans la boue des compromissions, des concussions et qui n'est qu'un prélude calculé pour l'édification d'un prochain totalitarisme.

Le surréalisme déclare, à l'occasion de ce nouveau forfait, qu'il n'a renoncé à aucune de ses revendications et, moins qu'à toute autre, à la volonté d'une transformation radicale de la société. Mais il sait combien sont illusoires les appels à la conscience, à l'intelligence et même aux intérêts des hommes, combien sur ces plans le mensonge et l'erreur sont faciles, les divisions inévitables : c'est pourquoi le domaine qu'il s'est choisi est à la fois plus large et plus profond, à la mesure d'une véritable fraternité humaine.

Il est donc désigné pour élever sa protestation véhémente contre l'agression impérialiste et adresser son salut fraternel à ceux qui incarnent, en ce moment même, le devenir de la liberté.

Adolphe ACKER, Yves BONNEFOY, Joë BOUSQUET, Francis BOUVET, André BRETON, Jean BRUN, J.-B. BRUNIUS, Eliane CATONI, Jean FERRY, Guy GILLEQUIN, Jacques HALPERN, Arthur HARFAUX, Maurice HENRY, Marcel JEAN, Pierre MABILLE, Jehan MAYOUX, Francis MEUNIER, Maurice NADEAU, Henri PARISOT, Henri PASTOUREAU, Benjamin PERET, N. et H. SEIGLE, Iaroslav SERPAN, Yves TANGUY.

89 'Liberté est un mot vietnamien', April 1947, a tract written by Yves Bonnefoy, André Breton, Pierre Mabille and signed by twenty-five people, and which called for the end to 'the Imperialist war' in Indochina which had begun in 1946.

Negation, not even Nothingness, though it bears a likeness to it; it would be more correct to call it the Impossible or, if you like, the imaginary point where dream and waking, the real and the fictitious, the objective and the subjective, merge.[29]

His depiction of a Surrealist nothingness was quite different from his own Existentialist concept of nothingness, of course: Surrealist nothingness may be understood as a wanton destructiveness and an abandonment of individual responsibility to any moral imperative; Existentialist nothingness, or 'pour soi', may be understood as a synonym for the conscious seizure of any moral imperative.[30]

It is understandable that Sartre would have misgivings about Surrealism, however.[31] Surrealism was a movement whose psychoanalytic interests automatically alienated it from an existential framework. In insisting on the relevance of the unconscious to conscious life, the Surrealists dissolved subjectivity, breaking down the potential for Sartrean engagement and action: their insistence that one's situation was manipulated by external or subconscious activities removed the element of responsibility so central to the Sartrean project. Sartre argued that Surrealism only distanced literature and the reader from the human condition, and so removed itself from cultural responsibility. As Sartre expressly stated that literature must discover the absolute in the relative, he was evidently dissatisfied with what he perceived as Surrealism's aloofness from cultural responsibility and its refuge in such seemingly abstract concepts as Eros, myth, magic, or the sacred. Sartre insisted that good authors were those who had seized the crisis of language prompted by the war to pose the question 'What are the relationships between ends and means in a society based on violence?'[32] Perhaps he was not familiar with Breton's wartime writings, especially the 'Prolegomena to a Third Surrealist Manifesto or Not' and *Arcane 17*, texts which did address the human condition, the need for a new direction, a new better reality – albeit in a very different style to Existentialist art and literature.

Unsurprisingly, the Surrealists retaliated, notably in two collective tracts, namely: 'Liberté est un mot vietnamien' in April [89] and 'Rupture inaugurale' in June 1947. The former tract was the first collective one to be issued since Breton's return to Paris, and offered the first opportunity to counteract the accusations of political and cultural impotence issued by Tzara the previous month. It was signed by twenty-five people including the Main à Plume figure Adolphe Acker, and it articulated the Surrealists' concept of political morality and their stance against the 'bloody ignominy' witnessed in the 'imperialist war' in Indochina which had begun in 1946. It attacked bourgeois imperialism, but also the ambiguous stance of Communists towards the war.[33] The second lengthier tract, with fifty-one signatories, involved a more thorough statement on political and cultural liberty against 'all partisan politics'.[34] The frontispiece paid tribute to Sade, the Surrealist icon of independent poetic revolution: it was a photograph of the ruins of Sade's hilltop chateau in Lacoste, probably taken by René Char on his visit there in 1931, with the following caption:

The hard stone profile of the Marquis de Sade still looks at the horizon, at everything that has vanished for him on that plain where men make prisons in which to lock those who have loved.[35]

'Rupture inaugurale' attacked the French Communist Party for adopting bourgeois methods and weapons; it criticized the widespread reactionary condemnation of Germany by French diplomats and Communists, arguing that while that country may have produced Hitler, it also produced Hegel, Marx, Stirner, Freud, Novalis, Nietzsche, Karl Liebknecht and Rosa Luxembourg; and it pointed out that Surrealism's past experience with the Communist Party had proved problematic because the Surrealists were concerned, primarily, with the total – and uncompromising – liberation of man, which was impossible within the confines of a party-political agenda. For the Surrealists the proletarian revolution was a means to total liberation – not an end in itself. Finally, it made the point that morality would not change with an economic revolution alone – it needed a cultural revolution too, one that united the imaginary and the real, the expressible and the inexpressible, reason and passion. This tract was published three months after Tzara's attack on Surrealism and two months after Sartre's. Hence it may be seen as an attempt to counteract both authors' criticisms of the movement and to challenge the general bias of the French Communist Party towards the movement. It also retaliated against 'Monsieur Sartre' and his criticisms of the movement in questioning the computability of Existentialism and Communism, and held up the writings of the Marquis de Sade and Freud as the key figures for the doctrine that would succeed Christianity. In an interview in 1948, Breton explained that 'Rupture inaugurale' expressed a refusal to be torn between inefficiency and compromise – that is a refusal to be labelled impotent and to be pressurized into political compromise.[36] These tracts signalled the Surrealists' firm line on party politics, their dogged faith in all that FIARI and Péret's *Le Déshonneur des poètes* had called for, and, as we shall now see, their continued faith in a politics of Eros which would soon be expressed in their international exhibition, opening the month after publication of 'Rupture inaugurale'.[37]

On 7 July 'Surrealism in 1947' opened at the Galerie Maeght, 13 rue de Téhéran, Paris with such crowds and so many photographers that apparently the poet Jacques Prévert 'commented that anyone would think the photographers were photographing each other'.[38] According to Adrian Maeght, the son of Aimé Maeght, his father chose to hold the exhibition out of nostalgia for his own youthful interest in Surrealism, notably Surrealist literature. His father viewed Surrealism as an important avant-garde movement and many of the authors he had published as an editor and artists he represented as a gallerist had 'traversed Surrealism' in some form or other. Maeght's support of Surrealism at a time when many were negative towards it was significant. As Adrian Maeght, then in his late teens, recalled: 'After the war there was a lot of antagonism towards Surrealism as it was anti-politics, anti-Stalin, anti-doctrinal....It was an unusual time when everyone who was for the Communist Party was good and everyone who was against it was bad.' Yet his father recognized that, as a result, Surrealism also represented a 'certain liberty'.[39] In a letter to the artist Enrico Donati, dated 3 February 1947, Aimé Maeght certainly wrote of 'Surrealism in 1947' in terms that evoke a *prise politique*, describing it as 'A point of departure, the taking of a focused and unequivocal position.'[40]

Breton's invitation to artists to participate in the exhibition was equally unequivocal. It was to present to the public Surrealism's 'New Myth' of the 'Great Transparent Ones', who had magical powers, written of in the 'Prolegomena to a Third Surrealist Manifesto or Not' (1942).[41] Of course the exhibition also needed to counteract Maurice Nadeau's *Histoire du surréalisme*, in which he pronounced the death of the movement, and the general public's and critical perception that Surrealism was no longer a cultural power broker. But in turning to myth and magic the Surrealists indicated that while they had not wavered from their initial, revolutionary stance of the 1920s, they were attempting to address the horrors of the recent war and to offer a new direction out of the French nation's despair.

During the war the Surrealists voiced their stance on myth and magic, respectively, in the magazine *View*, stating that myths were 'alive so long as men believe in them. Out of them come new deeds, new realities, because myth is creative' and that magic was 'the means of approaching the unknown by other ways than those of science of religion.'[42] Essentially, myth and magic offered metaphoric discourses to the Surrealists to address history but also the need for change. Furthermore, as Whitney Chadwick has pointed out, the Surrealists viewed myth – and, I would add, magic – 'in the French sense, in which myths are constructed from all the versions of a story, rather than the somewhat narrower English tradition in which a myth is identified as such primarily through its origins and historical meaning.'[43] As such, the 1947 exhibition could look to Greek and medieval myths, occultist and alchemical references, and allow a group of relatively disparate, international artists to exhibit very different art styles and subject-matters whilst always sharing a common pursuit.

In their recourse to myth and magic the Surrealists were still indebted to the ideas of Freud, who wrote of the psychic significance of both in *Totem and Taboo*: *Resemblances Between the Psychic Lives of Savages and Neurotics* (1913). Here Freud discussed myth in terms of primitive peoples and the infantile psyche, depicting it as collective wish-fulfilment loaded with symbolism and as a phenomenon that saw a decline with the rise of civilization. He explained magic, spirits and demons as projections of man's own emotional impulses. For Freud, myth and magic were signs of the primitive and were repressed in the name of civilization, but like totem and taboo, both return in the modern age in the religions, manners and customs of civilized people. The Surrealists' embrace of the primitive, irrational nature of myth and magic was in keeping with their use of Freudian psychoanalysis for social and political subversion, for their politics of Eros. For myth, magic and the themes that the Surrealists used to link them – *initiation* – had uncanny characteristics. They played on the uncanny theme of unveiling, of making the secret come to light. Freud explains the uncanny as relating to 'the belief in the omnipotence of thoughts and the technique of magic based on that belief', stating that an uncanny experience can occur 'when primitive beliefs which have been surmounted seem once more to be confirmed.'[44]

Breton's notion of initiation had certain 'feminine' qualities to it too as it was influenced by the recent publication of René Guénon's *Aperçus sur l'initiation* (1946) in which initiation was presented as a rebirth and a 'regeneration'.[45] Guénon wrote about initiation in terms of ritualistic stages through which a spiritual knowledge is gleaned, and presented symbolism, ritual and myth as key ingredients to initiation. Breton also looked to Frazer's *Golden Bough* for this exhibition, citing his definition of magic as 'the mother of freedom and truth' in the catalogue.[46] This concept of initiation as a rebirth and of magic as a feminine power that was not hysterical or monstrous (as in the 1938 exhibition) but healing and enlightening again reminds us of Freud's double-sided conceptualization of the uncanny (the womb/tomb, fantasy of intra-uterine experience/fear of castration dichotomy). In this exhibition the Surrealists presented a labyrinthine, intra-uterine space as utopic. Recognizing the prophetic nature of the 1938 exhibition, they now turned to the power of the feminine in the terms of Breton's wartime *Arcane 17*, as discussed and cited in the Introduction to this book: 'it rests with the artist to make visible everything that is part of the feminine, as opposed to the masculine, system of the world.'[47] All this is key to our appreciation of the exhibition design and installations, and how the uncanny was again staged through the feminine, just as Breton evoked the redemptress Melusina in *Arcane 17* too.

While the tone of both exhibitions may have been different, the Maeght gallery space took on a feminine form like that of the 1938 exhibition in its non-linear, labyrinthine layout so that Surrealist creativity was presented spatially and symbolically as procreative. Breton and Duchamp conceived of the *mise en scène* for the exhibition but it was Kiesler, the architect who believed in the 'primordial unity' of man's 'creative consciousness' and his environment (as expressed in his designs for Peggy Guggenheim in 1942), who succeeded in bringing those ideas into the third dimension and adding his own.[48] He was helped by 'an extraordinary, ingenious craftsman who could tackle anything', known as 'Zigoto'.[49] Kiesler left New York for Paris to design the exhibition (Duchamp remained) and spent four months ensuring everything went according to plan and to his vision, which also spoke to this concept of rebirth. In 1946, Kielser wrote of the significance of the spiral in architecture as a natural, potent form, describing it as 'Continuous motion from within its own force. Power of birth and re-birth.'[50] Indeed, Kiesler's explanation of his personal turn towards natural, spiral forms in the aftermath of World War I might equally apply to the conditions that led the Surrealists to turn towards the feminine and new forms and myths after World War II:

> I was living in Paris after the First World War. Everybody was concerned with problems of reconstruction: youth, particularly with ideas of resurrecting the spirit massacred....[51]

Accordingly, the gallery space was orchestrated so that the spectator was led through a spiritual rebirth, progressing from the historical into the new in a labyrinthine series of rooms. So a path was mapped out for the public which began by presenting Surrealism's artistic and literary heritage, then pre-war Surrealism, followed by a central egg-shaped room devoted to superstition, and finishing with the new and mythological in the form of a room with altars and totemic sculptures.

The spectator's experience of the exhibition is best understood as a series of 'stages', in keeping with the concept of initiation. It first involved ascension into true, contemporary Surrealism, via twenty-one red stairs, each decorated to look like the spine of a book, representing the twenty-one major arcanes of the Tarot and the 'forefathers' of Surrealism. Thus the spectator stepped from the first tarot card, 'The Magician' (represented by Charles Maturin's *Melmoth ou l'homme errant*) to the last card, 'The World' (represented by Isidore Ducasse's *Complete Works*). In between, were such works as Rousseau's *Rêveries d'un promeneur solitaire* (representing 'The Empress' card), Fourier's *Théorie de quatre mouvements* ('The Star'), Apollinaire's *L'Enchanteur pourrissant* ('Death'), Jarry's *Ubu Roi* ('The Devil') and Baudelaire's *Les Fleurs du mal* ('The Pope'). Sade was duly represented too, his *Justine* being chosen to represent 'The Chariot' card. In sum, on entering the upper gallery space, the spectator had effectively taken the first step in initiation. This was symbolized by the fact that the stairs were 'swept from above by the light of a small revolving lighthouse' dramatically symbolizing Surrealist enlightenment or 'illumination'.[52] The upper space displayed examples of pre- to post-war Surrealism: Calder mobiles hung from the ceiling, paintings by Matta, Tanguy and Miró were on the walls, and Arp's biomorphic *Fruit of the Moon* (1936) sculpture sat on the floor.

This large white-grey, aluminium sculpture proved a dramatic focal point – as one critic put it, it appeared as if it had 'fallen from another planet'.[53]

The spectator then entered the Room of Superstitions, envisaged by Duchamp as a grotto and designed by Kiesler as a space of magic and 'continuity-architecture-painting-sculpture'.[54] The walls were covered with black drapes, paintings could be seen through openings, a blue-green light filled the room and, according to Sarane Alexandrian, the room had 'a disturbed and disturbing atmosphere'.[55] Like the 1938 exhibition, this was an important, central space which would initiate the unwitting spectator into a Surrealist world vision. It was oval in form and, as noted by Jean Arp in his essay in the exhibition catalogue, resembled a large egg in which the spectator was enveloped 'like in the bosom of his mother'.[56] Spatially, the room was emphatically maternal. It had an uncanny edge to it which was key to Kiesler's architectural design and philosophy. As Yehuda Safran has written, Kiesler's was a 'Promethean model whereby a new conception of human knowledge through creation would enlighten the conscious self and wake the imagination to the reality which lies behind or in familiar things'.[57] Furthermore, when Kiesler wrote of magic and 'the life force' in his essay 'Endless House – Space House' in *VVV* in 1944, he evoked the dynamic relationship between the body and space. His idea of magical architecture was based on an idea of 'structures in continuous tension…to shelter those "continuous mutations" of the life-force'.[58] It was a room which was intended to expose man's psychic need for ritual and superstition and the essential role the arts had to play in satisfying that need; it was meant to present the spectator with a series of tests ('cycle théorique des épreuves').[59] It also symbolized the breakdown of man's relationship with nature, one that Kiesler was eager to rebuild – this was symbolically captured in a curving path and with those dark drapes and the blue-green light, the space was almost like a wood at night.

Max Ernst's *The Black Lake*, was painted on the floor. It was intended as a symbolic source to nourish anguish, and around it were 'ranged shapes which represented the atavistic fears of mankind'.[60] The details in this Room of Superstitions again evoked those feminine, uncanny qualities we saw in the 1938 exhibition: dim lighting, the creation of a natural, grassy and wet environment within a building, and a sense that the truest Surrealist environment was the city of flea markets, dark alleys, mysterious encounters and irrationality. As always, the Surrealist space was the very antithesis of the modern gallery, big department stores and official exhibitions.

Sculptures were also present in this room and typified Surrealism's interest in the totemism of Native American and Oceanic cultures. David Hare's life-size sculpture, *Anguish-Man*, built for the exhibition, captured the anxiety of man in its emaciated, crude figuration, and demonstrated a debt to the primitivist standing figures of Giacometti, whom he had recently befriended in Paris. Kiesler's giant plaster *Anti-Taboo Figure* and Kiesler, Etienne Martin and François Stahly's *Totem of Religions* [90 & 91], made of wood and rope, were also built specifically for the exhibition and stood like a primitive icon and crucifix respectively. Yves Tanguy's *The Ladder Announcing Death* was also here: a bizarre, abstracted ladder with staggered screens held upright with cord, reaching towards the ceiling. Hans Arp's installation piece, an architectural cascade made of wide strips of paper painted by Joan Miró and with abstract forms intended to symbolize superstitions, also stood alongside these sculptures, continuing Kiesler's curvilinear design [92]. The sculptures demonstrated the Surrealists' fascination with ethnography too, particularly its

 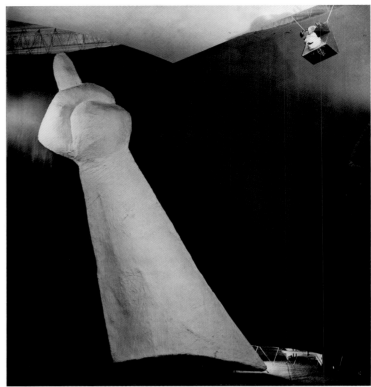

90 **Etienne Martin, *Totem of Religions*, executed for the Room of Superstitions, 'Surrealism in 1947' exhibition, Galerie Maeght, 13 rue de Téhéran, Paris, 7 July – 30 September 1947. The model also wears the 'false breast', from Marcel Duchamp and Enrico Donati's *Please Touch* luxury exhibition catalogue, as a titillating g-string.**

91 **Frederick Kiesler's *Anti-Taboo Figure*, Room of Superstitions, 'Surrealism in 1947' exhibition. Photo by Willy Maywald.**

92 **Installation view of the Room of Superstitions, 'Surrealism in 1947' exhibition: David Hare, *Anguished Man*; Roberto Matta, *The Whist*; Joan Miró, *The Rigid Cascade of Superstitions;* Yves Tanguy, *The Ladder Announcing Death*, all 1947. Photo by Willy Maywald.**

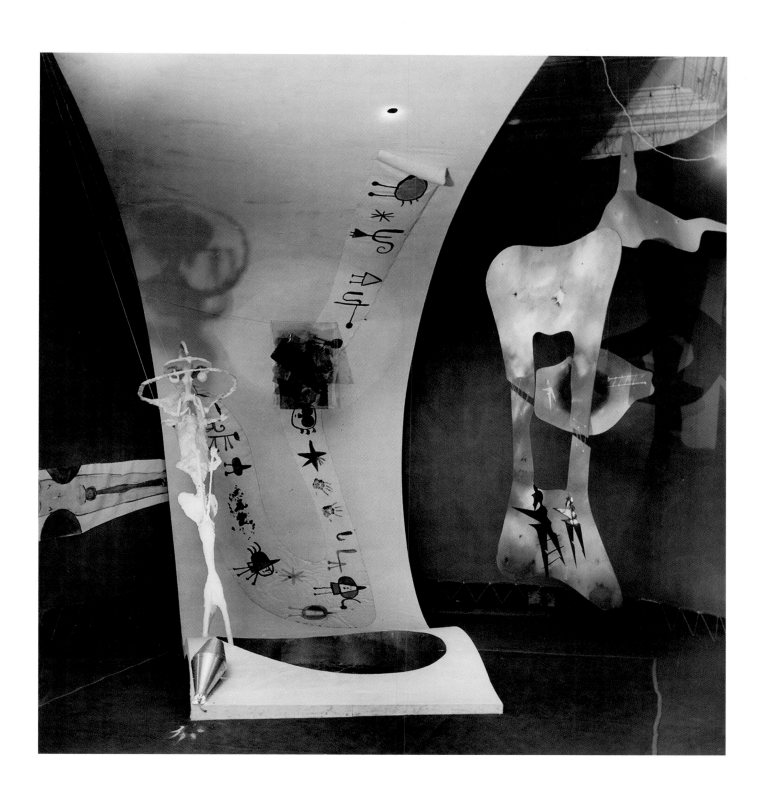

93 **Marcel Duchamp and Frederick Kiesler,**
The Green Ray, photo-collage in the Room of
Superstitions in the 'Surrealism in 1947' exhibition,
Galerie Maeght, Paris, 1947. This object was
indebted to Jules Verne's story of 1882 and was
constructed by Frederick Kiesler on Duchamp's
behalf. Photo by Denise Bellon.

94 **Alberto Giacometti,** *Invisible Object (Hands*
Holding the Void), 1934–5. Giacometti came to
Paris from Geneva in 1922 and from 1930 to
1935 associated with the Surrealists, producing
erotically charged sculptures. *Invisible Object*,
which incorporates a found eye-protection mask,
was celebrated by Breton in *L'Amour fou* (1937)
and was exhibited at the 1959 EROS exhibition,
Galerie Daniel Cordier, 8 rue de Miromesnil, Paris,
15 December 1959 – 29 February 1960.

concern with 'self-ethnography' to use James Clifford's term (the act of writing one's existence 'in a present of memories, dreams, politics, daily life'), and the logic that for primitive man vision and reality are one.[61]

The idea of the 'primitive eye' was key to other objects on show. As Breton asserted in his 1928 essay 'Surrealism and Painting', the Surrealist 'eye' was to exist 'in its savage state', so that moral values could be exposed as contingent and the virtues of the irrational explored and celebrated.[62] Most importantly, this new way of seeing demanded an active role for the spectator. It reinforced the idea that the spectator must complete the work of art and expose him/her self to the possibility of experiencing a new reality in the process. Next to Kiesler and Martin's *Anti-Taboo Figure* was *The Green Ray*: a peephole view, designed by Duchamp and constructed by Kiesler, which also seems to have been homage to the 'primitive' (pre-scientific) mind [93].[63] This installation was an optical illusion devised by Duchamp using sheets of blue and yellow gelatine, and intended to produce an optical phenomenon: a flash of green, similar to that which appears just as the sun sets. The title referred to a story by Jules Verne, *The Green Ray* (1882), in which a young woman decides between two lovers, a scientist and an artist, on the basis of her quest for the green light that appears on the horizon before sunset. When the scientist informs her that this phenomenon is no more than an optical illusion, she chooses the artist as her lover.[64] The spectator in the exhibition was to abandon reason and scientific logic and look through the primitive eye.

Roberto Matta's painting *Dream, or Death* (1945) also hung in the Room of Superstitions and also had an intra-uterine dimension. Here the public was confronted with a painting which seemed to emphasize the element of psychological horror and enlightenment he had evoked almost ten years earlier in his 1938 *Minotaure* article. It depicted a woman with schematic breasts, lying horizontal as her womb is torn from her, her hand holding an egg or philosopher's stone, her mouth open, suggesting agony and ecstasy – perhaps the very essence of birthing. The image may be related to Giacometti's sculpture of 1934, *Invisible Object* (*Hands Holding the Void*) the plaster cast of which Matta had recently purchased [94]. That sculpture, with its nubile female in a frontal pose, reminiscent of Egyptian art and seeming to be either kneeling or caged, her head made from a metal eye-protection mask found at a flea market, had entranced Breton when he first saw it in Giacometti's studio. It is described by him in *L'Amour fou* as an embodiment of the dynamics of desire itself, specifically 'the very emanation *of the desire to love and to be loved* in search of its real human object, in its painful ignorance', in all its fragility and contained dynamism.[65] The 'void' of the work's title may be an insistence on the impossibility of defining desire, or the metaphysical: when viewed alongside Matta's painting we sense a common quest for the alchemy of desire, but also the desire for the spectator to try to make sense of it all.

Matta's *Starving Woman* (1944) was also on display in the exhibition and took erotic expression further. The painting portrays a woman, her head balanced on a table, her jaw gaping, as she bites her nails. Captured in Matta's leitmotif, elongated, totemized style, the swirls of paint about her head emphasize the angularity of her form – an angularity that echoes Hérold's wartime crystalline figures and their angst. For Matta's use of technology as symbol for warfare and barbarism (in his wartime art) may be viewed as a reference to its recent abuse with the atomic bomb and as demonstrating his belief that art's responsibility was 'to show man in his social situation'.[66]

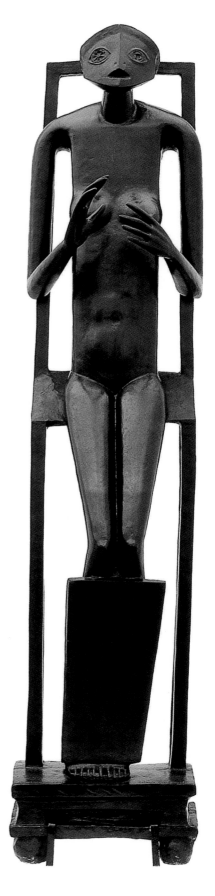

95 **Max Ernst,** *Euclid*, 1945.

A painting of *Euclid* (1945) by Max Ernst, the artist acknowledged as the 'Magician' of the Surrealist group in the April 1942 edition of *View*, continued this assault on science and the production of knowledge. The painting could also be seen if one drew back a window of cloth cut in the drapes: an angular, abstracted portrait of the mathematician with an inverted pyramid for a face under a dramatic, if not dandy-like, hat with roses and wearing a baroque costume [95]. Nicolas Calas, writing in November 1946, states that it is 'reminiscent of portraits by Holbein – unless it is a reactivation of the child's vision of its grandmother' and 'a challenge to Euclidean geometry and the use of it made by cubism and abstract art'.[67] The fig leaf, usually used to cover the sex of an ancient statue now becomes a mask, thus adding, for Calas, 'a satirical and "venetian" note to the violent anti-classical spirit of the picture'.[68] Considering the Room of Superstitions overall, we see how Kiesler's vision of painting, sculpture and architecture merging as one was successfully realized. Little wonder that the critic Pierre Guerre, in a review in *Cahiers du sud*, described the space in magical terms, emphasizing the theatrical use of light and sense of adventure and revelation for the spectator.[69]

The next initiatory stage was the Rain Room, which was conceived by Duchamp and continued this theme of rebirth, purification and renewal. It was divided into two spaces by 'curtains of rain' which fell onto a floor of duckboards. Artificial grass also decorated the room and there was a billiard table which you had to pass as you left. The table was meant to be in constant use according to Sarane Alexandrian's account.[70] However, it soon became useless, according to Marcel Jean, 'since the public had – of course – pocketed the balls'.[71]

On leaving the Rain Room, and before entering the next space, the spectator was greeted by Jacques Hérold's sculptural rendition of Breton's 'Great Transparent Ones' [96]. Here, Hérold portrayed Breton's 'New Myth' within a fragmented, crystalline, androgynous form that he intended to represent the mutilated form of the post-war world.[72] He had hoped to construct this sculpture in glass or transparent plastic, but as both materials were too expensive (the figure was 1.83 metres or 6 feet in height) he constructed it in plaster and later it would be cast in bronze. It was an intentionally imposing presence in the exhibition. As Hérold wrote in the exhibition catalogue, it was emphatically oppositional in its hard form and the very opposite of Dalí's soft forms (and of course by extension opposed to Dalí's loyalty to Franco's regime):

> The soft world stopped living in 1944. I oppose to the soft structures of Dalí, the object made in the form of a spike, broken glass, shear blades, crystal. A cutting hand, a stabbing.[73]

As noted in the last chapter, Hérold's *Flayed Figures* (1943) began his crystallizing process of flaying the body. His later *Maltraité de peinture* (1957) further explained the symbolic significance of his post-war crystallization in terms of the need for art to reflect brutal reality. Hérold's *Great Transparent One* sculpture may be read as symbolically capturing the angst of post-war society. It embodied the astral and the symbolic with a cavernous, wailing face, triangular breasts and solar appendages (a star and crescent at its collarbone), but with its swollen belly (with a mirror in it) and its facial features shattered into parts (an eye, an ear, a nose, a finger, a tongue) it shattered the myth of spiritual unity and universality.[74] Two elements of the work could be read as symbolic of hope however: namely a piece of coal in its left hand and a plate holding two eggs, an offering, which was placed at its feet in the exhibition. Both were alchemical references: to fire with

which base metals turn to gold and to the two hemispheres of the earth.[75] The sculpture represented the fallibility of man, faced with the knowledge that he is not the centre of the universe and cannot control it, and that in the face of great disturbances and war he is, as Breton wrote in the 'Prolegomena to a Third Surrealist Manifesto or Not', 'powerless to be anything but a victim or a witness'.[76] This was the guilt-ridden truth that faced all of Paris in 1947.

Having passed by Hérold's sculpture, an altar to Breton's new vision, the spectator had entered the final stage, the Labyrinth of Initiations, which was also devised by Breton. This was a rectangular room divided into twelve octagonal spaces, based on the votive altars of pagan cults and each corresponding to a sign of the zodiac, from Aries to Pisces, and representing a Surrealist mythical being or object capable of being endowed with mythical life. Brauner, Breton, Frédéric Delegande, Ernst, Jindrich Heisler, Hérold, Lam, Matta, Francis Miller and Toyen were the main artists to contribute to the twelve altars and their myths. The altars were to be modelled on altars used by 'pagan cults, (Indians or voodoo, for example)' and were listed from one to twelve (and the sources indicated) by Breton in his invitation to artists: the Worldly Tiger (*Le Tigre mondain*, from Jean Ferry's story of the same title), the Hair of Falmer (*Le Chevelure de Falmer*, from Chant IV of Lautréamont's *Les Chants de Maldoror* of 1868–9), the Suspicious Heloderm (*L'Héloderme suspect sur le cactus tonneau*, a reference to Gila Monster and Barrel Cactus), Jeanne Sabrenas (the heroine of Alfred Jarry's 'La Dragonne'), Léonie Aubois d'Ashby (from Rimbaud's 'Dévotion'), the Secretary Bird (*L'Oiseau Secretaire ou Serpentaire*, a subject, Breton noted, that was 'dear to Max Ernst'), the Juggler of Gravity (*Le Soigneur de Gravité*, an element of Duchamp's *Large Glass* of 1915–23), the Condylurre (explained by Breton as 'the crazed crone of old authors' and 'star nosed mole'), Brauner's *Wolf-table*, Raymond Roussel, the Great Transparent Ones, and the Window of Magna sed Apta (from George du Maurier's 'Peter Ibbetson').[77] The design of these altars was also specified. Each had to be structured in harmony with its subject-matter, to house a figuration of the subject (a painting, sculpture or object), and to evoke the cultural ambience of its subject with suitable relics, such as crucifixes. And a corresponding sign of the zodiac, signified by specific colours and stones, was to be visible on each altar's frieze.

If we look at some of these altars we better appreciate their fantastic conflation of literature, art, magic and pagan ritual. The second altar, entitled *The Hair of Falmer* was constructed by Wifredo Lam [97]. Here a four-breasted torso with two arms holding large knives in their hands, topped with abundant tresses of hair, stood on an altar as if in some sacrificial ceremony. Before it were food offerings, behind it an inverted crucifix. The altar paid homage to Maldoror's encounter with Falmer, a fourteen-year-old boy, who was hung from the gallows by his beautiful blond hair for three days and subjected to tarring and whippings by women. Maldoror cuts him down and in so doing cuts his hair which then takes on a haunting fetishistic power as a symbol of physical torture.[78] Hérold contributed a 'sculpture physique' to this altar, a golden plate with a fork standing in it and the inscription 'five grams of sun'.

The fifth altar was also literary in dedication. It paid homage to Rimbaud through the character of Léonie Aubois d'Ashby from his poem 'Dévotion' in his collection *Illuminations* (1886) [98].[79] The altar was designed by Francis Miller, who had befriended Tzara and Bellmer in the south of France in 1945 and who was part of the Surrealist group from 1947 until 1950. However, Breton had conceived it and he chose Rimbaud because of the element of the sacred in his work.[80] Hérold

96 **Jacques Hérold, *The Great Transparent One*,** 1947. Hérold's futuristic creature made an imposing impression at 1.83m. For the exhibition it was made of plaster as neither the artist nor Aimé Maeght could afford to cast it; a bronze version was made later.

97–99 **'Surrealism in 1947' exhibition, Galerie Maeght, Paris, 1947.**
Above: Wifredo Lam, altar to *The Hair of Falmer*
Middle: André Breton, altar to *Léonie Aubois d'Ashby*
Below: Roberto Matta, altar to *The Juggler of Gravity*
Photos by Denise Bellon.

also played a part in this altar, contributing an object entitled *Rimbaud's Tie*, which was a tie made of grass.

Other altars were devoted to artists. The sixth altar, entitled *The Secretary Bird or Serpentine* [101], was dedicated to the 'Bird-Superior', Max Ernst, and the Virgo zodiac sign. Brauner's *The Lovers* (1947) [100] took pride of place on it. It represented two figures from the Tarot: 'The Magician', with his coins, chalice, sword and staff, and the 'Papesse' (Popess) with her tiara, pontifical habit, book and throne. As Verena Kuni has observed in her reading of this work, Brauner had added to the traditional iconography of the Tarot, lending it a specific Surrealist and amorous quality to both characters.[81] The Magician does not wear a magician's cape or hat but instead his chest is covered with snakes, his hair bears the symbol of infinity and a volcano erupts from his mind. These are personal attributes typical of Brauner's repertoire in the 1940s and used to indicate his vision of the artist-magician. In addition, a note on the reverse of the painting states that Mount Etna had just erupted and so Brauner seems to have included the volcano as a sign of objective chance, which endows the work with even greater magical significance. Similarly, the Popess's bird's head, the lunar characters which refer to her planetary referents, and the scissors and book on her lap, suggest her divine power over life and death. The numbers 1713 are inscribed at the base of her throne, written like the initials of André Breton. Brauner also depicts the Magician and the Popess with their respective signs and symbols, as complementary male and female figures respectively, whose unison against a dark landscape promises future creativity. The words 'Liberty, Magic, Destiny' denote the hope that surrounds the image, and indeed the exhibition for which it was intended, just as the words 'Past, Present, Future' insist on the cycle of life, the power of magic at that moment in 1947 and the chance of liberty and rebirth in the future. Brauner noted the magical significance of the magician's baton (which bears the sun and moon on it) as a sign of conciliation between the 'two principles, Patriarchal and Matriarchal'.[82] Significantly, the feminine spirit is both the victimized past and the promise of a better future, as Brauner explained in his notes on the painting:

> She has the head of an aggressive bird (a Secretary bird) to show that following the oppressions that she has sustained through all of human history because of an almighty and responsible patriarchy – her only defence is this castrating aggressiveness, provisional symbol of her current struggle for her life, plunging her lover in his relations with her, into guilt and fear.[83]

The painting hung below the altar; on top he put a hawk-like bird, a totemic woman in the grasp of his claws. To its side stood an object placed there by Hérold, a small classical sculpture of a Madonna and Child linked by a serpent.

Roberto Matta made the seventh altar, under the sign of Libra and entitled *Juggler of Gravity* [99], which was a homage to Duchamp's *Large Glass* and the *Juggler of Gravity* Duchamp had planned to be an element of that work but which he had never realized. Matta based his altar on Duchamp's drawings and the resultant object was made up of a pedestal table with one leg propped on a breast on a plate so that it was tipped at an angle and with a ball on it defying the laws of gravity. Around it were various Duchamp referents – a flat iron inscribed 'a refaire le pass', a cheese grater and twine, and an evocation of his *Three Standard Stoppages* (1913–14).[84] Duchamp's retinal play and defiance of the laws of nature were 'worshipped' within this gravity-defying altar.

100 **Victor Brauner,** *The Lovers*, 1947. Brauner's painting hung below the altar entitled *The Secretary Bird or Serpentine,* dedicated to Max Ernst, and the Virgo zodiac sign. It portrayed two figures from the Tarot, 'The Magician' and 'The Popess'. The words 'Liberty, Magic, Destiny' and 'Past, Present, Future' insist on the power of magic at that moment in 1947 and the chance of liberty and rebirth in the future.

101 **Victor Brauner, altar to** *The Secretary Bird or Serpentine*, 'Surrealism in 1947' exhibition, Galerie Maeght, Paris, 1947. The altar housed a hawk-like bird, a totemic woman in the grasp of his claws, and to its side a small classical sculpture of a Madonna, Child and serpent. Below hung Brauner's painting *The Lovers* (1947). Photo by Willy Maywald.

102 **Victor Brauner, *Wolf-table*, 1947.**

The ninth altar was dedicated to Victor Brauner's *Wolf-table* object and the star sign Sagittarius [102 & 103]. The object took the form of a wolf whose head was at one end of a wooden table, facing his bushy tail and scrotum on the other, his feet metamorphosing out of the table. It was an object that had appeared in two earlier paintings by Brauner: *Fascination* (1939) and *Psychological Space* (1939), the former being praised by Breton, in an essay of July 1946, as 'that famous table (*Psychological Space*, 1939) screaming over its shoulder at death and displaying proudly a bulging scrotum' and as anticipating the terror of the war to come.[85] For Breton, Brauner's art of this period (c.1939–46) had a 'twilight' power and could be linked to the iconography and myths of Native Americans and occultism, all the while involving 'all the powers of the *self* in order to exorcise all those powers of the *impersonal* which are increasingly harmful to us.'[86]

Finally, after this spiritual pilgrimage, the visitor was to be provided with material sustenance, a Surrealist meal in a Surrealist kitchen, a type of reward after the initiation, or a sign of spiritual replenishment and knowledge of the Self.

103 Victor Brauner, *Ceremony*, 1947. In 1942,
Brauner wrote 'My strange works hold the secret
of the future world to come, of a free incongruous
mythology that exists in our subconscious and
with an indistinct forewarning.' Here, the future is
painted as the fusion of opposites as male and
female, sun and moon, birth and death are joined
in a tribal ceremony.

104 **Enrico Donati, *Fist*, 1946.**

According to Marcel Jean the idea was unrealized, just as the idea to have paintings by 'Surrealists despite themselves' (Bosch, Arcimboldo, Blake, Henri Rousseau, Carroll), and those who had 'ceased to gravitate in the movement's orbit' (such as de Chirico, Masson, Picasso, Dalí, Paalen, Magritte and Dominguez) was not carried out either.[87] However, the exhibition did end with a literary room of Surrealist documents, photographs, objects and first editions of books. Even Aimé Maeght's office was turned into a gallery space.

The exhibition introduced many new artists to the Parisian public, notably Enrico Donati, the Italian artist who had quit Europe for New York in the spring of 1940. There he befriended Duchamp and the Surrealists, and in 1945 he helped Duchamp design the window display at Brentano's, New York, for the promotion of their expanded French edition of Breton's book of essays, named after his 1928 essay, *Surrealism and Painting*. Donati's *Fist* (1946), a gargantuan bronze clenched fist with two glass eyes in its grasp, reminiscent at first of a Rodin sculpture only to then appear like a monstrous face, made a dramatic impression [104]. A second sculpture, *The Evil Eye* (1947), placed in the Room of Superstitions, was equally startling and continued the Surrealists' 'primitive eye' theme [105]. Also on show were sculptures by Maria Martins, the wife of the Brazilian ambassador to the United States. She had trained with Oscar Jespers in Belgium and was famously honoured by Duchamp when he presented her with an edition of his *Boîte-en-valise* in which he included a once-off miniature abstract painting made of ejaculate on celluloid backed with black satin.[88] Martins's bronze sculpture *The Path, the Shadow, Too Long, Too Narrow* (1946) embodied the female principle by drawing on Amazonian legends and Nature's rhythm of life and death [106]. The snake was a key motif in many of her sculptures, usually a reference to the Amazonian snake goddess, but here the snakes entangle the male and the female turns her back to him. Like Giacometti's *Invisible Object*, her hands reach out to touch space while at

105 **Enrico Donati,** *The Evil Eye*, **1947. Breton
welcomed Donati into the Surrealist group after
meeting him in New York in 1942 and in his
1944 essay on the artist stated, 'I love the
paintings of Enrico Donati as I love a night
in May.'** *The Evil Eye* **stood in the Room of
Superstitions, 'Surrealism in 1947' exhibition,
Galerie Maeght, Paris, 1947.**

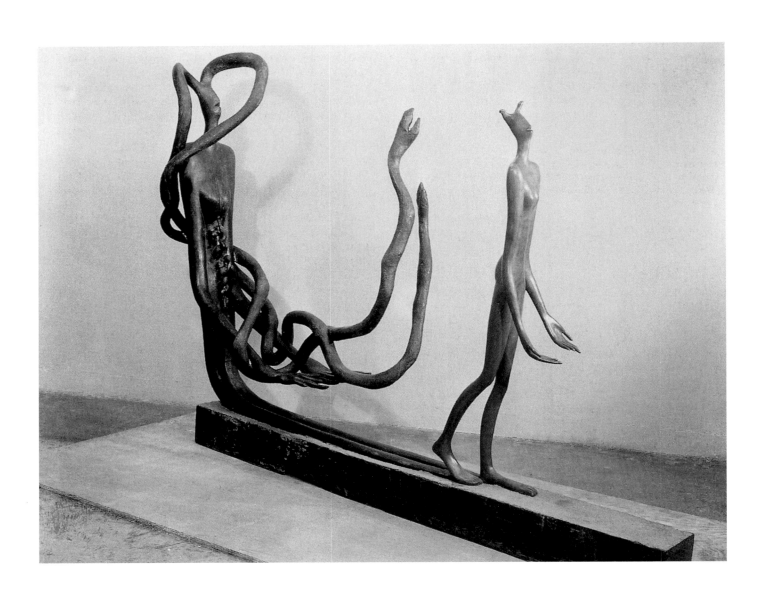

106 **Maria Martins,** *The Path, the Shadow, Too Long, Too Narrow*, 1946. Maria fused human and plant forms in her sculptures, leading Breton to write in his 1947 essay on her: 'Maria owes nothing to the sculpture of the past or the present – she is far too sure, for that, of the original rhythm which is increasingly lacking in modern sculpture; she is prodigal with what the Amazon has given her – the overwhelming abundance of life'.

107 **Maria Martins**, *The Impossible III*, 1946.

PRIÈRE
DE
TOUCHER

LE SURRÉALISME EN 1947

108 **Marcel Duchamp and Enrico Donati,** *Please Touch*, **cover of 'Surrealism in 1947' exhibition catalogue, made of foam rubber breast and velvet mounted on board. The idea for this erotic luxury edition of the exhibition catalogue was Duchamp's though it was developed by Donati. He purchased 999 'falsies' (foam-rubber breasts), from a warehouse in Brooklyn, and painted them with Duchamp to give them a more natural appearance before gluing them onto swatches of black velvet so that they looked like a breast peeking out from an evening dress. Where art exhibitions usually warn the spectator 'Do not touch', here Duchamp and Donati did the opposite in putting a sticker on the back of the catalogue which invited the public not only to look but to 'please touch'.**

the same time male and female, new life and the grip of death, are inseparable. Another sculpture, titled and reproduced as *Impossible* (1946) in the exhibition catalogue, continued this alchemical fusion of the sexes [107]. It depicts a man and a woman in an aggressive embrace, their faces crystallizing into bronze strips and their torsos interlocked. As in Matta's two paintings, the life and death drives, Eros and Thanatos, seem in conflict here. Breton, who came to know Maria Martins's work through Duchamp in 1943, described her sculpture in 1947 as, 'at the very roots of the sacred'.[89] Her art reminded him of the rhythm of Haiti, and he found it to be infused with desire. Related works on this theme by Ernst, Brauner, Man Ray and others were displayed and were complemented by paintings by Wifredo Lam and the Haitian artist Hector Hippolyte. One gets the sense that Breton, like Péret, was keen to promote non-European art – perhaps seeking to evoke throughout the exhibition that 'night in Haiti' when he was so struck by the Haitians' 'resolute soul'.[90] The inclusion of art by insane patients, lent by Doctor Gaston Ferdière, and the young artists Francis Bott, Roger Brielle, Iaroslav Serpan, Ramsès Younane and Jean-Paul Riopelle, selected for their work in automatism, indicated that the exhibition was not only reaching back to the first years of the movement but also opening the way to new artistic directions.[91]

To better appreciate this multifaceted exhibition and the many mythological and magical nuances of its exhibition space, the spectator could purchase the catalogue on the way out. The luxury edition was an *objet d'art* in itself, with engravings and lithographs by several Surrealists. It was designed by Duchamp and Enrico Donati and the black velvet cover was adorned with hand-coloured foam-rubber breasts [108], so-called 'falsies', shipped over from the US, and collected by a young Adrian Maeght who was terribly embarrassed when a number of them fell on the ground as they were being inspected by customs.[92] The ordinary edition, of which about 5,000 copies were printed, simply had a black-and-white photograph of the same breast cover. They titled it 'Prière de toucher' (Please Touch). Donati explained the construction of the object:

> Duchamp created a plaster, then came to see me and said 'I would like to put this on the cover'. I made them all and painted every nipple. I put in the black velvet because I thought it looked naked. I said to Marcel, 'Please Touch', and he said 'Prière de toucher', and that was it.[93]

The catalogue continued the Surrealists' subversion of the 'white cube' exhibition space and the aura around the gallery-going experience. Normally signs in galleries and museums read 'Do Not Touch': here the catalogue stated in block letters the very opposite. Given the erotic dimension to the catalogue – a breast which one literally cupped in order to hold the book – this subversion took on a wonderfully humorous aspect, allowing the spectator to enact a 'double taboo' (touch and touch the forbidden, so to speak). Yet as a disembodied breast backed on black velvet it went beyond titillation, continuing the Surrealist history of uncanny objects where the familiar is made strange. Like Oppenheim's *Object (Déjeuner en fourrure)* it had a macabre quality to it, suggesting desire but also violence or mutilation, even the uncanny fear of male castration. This sign and symbol of woman, this reminder that it is woman who is the uncanny embodied, is in keeping with the inherent feminine nature of Duchamp's organic grotto idea for the exhibition, Kiesler's egg-shaped Room of Superstitions, the altars' evocation of primitive cultures and the hysteria of voodoo. The catalogue suggested that touch was central to the exhibition and courage, the courage to touch. It might be seen as a further step in the Surrealists' initiation of the public. Certainly it was a provocative reminder of their faith in desire and Eros in a bleak post-war Paris of strikes and shortages. As Jacques Kober, who managed the Maeght gallery, wrote to Donati in May 1947: 'The cover that you have made up is altogether revolting, it is marvellous in a world that is eating away at itself.'[94]

The catalogue's thirty-eight essays expanded on the exhibition's themes and intentions. In the 'Prolegomena to a Third Surrealist Manifesto or Not' Breton had stated that because of his vision of a new myth 'accusations of mysticism are sure to be brought against me'.[95] His opening essay in the catalogue seems to have attempted to avert such accusations in clarifying the sacred element of his new myth. Its title, 'Devant le Rideau', also alluded to the exhibition in suggesting the theme of unveiling, and the idea that poetry and art were like a beacon. As if to establish the continuity of the movement despite the war years, Breton began with reminiscences on the last international exhibition in Paris of 1938 and dismissed the 'recent appearance' of Existentialism. He then explained the exhibition's aesthetic, and how its 'initiatory' emphasis was intended to emphasize the interdependence of aesthetics and morality in evoking such authors as Sade, Fourier, Lautréamont and Jarry. His essay summarized the exhibition itself as a 'spiritual parade' before which the spectator had to judge his own faith.[96]

The second catalogue essay, entitled 'Le Sel répandu' was by Benjamin Péret. He wrote that all superstitions are linked by a 'poetic conscience' and presented a classification of common superstitions (a black cat, the number 13). Among the superstitions he addressed were those explained as based on magic and superstition (e.g. the supernatural powers of body parts such as hair, blood and nails, to walk on excrement with your left foot brings happiness or to touch the hump of a hunchback brings happiness).[97] Péret noted all this amid an acknowledgment of the atrocity of war and the shadow Hiroshima still cast over the world.[98] Jules Monnerot's essay 'Contre la peur d'imaginer' addressed the themes of subjectivity and the need to protect the liberty of the imagination itself. Arpad Mezei's essay 'Liberté du Langage' emphasized the fact that words are made of signs and signification and as such are often rooted in ancient referents and so loaded with power and potential.[99] An essay by Georges Bataille on the 'Absence of Myth' indicated his renewed interest, and friendship, with the Surrealists. Bataille recognized the Surrealist belief in myth as an essential ingredient for contemporary society and the value of myth in answering man's fear of the infinite as the 'absence of God is no longer a closure: it is the opening up to the infinite'.[100] Henri Pastoureau's essay 'Pour une offensive de grand style contre la civilisation chrétienne' was equally positive. It distanced Surrealism from Christianity and Marxism and emphasized intuition and a new philosophy of life.[101]

Essentially, the exhibition catalogue emphasized the immense need of society for a spirit of belonging, in presenting a new myth to replace old, superstitious myth. This was not an insular perspective – myth was under consideration by other intellectuals too in the aftermath of the war. In 1947 the Marxist writer Henri Lefebvre wrote of the need for myth in his *Critique of Everyday Life* (1947), where he explored elements of the everyday – myths, religious ceremonies, Charlie Chaplin films, Surrealism – as the key to the science of man. Like the Surrealists, he recognized that ritual and myth had lost their sacred aura in modern society and had become secularized:

> What remains of ritual and myth? A date, a vague impression of birth,
> of hope, of grandiose drama – the idea of an all-powerful god who is
> nevertheless mysteriously destined to be born and to die.[102]

Lefebvre decided that Surrealism was an important 'symptom' of the search for
the sacred in modern society. He was critical of what he saw as Surrealism's
frequent superstitious over-valuation of myth at the expense of everyday life,
but his exposition of modern society's organization according to 'the law of the
transformation of the irrational' echoed the Surrealists' presentation of myth
to the French people in their 1947 show.[103] Lefebvre was therefore critical but
respectful of Surrealism. Indeed, many responses to the 'Surrealism in 1947'
exhibition were mixed. A letter from David Hare to Donati dated 14 August 1947
suggests the torn emotions of the French public:

> The general public accepts [Surrealism], not as anything new but as
> past history which they never very clearly understood but which they
> have come to accept not because they have understood it but partly
> because they have become accustomed to it and perhaps mostly
> because they say to themselves 'After all, it is French, it diveloped [sic]
> in France and now it has come back again. We are pleased to have it
> back because it belongs to us but how could one expect us after what
> we have been through in the war to take it very seriously.' This is the
> general attitude and as a consequence the gallery is at all times
> crowded but not with people really interested or even with those
> realy [sic] against.[104]

A positive embrace of the returned Surrealism was voiced by reviews such as
the *Gazette des Lettres*. It heralded the exhibition by dedicating a full edition to
Surrealism and the show just a few days before the opening. The edition included
Breton's outline of his 'Initial Project' for the exhibition (illustrated by Magritte's
Key of Dreams of 1930) and excerpts from *Arcane 17*. Gaëton Picon's article, entitled
'Le Surréalisme et l'espoir', urged readers to admit that Surrealism was the ultimate
manifestation of human enthusiasm and had an absolute spirituality that was much
needed.[105] Jean-José Marchand wrote of the history of Surrealism from 'l'époque
des sommeils' (the period of sleeps) in 1922, when the Surrealists experimented
with sleeping-fit sessions to create automatic texts and drawings, to the activities
of the Main à Plume during the war, describing 1947 as 'the year of hope' for
Surrealism.[106] Camille Bourniquel, writing in *Esprit* in November, conceded that
while the war had killed all previous notions of 'scandal', many were surprised at
the direction of Surrealism towards esotericism, Gnosticism and the 'science of
numbers and magic'.[107] He concluded that Surrealism was like a Church under
attack which resorted to its essential doctrine of realism and black magic as a
means of self-defence. Within the walls of the gallery, and in the knowledge of
the war, Occupation and Hiroshima, Bourniquel suggests that the exhibition offered
a reprise through an 'emancipatory magic' while also criticizing the moroseness
of the day.[108]

Others were less willing to consider the emancipatory potential of Surrealism
in a post-war world. Albert Palle wrote in *Le Figaro* that Surrealism had lost its
cultural relevance: 'We are no longer moved by it...the enormous destruction of the
world which we lived through during the dark years has emptied Surrealism of its
explosive force.'[109] Marie Louise Barron's review in *Les Lettres françaises*, nine days
later, painted a ridiculous portrait of Surrealism as a little old widow wearing a

young woman's pink hat on top of her grey hair. Barron was unimpressed by the display of three artificial breasts in the Maeght gallery window and by the fact that one had to pay to view the exhibition. She noted that the entrance fee of 50 francs was less than an evening at the funfair, the *Foire du Trone*, but not such a spectacle for one's money. She thought it was a '*parti pris* to shock but shocking no one any longer'.[110] However, she did paint a wonderful image of the disorienting nature of the exhibition. The Surrealists had successfully created a space that was bizarre and non-Western at a time when France was sliding into nationalistic conservatism.

Perhaps the worst critique came from members of the Surréalistes Révolution-naires, a group calling themselves 'revolutionary Surrealists' as they were both surrealist and communist. The group was launched with Christian Dotremont and Jean Seeger's tract 'Pas de quartiers dans la révolution', published in Belgium in the third and last issue of Dotremont's review *Les Deux Soeurs* on 7 June 1947 (and reprinted in *Le Drapeau rouge* on 9 July 1947). The tract was followed by another, 'Le Manifeste des surréalistes-revolutionnaires en France', with eighteen signatures, including many ex-members of the Main à Plume group, which again insisted that recognition of the Communist Party was fundamental to revolution, and on 1 July 1947 by 'La Cause est entendue', a Belgian and French tract issued against the 'Surrealism in 1947' exhibition, which insisted that it was a show of Surrealism of 947 – not 1947.[111] Even Aimé Maeght and Kober signed their petition against the exhibition. In a letter to Kiesler dated 17 May 1948, Jacques Hérold interpreted the petition as a Stalinist development, opining that the young group would not last long, and reported that he had heard Maeght complain that his business and reputation had suffered because of the show.[112]

However, despite the mixed responses to the exhibition it was successful in attracting new young members to the Surrealist group. Marcel Jean wrote that 'for several months an absolute mob of young people jammed the café which André Breton had begun to patronize once more'.[113] Breton even drew up a questionnaire in a café session to give to writers and artists who wanted to join the group. It had eight questions including 'What exactly, at the present time, do you expect of Surrealism?'[114] As Martica Sawin has documented, Jean Schuster was one such youngster keen to become part of this avant-garde group. Schuster was only sixteen in 1947 and went to see the exhibition having discovered a book on Surrealism at a friend's home. He obtained Breton's address from the gallery, went to his apartment block at 42 rue Fontaine where he found a note beside Breton's name saying that one had to make an appointment. Schuster duly did this and was given a rendezvous for 5.45 p.m. at the Surrealists' regular café in Place Blanche. This allowed the young man to talk to Breton for fifteen minutes before the normal daily six o'clock gathering.[115] Soon Schuster would be showing Breton his poetry and would eventually become Breton's right-hand man. Breton always respected the vital role of young minds for Surrealism and revolution. Indeed, Marcel Jean noted in a letter of November 1947 that the subject of one of these café meetings was 'the problem of youth', and in a letter in January 1948 that 'The ebb of young surrealists is rising like a September tide.'[116]

Breton had expressed the belief in the 'Prolegomena to a Third Surrealist Manifesto or Not' that in the aftermath of the war man needed to be presented with 'the broadest utopian landscape in order to make this animal world understandable'.[117] In two essays written in 1947, 'Second Arche' and 'Comète Surréaliste', he politicized the themes of myth, magic and the sacred in his criticism of *engagé* art. In 'Second Arche', a text which was included in the catalogue when part of the exhibition travelled to Prague, Breton insisted 'ART MUST NEVER TAKE ORDERS, WHATEVER HAPPENS!', taking a firm stand against art that serves party politics.[118] His stance against an art of 'commitment' is clearly a stance against art which serves the Communist Party. In 'Comète Surréaliste' he also pronounced the Surrealist aesthetic as one devoted to the liberation of man, morality and human understanding and insisted on the need for artistic freedom. He explained the 1947 exhibition as an attempt to confront the various aspects of the movement since its beginnings to see if it had proved anything and to assess how the war had affected its agenda.[119] Here, again, he expressed distaste for the political corruption or indoctrination of artists and writers, and insisted, as Péret had, on 'the honour of poets and artists'.[120] He ended the essay on a note that made the politics of the exhibition's recourse to myth and magic and the uncanny clear: the Surrealists wanted nothing less than 'a total renewal of mores, to reshape human understanding'.[121] If the Communist Party was not impressed the younger generation certainly was. The exhibition offered something new. It presented a new myth, one based on magic, superstition and initiation as a means of instilling the spirit of life in a people who had been traumatized by death. This vision of liberty would grow and over a decade later would recombine in the eighth international Surrealist exhibition of 1959, as we shall see in the next chapter.[122]

109 Marianne Van Hirtum, Radovan Ivsic, André Breton, Jean-Jacques Lebel and Elisa Breton at the inauguration of the monument to Guillaume Apollinaire by Pablo Picasso, Paris 1959. Photo by Pablo Volta.

110 Jean-Jacques Lebel, *André Breton and Guillaume Apollinaire (dream of 30 June 1956)*, 1956. Lebel's collage-drawing refers to a dream he had in which Breton (represented by the wolf, a cut out) and Apollinaire (whose portrait is drawn on the right) appeared and Breton said 'la vie est courte' ('life is short').

CHAPTER FOUR

Embattled Eros

The only art worthy of man and of space, the only one capable of
leading him further than the stars...is eroticism.
  André Breton, *Exposition InteRnatiOnale du Surrealisme*, 1959[1]

The 1959 international Surrealist exhibition, dedicated to the theme of Eros and
launched with a testimony to the Marquis de Sade, ran from 15 December 1959 to
29 February 1960. It was conceived and mounted at a time when the Surrealist group
was becoming increasingly politicized due to both the influence of the young men
and women who continued to join it and the controversy surrounding the Algerian
War, which plunged France into a prolonged national crisis from 1954 to 1962.

The war in Algeria directly undermined the official ideology of the French
Republic which saw France as *une et indivisible*.[2] Just as France's experience of
World War II had often been characterized through corporeal language, including
metaphors of corruption, terror and purging, so was public discourse surrounding
the Algerian war dominated by metaphors of the corruption and disease of the
nation. As the war intensified, it directly contributed to the economic destabilization
of the Fourth Republic, undermining government programmes in education, social
security, regional development and other areas of national life, and contributing
to significant inflation and rising budget deficits.[3] But it was the immorality and

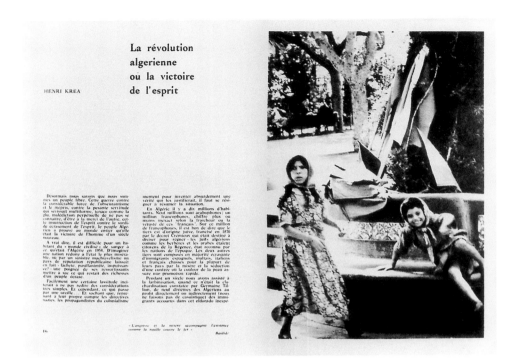

La révolution
algerienne
ou la victoire
de l'esprit

HENRI KRÉA

111 **Double page in** *Front unique*, **review format, no.1, Milan, 1959, with an essay by the Algerian poet Henri Kréa.**

hypocrisy of the war which incensed the Surrealists and motivated their vocal opposition to it. While many intellectuals had been slow to protest, the Surrealists defended the Algerian right to independence from the outset. Continuing the anti-colonialist stance they had voiced in their opposition to the war in Morocco in 1925 and the war in Indochina in 1947, on 9 December 1954 they joined one of the first committees set up to oppose the war, the Comité de Lutte Contre la Répression Coloniale, founded by the anarchist George Fontenis. Over the next several years, opposition to the war coloured much Surrealist activity, but was especially visible in the tracts and journals which they published.

In 1956, in the first edition of the new Surrealist review *Le Surréalisme, même*, Breton's opening essay, 'Pour la Défense de la Liberté', honoured and supported those battling against 'colonialist repression'.[4] In 1958, Jean Schuster and Dionys Mascolo published *Le Quatorze Juillet* which ran for three editions, and which was a vital voice of resistance, denouncing the war in numerous ways. The title was suggested by Breton who contributed to the review along with Robert Benayoun, Jean-Louis Bédouin, Gerard Legrand and Benjamin Péret, as well as the young artist Jean-Jacques Lebel who joined the Surrealist movement in 1956 [109 & 110]. External contributors included such established cultural figures as Maurice Blanchot, Marguerite Duras and the sociologist Edgar Morin. The first edition of July 1958 included an article by Maurice Nadeau exposing the use of torture by the French army in Algeria, and in the second edition of April 1959 a survey prepared by Breton, Blanchot, Mascolo and Schuster was published, addressing the complacency of intellectuals' attitudes to the current political scene. The third and final issue printed the responses to the survey provided by intellectuals such as the writer Pierre Klossowski and editor Jean Paulhan. It also named seventy-one others who had been sent the survey but had not replied. Through the review Schuster and his entourage encouraged intellectuals to play a more active and oppositional role.

Front unique was another vital voice of dissent. It began as a poster-size broadsheet published by Jean-Jacques Lebel in Paris and Florence from 1955 to 1958. Its second incarnation was as a review launched in the spring of 1959. This was published in Milan by Lebel and the gallerist Arturo Schwartz. Lebel was one of the most prominent young members of the Surrealist group although he was also affiliated to the anarchist Noir et Rouge group and would gradually evolve away from Surrealism in the 1960s. The spring 1959 edition of *Front unique* included essays by Breton, Picabia, Péret, Bédouin, Jaguer and others, illustrations by Brauner, Carrington, Ernst, Lam, Tanguy and Matta, and a key essay by the Algerian poet Henri Kréa, 'La révolution algerienne ou la victoire de l'esprit' [111].

In June 1959, to coincide with the opening of an exhibition of Edouard Jaguer's Phases group, which would tour three cities in Poland that summer, the Surrealists issued a tract entitled 'Message des Surréalistes aux intellectuels polonais'. The Phases group had their own periodical, of the same title, which had been launched in 1954 and which gave a voice to artists, including Surrealists (e.g. Hérold, Lam, Toyen), excluded members (e.g. Matta), as well as other artists, such as those of the CoBrA group (e.g. Pierre Alechinsky). As Durozoi notes, Phases embraced Italian, Spanish and East European artists and activities, and acted as a sort of guide to Surrealism for many artists.[5] Thus it was a useful voicebox for the Paris Surrealists and the perfect way for them to launch their tract and reach out to their European comrades. The tract was also recorded by Breton, broadcast twice on Polish radio and published in the journal *Plastyka* in Cracow. Attacking what it called the 'dead culture' as promoted by the Minister of Culture, André Malraux, the tract denounced French imperialism in Algeria and called attention to what the Surrealists saw as imperialism's corrosive effect upon France's republican values. As Surrealists they honoured internationalism and a true revolutionary spirit, but believed:

> However, the truth, today, is that the fire of liberty does not stir anymore in France. It is necessary to finish with the sentimentalism of History as long as it gives sustenance, everywhere in France, to the belief that France is still a guardian of emancipatory tradition.[6]

On 1 September 1960 a second, more pointed, attack was issued by 121 intellectuals, including Surrealists, entitled the 'Déclaration sur le droit à l'insoumission dans la guerre d'Algérie', more commonly referred to as the 'Déclaration des 121' [112]. It too denounced the French government's colonial politics and demanded an end to the reign of terror in Algeria. It insisted on the right of French men to refuse to fight in the Algerian War and argued that the cause of the Algerian people was that of all free men. It described the war as a war of independence, of liberty versus racism, which was perverting the French nation in forcing it to collude in torture and tactics comparable to those of Hitler. The declaration called for resistance to the war outside of official party lines and inspired by individual moral conscience alone. The Surrealists and their supporters were key players in this political stance: the tract was drawn up by Dionys Mascolo and Jean Schuster, Maurice Blanchot made modifications, and the final version was agreed on at a meeting between Breton, Mascolo, Schuster and Claude Roy. It was then printed and sent out to intellectuals to enlist their support by signing. All Surrealists of French nationality signed it including Jean-Louis Bédouin, Yves Elléouët, Edouard Jaguer, Jehan Mayoux, André Masson and José Pierre.[7]

The declaration, described by Simone de Beauvoir as the 'reawakening of French intelligence', signalled a powerful unification of intellectuals in Paris against the

Déclaration sur le droit à l'insoumission dans la guerre d'Algérie

« LES 121 »

Un mouvement très important se développe en France, et il est nécessaire que l'opinion française et internationale en soit mieux informée, au moment où le nouveau tournant de la guerre d'Algérie doit nous conduire à voir, non à oublier, la profondeur de la crise qui s'est ouverte il y a six ans.

De plus en plus nombreux, des Français sont poursuivis, emprisonnés, condamnés, pour s'être refusés à participer à cette guerre ou pour être venus en aide aux combattants algériens. Dénaturées par leurs adversaires, mais aussi édulcorées par ceux-là mêmes qui auraient le devoir de les défendre, leurs raisons restent généralement incomprises. Il est pourtant insuffisant de dire que cette résistance aux pouvoirs publics est respectable. Protestation d'hommes atteints dans leur honneur et dans la juste idée qu'ils se font de la vérité, elle a une signification qui dépasse les circonstances dans lesquelles elle s'est affirmée et qu'il importe de ressaisir, quelle que soit l'issue des événements.

Pour les Algériens, la lutte, poursuivie, soit par des moyens militaires, soit par des moyens diplomatiques, ne comporte aucune équivoque. C'est une guerre d'indépendance nationale. Mais, pour les Français, quelle en est la nature? Ce n'est pas une guerre étrangère. Jamais le territoire de la France n'a été menacé. Il y a plus: elle est menée contre des hommes que l'Etat affecte de considérer comme français, mais qui, eux, luttent précisément pour cesser de l'être. Il ne suffirait même pas de dire qu'il s'agit d'une guerre de conquête, guerre impérialiste, accompagnée par surcroît de racisme. Il y a de cela dans toute guerre, et l'équivoque persiste.

En fait, par une décision qui constituait un abus fondamental, l'Etat a d'abord mobilisé des classes entières de citoyens à seule fin d'accomplir ce qu'il désignait lui-même comme une besogne de police contre une population opprimée, laquelle ne s'est révoltée que par un souci de dignité élémentaire, puisqu'elle exige d'être enfin reconnue comme communauté indépendante.

Ni guerre de conquête, ni guerre de « défense nationale », ni guerre civile, la guerre d'Algérie est peu à peu devenue une action propre à l'armée et à une caste qui refusent de céder devant un soulèvement dont même le pouvoir civil, se rendant compte de l'effondrement général des empires coloniaux semble prêt à reconnaître le sens.

C'est, aujourd'hui, principalement la volonté de l'armée qui entretient ce combat criminel et absurde, et cette armée, par le rôle politique que plusieurs de ses hauts représentants lui font jouer, agissant parfois ouvertement et violemment en dehors de toute légalité, trahissant les fins que l'ensemble du pays lui confie, compromet et risque de pervertir la nation même, en forçant les citoyens sous ses ordres à se faire les complices d'une action factieuse ou avilissante. Faut-il rappeler que, quinze ans après la destruction de l'ordre hitlérien, le militarisme français, par suite des exigences d'une telle guerre, est parvenu à restaurer la torture et à en faire à nouveau comme une institution en Europe?

C'est dans ces conditions que beaucoup de Français en sont venus à remettre en cause le sens de valeurs et d'obligations traditionnelles. Qu'est-ce que le civisme, lorsque, dans certaines circonstances, il devient soumission honteuse? N'y a-t-il pas des cas où le refus de servir est un devoir sacré, où la « trahison » signifie le respect courageux du vrai? Et lorsque, par la volonté de ceux qui l'utilisent comme instrument de domination raciste ou idéologique, l'armée s'affirme en état de révolte ouverte ou latente contre les institutions démocratiques, la révolte contre l'armée ne prend-elle pas un sens nouveau?

Le cas de conscience s'est trouvé posé dès le début de la guerre. Celle-ci se prolongeant, il est normal que ce cas de conscience se soit résolu concrètement par des actes toujours plus nombreux d'insoumission, de désertion, aussi bien que de protection et d'aide aux combattants algériens. Mouvements libres qui se sont développés en marge de tous les partis officiels, sans leur aide et, à la fin, malgré leur désaveu. Encore une fois, en dehors des cadres et des mots d'ordre préétablis, *une résistance* est née, par une prise de conscience spontanée, cherchant et inventant des formes d'action et des moyens de lutte en rapport avec une situation nouvelle dont les groupements politiques et les journaux d'opinion se sont entendus, soit par inertie ou timidité doctrinale, soit par préjugés nationalistes ou moraux, à ne pas reconnaître le sens et les exigences véritables.

Les soussignés, considérant que chacun doit se prononcer sur des actes qu'il est désormais impossible de présenter comme des faits divers de l'aventure individuelle; considérant qu'eux-mêmes, à leur place et selon leurs moyens, ont le devoir d'intervenir, non pas pour donner des conseils aux hommes qui ont à se décider personnellement face à des problèmes aussi graves, mais pour demander à ceux qui les jugent de ne pas se laisser prendre à l'équivoque des mots et des valeurs, déclarent:

— Nous respectons et jugeons justifié le refus de prendre les armes contre le peuple algérien.

— Nous respectons et jugeons justifiée la conduite des Français qui estiment de leur devoir d'apporter aide et protection aux Algériens opprimés au nom du peuple français.

— La cause du peuple algérien, qui contribue de façon décisive à ruiner le système colonial, est la cause de tous les hommes libres.

government-condoned use of torture and genocide in Algeria.[8] Along with the
Surrealists, other signatories included de Beauvoir herself, Marguerite Duras,
Michel Leiris, Jean-Paul Sartre, Alain Resnais and Alain Robbe-Grillet. Originally
distributed as a pamphlet, no publishing house in France dared print the tract, as
the government threatened the severest penalties for any press which did. *Les Temps
modernes* published two blank pages with a note explaining that while the journal's
management was willing to risk publishing it, the journal's printers had refused to.[9]
Within a month twenty-nine of the signatories had been arrested and numerous
others working in such fields as cinema, the media and education were blacklisted.
Breton wrote to the judge in charge of prosecutions in the case, stating defiantly:

> I declare myself one of the co-authors and specify that by signing it I
> implicitly undertook to do everything in my power to disseminate it.[10]

As the case of the 'Déclaration des 121' indicated, one of the first casualties
of the Algerian War was freedom of information. Newsreels were censored,
Radiodiffusion-Télévision Française came under strict governmental control,
and public meetings, films and literature dealing with the Algerian cause were also
restricted.[11] Between 1954 and 1963 approximately thirty-five books were seized
for addressing the subject of the Front de Libération Nationale (FLN, the Algerian
National Liberation Front), or related issues such as torture, and two-thirds of these
books were published by presses with 'underground' reputations such as Maspero
or Editions de Minuit.[12] Indeed, even when the press fought against seizure of
their editions and confiscation of their journals, the judicial system condoned such
censorship as protection of the state, deeming these banned publications treasonous.
Hence, when several organizations sued the Prefect of Police, Maurice Papon, for
seizing a pamphlet on torture in 1959, the judge ruled that 'the massive distribution
of printed matter accusing French troops of atrocities constituted a crime.'[13]

One of the most important publications to be repressed was *La Question* by
Henri Alleg, the editor of *Alger républicain* from 1950 to 1955. The book, published
in February 1958, sold 60,000 copies before being seized by the authorities. In it
Alleg detailed his imprisonment and gruesome torture at the hands of French
paratroopers in Algeria following his arrest on 12 June 1957. In his preface, entitled
'Victory', Jean-Paul Sartre asserted that Alleg's book powerfully exposed 'the
intolerable truth about torture'.[14] Sartre compared the atrocities committed in
Algeria to those suffered by French men and women at the hands of the French
Gestapo at their Parisian headquarters in rue Lauriston. The French, he argued,
could not stand idly by as Algerians were being systematically tortured by the
French army with equal brutality. This 'terrible truth' had to be faced, as 'Anybody,
at any time, may equally find himself victim or executioner.'[15]

Simone de Beauvoir also campaigned against the use of torture in the Algerian
War. She voiced outrage for one militant woman who was the victim of French army
brutality, Djamila Boupacha, whom, it was alleged, confessed to planting bombs for
the FLN. However, her confession was made under physical and sexual torture,
including rape. De Beauvoir documented her disgust at the French nation in these
years in her autobiography: 'This hypocrisy, this indifference, this country, my
own self, were no longer bearable to me. All those people in the streets, in open
agreement or battered into a stupid submission – they were all murderers, all
guilty.'[16] De Beauvoir learned of Boupacha's case from the Algerian feminist lawyer
Gisèle Halimi, and was asked to write an article demanding an inquiry. Her article
was published in *Le Monde*, although it too was subjected to censorship. Certain

112 *Déclaration sur le droit à l'insoumission dans la guerre d'Algérie*, 1960. The 'declaration of 121' intellectuals against the Algerian war was published in *Front unique*, no.2, Milan, 1960.

changes to de Beauvoir's text were made by the editor, Monsieur Gauthier. She recalled his response to her frank description of Boupacha's rape: 'he asked me to change the word "vagina", which was the one Djamila had used, to "womb"….M. Gauthier added, that I had written "Djamila was a virgin"; would I not paraphrase this somehow? I wouldn't. They printed those four words in parenthesis.'[17] De Beauvoir took this as evidence that the French bourgeoisie was less concerned with the injustice done to Boupacha than with the sexual aspects of her character, the question of whether or not she was a virgin. When de Beauvoir raised the case with the assistant to the Minister of Justice, Monsieur Patin, he claimed that a photograph of Boupacha 'between two ALN soldiers with their guns in their hands' was proof of her sexual impurity.[18]

State-sponsored torture, censorship and the high-profile cases of Alleg and Boupacha all had marked effects on Surrealism, reinforcing and adding yet more complex layers to its focus on the body as theme. In 1962, Roberto Matta was awarded the Marzotto prize in Italy for his *La Question Djamila* (1957) which was exhibited at the second *Documenta* of Kassel in 1959. Jean-Jacques Lebel pasted in a fragment of the 'Déclaration des 121' and painted Boupacha's rape in his contribution to the collective work *Le Grand Tableau antifasciste collectif* (1960), executed along with fellow artists Enrico Baj, Roberto Crippa, Gianni Dova, Erró and Antonio Recalcati [113].[19] Lebel's image of Boupacha's rape consisted of an elaborately drawn and multi-coloured abstraction of the splayed legs of a woman lying prone with the word 'Liberté' scrawled at her head. The image drew attention to the sexual resonances which the Orient continued to hold in the French public imagination in the 1950s and which had infuriated Simone de Beauvoir. It also rebuked the timelessly beautiful Oriental nude which had been a mainstay of the French classical tradition in art since the nineteenth century, especially in the work of Jean-Auguste-Dominique Ingres and Eugène Delacroix. The degree to which the Orient was imagined in terms of erotic submissiveness has been attested by Edward Said. In *Orientalism* he emphasized the degree to which French imperialism was legitimized by such literary representations as Nerval's *Voyage en Orient* and Flaubert's *Salammbô*, in which the Oriental woman played an important role as 'a disturbing symbol of fecundity, peculiarly Oriental in her luxuriant and seemingly unbounded sexuality'.[20] Building on Said, Linda Nochlin has explained in *The Politics of Vision* that the Near East, whilst an actual place of French colonization, was also 'a project of the imagination, a fantasy space or screen, onto which strong desires – erotic, sadistic, or both – could be projected with impunity'.[21] For example, Delacroix's *Death of Sardanapalus* (1827–8) depicts, in a palette dominated by violent reds, the despairing massacre by the Assyrian king after his defeat in battle of his female slave-concubines who are killed with orgiastic skill and flair [114]. We find such Orientalism and its continued political relevance being explored one hundred years later in Picasso's reworking of Delacroix's *Les Femmes d'Alger dans leur appartement* (1833) in a series of twelve canvases, *Les Femmes d'Alger* (1954–5) [115]. Picasso also produced a portrait of Djamila Boupacha in 1961 which was reproduced on the cover of the 1962 Gallimard edition of de Beauvoir's essay on Boupacha and in Aragon's *Les Lettres françaises* on 8 February 1962. Where Algeria was presented predominantly in Orientalist terms in mainstream culture – as an immoral, feminized threat to French hegemony or as a feminine space in need of protection – avant-garde artists could exploit such associations as a means of voicing dissent.

Indeed, Kristin Ross has pointed out the degree to which the Algerian War was characterized in French public life as a domestic dispute between husband (France) and wife (Algeria) in which Algeria was implied to be a feminine subordinate in need of swift and firm handling in order to be brought to order. The Algerian independence movement was blamed for 'the destruction of the household'.[22] The Algerian War came to a climax in May 1958 when, with the revelation that French soldiers taken prisoner by the FLN had been executed, the French right staged a resurgence which propelled Charles de Gaulle back into power in June. De Gaulle promised constitutional and colonial reform, a rejuvenation of the national image, and a return to economic stability. Now an elder statesman at sixty-seven years of age, he embodied reverence for the nation, Church and family.[23] He declared in a tone of paternal benevolence, 'Formerly, the nation from its heart placed confidence in me to lead it to safety. Today, as it faces grave new difficulties, let it know that I am ready to assume the powers of the Republic.'[24]

The election of de Gaulle, from the point of view of the Surrealists, only exacerbated the crisis in which France was immersed and seemed to entrench further the dominance of conservative, bourgeois values. In this context the 1959 EROS exhibition constituted a decisive intervention. It was based around an elaboration of long-standing Surrealist notions of the erotic, now extended into an examination of the Sadean erotic. However, Sade was invoked on artistic and political grounds: his revolutionary, supposedly 'obscene' philosophy was used as a metaphoric means of shedding light on the political 'obscenities' of the day.

Just prior to the exhibition, the Surrealists explored the erotic in their 'Enquête sur le strip-tease', published in *Le Surréalisme même*, between autumn 1958 and 1959. The inquiry, reminiscent of the pre-war *Recherches sur la sexualité* (1928–32), was prompted by Roland Barthes's assertion in *Mythologies* (1957) that striptease 'under the guise of inducing and inflaming desire, tends to dispel it by the use of exoticism'.[25] Barthes suggested that one of the attractions of the striptease for the spectator was its 'delicious terror':

> We are dealing[...]with a spectacle based on fear, or rather on the pretence of fear, as if eroticism here went no further than a sort of delicious terror, whose ritual signs have only to be announced to evoke at once the idea of sex and its conjuration.[26]

For Barthes striptease tempted spectators with profane, illicit titillation, or 'a touch of evil' with fetishistic trappings (furs, fans, gloves, stockings, feathers, hats), but never posed a fundamental threat to the 'Moral Good'.[27]

The Surrealists, of course, wanted to go much further and to do away with the 'Moral Good' altogether. In its recourse to Sadean imagery and philosophy, the 1959 EROS exhibition staged its own 'philosophy in the boudoir'. In his 1795 novel of that name, Sade recounts the story of the innocent virgin Eugènie, who is schooled by libertines to become a violent heroine who will turn against morality and torture her own mother. As part of her education Eugènie is made to listen to a tract, 'Yet Another Effort, Frenchmen, If You Would Become Republicans', which parodies the rhetoric of the French Revolution, attacks morality and the Church as the 'cradle of despotism', denouncing capital punishment. The tract presents echoes of Sade's revolutionary call: that man and woman should live by Nature and libertinage be permitted for all. The Surrealists undoubtedly recognized that the Sadean universe and its relentless exploration of sexual domination are emblems for exploitation itself and all forms of corruption, notably political corruption. This took the form of

113 **Erró, Enrico Baj, Roberto Crippa, Gianni Dova, Jean-Jacques Lebel and Antonio Recalcati,** *Le Grand Tableau antifasciste collectif*, **1960. This collective painting, a manifestation against the Algerian War, was seized by the Italian police who kept it for some twenty-four years. Lebel's depiction of Djamila Boupacha is in the top left corner of the painting.**

114 Eugène Delacroix, *Death of Sardanapalus*, 1827–8. In this depiction of the orgiastic destruction of Sardanapalus' kingdom and worldly goods, Delacroix stages the Orient as an exotic, lascivious land.

115 Picasso, *Femmes d'Algers*, 1955. Picasso's reworking of Eugène Delacroix's *Les Femmes d'Alger dans leur appartement* (1833) explores the West's fascination with the Orient, notably the association between the conquering of a land and people and the sexual possession of an Algerian woman in her domestic space. Picasso produced a series of paintings and lithographs based on Delacroix's original during the first months of the Algerian War, from December 1954 to February 1955.

116 Mimi Parent, Poster for EROS exhibition, Galerie Daniel Cordier, 8 rue de Miromesnil, Paris, 15 December 1959 – 29 February 1960. André Breton invited Parent to design the poster for the exhibition which shows her 1959 fetish-object *Masculine-Feminine*.

117 Mimi Parent, *Masculine-Feminine*, 1959. Parent's object enacts a gender 'troubling' in addressing cross-dressing and the fetishistic power of hair in a male tie made from female hair – Parent's own.

a gigantic 'return of the repressed' in opposition to the war, torture and censorship, drawing upon the work of a great writer and revolutionary who wrote about all of those in an earlier context. For the Surrealists, Sade, as Carolyn J. Dean has written, was 'synonymous with a persecuted truth.' They 'used him as an emblem of the affirmative force of the libido and as a tragic symbol of the power of censors and of bourgeois defenders of the state and the family in particular.'[28]

The postcard-size invitation to the exhibition warned visitors of the nature of the event they were about to experience in the Galerie Cordier on 8 rue de Miromesnil. It revealed the exhibition's theme as Eros through typography – Exposition inteRnatiOnal du Surréalisme – and a pink-tinted photograph of the curvaceous body of a young female. The poster for the exhibition alluded to the erotic but a specifically Sadean erotic with a photograph of a tie made of female hair viewed against the collar of a white shirt and lapel of a black suit, the sex of its wearer undisclosed [116]. The hair was sexually suggestive, but also macabre, hinting at a scalp or trophy of some sort. Superimposed on the photo, the location and dates of the exhibition were highlighted, again in pink. The object, entitled *Masculine-Feminine*, was made by a new member to the group, the Canadian Mimi Parent, and had been chosen for the poster by Breton [117].[29] Black, pink, nudity, cross-dressing: clearly this exhibition promised a provocative return to the theme of Eros. In addition, Daniel Cordier's gallery already had a reputation for avant-garde erotic art. Cordier, who had been the secretary to Jean Moulin, the wartime Resistance leader, opened his first gallery in 1956 on the rue de Duras, moving to this larger location in May 1959 where he exhibited Hans Bellmer, Jean Dubuffet, Öyvind Fahlström, Henri Michaux, Bernard Réquichot and others. He opened the gallery with the intention of patronizing abstract art (which was the vogue for collectors in 1950s Paris), but had been drawn to these more controversial, erotic artists instead:

> If, in opening this gallery, I had the intention of showing works
> that pleased me and that were a part of their time from the point
> of view of abstraction, imperceptibly I drifted according to the will
> of my character and my curiosity towards a painting of attack,
> whose visible or hidden spirit is eroticism, which remains the
> most energetic fermenting agent of the conscience.[30]

He hoped his exhibitions would change the art scene, and direct it away from bland historical retrospectives towards topical thematic shows.[31] According to Mimi Parent, Cordier was very generous and open-minded when it came to facilitating the exhibition. Parent was heavily involved in the staging, notably in creating a crypt dedicated to fetishism, while Oppenheim was given her own room to stage 'an inaugural feast', as we shall see. The key organizers were André Breton and Marcel Duchamp, with the young José Pierre acting as assistant. The 'chief-operator' of the exhibition who oversaw everything was Pierre Faucheux, the associate producer was Georges Fall, others involved in the production included Robert Benayoun (hanging), Françoise Aullas (special effects), and François Dufrêne and Radovan Ivsic (sound). As Breton explained in the catalogue, the exhibition's motto was that art was to seize life and all its contradictions and build on Eros as 'a privileged place, a theatre of initiations and prohibitions, where the deepest processes of life play themselves out.'[32]

The exhibition was viewed as spatial from the outset, as a 'a game of individual entrances and exits', playing on the viewer's inhibitions through uncanny tactics, namely allusion and surprise.[33] Its *mise-en-scène* denied any 'safe' distance between

EXPOSITION INTERNATIONALE
DU SURREALISME 1959-60
Mimi Parent

118 **Jean Benoît and Mimi Parent, Montreal, 1943.**

the spectator and the erotic. It led the viewer into a gallery space which had all the hallmarks of a striptease (with soft music, sweet smells and fetishes), but which then began to subvert that controlled environment by introducing more threatening motifs, such as cannibalism, Sadism and masochism. The space flouted the double-edged nature of the erotic desire of the feminine: as enticing *and* threatening. As the spectator progressed through the exhibition, he/she followed an 'intra-uterine' path, reminiscent of the 1938 exhibition, which culminated in a lavish collective feast displayed on the naked body of a beautiful woman.

Significantly, the exhibition was intended to capture two aspects of eroticism: eroticism as that part of man's conscience which calls his own being into question; and eroticism as an experience which demands an equal sensitivity towards anguish as towards desire.[34] Young and old Surrealists were involved, from Tanguy to Breton's daughter Aube. Even the disfavoured Salvador Dalí, Roberto Matta and Victor Brauner were welcomed back for the exhibition.[35] Seventy-five artists contributed in all, hailing from nineteen countries. Cordier's links with New York ensured Jasper Johns, Robert Rauschenberg and William Copley were invited to show; the other Americans involved were Man Ray, Dorothea Tanning, Joseph Cornell, Arshile Gorky and Louise Nevelson. The inclusion of *Art Brut* artists Alöyse and Friedrich Schröder-Sonnenstern demonstrated an unrestrictive view of Surrealism not as an art style or school but as a perspective on the world.

The opening of the EROS exhibition also testified to Surrealism as a way of life, a philosophical outlook or primitive vision: a performance by Mimi Parent's husband Jean Benoît, also from Montreal [118]. It was entitled 'Execution of the Testament of the Marquis de Sade'. Benoît made the costume several years before he put it to use on this occasion. Indeed, it was on seeing photographs of Benoît's costume that Breton personally invited him to become a member of the Surrealist group. Benoît's puritanical upbringing gave him a particular understanding of Sade, whose *120 Days of Sodom* he read soon after emigrating to Paris from Montreal in 1948. Benoît was attracted to Sade both as a means to understanding his own sexuality and as an assault on bourgeois morality and good taste.[36] His performance was held not in the Cordier gallery but in the apartment of Surrealist poet Joyce Mansour on the night of 2 December, the 145th anniversary of Sade's death. The performance was a theatrical re-enactment of the burial of Sade who had desired to be laid to rest in an unmarked copse within the grounds of his beloved estate at Malmaison, without any autopsy and without any ceremony. Sade had wished that all traces of his tomb be gradually erased by Nature itself.[37] However, as Maurice Lever has explained, on his death and against his wishes, the Marquis was given a religious burial in the cemetery of Charenton, 'at the far eastern end, almost on the banks of the Saut-du-Loup separating the cemetery from the forest of Vincennes. The grave was covered with a stone on which no name was engraved and which had no ornament other than a simple cross.'[38] Obviously, this burial went against Sade's expressed wishes. It was Benoît's aim to protest the contravention of Sade's wishes and to give him, by re-enactment, the atheistic burial he wanted.

Benoît forbade any reporters or photographers to be present, or for the performance to be captured on film by any of the Surrealists present, apart from the photographer Gilles Ehrmann.[39] This was a performance to be experienced in the flesh by a number of invitees, paying homage to Dada actions at the Cabaret Voltaire in Zurich in 1916, to Hélène Vanel's performance at the 'International Surrealist Exhibition' of 1938, and to Antonin Artaud's concept of a 'theatre of cruelty' [119].

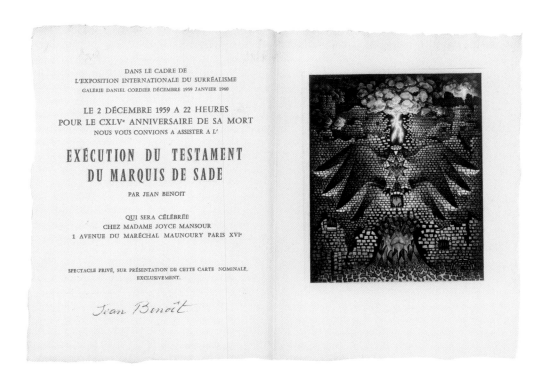

119 **Jean Benoît, Invitation to** *Execution of the Testament of the Marquis de Sade*, **2 December 1959.**

Like those, it challenged the traditional spectator-performer relationship by putting the audience on edge, presaging the Happenings of the 1960s in its combination of text, improvised physical action and sensational *mise-en-scène*.[40] Indeed, the subversive intent of the performance was explicit, centring as it did around an elaborate striptease performed against the background of quotations read aloud from Sade, his Surrealist biographers Maurice Heine, Gilbert Lely and Breton, each proclaiming the revolutionary potential of Sade's (imaginary) sexual terror and attacking intellectuals who had criticized or sublimated Sade's revolutionary morality.

Benoît's costume for the performance was made of paper, felt, wood, metal, black dye and an old nylon stocking [120–122]. Benoît wore a squid-like mask which was reminiscent of tribal headgear, particularly the masks of the Dogon and Kwakiutl.[41] He carried wings, wooden panels and an iron phallus with the letters S-A-D-E on it. The performance began with a blaring soundtrack capturing the turbulence of the city which had been recorded by poet Radovan Ivsic. The soundtrack was described by the French writer and historian Annie le Brun as evocative of a volcano. It was an image which expressed both the words of Sade – 'One day, examining Etna, whose breast vomited flames, I wanted to be that famous volcano' – and the rallying cry of Breton, 'The Marquis de Sade returned to the inside of the volcano during an eruption.'[42] As the music reached a crescendo, Benoît appeared and Breton began to read the testament of Sade, wherein the Marquis called for an unmarked grave. As Breton finished reading, the striptease began, with Parent removing Benoît's costume, piece by piece, and Jean-René Major reading out the symbolic significance of each (as annotated by Benoît).[43] When he took off his mask, the 'totem of the free man', Benoît revealed his war-painted face, his choice of strong colours emphasizing his piercing blue eyes.

Benoît continued his Sadean 'striptease' by removing the massive medallion he wore about his neck. This medallion was dedicated to Breton, Lely and Heine,

120 Jean Benoît in costume for *Execution of the
Testament of the Marquis de Sade*, December
1959. Benoît's mask was reminiscent of tribal
headgear, while his wings, wooden panels and
large medallion symbolized the entrapment of the
individual in modern society and the imprisonment
of the revolutionary Marquis de Sade.

121 Jean Benoît performing *Execution of the
Testament of the Marquis de Sade*, 2 December
1959. Once he had stripped himself of his
costume, Benoît stood naked before his
audience wearing only body paint and a large
phallus which spurted a bouquet of five flowers
each inscribed with a letter, spelling A-M-O-U-R.
Photo by Gilles Ehrmann.

and to Lely's prophetic words, written in his 1952 biography of the Marquis de Sade: 'Everything that Sade signs is love.' Then he removed the vest which was decorated with painted black arrows, a heart and teardrops. It was explained in the performance notes that this painted heart had to be purged of its tears, which were symbolic of pathos, and ideas of nation, family and religion – all the dogmas of which Sade and the Surrealists vowed to purge society. The crutches and the wooden panels, between which Benoît was shackled, were then removed. They were symbolic of man's state of spiritual slavery, and the large womb-like protrusion represented procreation and the untapped potential of pregnant womanhood:

> Life. Egg, oval, pregnancy, fertility. Ovums and spermatozoids who
> come together. Eyes, teats, navel, anus, etc...

The association between life, Eros and the womb was also a reference to Sade's observation that:

> It is in the breast of the mother that the organs are manufactured
> which make us susceptible to such and such fantasy...[44]

Benoît stood, stripped, his flesh painted with arrows, all pointing towards a star at his heart, and surrounded only by his tomb, the closet-container of the costume, holding up a large branding-iron, and wearing his phallus, or 'membre viril' (described, in the catalogue, as having the proportions of two characters from Sade's *120 Days of Sodom*: Brise-cul and Bande-au-ciel) which spurted a bouquet of five flowers each inscribed with a letter: A-M-O-U-R.[45] Finally, Benoît raised the hot iron and burned the letters S-A-D-E onto his chest, sacrificing his flesh as the ultimate finale to his Sadean testimony. No sooner had Benoît removed the iron than Matta stepped forward, moved by the intensity of the performance, and thrust the hot iron at his own chest too.[46] The question was posed as to whether Simone de Beauvoir, who had dared ask 'Faut-il brûler Sade?' (1951) and had imposed too 'rational' a reading on Sade for Benoît's taste, should be burned too.[47] The reply was a joyous 'Oui, sur la fesse' (Yes, on the buttock)!

Benoît's costume and performance was a tribute to the revolutionary ideas of Sade and the 'primitive' culture and mentality that the Surrealists favoured over Western, scientific rationalism. It had all the details of a shamanistic rite of initiation and replaced consumer culture's repression of the erotic with the transgressive, Sadean erotic. It emphasized the repressive rule of nation, family and religion, and the untapped potential of the feminine. The primitive nature of his performance was undoubtedly based on his ethnographic training, with Parent, at the Musée de l'Homme, but it also emphasized the Surrealists' belief in the potential of primitivism as a state in which man has not yet been corrupted by logic and still has faith in Eros.[48] The political message of the performance was even to be seen in the detail Benoît insisted upon. For instance, he specified in his notes that the best papier mâché used in making the costume was made of *L'Humanité* and *Le Figaro* – in his view, Communist and Catholic papers respectively, both better for pulp than reading. According to Benoît, all critics of Sade should be branded with hot irons. He listed in his notes, as exemplary culprits, Paul Bourdin, Jean Desbordes and Louis Parrot. Simone de Beauvoir was to be branded for her neglect of the 'poetry' of Sade, and Paul Claudel was to be burnt on *both* buttocks.[49]

While Benoît's homage to Sade was not performed for the public, the posters and invitations for the exhibition drew huge crowds when the Cordier gallery doors opened thirteen days later. Indeed, crowds took over the street, even though entrants had to pay an entrance fee of 500 old francs (*c.*5 new francs) and were let

122 **Jean Benoît with his costume for** *Execution of the Testament of the Marquis de Sade* **hanging on the interior wall of the EROS exhibition, Galerie Daniel Cordier, Paris, December 1959.**

into the gallery at fifteen-minute intervals. Initially, the public entered a chamber with rosy-coloured walls and ceiling, which had been conceived of by Duchamp and designed by Pierre Faucheux so that it rhythmically breathed in and out (with air pumps), and had a floor of sand.[50] Here, pride of place was given to Hans Bellmer's *Doll*, which was suspended from the ceiling like a Sadean victim, her body manipulated and contorted to appear as a double-legged creature, the monstrosity of her form only offset by two pairs of girlish shoes and socks and the vacant stare of her face [123]. This object immediately exploited the disturbing uncanny power of the fragmented body, the automaton. Bellmer's photographic portraits of his lover, the artist and writer Unica Zürn, in which her naked breasts and body are bound with string, were also exhibited in the exhibition [124]. Such sadistic imagery could only have augmented the erotic tension of the spectator looking up and seeing this doll trussed up like a chicken.[51]

This space gave way to a green corridor through what the historian Robert Benayoun recalled as 'a "vaginal" door with beads of dew opening up onto a labyrinth inhabited by sighs and swoons.'[52] Here, in this labyrinthine space, the walls were draped in green velvet and the sensation of a sexual passageway was augmented by the inclusion of stalactite and stalagmite-like forms [125]. More special effects were employed: a recording of female sighs, moans and groans, and the recurrent proclamation 'Je t'aime', recorded by Radovan Ivsic and performed by four female actresses, was played on a loop.[53] To add to this mood, a perfume by Houbigant, aptly called 'Flatterie', was sprayed into the air. All the senses were assaulted, as in the 1938 exhibition, but now the 'penetrative' mood, drawing the spectator deeper and deeper into a vaginal arena was all the more dramatic and excessive. To the right of the entrance of this space was Joan Miró's *Sleeping Object* (1936) [127], a segment of tree trunk painted blood red with the female sex/eye marked out in black against bone-like white, topped

123 **Hans Bellmer,** *The Doll*, **1932–45.** Bellmer's doll with its many limbs and orifices made a dramatic, monstrous impression on the spectator as he/she entered the Galerie Cordier. It was suspended from the ceiling while the walls around breathed in an out thanks to hidden air pumps.

124 **Hans Bellmer,** *Unica Ligotée*, **1958.** Reproduced as 'Keep Cool' on the cover of *Le Surréalisme, même*, no.4, 1958, this disturbing image of Unica Zürn recalls Bellmer's description in *Petite Anatomie de l'inconscient physique ou l'anatomie de l'image* (1957) of a photograph 'where a man, in order to transform his victim, had blindly bound, crosswise, thighs, shoulder, breast, back and stomach with a tightly pulled steel wire and produced swollen pads of flesh, irregular spherical triangles, cut along folds and unclean lips into the body, created multiple breasts which had never been seen before in indescribable places'.

125 **Interior of EROS exhibition, Galerie Daniel Cordier, Paris, 1959–60, with Miró's** *Sleeping Object* **(1935–6) just visible on the right and Giacometti's** *Invisible Object* **(1934–5) and Rauschenberg's** *Bed* **(1955) in the background.**

with a male machine made of a metal spring, gas burner, chain, manila and string, all assembled to look like the bizarre juxtaposition of two lovers, two opposites, and yet also looking like a tortured torso or mutilated limb. This work was from Breton's own collection, and reinforced the tension between Eros and Thanatos. Further on, the spectator could view paintings by Simon Hantaï and Max Walter Svanberg and two paintings by Pierre Molinier, both of which were chosen specifically by Breton for the exhibition: *Succubus* (1950) and *The Flower of Paradise* (1955).[54] *The Flower of Paradise* had a prominent position in this space and depicted two elongated female nudes, both with stockings and red nails.[55] It depicted the escapist, desirous potential of the female body as a 'paradise'. In contrast, *Succubus* was an image of grotesque, abject femininity: black-haired and black-stockinged, with pouting red lips, strangling a male species, who is caught in her snake-like grasp.[56] Molinier's imagery seduced, only to then horrify, the gaze.

Finally, at the end of this green velvet space, leading into the next, the public were faced with perhaps one of the most striking juxtapositions in the exhibition, Alberto Giacometti's *Invisible Object (Hands Holding the Void)* of 1934–5 and Robert Rauschenberg's *Bed* of 1955, which stood side by side. We recall that the former object was, for Breton, about the 'desire to love and be loved'. In contrast, Rauschenberg's *Bed* [126], standing taller than Giacometti's sculpture at some two and a half metres (8 ft) was an assemblage piece, or one of his 'Combines' as he termed them, and a much more abject affair. *Bed* involved a combination of oil paint and pencil messily splashed on found objects (a pillow, quilt and sheet) on wood supports. It married the Duchampian found object with the gesturalism of Abstract Expressionism, but it also had an element of Surrealist black humour in its use of the artist's own cast-off bedding, 'stained' with paint. Although the *Bed* may be interpreted as the signature of Rauschenberg's own (sexual) creativity,

126 Robert Rauschenberg, *Bed*, 1955. Thanks to Daniel Cordier's connections in New York, Rauschenberg was invited to exhibit in the 1959 EROS exhibition. The *Bed* combines the found-object (his own bed and bedding) with Abstract Expressionism (the gestural, stain-like daubs of paint) and made a dramatic contrast to the 'classical' 1930s Surrealism of Giacometti's *Invisible Object* which stood beside it.

127 Joan Miró, *Sleeping Object*, 1936. With its blood red carob trunk, metal spring, gas burner, chain, manila and string, this object was part of Miró's macabre painting-objects and 'savage paintings' of the mid-1930s and relates to the fascination at the time of both Surrealists and 'dissident' Surrealists with the Marquis de Sade. It was purchased by Breton in 1936.

128 **René Magritte, *Invisible World*, 1954. Magritte defies our rational expectations in this image of a rock in an interior by the sea as art is shown *not* to be a window on the world and as time and space stand still. The title is best understood in light of his statement of 1964 in a letter to André Bosman – 'Mystery is invisible'.**

a form of self-portrait perhaps, the juxtaposition of art works dramatically posed a very explicit, raw eroticism with a metaphysical one.

The spectator was then led on through a cavernous path where a number of paintings by Miró, Ernst, Dalí, Lam, Svanberg and others hung. This line-up included more oblique canvases such as René Magritte's *Invisible World* (1954) [128] and Yves Tanguy's *The Heavy Palace* (1935). These paintings exemplified the two stylistic poles of Surrealist painting: superb illusionism offset by bizarre juxtaposition and scale in the former, and biomorphism where colour, a low horizon line and abstracted forms led the spectator into an inscape of the mind, in the latter. Like all the works in the exhibition, both were only dimly lit with spotlights. From this dramatic space, one was led deeper into the erogenous zone, where green velvet turned to black fun-fur and one found oneself in the second main space: a crypt-like haven, designed by Mimi Parent. This seems to have been a very macabre but beautiful space. For one critic it evoked the artificial grottoes in the Boboli Gardens behind the Pitti Palace in Florence, the *Slaves* of Michelangelo and the *Venus* of Giambologna; it also echoed Baudelaire's erotic novella on a young writer's romance with the beautiful *La Fanfarlo* (1847), where she and her decadent abode represented a space where everything was soft, perfumed and dangerous to touch.[57] Another critic wrote that it was an 'indescribable space', half-forest, half-grotto.[58] A third described it as a chapel to erotic fetishism.[59] It housed a reliquary to fetishism: a wall of objects [129] made specifically for the exhibition, including Meret Oppenheim's *The Couple* (1956) [131] and Parent's *Masculine-Feminine* object.

Oppenheim's *The Couple* was an assisted ready-made, a pair of worn brown leather boots attached at the toes. This work illustrated an article on the Hermaphrodite in the exhibition catalogue, an association which, combined with the title, again presented the viewer with a paradoxical display of sexuality. The object could be read both as symbolic of a forced union or of an ideal, inseparable. As already noted, Mimi Parent's *Masculine-Feminine* was reproduced on the poster advertising the exhibition. The object – a tie made from female hair – continued the exhibition's atmosphere of tension between the nurturing and destructive feminine. On the one hand, it played on the traditional, poetic and painterly associations between flowing hair and sexual desirability (one thinks of Titian, the Pre-Raphaelites, or the Symbolists) and it evoked male fantasies for female pubic hair (Freud labelled such a fantasist a 'pervert', a 'Coupeur de nattes', and proposed that Leonardo da Vinci suffered from the obsession).[60] On the other hand, as this sensual female hair was tied into a distinctively male form (the tie), *Masculine-Feminine* also seems to explore cross-dressing or lesbianism, or perhaps to be a homage to women who rejected their prescribed sexual role (in evoking women who chose to crop their hair and wear shirts and ties, such as Gertrude Stein, for example, who like Parent left North America for liberal Paris).[61] Parent's object may be read as questioning the social construction of gender and as insisting that gender opposites were better viewed as permutations available to both sexes.[62] Transvestism subverts the phallus and presents it as a stage prop, an accessory that is not fixed, but charged.[63] Parent's object is emphatically uncanny as the familiar made strange: it enacts an archetypal female sexuality and yet perverts it in sculpting hair into a tie; one reaches for the tie and instead finds silky hair, conjuring up the tactility of female hair and male chest hair simultaneously. *Masculine-Feminine* may be seen as denying the myth of original wholeness,

129 **Fetish wall, Interior of EROS exhibition, Galerie Daniel Cordier, Paris, 1959–60.** Mimi Parent's *Masculine-Feminine* object can be seen second from left at the bottom and Adrien Dax's *Reliquary* in the middle of the second column from the right.

130 **Frida Kahlo, *Self-Portrait in Red and Gold Dress*, 1941.** Kahlo was described by Breton in 1938 as 'a ribbon around a bomb', but the Mexican artist claimed she was not a Surrealist – her life was simply surreal. Suffering from polio at the age of seven, which damaged her right foot, and a horrific streetcar accident at the age of fifteen, which left her partially crippled, she endured some thirty-five operations on her spine and foot and an adult life of pain. The self-portrait dominates her *oeuvre*, allowing her to master female and Mexican identity, address her physical and psychic pain, and portray the cruel duality of Nature (life/death, fertility/barrenness) which affected her daily.

insisting that the phallus may be located in the male and/or female, and that one can be the subject and object of desire simultaneously. Of course, hair, and its fetishistic qualities, was used by many women Surrealists to voice their dissatisfaction with society and sexual power structures – one only has to think of Frida Kahlo's moustached self-portraits with their dramatic eyebrows and sculpted hairstyles [130] or Léonor Fini's women's leonine locks; equally Duchamp's iconoclastic *L.H.O.O.Q.* of 1919 and Man Ray's photographs of him as 'Rrose Sélavy'. One could also suggest that this object continued Surrealism's primitivist aspirations for the erotic (to merge the material and the spiritual), for the organic object also evoked tribal art – for example, pre-Columbian masks and helmets used in ceremonies were often adorned with human hair trimmings.

The spectator entering this crypt, and seeing these bizarre objects boxed up in a reliquary, effectively stepped into the ultimate feminine, uncanny space, its dark fur suggesting one had stepped into the female sex itself. This was a space designed by a woman which allowed the female spectator to re-enter her own mythological self, the feminine body which patriarchy had confiscated from her, thus presaging the performance art of later women artists such as Carolee Schneemann. Yet the space contained objects designed by both women (Elisa Breton, Micheline Bounoure, Joyce Mansour, Nora Mitrani, Oppenheim, Parent) and men (Breton, Matta, Adrien Dax [132], Radovan Ivsic), and as such conformed to Parent's non-essentialist vision of eroticism as the domain of men and women alike.

Parent's fetish room was not the finale however. The last room was decorated in blood-red velvet which gave it an immediate, abject, impact while red railings divided the space in two. Benoît's Sadean costume hung on the walls, and behind the railings lay a real naked female stretched out between two burning candles on a table, as if ready for a sacrificial ritual. She was Meret Oppenheim's *Cannibal Feast* – a model, painted gold, her hair strewn with blue flowers, leaves and jasmine, and

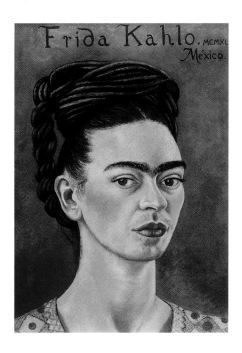

131 **Meret Oppenheim**, *The Couple*, 1956.
Oppenheim's first object since 1936, *The Couple*
continued her fascination with the fetish object as
two leather boots are given a human character in
their state of half-undress and their passionate
'kiss'. Oppenheim later produced a further
variation of the object which continued its erotic
humour: *The Couple (with egg)* (1967), consisting
of black laced, attached boots and their 'egg'
offspring made from their cut-off tips and nesting
on shoelaces.

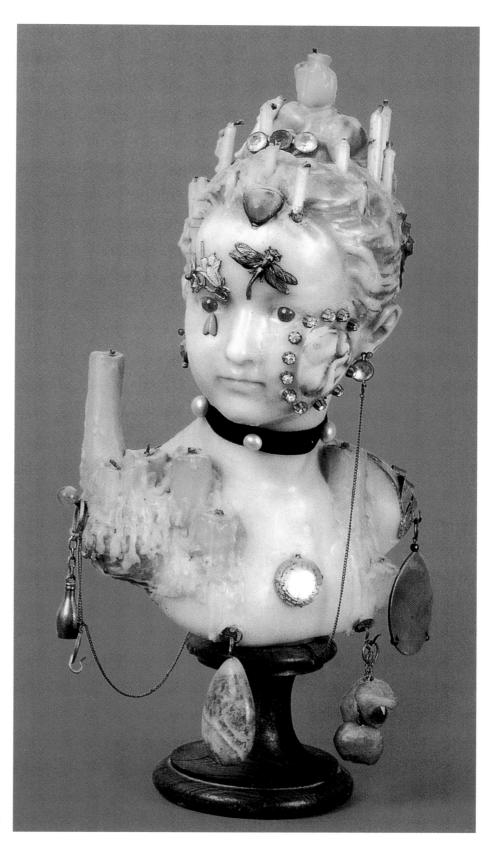

132 **Adrien Dax**, *Reliquary*. Dax (1913–79), came to Surrealism in the late 1940s and contributed to reviews and collective events. His object, which was displayed on the Fetish wall in the 1959 EROS exhibition, is fittingly uncanny in its Gothic layering of a classical female bust.

surrounded with exotic food and fruits [133]. She had preserved fruit at her neck, *petits fours* and sweet biscuits between her breasts, and slices of orange, strips of roast chicken, prawns, and lobster in scallop shells on her stomach. Champagne-filled glasses stood by her sides and two cooked lobsters crouched on her legs. The element of titillation and trepidation around the installation was emphasized by all the critics who described the woman with her eyes closed, lying totally still while a group of people ate the food from her body.

Oppenheim created a space within which the spectator had to confront his/her desires: whether to gaze at the woman, to identify with her, or to join in a tribalistic ceremony?[64] Indeed, the *Cannibal Feast* began as a *Spring Banquet* among friends in Bern in April 1959. The work presented the feminine as a banquet. For Mikhail Bakhtin the banquet is a site of free speech, communal gaiety and the celebration of life, marked by the grotesque, excessive enjoyment of food and drink:

> Man's encounter with the world in the act of eating is joyful,
> triumphant; he triumphs over the world, devours it without being
> devoured himself. The limits between man and the world are erased,
> to man's advantage.[65]

For Bakhtin, the banquet is a moment of 'the triumph of life over death. In this respect it is equivalent to conception and birth.'[66] The sense of the banquet as life-giving and nurturing as well as excessive and grotesque is present in Oppenheim's work, although it must be acknowledged that Oppenheim herself was not entirely convinced that all spectators of the work took it in the correct philosophical spirit.[67]

Oppenheim took the Surrealist object to operatic extremes, not merely suggesting the desired female through its substitute, an artistic *representation*, but presenting us with a real woman's body, complete with the smell of flesh, sweat, makeup, fruit and alcohol merged. The 1938 Surrealist exhibition had displayed many mannequins in suggestive poses, with Duchamp's mannequin raising the taboo of cross-dressing and Masson's mannequin the taboo of bondage. The 1947 Surrealist exhibition had explored the tabooed nature of the female body with Duchamp and Donati's 'Prière de toucher' catalogue. In placing a real woman at the heart of the 1959 exhibition Oppenheim further defied society's attempts to contain sexuality and, through the motif of the eating of food, produced an installation which could be read both in terms of the commodification of the female body in consumer society and the eternal rejuvenation of Nature which the female body allows.

The provocative nature of the exhibition was reinforced by the luxury catalogue, fifty of which were produced. Titled *Boîte alerte* ('emergency box', and a pun on *boîte à lettre*, letter box), this was conceived of and constructed by Parent and had the appearance of a small green letter box [134]. It was no ordinary letter box however, as was intimated by its label – 'missives lascives' ('lascivious letters', a label added by Duchamp).[68] Inside were a number of erotic letters and objects. It contained two records on which poems had been recorded: Benjamin Péret's 'La Brebis galante' and Joyce Mansour's 'L'Ivresse religieuse'; colour lithographs by Dax, Miró, Svanberg and Toyen; coloured postcards by Hans Bellmer, Dalí, Gorky, Miró and Clovis Trouille; an envelope with the capitalized word 'HAUT' on it, which contained a black nylon stocking ('un bas'). An envelope, with 'Usage Externe' written on it, contained the typescript of an erotic short story by André Pieyre de Mandiargues entitled 'La Marée', and another envelope contained Mansour's erotic short story 'La Pointe'. These poetic explorations of the erotic were counterbalanced by other more macabre inclusions, such as a copy of an

133 **Meret Oppenheim's** *Cannibal Feast* **installation, EROS exhibition, Galerie Daniel Cordier, night of 15 December 1959. On the opening night of the EROS exhibition, a live model painted in gold lay stretched out as the** *Cannibal Feast* **in a velvet-lined room, surrounded by fine food and champagne as three men and two women (making up three 'couples' according to the artist) ate from her. This was the erotic finale to the exhibition. On subsequent nights, three wax mannequins were staged in the room: one for the naked model, dressed only in food, and two male diners dressed in tuxedos.**

article from a medical review on a Bolivian woman who had been infibulated on the orders of her husband – a procedure which indicated that the husband had paradoxically mutilated the very organ that he prized. Also macabre was a typed letter with words blackened out to indicate the idiocy of censorship. The box also contained Duchamp's signed found object, *Couple of Laundress's Aprons*, with genitalia peeping out from behind tartan cloth flaps. This couple was based on a pair of late eighteenth-century purses. Finally, the box included a copy of the enigmatic telegram that Duchamp had sent to Breton from New York before the opening of the exhibition:

> Je purule tu purules la chaire purule grace à un rable
> de vénérien qui n'a rien de vénérable rrose.

According to José Pierre, the telegram was generally accepted as nonsensical, but it may have harboured a rather macabre bodily message in its evocation of a corrupt, infected (venereal) body.[69] Each of these objects served to depict Eros from historical, psychiatric and moral perspectives.

There was also a slim collection of essays by over thirty Surrealists, including one explaining Benoît's *Testament* entitled 'Dernière heure', and with a concise erotic dictionary (entitled *Lexique succinct de l'érotisme*) at the back which explained the various meanings of eroticism: from medical discourse (hysterical

134 Mimi Parent, *Boîte alerte*, 1959. For the catalogue of the EROS exhibition, Galerie Daniel Cordier, Paris. Parent designed a small green letter box. Its punning title, *Boîte alerte –* emergency box or *boîte à lettre,* letter box, indicated the Surrealists' black sense of humour and desire for the exhibition to be interactive. Marcel Duchamp came up with the idea for the object's subtitle – *missives lassives,* or lascivious letters, an allusion to the many erotic texts and objects inside.

patients deemed to be suffering from erotic madness), to literature (erotic love poetry), to psychiatry (an exaggerated sense of genital instinct), to an appreciation of the erotic as an individualistic phenomenon which is uncategorizable in terms of society's logic and morality.[70] Unsurprisingly, obscenity was defined as relative.[71] The Sadean emphasis of the exhibition was also pronounced in the dictionary where the Marquis de Sade was defined as a 'Visionary, Moralist and Revolutionary'.[72] Clearly, the catalogue intended to lead the viewer into a self-conscious position *vis-à-vis* the erotic, the political and the moral state of the nation.

This self-consciousness was supposed to facilitate reflection on and enjoyment of the sexual repressed but, given the charged political climate of the day, no doubt carried with it meanings which had more to do with the colonial repressed. Edward Said, as observed above, drew attention to the reliance of French colonial attitudes towards the Orient upon a sense of the Arab as sexual Other, but Said also powerfully demonstrated that one of the intellectual bases of French colonialism was a sense of the Arab colony as spatial alter ego too.[73] This took the form of a conviction that French rationalism, science and technology were innately superior to what French colonialists – administrators, the military, businessmen – saw as the innate disorder and mysteriousness of Oriental territories and the fundamental disorganization of life in them. The spatial hierarchy and the sexual one often went hand in hand. As Patricia Morton has documented, both were evident in the 1931 Colonial Exposition held in Paris, where the spatial layout of the pavilions of Morocco, Algeria and Tunisia 'formed a kind of Exposition Casbah' upon which a logical, campaign plan-like order was enforced.[74] The Surrealists took a stand against the Colonial Exhibition and its 'civilizing mission' in their counter-exhibition of 1931, 'The Truth about the Colonies', and in two manifestos 'Ne visitez pas l'Exposition Coloniale' and 'Premier Bilan de l'Exposition Coloniale' [135 & 136].[75] The 1959 EROS exhibition not only continued the Surrealists' conception of the primitive as a state of mind that offered a radical alternative to modern rationalism, it also indicated their solidarity with all things Other in exploiting the colonialist association between the colonized, spatial dis-order and sexual immorality.

A number of essays in the catalogue explored the exhibition's subversion of traditional, patriarchal, rational society. In his introductory essay, Breton claimed that eroticism was the 'highest common factor' in Surrealist art since its beginning. Indeed, he referred to Emmanuelle Arsan's celebrated novel *Emmanuelle* (1957) as exemplary of the individual's erotic quest. It told the Sadean story of a nineteen-year-old girl married to a strait-laced colonial diplomat in Bangkok who pursues her own sexual exploits outside of marriage with strangers, women friends and an older man, Mario, who becomes her instructor in *jouissance*.[76] In his essay, Guy Doumayrou continued the Surrealists' fascination with erotic space in his design for an elaborate, utopian city, reminiscent of the French neoclassical architect Claude Nicolas Ledoux's plan of Chaux, an ideal city for the salt mines of the Franche-Comté.[77] This plan depicted a modern city that was essentially an epic sexual institution (indeed, the plan of the utopia resembled an erect phallus penetrating a vagina). The city would dispel moral taboos and would be structured through collectives or communes. In this utopia impulse was to be followed, flowers would bloom throughout the year, music would always be played, and perfume and erotic imagery abound.[78] The city was mapped out as a range of enigmatic spaces each of which could be penetrated and explored for its revelation of erotic delight, including the 'l'oeuf révèlateur' space and the 'chambre des délices'.[79] Here Doumayrou's plan

evoked Fourier's utopian plans for an ideal universe wherein the four elements would be in harmony and the senses given free reign.

The catalogue essay by Man Ray also explored corporeal-erotic space, presenting an image of the lips of the mouth as comparable to two people meeting, entwining and revealing their teeth. And Jean-Louis Bedouin, in his essay entitled '1 + 1 = 1', in which he described the female body as a locus for signs and symbols, asserted that

> the woman's body is the mediator *par excellence*, since it alone allows
> me to overcome the full distance that separates me from the world,
> like a river whose two branches unite to embrace an island.[80]

With such a provocative exhibition space and intriguing catalogue the EROS show attracted extensive press coverage both nationally and internationally.[81] Jean-Jacques Lévêque, in his review of 1 January 1960 in *L'Information* described the exhibition in terms of bizarre spaces and psychological states, albeit seeing it as outmoded: 'Here is an exhibition which gives away an old spirit of thirty years....Eroticism seen by Surrealism does not surpass the level of the bazaar side-passage, of the psychiatrist's office, of the little hell of the well-heeled man.'[82] Yvonne Hagen, writing for the *New York Herald Tribune*, claimed that visitors would find 'a glittering sight with distractions, jokes and side shows that will amaze, astound and shock them like a trip through a ghost tunnel at Luna Park'. However, she continued that this 'revival of Surrealism' demonstrated that 'Surrealism is no longer an attraction to major talent.'[83] Other critics compared the exhibition to the atmosphere of the waxworks museum in Paris, the Musée Grévin, though such comparison had also attended the 1947 international Surrealist exhibition.[84] Despite some suggestions that Surrealism was decaying, the movement had not lost its power to shock. Several reviews deemed the exhibition to be an 'outrage to good morality', and an insult to French identity. One critic stated that the exhibition was a

135, 136 **Photographs of the Surrealist 'The Truth About the Colonies' exhibition, Paris, September 1931, published in *Le Surréalisme au service de la révolution*, no.4, December 1931. Designed by Yves Tanguy, André Thirion, Paul Eluard and Louis Aragon, 'The Truth About the Colonies' exhibition took a stand against the official Colonial exhibition that year. Marx's axiom 'A people that oppresses another cannot be free', was proclaimed in the main exhibition room, which displayed African, Oceanic and American objects and 'European fetishes' (*Fétiches européens*) – including a statuette of a black child with a begging bowl. Records of popular songs, Polynesian, Asian and rumba music were also played.**

threat to the youth of France and the reputation of France internationally.[85] In the paper *Finance* the exhibition was criticized as an insult to the Minister of the Interior.[86] *Libération* also accused the Surrealists of immorality and blackening the name of art.[87] A critic in *La Nouvelle Revue française* even described it as an exercise in 'vulgar pornography' somewhere between the 'Grand-Guignol and the whore house'.[88]

The socio-political power of Surrealist art remained as did Surrealism's status as a champion of revolutionary sexual liberty, especially at a time of acute censorship. The repression of the day, which surrounded representation and discussion of the Algerian War, also encompassed erotic literature. In December 1956, Jean-Jacques Pauvert, the publisher of the review *Le Surréalisme, même* was put on trial for publishing four volumes of the Marquis de Sade's writings – *Philosophy in the Boudoir, Justine, Juliette* and *120 Days of Sodom* – works that were deemed, like the EROS exhibition, to be an 'outrage to good morality'. To publish Sade was to incite anarchy and despite the testimonies of several intellectuals, including Breton, Pauvert was fined and the Sade volumes seized.[89]

Central to both the conservative tendencies of the French state and to the revolutionary aspirations of the Surrealists was an interest in the youth generation which exploded in numbers and influence in society in the 1960s. Both sides knew that the youth population was essential to the political status quo in France and, at least at the beginning of the decade, significant numbers of young men continued to be called up for military service in Algeria. Minister of Culture André Malraux made a conscious effort to promote a respectable youth culture through, for example, the 'Biennale des Jeunes' at the Musée d'Art Moderne, which brought together artists under the age of thirty from forty-two countries and which opened two months before the EROS exhibition, on 2 October 1959. This event was marked by a tension between the recognition of the young work of by-now 'old masters' such as Braque and, on the other hand, the new directions being laid out by artists such as Yves Klein, Jean Tinguely and the *Nouveaux réalistes* [137].

Of course, as the 1959 EROS exhibition demonstrated, Surrealism still had the power to attract young minds [138]. In their collective declaration of February 1960, 'Des Biscuits pour la route', the Surrealists pointed out that revolution was a state of mind not age, arguing that Surrealism encompassed many generations and intimating that they welcomed the possibility of a new generation taking up the Surrealist challenge.[90] At the beginning of the 1960s there were already signs of an impending explosion of emancipatory philosophy and activity. The question was to what degree this would be explicitly Surrealist or to what degree Surrealism would be overtaken by other movements.

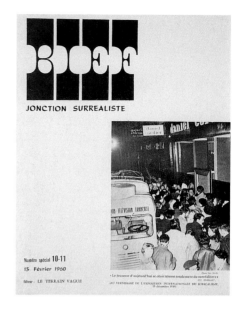

137 Jean Tinguely, *Metamatics no.17*, 1959. Tinguely's clever machine for printing automatic expressionist art was exhibited on the Trocadéro Esplanade at the Biennale de Paris in October 1959.

138 Cover of *Bief, jonction surréaliste*, numéro spécial 10–11, 15 February 1960. The photograph on the cover of this Surrealist review is of the large crowd outside the Galerie Daniel Cordier, 8 rue de Miromesnil, Paris, for the opening night of the EROS exhibition on 15 December 1959.

139 Ben Vautier, *Brushing Teeth after Mystery Food* at the Fluxus Festival of Total Art and Comportment, Nice, 1963. In a typical Fluxus performance, which is simple, unpretentious and playful in its absurdity, Vautier brushes his teeth after eating a mystery food on a table on the street in Nice, his tidy bourgeois clothes (suit and bowler hat) looking subversively clownish in the process.

140 Pierre Faucheux, cover of 'Absolute Deviation' exhibition catalogue, Galerie de l'Oeil, 3 rue Séguier, Paris, 7 December 1965 – February 1966. Faucheux worked closely with the Surrealists in the 1960s and here designed a kaleidoscopic image of Charles Fourier, whose concept of *écart absolu* was the theme of the exhibition, for the cover of the catalogue.

CHAPTER FIVE

Absolute Deviation

> [T]he 1965 exhibition, although inspired by a certain pessimism with
> regard to man's remaining chances to triumph over the specious
> alienation where Domination was leading him, seemed to anticipate
> May '68 and the youth uprisings in other countries which preceded
> the insurrection in Paris.
>
> Philippe Audoin, *Les Surréalistes*, 1973[1]

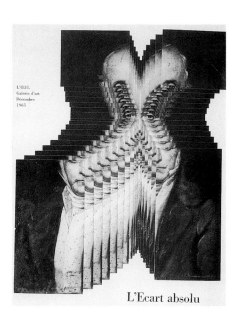

L'Ecart absolu

By the 1960s the Surrealist group had moved headquarters in Paris, from boulevard
Montparnasse in the *rive gauche* to a new café called La Promenade de Vénus, on
the corner of rue du Louvre and rue Coquillière, near Les Halles. The group had
new young, international members, including Jorge Camacho (Cuba), Konrad
Klapheck (Germany), Mimi Parent and Jean Benoît (Canada), and the French artist
Jean Terrossian. Several new Surrealist reviews had been published since Breton's
return to Paris after the war – *NÉON* (1948–9), *Médium* (1952–5), *Le Surréalisme,
même* (1956–9), *Bief, jonction surréaliste* (1958–60), *Front unique* (review, 1955–60)
– and the 1960s saw the birth of another review, *La Brèche: action surréaliste*.[2] The
latter was founded in October 1961 with Breton as editor, and Benayoun, Legrand,
Pierre and Schuster as editorial committee. It ran for eight editions, until November
1965. The review promoted the philosophers the Surrealists had always looked to,

141 Jean-Jacques Lebel, *Parfum Grève Générale, Bonne Odeur*, 1960. In this collage, Lebel retaliated against the military brutality of the Algerian War, and the political and cultural brutality of capitalism and consumerism. His collage includes cut-out newspaper headlines, pin-up girls (a nude photograph of Eva Braun) and memorabilia (including a passport photograph of himself on the left looking up at a war plane, and a torn envelope from a letter by the painter Bernard Buffet to André Breton). Lebel's collage calls for the *'bonne odeur'* (nice smell) of a general strike in support of the Algerian liberation movement, the FLN.

notably Sade and Fourier, and it addressed contemporary fiction (the *nouveau roman*) and film (the *nouvelle vague*). It also continued to voice the Surrealists' political positions, as demonstrated, for example, by the publication of their tract in support of the Cuban revolution, 'L'Example de Cuba et la révolution' in December 1964. Here they wrote of a 'true revolution':

> A true revolution must transform mankind in its social and individual totality. It is not enough to destroy capitalist economic structures and install in power another class which exercizes its domination according to precepts inherited from the old society: the sanctity of work, love sacrificed to the reproduction of the species, cults of personality, the bureaucratization of the artist who is reduced to the role of a propagandist, and so on. [3]

The tract reiterated the Surrealists' revolutionary ambitions but also their readiness to be involved in a revolution outside the confines of the Surrealist group itself. It stated:

> SURREALISM HAS ALWAYS WANTED IN ITS OWN DOMAIN TO CATALYSE REVOLT[...]IT ASPIRES TO BECOME THE CONDUCTOR-WIRE BETWEEN MOMENTS OF THE REVOLUTION...[4]

This rallying call resonated with the post-war 'baby-boom' generation which was becoming increasingly politically mobilized. Surrealism came to act as a 'conductor-wire' for younger avant-garde groups including the Situationist International, Nouveau Réalisme, Nouvelle Figuration, Fluxus, and Jean-Jacques Lebel and the Happening 'tribe'. The Situationist International (SI), formed in 1957 from a few European avant-garde groups and led by Guy Debord, recognized the revolutionary progress made by Dada and Surrealism up until 1945 but insisted that new tactics, new situations had to be created. They railed against the 'society of the spectacle' and proposed the exploration of the 'psychogeography' of the city of Paris as a means to creating alternative anti-Establishment images and understanding modern urban society. The Nouveaux Réalistes, founded in 1960 by Pierre Restany, turned to social debris for inspiration in their art, while the Nouvelle Figuration group, launched by the Parisian art-dealer Mathias Fels in an exhibition in 1961, analysed images, often popular cultural iconography, as mediators of power structures. Fluxus, a group formed in 1961, interrogated language and action through intellectual but often humerous anti-art objects and performances. Jean-Jacques Lebel had moved increasingly towards political militancy in his art and life, his collage work of 1960, *Parfum Grève Générale, Bonne Odeur* [141], fusing critical references to Hitler's 'vie amoureuse', US air force bombers, the shooting of an Italian striker by Italian riot police, Playboy bunnies and Surrealism (the fragment of an envelope sent to Breton by Bernard Buffet with photographs of works of art in it – which Breton tore up on receiving), and presaging the 'general strike' that would come eight years later. His Happenings, begun with *L'Anti-Procès* in Venice in 1960, called upon artists and society to subvert regimes through an Artaud-like theatre of excess based upon large-scale, collective performances, often graphic in nature and linked to an explicit attack on the bourgeoisie and the state. Most of these avant-garde groups were linked by Neo-Dadaism and an urgent need for concrete action. This might take the form of the artistic destruction of vehicles by the Nouveau Réaliste César in *Automobile Compression* (1960) or the public brushing of teeth on a sidewalk by the Fluxus artist Ben Vautier in *Brushing Teeth after Mystery Food* (Fluxus Festival of Total Art and Comportment, Nice, 1963) [139].

The new artistic movements, or revolutionaries as many would have preferred to be called, were engaged in analysis of the image as a product of consumer society and were preoccupied by the coercion of the artist into that consumerist hegemony. However, this subversive spirit was also indebted to Surrealism. Like the Surrealists, the artists involved in these new movements were all concerned with transforming life by art or art by life; they all shared a utopian vision; they rejected traditional art in favour of the found object or chance; and many turned to the erotic as a means of cultural and political subversion. Notably, Jean-Jacques Lebel and the Happening 'tribe' aimed to dialectically advance Surrealism and its politics of Eros, to orientate it towards social revolt, ultimately radicalizing it in their involvement in the much larger movement of May 1968.

A number of publications which were influential upon the 1960s generation also spoke to Surrealist concerns and themes, notably the destructive nature of consumer society, the political potential of Eros and the hermeneutics of freedom in general. While the first volume of Henri Lefebvre's three-volume *Critique of Everyday Life* (1947) was re-printed in 1958, the second volume of *Critique of Everyday Life* was published in 1961.[5] The first volume of the work presented an introduction to the concept of everyday life which, for Lefebvre, was the proper domain of revolutionary Marxist thought and action, updated to address not only the alienation of the worker in capitalism but of the consumer. In the second volume Lefebvre extended his portrayal of society and the individual as having been gravely damaged by excessive industrial and technological development. In his writings, and in his role as lecturer at the University of Strasbourg and then at the University of Paris at Nanterre, Lefebvre became a key spokesperson for the aims and ideals of May 1968. Although he had criticized Surrealism in 1947 for what he saw as its frequent aloofness from the urgent social issues of everyday life, his writings nonetheless showed an appreciation of the Surrealist tradition, and the evolution of Surrealism in the 1960s, especially through its interaction with new, younger avant-garde groups, would bring it closer and closer to life on the street.

In 1961, Georges Bataille mixed anthropology, literary analysis, art history and philosophical inquiry in his study of erotic excess, *The Tears of Eros*.[6] He examined the relationship between the torturer and the victim in a variety of sacrifical and sadistic rituals in both ancient and modern societies, concluding with a particularly macabre chapter in which he describes voodoo sacrifices in Africa and the Chinese torture ritual of 'Cent Morceaux'.[7] Bataille deliberately concluded the book with examples of extreme violence. He wanted the reader to end with a sense of atrocity. The resonance of Bataille's work with the contemporary reader undoubteldy stemmed, at least in part, from the continuing violence of the Algerian War. Indeed, the Algerian War was much on Bataille's mind when his own daughter, Laurence, was arrested and jailed for protesting against it while he was writing the book.

Herbert Marcuse's *Eros and Civilization* (1955) was first published in French in 1963 and it too presented a political understanding of Eros, entailing a 'philosophical inquiry into Freud' (especially Freud's *Civilization and its Discontents*, 1930), but going beyond Freud in always relating the psyche to the possibility of huge social transformation.[8] Marcuse started with Freud's definition of 'civilization' in terms of the suppression of the pleasure-principle in favour of the reality-principle. However, Marcuse merged psychoanalysis with Marxism to define the reality-principle as the conforming of a population to the demands of capitalist society and he proposed a revolutionary reworking of Freud which aimed to liberate the individual from those demands.[9] For Marcuse, art could be one of the most important means to the creation of a non-repressive society in so far as it allowed the individual to embrace his or her psychic pasts, and make visible the return of the repressed, in order to liberate him-/herself. Marcuse was determined to show how the psychological category of repression was a political category in post-industrial capitalist society. He presented the liberation of Eros as a vital step in the establishment of a society underpinned by liberated desire, new forms of human communication and the positive reorganization of work:

> the elimination of surplus-repression would *per se* tend to eliminate,
> not labour, but the organization of the human existence into an
> instrument of labour...the liberation of Eros could create new and
> durable work relations.[10]

Eros and Civilization, along with Marcuse's later *One Dimensional Man* (first published in French in 1968), became a defining text for a generation of young professors and students.[11]

As Alain Joubert acknowledged in his account of this period of Surealism's history, Marcuse undoubtedly shared concerns and themes with the Surrealists in the 1960s.[12] Many of Marcuse's theories were similar to those of the Surrealists in their evocation of Eros: the Surrealists argued that the commodity impulse must be rejected in favour of the desiring impulse, and they believed that art's social role was to reveal the paralysis of man's desires by technocratic society. Marcuse, like the Surrealists, acknowledged the importance of Fourier's 'giant socialist utopia'.[13] A Marcusean-Fourierist vision of utopia was evident in the last major international Surrealist exhibition, the 'Absolute Deviation' (L'Ecart absolu), of 1965. Indeed, the chosen title of the show was coined by Fourier in his *Théorie des quatre mouvements et des destinées générales* (1808).

The 'Absolute Deviation' exhibition, held at George Bernier's Galerie de l'Oeil, 3 rue Séguier, was a protest exhibition from the start. It retaliated against the retrospective exhibition of Surrealism which had been organized by Patrick Waldberg at the Galerie Charpentier in Paris in April 1964. Waldberg's exhibition displayed the work of Surrealists (e.g. Hérold, Lam, Magritte, Masson, Matta, Miro, Molinier, Oppenheim, Tanguy), momentary-Surrealists (e.g. Alberto Giacometti, Maurice Henry, Henry Moore), and non-Surrealists (e.g. Hannah Höch, Paul Klee), as well as primitive artefacts (American and Oceanic masks, statues, dolls). In his accompanying catalogue essay, 'Le Surréalisme, Sources – Histoire – Affinités', Waldberg traced the history of Surrealism from the Romantics to Dada to the present day, viewing Surrealism as a style in which even artists such as Balthus could be included.[14] The Surrealists strongly objected to Waldberg's historicist view of Surrealism, proclaiming that their group was militant, avant-garde and up-to-the-minute. In a radio programme on 17 April 1964 about Waldberg's exhibition, Breton asserted that the 'Absolute Deviation' exhibition 'like those that preceded it, will oppose routine by insisting a priori more on the contributions of new artists than of those who already have been consecrated.'[15]

A similar confrontational tone was apparent in a collective tract drawn up by the Surrealists entitled 'Tranchons-en' which they would insert into the 'Absolute Deviation' exhibition catalogue. The tract stated that where previous exhibitions 'bore witness' to Surrealist activity at a given moment (listing the 1938 and 1947 exhibitions) or involved a 'particularly subversive theme as a pretext' (naming

142 **Max Ernst, 'The Woman with a Hundred Heads Opens her August Sleeve', from** *La Femme 100 têtes,* **1929. Ernst's collage novel relates to and takes images from nineteenth-century illustrated novels, investing the original imagery with fantastic erotic significance. Its title deliberately puns and may be read as 'La Femme cent têtes' (the hundred-headed woman), or 'La Femme sans tête' (the headless woman, the 'sans' exaggerating the element of violence here as it suggest 'sang', blood), or 'La Femme s'entête' (the stubborn woman).**

the 1959 exhibition), the exhibition of 1965 was 'a "combative" exhibition, which *directly* confronts the most intolerable aspects of the society in which we live'.[16] The new 'deviation' in the exhibition's title would begin when society acted on its own desires and rejected the trappings of capitalist society – herein lay the exhibition's debt to the philosophy of Charles Fourier.

Interestingly, the focal point originally planned for the 1965 exhibition was not Fourier but Woman – specifically, in Breton's words, 'on the exaltation of women and of love seen as a revelation: a possible irruption of Provençal courtliness in a world of boors and poor man's Don Juans'.[17] Breton, José Pierre, Radovan Ivsic, Joyce Mansour and others, planned an exhibition which traced the historical role of woman: poetic tributes to famous *femmes fatales* in pagan, medieval and Pre-Raphaelite depictions, and such works as Ernst's *La Femme 100 têtes* (1929) [142].[18] Plans for the accompanying catalogue also included a history by Breton of the representation of woman, an erotic account of woman depicted by the artist or 'La Femme à son miroir' by José Pierre, and a synopsis of woman in the eighteenth century versus woman 'modern style'.[19] The theme of consumerism, however, had arisen during discussions on the 'new woman' leading Breton to suggest Fourier as a theme.[20] In this discursive way, the exhibition 'Absolute Deviation' was born and the 'new woman' became a theme within it but largely in terms of her relationship to consumer capitalist society.

The exhibition poster and cover of the catalogue alerted the public to the philosophy behind the show. It was designed by Faucheux and depicted a *portrait harmonique* of Fourier, his face faceted and multiplied in a kaleidoscopic fashion [140]. Writing at the dawn of the nineteenth century and in reaction to the rationalist and Enlightened philosophy born of the French Revolution, Fourier was convinced that his theories on 'Harmony' would bring an end to mercantile civilization and the birth of a 'new social world'.[21] Fourier criticized society with all its scientific, materialist trappings and wrote of the need to discover, reveal and follow all of Nature's secrets so that a new society, founded on passion, could be born. In his *Grand Traité*, he wrote that politics must aim to 'find a new social order that ensures the poorest members of the working class sufficient well-being to make them constantly and passionately prefer their work to idleness'.[22] He believed that sexual harmony would lead to social harmony, and that the repression of passion, however perverse, would only lead to violence.

The title of the exhibition referred to the twelfth section of Fourier's *Le Nouveau Monde industriel et sociétaire* (1829), where the philosopher offers a succinct synopsis of the economic aspect of his philosophy in a shortened version of his theory and compares himself to Newton and Columbus, leading the world into new harmonious lands. This text was specifically cited by Breton in 'Générique', his preface to the catalogue:

> Columbus, to arrive at a new continent, adopted the rule of absolute deviation; he cut himself off from all known routes, he entered into a virgin ocean, without taking into account the fears of his century; let's do the same, proceeding by absolute deviation...[23]

Fourier's revolutionary methods of social analysis and social change were based on two key theories: 'absolute doubt' and 'absolute deviation'. The former referred to the absolute doubting of all opinions indiscriminately – and so the need to doubt civilization itself; the latter required the doubting and dismissal of the doctrines, teachings and moral codes of all previous thinkers and philosophers.[24]

Fourier had been a key influence on Breton since the war. He was included and praised in Breton's *Anthologie de l'humour noir*, as a liberal who had justly gained the posthumous recognition of Karl Marx and Friedrich Engel. He was the subject of a monograph by Breton, *Ode à Charles Fourier* in 1945, which was republished in 1961 with a critical introduction by Jean Gaulmier (which contextualized Fourier within the history of French literature from Baudelaire to the Surrealists). Fourier's *Théorie de quatre mouvements* was one of the initiatory twenty-one steps in the 1947 international exhibition, and in 1951 Breton again called on Fourier in 'an era of *inhumanism*', stating,

> I see Charles Fourier as a revolutionary only to the degree that he
> maintained and made sensible the idea that the whole cultural
> development of humanity has been effected in a sense which does
> not respond to any internal necessity, but only from pressures which
> might as well have been others, and differently exerted.[25]

Fourier's writings were the subject of several scholarly studies in the late 1950s and the following decade including not only Marcuse's *Eros and Civilization* but also Emile Poulat's *Les Cahiers manuscrits de Fourier* (1957) and Simone Debout-Oleszkiewicz's edition of Fourier's *Le Nouveau Monde amoureux* (1967) with an original drawing by Matta. By the mid-1960s, the Surrealists' faith in a utopian socialism had never been stronger. Of course Fourier's philosophy complemented the Surrealists' stance on Eros too: as Roland Barthes has noted, Fourier, like Sade, offered a philosophy and language based on the articulation of Eros and Psyche in opposition to social order.[26] The Surrealists insisted that radical change was possible via Fourierist desire and liberation from the technocratic mentality peculiar to capitalist society. Through their manipulation of the exhibition space in 'Absolute Deviation', its installations and individual works of art, they rejected bourgeois civilization and its unfettered consumerism.

In an exhibition which was thematically concerned with the dangers of consumption, it was appropriate that the Surrealists did not produce a luxury catalogue as they had for their 1947 and 1959 shows. Instead, the catalogue was presented with a relatively plain, not to say industrial, style of typography and illustration. This style was continued in Faucheux's designs for the Surrealist review *L'Archibras*, which was under discussion in 1965 and would be launched in April 1967. *L'Archibras* was the last official group review, being published until 1969, and it too paid homage to Fourier. The title was taken from Fourier's essay 'L'Archibras', which was printed in *La Brèche, action surréaliste* in December 1964. Fourier's essay complemented Surrealist ideology not only as a work which had been censored out of his *oeuvre* by Victor Considérant, Fourier's disciple, in 1848, but more so in its fantastic meaning. Fourier's archibras was an 'arm of harmony', a fifth limb with special powers. It had many of the functions of various animals' limbs and took the form of an immensely long tail/arm. He described it as a combination of an elephant's trunk and a monkey's prehensile tail, about 5m (16 ft) in length, with a little hand at the end (as strong as an eagle's claws). It allowed man to swim as fast as a fish, to climb tall trees and pluck fruit from branches. Most importantly, this mutant limb was the ultimate symbol of rehumanized man in the sunlit world that ends Fourier's *Théorie de quatre mouvements*.[27]

As mentioned above, Breton cited Fourier in his 'Générique' essay in the exhibition catalogue. Jean-François Revel's 'James Bond contre Docteur Yes', and Philippe Audoin's 'L'Air de fête' catalogue essays also demonstrated the Surrealists' application of Fourierist humanism to the context of the dehumanized world of the 1960s.[28] The neglect of morality in the face of consumerism was attacked in these essays, as was 'l'usure sans usage', and the worker's obsession with 'pastimes'. Revel proposed that 'pastimes themselves have become an industry' and he insisted that society's fascination with science fiction, the Cadillac and James Bond was destroying French individualism.[29] Similarly, Audoin criticized the mechanization of desire in society, where happiness had been reduced to another consumer item. He also directly stated that the exhibition was conceived in the spirit of Fourier and his notion of 're-orientation' of existing civilized forms towards a radical new departure.[30]

This re-orientation was evident in the installations, in particular, in the 1965 exhibition as found, everyday, mass-produced machines were fused and sprouted their own bizarre limbs to become totems to a new non-conformist world. Indeed, the Surrealists' critique of the leisure and consumer industries resulted in the two main exhibition spaces resembling nightmarish or Gothic shopping malls; slogans and gadgets were designed to attract the spectator's attention into dark macabre spaces where consumer machines, noise and spotlights turned passive consumption into a noisy, confrontational exchange.

The exhibition opened at 6.30 p.m. on the evening of 7 December. Over 2,500 people attended, including such aristocratic collectors as Marie-Laure de Noailles, Alix de Rothschild, la Duchesse de La Rochefoucauld and the glamorously clad artist Leonor Fini. The public entered the gallery from a courtyard covered with pebbles. Twenty boundary stones marked out the space, each lit from behind so that a twinkling grid was created. Under the direction of Faucheux, the main gallery had been dramatically transformed with black cloth covering the walls and spotlighting throughout. Ninety-three exhibits were crammed into the space, many of which were moveable/mechanized objects, so that reviewers emphasized the element of the amusement park or the 'penny arcade' about the exhibition.

In the first gallery space spectators entered they came face to face with a bizarre array of installations, each subverting the 'false elements' of society. The first one was a monstrous machine made by Faucheux with contributions by other artists. It consisted of a large glass case with objects behind a two-way mirror sorted into ten individual compartments in what was called the *Does-not-Computer* (*Le Désordinateur*) [143]. Specific compartments lit up when the spectator hit a button on a control panel in front of the glass case. Each button corresponded to certain questions which could be put to the 'computer' – for example, one could press a button captioned 'travail' (work) and a glass case with French baguettes in it would light up. Another button labeled 'natalité' (birth rate) when pressed lit up a glass case with seven stuffed rats in it joined by their tails. There were also a number of cases that lit up themselves, so that the machine flashed on demand and at random in the dark gallery. Each object, illuminated in its respective case, represented a prevalent flaw of French society, from its technocratic infrastructure to the myth of the 'New Woman' and her sexual emancipation. Ten texts in the exhibition catalogue explained each of the ten encased objects.

A decoy parodied the concept of the cosmos perpetuated by such publications as *Planète* magazine which Legrand deemed pseudo-scientific. An oval wheel, according to Alain Joubert, was intended to parody a society in which men loved their cars more than their wives. The rather grotesque object described above as a response to the birth rate, parodied the 'baby boom' of the 1950s, and as Raymond Brode wrote, the threat of over-population:

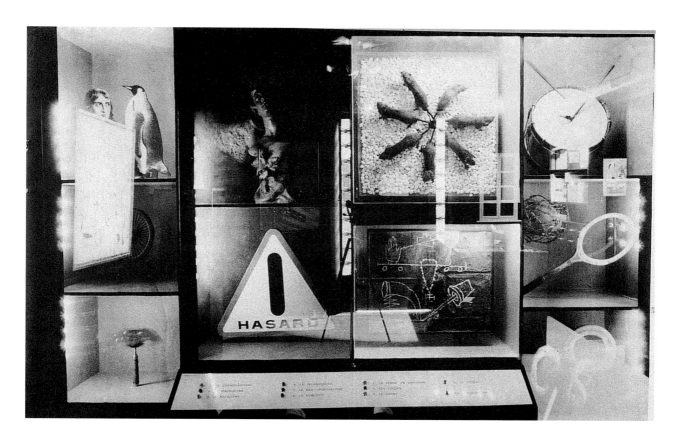

143 The *Does-not-Computer*, collective work, at the 'Absolute Deviation' exhibition, Galerie de l'Oeil, Paris, 1965–6. Photo by Suzy Embo.

More surely than the avatars of politics, the birth-rate generates a fascism of mass, a gloomy terror where high numbers invade the mind with their vile rumour and clog the horizon of bovine buildings.[31]

An alphabet of vagabonds, was, according to Benayoun, an alphabet of mock-scientific symbols, intended to parody 'American technology' and France's imitation of it. A broken drum illustrated the phrase by René Alleau, 'Break the drum of reasoning reason and contemplate the hole you've made', which was quoted by Philippe Audoin in his essay 'Haute Main'. It was symbolic of neo-spiritualism and the need to regain the sacred. An image of a one-armed Napoleon Bonaparte – 'Bonaparte Manchot' – along with the punning advertising slogan 'Bon appartement chaud' (good warm appartment), was introduced by Jean Schuster as a reflection of the corruption of public space by advertising and 'Malthusian economics'. It may have also been an allusion to the fact that aspects of the Napoleonic Code had recently been revoked – for example, new legislation in 1965 gave women more financial independence within marriage.[32] A figurine of the modern woman, labelled 'Femme Modern Style', might justify such an interpretation as it was explained by José Pierre in terms of sexual emancipation. The mannequin bust symbolized the need for woman to free herself from masculine hypocrisy, to adopt the tactics of the heroines of Sade and Jarry, and to combat the romantic representation of woman. A road sign (stating 'Hasard!') was included as a warning to the public that pastimes, the catchword of Parisian society in the 1950s and 1960s, were no more than an extension of work and its conditioning of man into an inert citizenship, according to Robert Lagarde in his explanatory text 'Ouvrir à deux battants'. A rugby ball encircled in barbed wire, made by Benoît [144], and a broken tennis racket, were the last objects to attack the *cadre*-type so vilified by Fourier. The rugby ball was interpreted by Radovan Ivsic as emblematic of the 'religion' of

144 **Jean Benoît,** *Antiquity at the End of the Twentieth Century*, **1965. Benoît's object, a rugby ball encircled in barbed wire, was exhibited in the *Does-not-Computer*, collective work, at the 'Absolute Deviation' exhibition, Galerie de l'Oeil, Paris, 1965–6.**

145 **Cover of *L'Archibras*, no.1, April 1967, designed by Pierre Faucheux.**

sport (presumably a pun on rugby as the 'jeu/dieu du peuple'), a new obsession he read as the channelling of people's energy into an activity where they might learn to enjoy watching and docility. The last case housed a sculpture of inter-twining baguettes. As mentioned above, it symbolized work and it was included to emphasize the warped ethics of society at large. In his accompanying text, Georges Sebbag wrote that it symbolized man's daily working for bread (i.e. money) and his resultant creative and spiritual inertia. Owing to the mechanization of his life, revolving around labour and consumerism, man cannot be inspired to react, let alone revolt.

In her article on the exhibition in *L'Archibras* in 1967 [145], Joyce Mansour described the *Does-not-Computer* as 'myth, ritual, and quest all at once'. She evokes her engagement with the machine, its two-way mirror and strange compartments, in wondrous, poetic terms:

> I will dive my eyes into the night without silvering, my fingers will
> waltz on the control panel and, finally liberated from the 'clear and
> simple solution' of the daily routine, I will leave in search of the exit.
> An exit. Any exit.[33]

But first she finds the second major installation in the exhibition. It too was a monstrous consuming machine – *The Consumer*, built by Jean-Claude Silbermann [146 & 147]. It greeted spectators as they moved into the second, main gallery space, having passed the *Does-not-Computer*. It stood 3.6m (12 ft) high and was crucifix-like in shape, its body made from a pink mattress. It had various features which alluded to the trappings of consumer society: sirens crowning the head like a halo, a television as a face, a taxi-radio bleeping as a voice, a washing machine for a stomach (washing newspapers), and a refrigerator as a heart, to the rear. In the refrigerator the spectator could see a bridal veil, dress and shoes as if emphasizing the loss of romance in the consumer age. It even had a licence plate at the back,

146, 147 Jean-Claude Silbermann's *The Consumer*, at the 'Absolute Deviation' exhibition, Galerie de l'Oeil, Paris, 1965–6. The front (left) of Silbermann's crucifixion-shaped object displays all its consumer-organs: a mattress-body, washing machine stomach, television face and halo of shrieking sirens. The rear (right) displays its refrigerator heart housing a bridal veil, dress and shoes. Photos by Marcel Lannoy.

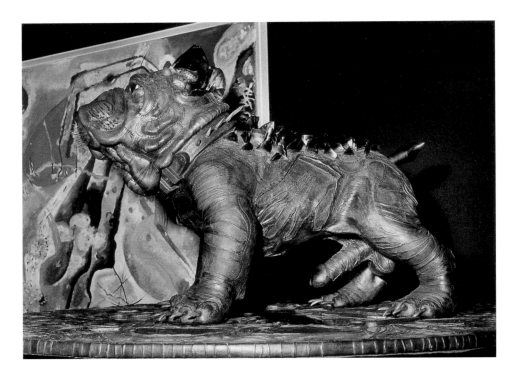

148 Jean Benoît, *Bulldog of Maldoror*, at the 'Absolute Deviation' exhibition, Galerie de l'Oeil, Paris, 1965–6. Part of Wassily Kandinsky's *Tache Rouge* (1914) can be seen behind Benoît's ferocious object. In her review of the exhibition, the Surrealist poet Joyce Mansour imagines Benoît's bulldog with its bloody claws bounding out of the show into the grass of Alechinsky's nearby *Central Park*.

mocking people's obsession with automobiles. To add to the drama of this creature, nearby neon lights assaulted the spectator's eyes, lighting up to read the word 'BIP' here and there in the room. This was the sound of the radio-voice – a constant piercing Morse code-like noise. Paintings hung on the walls, including de Chirico's *Metaphyscial Interior* (1917) and Max Ernst's *Idol* (1926). A large, boldly coloured painting with serpentine lines entitled *Central Park* (1965) by the Belgian Pierre Alechinsky also hung on the wall – the ex-CoBrA artist, who also spent time with the Phases group, was one of those listed by Breton as a Surrealist under the age of fifty in a contemporary *Arts* magazine article [149].

A sculpture of a bulldog by Jean Benoît, entitled *The Bulldog of Maldoror* [148], was also exhibited in this room. Standing on a pedestal, it took pride of place near *The Consumer* – a juxtaposition which led Mansour, in her article, to fantasize that the dog, with its bloody claws, would bound towards Central Park's alleys. The sculpture was life-size, modelled on a real bulldog that belonged to Benoît's local grocer, and inspired by Lautréamont's bestial portrayal of the universe in *Les Chants de Maldoror*. Benoît made the dog out of thick leather, with patches from the gloves of women and children, which he purchased at the flea market. The gloves were intended to evoke the power of the Sadist, particularly one pair, which were noticeably male in size and colour, and which were strategically located on the flanks of the sculpture to suggest a grip necessary for the sodomy of the dog:

> a pair, a masculine one: an attentive eye can see their impression
> on the flanks of the bulldog, oriented so that one easily guesses the
> nature of the caresses so lavished.[34]

Benoît also emphasized the Sadistic nature of the dog by endowing the sculpture with rough-edged glass ears and spikes (made from green wine bottles) and a black, erect phallus (made clearly visible by a mirror on a leather stand underneath the sculpture). Benoît's bulldog exploited the fetishistic quality of leather and the taboo

149 **Pierre Alechinsky,** *Central Park*, **1965.**

of sodomy. Alongside the monstrous machines, it acted as a reminder that the desire to create and destroy, Eros and Thanatos, are biological drives in us all.

Finally, the spotlit room contained a third imposing installation: a mock-triumphal arch, with only one supporting column. This was a mutilated version of the Arc de Triomphe and was entitled *Re-routed Arch* [150]. It mocked Chalgrin's monument to Napoleon's imperial capital of Paris and the French Grand Army by propping the arch on one wooden leg. It symbolized the fallibility of the French nation and its 'civilizing mission'. Viewers passed under the arch as they proceeded through the exhibition.

The next space, the vacated gallery office, was largely dedicated to precursors of Surrealism, including a Henry Fuseli (J.-H. Füssli) watercolour painting, undated but entitled *The Nightmare*, Charles Filiger's gouache painting *Salomon, 1st King of Brittany* and Eduard Munch's colour lithograph *Towards the Forest*. Above the paintings – again undermining the traditional viewing experience in forcing the spectator to look up and away from the paintings – a theatrical prop, a mammoth bone measuring some three metres (36 ft), hung from the rafters. A further annexe (across an alleyway to the rear of the gallery) housed an eclectic array of paintings, including Friedrich Schröder-Sonnenstern's undated coloured-crayon drawing *The Mystical Dance of the Swan-Dolls*, Crépin's *Painting on Canvas, number 126* (1941), Svanberg's beaded mosaic image *Portrait of a Star* (1965) [151] and collage *The Twinstars Strange Day in Ten Faces* (undated), Mimi Parent's *En Veilleuse/In Nightlight* (1965), and Jean-Claude Silbermann's *Au Plaisir des demoiselles* (1963-4) [152].[35]

Surrealist objects, old and new, continued to play a major role in the conceptualization of the international exhibition, as evidenced by the installations discussed. But objects exhibited in earlier international exhibitions returned again: Duchamp's *Why not sneeze Rose Sélavy?* (1921) and Wolfgang Paalen's *Articulated Cloud* (1938) reappeared (the former in a display case, the latter on a secretary's desk in the vacated office). Giacometti's presence was here too, this time in the form of the white marble sculpture, *The Exquisite Caress* (1932). Several new objects on show brought the sculptural and found object into a whole new arena. Most notable among these were a burned-wood sculpture by Augustin Cardenas entitled *After the Fire*, Tetsumi Kudo's macabre profile of a wax head or death mask entitled *Rainbow in a Cage*, and Robert Lagarde's *Brothel Towards the Courtyard: One Visits the Garden* (1965), an object depicting a female figure cut down the middle with the silhouette of a bottle cut out of her belly [154]. Two objects by Ugo Sterpini also bordered between a Dalí-like erotic humour and Nouveau Réaliste assemblages: *Sky-Sea-Earth* (1964), a dresser with windows made with doors taken from a car, and *Armchair with Armed Hand* (1965), a biomorphic stool with a woman's hand holding an officer's revolver [153]. Given that the latter piece was designed in such a way that the sitter could end up with a gun, held in a mannequin's hand, between his/her legs, this object seems a wonderful proto-feminist 'updating' of Kurt Seligmann's *Ultra Furniture* exhibited at the 1938 exhibition.[36]

Two notable absences from the exhibition were André Masson and Hans Bellmer (it is most probable that Bellmer was too ill to be involved in the exhibition and that Masson had simply distanced himself from the group by then).[37] Women Surrealists who participated included Toyen and Leonora Carrington. Carrington's oil painting *El Rarvarok* (1964) subverted patriarchal myth, depicting a Cinderella in a carriage, witches in a dark corner, priests on a balcony, and a fallen woman being hounded

by weasels. Carrington's work seemed to depict a woman's mythological lifecycle, between romance, taboo and the underworld. While a generation younger, Mimi Parent's *In Nightlight* (1965), mentioned above, also critiqued the cultural myths that continued to surround woman. It was listed in the exhibition catalogue with the subtitle 'We are such stuff as dreams are made on, and our little life is rounded with a sleep – Shakespeare.' The pyrogravure depicts a naked woman, standing on a horse, against a background of mystical skies, the sun and the moon. This Gradiva, captured in Symbolist-like style, seems to represent the Superwoman as it was juxtaposed in the catalogue with Jindrich Heisler's object *Le Surmâle* (1944) and a nineteenth-century watercolour of a sphinx by Gustave Moreau.

The subject of dreams and nightmares was not restricted to the image or installation, however – on the opening night, just after ten o'clock, a macabre performance occurred. Outside the gallery, the queuing crowds' attention was diverted towards a spotlit door to the left of the main entrance, suggesting some–thing was afoot. A nervous silence began to spread out among the crowd. Then the doors opened and a fantastic creature stepped out, moving slowly such that people wondered if it was a real man or an automaton: it was Benoît dramatically dressed as a *Necrophiliac* [155–157].

Just as he brought Sade to life for the 1959 exhibition, so Benoît brought a controversial 'erotic' figure, the necrophiliac Sergeant Bertrand, to life for the 'Absolute Deviation' exhibition. Sergeant Bertrand, like his predecessor Sade, was lauded by Benoît and the Surrealists as an individual who succeeded in defying society's rules in conceiving of a crime which had no judicial precedent. Simone de Beauvoir referred to the character Bertrand in her autobiography *Force of Circumstance* (1963). In one section, dated 17 May 1946, de Beauvoir described an evening she spent with Sartre, Jacques-Laurent Bost and Alberto Giacometti at the Golfe restaurant. She recounts how Giacometti told the tale of a nineteenth-century

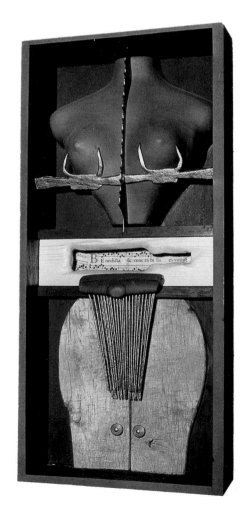

155, 156 **Jean Benoît as the *Necrophiliac*, at the opening night of the 'Absolute Deviation' exhibition, Galerie de l'Oeil, Paris, 1965. Photos by Marcel Lannoy.**

157 **Jean Benoît as the *Necrophiliac*, at the opening night of the 'Absolute Deviation' exhibition, Galerie de l'Oeil, Paris, 1965.**

pervert, a Sergeant Bertrand, who had a schizophrenic personality: respectable and gentle by day, necrophiliac by night. His obsession with corpses, particularly his mutilation and ingestion of dead women, had no precedent in court, and as a result his peculiar obscenity could not be fully judged. De Beauvoir and her colleagues discussed the problem posed by such a case: how does one judge obscene, unprecedented crimes?[38] A character who ignored social and moral doctrine, Bertrand had outraged the public even more by being a 'good citizen', an enforcer of law by day, and an 'evil' one, practising necrophilia in graveyards, by night. Benoît believed Bertrand captured the extreme, the excessive nature of desire.

Once again, Benoît's costume was intricate in its loaded symbolism. It consisted of a vast, tower-like-cape with shoulders bearing some thirty-nine tombstone crosses, and the illustration of a family vault inscribed with the names of historic heroines: Messaline, Louise Labé, Ninon de Lenclos, Pauline Borgèse, Jeanne Duval. Beneath this towering reliquary cape hung miniature black crows, birds which frequent Benoît's later macabre objects with disarming frequency and which may be attributed to his fascination with albino crows or simply to their Gothic connotations.[39] Other features of the costume included a phallic reliquary hung from the nape of the cloak (a sculpted phallus, which touched the ground like a devil's tail, pierced in the centre by the head of a doll-woman with the inscribed words 'Hommage au Sergent Bertrand'); and a heavy chain-belt from which digging implements hung. Benoît's feet and hands were gloved in claws, and in photographs he holds a witch-doctor-style staff to emphasize the split personality of Bertrand. The staff was equally ornate: at its tip, on top of a tarantula-style claw, stood two miniature figures: a female angel and a male devil, touching as they face each other.[40] Finally, the mask for the costume was in the form of a skull, with the image and texture of a moth. On the back of his necrophiliac costume, Benoît inscribed a phrase which made the tone of his performance clear – 'Mort, la vie te

guette' – that is, even in death one is trapped, stalked by life, and the body continues to be restricted by society's rules and taboos. These words were inscribed in an image of Bertrand's coffin, and were written underneath the portrait of a beautiful girl, skeletal heads and a crescent moon: an image of desire and pagan symbolism.

Benoît perceived this costume as another homage to Sade, as he explained in a contemporary letter to Lely:

> I have been dreaming for a very long time of illustrating every
> perversion in this way. Sergeant Bertrand, I am sure of it, carried in
> him all the seeds of a true sadist, he realized in material form some
> of the exploits that Sade calls – if my memory is correct – the 150
> murderous passions or the fourth class.[41]

Benoît moved among the crowd like the living dead – slowly, surely, staring ahead and not meeting their eyes. He then entered the gallery, staring at the objects behind glass, and the installations. Every now and then he roared 'Hou! Hou!' His presence was not witnessed by all and so the performance became another tantalizing and momentary aspect of the exhibition experience. At one stage he even looked out from behind the gallery window so that the crowd queuing outside in the street could see him. He then disappeared into the night.[42] Since the necrophiliac would devour his victims by night, his presence in a blackened gallery had a certain Gothic horror about it.

The 'Absolute Deviation' exhibition attempted to reawaken and permit man's baser desires and to insist that the consumer industry created and fed *false* desires. As previous international exhibitions had done, it entrapped spectators in an experience that played on their expectations and through bizarre juxtapositions turned many banal objects – a drum, rugby ball, baguettes – into subversive ones. In her article on the exhibition, Joyce Mansour wrote that spectators were called upon to interact with the art and concepts on display, as the exhibition encouraged the visitor to weave his/her own path of absolute deviation:

> It was and it is the responsibility of visitors to as much as participants
> in 'Absolute Deviation' to elaborate indefinitely upon this basic system
> (*trame*) and thereof to mark out paths of their own choosing.[43]

This was the poetic and political spirit of the show. Through their installations the Surrealists proclaimed that consumer society had forced the individual, unwittingly, into a passive state, where his/her life revolved around work and the weekend. They parodied the power of the advertising world and its monopoly on man's sense of dreams and freedom.

Alongside these major criticisms, key concerns were evident in the exhibition. Firstly, it challenged the role of woman in society in assessing the actual liberation behind her supposed modern, sexy identity. The subject of women's emancipation was a heated one in the 1960s as significant progressive legislation in France (finally) came about.[44] As noted above, a new marriage law was passed in March 1965 giving women greater financial independence. Contraception was legalized in December 1967, following regular campaigns for family planning since the 1950s.[45] Left-wing reviews insisted that the liberation of women would allow for sexual liberation (with contraception) and, therefore, moral liberation. Indeed, in an article in the PCF's *Partisans* review in 1966, it was argued that until woman was liberated man could not be liberated either, as sexual emancipation would negate the traditional exploitation of women by men and the capitalist exchange-system on which society as a whole was founded. This position articulated in *Partisans* drew on Simone de Beauvoir's belief that 'the liberty of woman begins in the womb'.[46] The article in *Partisans* argued both that marriage perpetuated the alienation of the sexes and that sex should not be equated with procreation.[47] Yet despite the new media image of women in the 1960s as controlling agents of their own bodies and budgets, they were caught between old and new stereotypes. As Claire Laubier has shown, consumerism is the key to our understanding of the condition (and conditioning) of women in France in the 1950s and 1960s. While the tension between woman's traditional, familial role and new, financially and sexually independent roles gradually became more and more evident, it was recognized that affluence in itself did little for women's rights.[48] The ultimate superficiality of consumerism and its supposed ability to fulfil the needs of women was exposed in the *Does-not-Computer*, with its pastiche bust of the 'Femme Modern Style' and in the assault on the washing machine – the domestic appliance *par excellence* meant to 'liberate' woman from the drudgery of housework – in *The Consumer*.

While the layout of the exhibition did not evoke a feminine, intra-uterine space, the emphasis in the exhibition was on the 'feminine' domestic world – family values, domestic appliances, the weekend and leisure activities, and the annual vacation. In some ways, the exhibition evoked a society similar to the one portrayed by Simone de Beauvoir in her 1966 novel *Les Belles Images* in that both were *exposés* of a changing French society and the general unease among French intellectuals about that change. The protagonist of de Beauvoir's novel, Laurence, has a family and career. She is an advertising executive who has her own car, a lover, and a family set-up which imparts the advertising image of domestic bliss – 'all grinning as though they were part of an American poster in praise of a brand of oatmeal.'[49] But she is still fraught with maternal guilt and unhappy with the superficiality of her married life: 'Love and motherhood constitute a violent emotional shock when you marry young and when a settled balance has not yet grown up between the intellectual and emotional aspects of your personality.'[50] The 'Femme Modern Style' was shown to be a highly superficial status.

Another key concern in the exhibition was with the history or legacy of Surrealism itself. The exhibition refused a linear, chronological mapping of Surrealism, offering a thematic, collective stance instead. In a satirical play, printed at the end of the catalogue, José Pierre captured the history of Surrealism in seven scenarios. He dramatized the subversion inherent in the emphasis on spontaneity and absurdity in the Surrealist aesthetic. He also indicated the Surrealist movement's recognition (and warning) of the increasing Americanization of France. The script of the play began in 1914 with two characters and one art masterwork – Giorgio de Chirico, Marcel Duchamp, and the *Mona Lisa*. It then moved into the 1920s and presented a fantastical conversation between Arp, Masson, Ernst, Miro and Man Ray in which Man Ray speaks of the power of a woman's smile to light up the 'darkroom' in which he lives. Then it presented a beach scene in which Magritte, Tanguy and a 'siren' (Gala) are engaged in a conversation, with Dalí arriving naked on a bicycle apart from a conquistador's helmet and the boots of a sewage worker. The fourth scenario marks the end of the 1930s and the war years with a long table around which Picasso, Dominguez, Paalen, Lam, Giacometti, Brauner, Matta and Péret sit and discuss the symbolic potential of an ice cube: Matta reads the ice cube as the earth, crossed with clouds of blood, presumably the clouds of war. The next scenario is America – with Breton, Gorky, Ernst, Tanning, Matta, Pollock, Masson and Aimé Césaire, set in the canyons

158 **Demonstration of some 25,000–50,000 people from Place Denfert-Rochereau to the Tomb of the Unknown Soldier at L'Etoile, Paris, 7 May 1968.**

of Colorado, and then post-war Paris, symbolized by a snow-covered Palais Royal. Toyen speaks of an elongated woman, freezing in the snow but with a vibrant red sex lighting up the dark night. The final act is the seventh scenario, the promenade of the Necrophiliac in the Père-Lachaise cemetery waiting for the moon before beginning his carnage. In the *finale* absurdity prevails and France confronts its American foe: we are presented with a frog that, to the joy of everyone, metamorphoses into Marilyn Monroe. This bizarre synopsis of Surrealism's history, from its Dada origins through to its insistence on the power of the feminine to re-enlighten the cold, harsh post-war world, to Benoît's transgression of taboo, maps out a very different and subversive history of Surrealism to Waldberg's tame one, while also lamenting the fact that the stars in the night sky, and the dreams they once inspired, had been replaced by the mass-media concept of stars – those of the Hollywood screen.

The *Does-not-Computer* made it clear that American culture was not the cause of France's demise, however. Indeed, France herself was mocked explicitly in the *Re-routed Arch*, a powerful reworking of the actual Arc de Triomphe as a symbol of France's downfall. The militant triumphalism of the Arc de Triomphe would again be undercut on 7 May 1968, at the beginning of that uniquely turbulent month, when between 25,000 and 50,000 students, teachers and other demonstrators would march to the Tomb of the Unknown Soldier singing *L'Internationale* [158].[51]

This was an aspect of the exhibition that the press did not emphasize, unsurprisingly. Indeed, the Surrealists pre-empted the press response by inserting three possible 'reviews' into the catalogue, each adopting a different stance – positive, negative and unsure – and printed on a different pastel-coloured piece of paper. The positive review, written by Audoin, printed on mauve paper and titled 'Filles de joie et publicains', feigned excitement, claiming, 'The Surrealists have made us better aware of the impossibility of the absence of God.' The indecisive review, written by Benayoun, printed on orange-coloured paper, and entitled 'Le Chou rouge et la chèvre noire', gave a detailed but dull documentation of the show. The hostile review, entitled 'Le Capharnaüm obscurantiste ou les égarements de l'intelligence', printed on yellow paper and penned by José Pierre, adopted a satirical tone, mocking Surrealist objects (such as Duchamp's fly-eaten *Still Life*) and emphasizing the poor quality of the work on show.[52]

In actuality, newspapers seem to have emphasized the theatricality of the exhibition in illustrating reviews with photographs of Benoît in his *Nécrophille* costume, his *Bulldog*, and the installation-machines. Many reviewers of the exhibition perceived it as Breton's revenge on Waldberg, and, no doubt conscious of Breton's age, acknowledged his role in the history of French modernism. Paul Waldo Schwartz, writing for the *New York Times International Edition* wrote,

> At 69, Breton himself remains an indefatigable montage of François Villon, Lenin and Boss Tweed, with mellifluent overtones of the elder poet. Remarkably enough he remains the archpriest of a present as well as past Surrealism.[53]

Frank Elgar writing in *Carrefour* on 22 December, perceived the exhibition as an authentic Surrealist show but wondered why it included so many examples of Expressionism (Munch, Kandinsky, Alechinsky) and Duchamp's Dadaist ready-mades.[54] The review *L'Arche* also presented the exhibition as the official manifestation of Surrealism and as a significant display of the work of young surrealists. The reviewer also found an existential element in the exhibition: 'There is, indeed, in this militant surrealism of André Breton and his friends, a purely existential element that most of our supposed existentialists have never known.'[55]

Some critics focused on the pertinence (or not) of the exhibition to contemporary culture. Marc Albert-Levin suggested that Surrealism was already in the streets of Paris and so did not need such a manifestation. He wrote that since sex dominated women's magazines – noting the recent cover of *Elle* magazine which asked if sex education should be taught in schools – and as young girls now happily sat on the metro chatting about whether 'sensuality is part of compassion or conversely', that Surrealism's role as 'sexual educator' was no longer needed.[56] A critic writing in the *New York Herald Tribune* under the name 'C.C.', also questioned the need for Surrealism in 1965. The critic noted that in taking over from Dada, the Surrealists 'rightly felt the public at large had to be shaken awake' but also wondered, 'Does that still hold for today's young artists, when the public at large has perhaps outstripped them in ways of protest?' Here the critic was referring specifically to protests over the French elections in 1965 and the radical form of protest involving 'human self-sacrifice by fire' in the West and East – the latter presumably a reference to the famous case of the self-immolation of the Buddhist monk Thich Quang Duc in Saigon in June 1963. The critic concluded that the exhibition was worth seeing 'for its overall agitated effect'.[57]

Other critics also assessed Surrealism within the specific climate of the mid-1960s. Otto Hahn, writing the weekly review in *Arts*, wondered whether Surrealism could engage with the 'synthetic' quality of society – a society of meat under cellophane, cosmetic surgery, artificial insemination, juke boxes and the HLM (*Habitation à Loyer Modéré*). He decided that Surrealism's inclination towards ancient techniques (presumably painting, the object and the very notion of the exhibition itself), despite using them to subversive ends, was still not radical enough. In praising younger avant-garde groups and strategies, where the focus was on the need to decondition society, his review also implied that Surrealism was still too concerned with the spiritual. Robbe-Grillet's novels, Rauschenberg's objectivity, the 'prototypes' of Victor Vasarely, the banality of Pop Art, Martial Raysse, the avant-gardism of Godard, the Rolling Stones and the Happening all win his praise.[58] In a review in *L'Express* the following week, Hahn continued his polemic, insisting that artists needed to visit a factory or the slums in the suburbs if they were really to speak to society. His leaning was evidently towards art in the street, out of the confines of the gallery space, for he described the exhibition as a 'mise en scène haute couture'.[59] He wrote that the exhibition was a little pompous, the proclamations detracting from the content:

> This type of bragging is, in any case, in the Surrealist tradition: having produced, individually, works of the first order, in their group manifestations they have done nothing but rival with the uproar of students. In visiting the exhibition, it is therefore necessary to steer clear of the prefaces and proclamations and not to be affected by intentions which are too plainly pronounced.'[60]

François Pluchart, writing in *Combat*, adopted a suitably Marxist critique. He emphasized that the price of entry to the exhibition was the same as the cost of going to see the latest Godard film, and that to buy the catalogue – which he claimed was necessary to understand the show – would cover the cost of attendance at the cinema for fifteen days.[61] The same criticism was levelled at the exhibition by André Ferrier, writing in *Le Nouvel Observateur*. Because of its eight-franc entry fee,

he described it as the most expensive exhibition in the world and noted that one needed to purchase the catalogue since the works were not displayed 'by the usual labels'.[62] In sum, most critics emphasized the generational struggle in their review, acknowledging Breton as the father (or anti-father) figure for younger avant-garde artists but questioning Surrealism's legacy in the midst of a burgeoning youth culture in which it seemed that a new-wave film or a Happening had greater mass appeal than an exhibition. Yet new-wave filmmakers and Happening artists were ever-conscious of Surrealism and its legacy and the need to lead culture in new directions. As Joseph Balsamo (Daniel Pommereulle) states in Jean-Luc Godard's *Weekend* (1967) [159]:

> You remind me of those who wouldn't move André Breton when he
> was dead....I am here to inform these Modern Times of the
> Grammatical era's end...and the beginning of Flamboyance...

Breton died on Wednesday, 28 September 1966. He was buried on 1 October, in Batignolles Cemetery, with the simple epithet on his granite headstone: 'Je cherche l'or du temps' ('I seek the gold of time'). His death would inevitably seem to signal an end of Surrealism, and at a fitting moment since counter-cultural radicalism was nearing its height. Breton was seventy when he died – three times the age of most of the young students and artists who would take to the streets of Paris two years later in May 1968 – but as Godard suggested, the death of Breton did not signal the end but a new beginning. Jean Paulhan, in his contribution to a special edition of *La Nouvelle Revue française* published in May 1967 to commemorate Breton, recognized this too. He spoke of Breton as a modern genius but also recognized the huge 'renaissance' that Breton's death might facilitate, concluding his essay with the ominous statement, 'Breton is dead. Everything is beginning again.'[63]

Certainly, Breton's death seemed to signal an end of an era for the avant-garde itself. Guy Debord and the SI had already indicated that their movement was not just the heir to Surrealism, but also its vanquisher. The SI came to new public attention the same year as Breton's death when it took a key role in student political activism. In Strasbourg in the summer of 1966 a few Situationists took over the local student organization, converting around one hundred students and inspiring the SI member Mustapha Khayati's manifesto 'De la Misère en milieu étudiant, considérée sous ses aspects économique, politique, psychologique, sexuel et notamment intellectuel et de quelques moyens pour y remédier.' Over 2,000 copies of the manifesto, published by UNEF, were distributed in Strasbourg alone.[64] In 1967, Debord's *La Société du spectacle: la Théorie situationniste* and Raoul Vaneigem's *Traité de savoir-vivre à l'usage des jeunes générations* were also published, and by 1968 the Situationists were the most prominent avant-garde group involved in political action.[65] Like many of the younger avant-gardes of the 1960s, their thinking and practice too were indebted to Surrealism, as well as to its precursors, including Sade and Lautréamont.[66]

The Situationists' interest in Sade, insistence on spontaneity, chance, urbanism, and the creation of situations in which the individual might free himself from repression, demonstrated significant continuity with the Surrealist aesthetic. In the 1950s, Debord had collaborated with the Belgian Surrealists on the review *Les Lèvres nues*, making a 90-minute film in homage to Sade entitled *Hurlements en faveur de Sade* (1952), which was in keeping with the Surrealists' fascination with Sade as a figure of revolt and which was documented in the review in 1955.[67] In 1966 Khayati also acknowledged the importance of the 'Sadism' of the Dadaists and Surrealists when it came to language: 'Following Sade, they asserted the right to say *everything*, to liberate words and "replace the Alchemy of the Word with real chemistry" (Breton).'[68] Where Breton's *Nadja* displayed a Baudelairean *flânerie* in its depiction of Paris, a joy of aimless wandering, meeting strangers and discovering new parts of Paris, Debord too was fascinated by the revelatory powers of the city. The Situationists' concept of *dérive* (drift or drifting), defined in 1957 as 'the practice of a passional journey out of the ordinary through rapid changing of ambience', was a way of countering modernist spectacle and creating new passagemways in society, but it had many traces of Breton's pursuit of the 'chance encounter' in *Nadja* too.[69] Debord explained how 'Chance plays an important role in dérives': it was by nature random, and open to the 'possible rendezvous' with a complete stranger.[70] Equally, the definition of *situation*, so central to the group's identity, seemed to echo the Surrealists' rhetorical style and desire to transform the world: the Situationists insisted 'First of all we think the world must be changed. We want the most liberating change of the society and life in which we find ourselves confined.'[71]

These concepts, and their debt to Surrealism, were also evident in the Situationists' approach to space too, specifically to the city space. Simon Sadler has observed the influence of Matta for the Dutch artist Constant Nieuwenhuys, a founding member of the SI, and his designs for a utopian city, *New Babylon* (1957–74) [160]. Constant's project was a revolutionary plan for a new urbanism, as the title of this project indicated – referring to Grigory Kozinstev and Leonid Trauberg's 1929 silent film of the same name, which was a socialist view of the Franco-Prussian War and celebration of the Paris Commune of 1871. In vision, Constant's *New Babylon* might be compared to Fourier's *phalanstère*; in form (if we consider Constant's drawings) it is comparable to the spatializations of Matta's late 1950s paintings, such as his *Eleven Forms of Doubt* (1957).[72]

However, the Situationists were eager to distance themselves from Surrealism. They claimed Surrealism's revolutionary potential had declined between 1930 and World War II, and became increasingly liquidated after the war. While acknowledging the importance of Surrealism's advance of the sovereignity of desire and surprise, they felt its revolutionary potential suffered due to its emphasis on the unconcious. In contrast, the Situationist would work with the material environment, creating situations instead of exploring the uncanny potential of the city, architecture and space. As a result, they insisted that 'surrealism was only the beginning of a revolutionary experiment in culture.'[73] In this way, as Peter Wollen has written, the SI project was largely 'that of relaunching Surrealism on a new foundation, stripped of some of its elements (emphasis on the unconscious, quasi-mystical and occultist thinking, cult of irrationalism).'[74]

If we can find Surrealist space in Situationism, we must turn to the Happening to find Surrealism's politics of Eros. The Happening was essentially an informal theatrical art form, based upon non-professionalism and spontaneity in performance, and generally held in limited spaces for limited audiences.[75] While most accounts agree in acknowledging New York as the birthplace of the Happening, it had an almost simultaneous evolution in Europe and, indeed, many of the Happening's most important cultural precursors were European. It combined the attack on the repressive nature of language and the attempt at subversive linguistic transformation effected by Dada, Kurt Schwitters's 'Merz theatre', which tried to break down traditional distinctions between stage-set, text and score, and Antonin Artaud's 'theatre of cruelty', which sought to eradicate the hierarchy between subject and object in performance.[76] While the legacy of Dada was always important to the Happening, the Happenings of Paris-based Jean-Jacques Lebel were more clearly influenced by Surrealism, especially as Lebel's European Happening (a term he adopted in 1962), like Surrealism, used space and art as a means of alerting the public to the subversive power of Eros.[77] Furthermore, Lebel was quite literally reared among the Surrealists, since his father, Robert Lebel, was not only a friend of Breton but also an art historian and the author of the first monograph on Duchamp, published in 1959. When World War II broke out, Robert Lebel took his wife and son to New York where, as we have seen, he worked with Breton as a broadcaster on Voice of America. In New York, Breton would bring the young Jean-Jacques and his own young daughter Aube (they went to the same school) to such events as the Broadway production of the musical *Hellzapoppin* – Olsen and Johnson's smash-hit farce in which the audience was bombarded with eggs and bananas, terrorized with rubber snakes and warnings about spiders on the ceiling, and in which clowns walked up and down the aisles in the intermission. Over a decade later, in 1956, Jean-Jacques Lebel would join the Surrealist group, signing the manifesto 'Hongrie: Soleil levant', contributing to Surrealist reviews, exhibiting in the 1959 EROS exhibition and organizing an international Surrealist exhibition in Milan in April–May of that year.

In December 1958, in the Surrealist review *Bief*, Lebel voiced a 'fraternal salute' to the anarchist review Noir et Rouge as a group which shared Surrealism's struggle. Several members of the Surrealist group had contacts with anarchists at this time. Breton was still friendly with the anarchist George Fontenis, Schuster contributed to anarchist journals, Mayoux was a militant syndicalist, and Péret was associated with Noir et Rouge until his death in 1959. The Noir et Rouge group appealed to a diverse constituency beyond narrow anarchist circles, combining a commitment to revolutionizing social and economic structures (through workers' councils, agricultural collectives, etc.) with an interest in 'revolutionizing social consciousness'.[78] In 1964, Jean-Louis Bédouin would state to a Fédération Anarchiste militant, Jean-Louis Gérard, that the fraternal bonds between the Surrealists and anarchists had 'never been exhausted or loosened'.[79]

By 1960 Lebel found the Surrealist group restrictive and was happy to leave. The Surrealists published a tract entitled 'Tir de Barrage', releasing him so that he could 'fly into the arms' of 'militant revolutionaries'.[80] In his own words, he was excluded for his 'anarchism and maladaptation to all types of authority', including the authority of Breton.[81] However, Breton remained a mentoring presence in Lebel's life, and Surrealist philosophy, notably its politics of Eros, remained an influence on his work. To give two examples: in his poster-statement for his 1963 exhibition (and accompanying manifestations) at the Galerie Raymond Cordier in Paris, Lebel launched into an attack on Hitlerism, Stalinism, Hiroshima, kitsch, consumer culture and the general suppression of the individual through the two words which, he said, unravelled the pathway to the jungle of life – 'Eros' and 'Thanatos'; and in 1966, the year of Breton's death, he published *Le Happening* in which there are obvious debts to Breton's view of Surrealism and its revolutionary potential.[82] Lebel wrote that the Happening, like Surrealism, was a way of living rather than a school or movement, that the artist was an 'unveiler' in society, uniting 'the real and the imaginary', Eros and Thanatos, and that art would liberate myth and the subconscious in society. Lebel wrote of his desire to cross forbidden territories in his art and to turn to the primitive and outsider art. He also referred to Bataille's theories on eroticism and to Marcuse's assertion that the liberation of Eros was central to the liberation of man from totalitarian society, whether capitalist or communist.[83] In short, Lebel's ideas were infused with Surrealist ideas, ambitions and terminology. Members of the Surrealist group recognized this and supported his new direction: Marcel Duchamp, Man Ray and Max Ernst went to see Lebel's Happenings and praised them, as did Victor Brauner who rhapsodized in 1961:

> Lebel's is a vibrating creative destiny, he has the pre-existing ardour of
> the fundamental demands of 'interiority' (freedom, violence, disorder,
> dialectical movement), reaching for the unliveable exterior world to be
> destroyed....Lebel, at desire's exact source (purity and youth) wants to live
> for he is not chained to slogans nor to any conformism nor to any integration
> compulsion...[84]

The main difference between Surrealism and Lebel's Happenings was that Lebel did not choose to convey ideas through the represented, metaphoric, erotic, liberated, body – he chose to represent ideas through the real, sexually explicit, performative, liberated body. Breton was critical of Lebel's explicit use of the body, but when one of Lebel's performances led to the artist's arrest, he did not abandon his 'prodigal son'.

The arrest took place when Lebel organized a Festival of Free Expression in Paris in April 1966, in which he orchestrated a Happening entitled *120 Minutes dedicated to the Divine Marquis* [161–164]. Just as Masson, Toyen, Bellmer, Hérold, Benoît and other Surrealists, as well as Debord, had turned to Sade, the 'Surrealist in Sadism', so too did Lebel. The Happening was aimed 'at the exorcizing of the anal rituals of merchandise and the authoritarian structure of capitalism'.[85] The Happening's debt to Surrealism was not just in the guise of Sade however, it was also in Lebel's use of space, chance encounter and surprise.

By chance, Lebel secured the Théâtre de la Chimère as the venue for his Happening – a space owned by Madame Martini, the widow of a Corsican gangster, who ran a number of strip-shows and bordellos in Pigalle, and which, ironically, was located on the ground floor of the very same building Breton lived in, 42 rue Fontaine.[86] According to the principle of the Happening, Lebel created a space in the Théâtre within which the volunteer actors decided on their individual activities; there were twenty-six participants who met several times prior to the Happening, including Denise de Casabianca, the film editor of Jacques Rivette's *La Religieuse*, which had just been banned for its blasphemous eroticism; Cynthia, a transsexual prostitute who worked in Pigalle; and a woman who asked Lebel if she could participate and sing soprano, and another with a desire to strip.[87] Together they drew up a rough chart of ideas and actions. On the night of the Happening, the audience entered the theatre through the stage door, which was flanked by two massive shanks of bloody meat. Here the Surrealists' recourse to the feminine uncanny entered new territory. This was (literally) a bloody entry into a womb-like space, a symbolic re-naissance, or more accurately what Lebel hoped would be a 'de-naissance', an attempt to exorcize civilization from the individual and lead him/her into 'a cosmic Zen or womb', a space of formlessness.[88] This was just the first stage, however, as one next entered a world of flashing strobe lights, jazz music and surreal film projections. Sugar cubes laced with LSD were handed around as

161–164 **Jean-Jacques Lebel and others,**
120 Minutes dedicated to the Divine Marquis,
Happening performed at the Théâtre de la
Chimère, 42 rue Fontaine, Paris, April 1966.

activities began from every side of the small space within which about five hundred people had congregated. Lebel and his co-conspirator Bob Benamou began to spank two girls, simultaneously in rhythm – beating out *La Marseillaise*. Once people recognized the tune of the French national anthem they began to hum along laughingly, then roles were reversed, and the two girls continued the rhythm on the bare buttocks of the two artists.

Elsewhere, excerpts from Sade's *120 Days of Sodom* were sung in a soprano voice by an unseen singer; she then seemed to appear as spectators looked up to see a naked woman urinating down from the rafters onto people below. This was a different woman however, a Sadean 'twin'. Meanwhile, three nuns entered wearing the yellow star of David – an obvious attack on the censorship of *La Religieuse*. They washed themselves, as prostitutes do before a client. Two departed, one remained, Cynthia, who continued to wash herself meticulously with her back to the audience, before presenting herself to them, half-clad as a nun. In the meantime, the singer's act had changed – a microphone had been placed at her stomach as she lay on the table covered in cream and her gyrations echoed throughout the room. She proceeded to slip on a G-string emblazoned with the star of David and donned a mask of de Gaulle. With the outstretched hands of a martyr she parodied the French Republic: Marianne, bare-breasted and marching forth, with a reminder of the Jewish victims of concentration camps between her thighs.

Cynthia had now stripped totally and had begun autosodomizing herself with vegetables. The nun Justine had revealed herself to be the Sadist Juliette! With her bobbed hair and slim figure she created chaos when she turned around to the crowd and they saw that she was in fact a transsexual with female breasts and an erect penis. One man in the audience even fainted and had to be removed by a stretcher over the heads of the crowd.[89] The obscenity of this act was profound. Even in the strip-shows in Pigalle Cynthia would not have been permitted to exhibit herself in such a fashion because full frontal nudity was illegal and real sexual engagement was taboo. The irony of this Happening was that it was put to an end by the brothel-owner Madame Martini who called the police to stop this 'affront to public decency'. Lebel was arrested for his Sadean representation of 'the Republic in danger', the sexually graphic nature of his Happening and the use of hallucinogens. But this was the power of the new art form, Lebel believing that sexual 'obscenity' was the only way to reveal the true nature of society. Arrest was an inevitable risk, but Lebel and his friends believed that 'it was fundamental to be anti-patriotic...to shit, literally, on France.'[90]

A petition – a common, but still effective, method of protest in the 1960s – was organized to stop the trial of Lebel for orchestrating the Happening. A declaration against his arrest and the policing of Happenings was sent around to artists and literati, stating that the accusation that the Happening was 'contrary to accepted standards of good behaviour' and 'offensive to the Head of State' had to be challenged, and that the policing of such events constituted 'a clear and intolerable attack on the freedom of the mind'. The declaration was signed by intellectuals and artists, including Jean-Paul Sartre, Simone de Beauvoir, Eugène Ionesco, Michel Leiris, Jacques Prévert, Eric Rohmer, Jacques Rivette, Jean-Jacques Pauvert, Edgar Morin and Noël Arnaud. The Surrealists who signed it included Marcel Duchamp, Maurice Nadeau, Gérard Legrand, Joyce Mansour, José and Nicole Pierre, Alain Joubert and Patrick Waldberg. André Breton signed it too. The petition was successful and, to avoid a public scandal, Lebel was released.

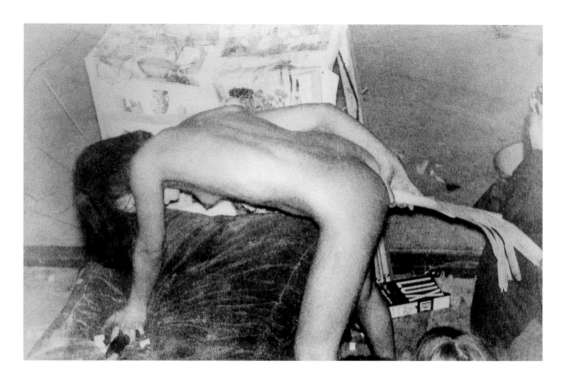

In the EROS exhibition, Sadean desire was portrayed as the redeemer of society. Spectacle, in the form of Oppenheim's naked *Cannibal Feast* and Benoît's sacrilegious *Testament to the Marquis de Sade*, had been indulged and the spectator had been forcibly embraced into a fetish reliquary and womb-like gallery space. In the 'Absolute Deviation' exhibition, Fourierist passion was advocated, the trappings of consumer society mocked and Benoît's performance was, again, a proto-Happening in itself. In other words, the Surrealists, as we have seen, had already bridged many of the gaps between art and life that new art movements in the 1960s had identified. They had broken down traditional linguistic syntax, challenged the hierarchical gallery space, and brought art into the domestic realm and the domestic realm into art. Lebel and his Happening colleagues took the language of Surrealism and its affinities with Sade and, influenced by contemporary politics, rearranged it to a new end. As such there was undoubtedly a vandalism inherent in Lebel's Happening, in its caustic use of Duchampian wit and excessive use of the Sadean aesthetic. Lebel had extended the boundaries of the Surrealists' radical use of the exhibition and Breton's concept of initiation, for in his Happenings the spectator was not to leave in self-knowledge but in self-disgust.

Lebel's arrest was not the only instance of the state's tendency to attempt direct political control of art at the time. His arrest occurred in the same month that *La Religieuse* was banned. The previous year, Jean-Luc Godard's film *Pierrot le fou* (1965) [166] had caused a public uproar and been restricted to viewers over the age of eighteen due to its 'political and moral anarchism'. In a public letter to the Minister of Culture, André Malraux, published in *Le Nouvel Observateur*, Godard described France as ruled by a 'Gestapo de l'esprit'.[91]

The neo-Surrealist review *Rupture* showed its support for Lebel in an article entitled 'Qui vive'. In fact, *Rupture* wanted to follow Lebel's example, to seize the original Surrealist 'spirit of revolution' and to continue to be the 'Defender and

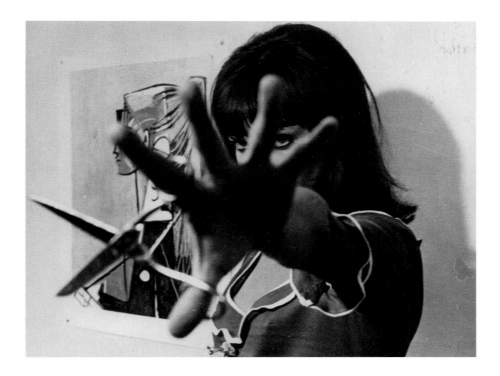

Inventor of Liberty.'[92] *Rupture* called for a renewal of Breton's and Trotsky's FIARI of 1938.[93] Breton and his group rejected the idea, but they did demonstrate their support for Lebel by signing the petition. The next time Lebel's name and face would seize the attention of the press was in May 1968, as the leader of the group that took over the Odéon [165 & 167]. However, even then, as he marched the streets of Paris protesting against de Gaulle and all that he stood for, he recognized that he also marched in defence of Surrealism and poetry itself overflowing into the streets. As he stated in a recent interview:

> In fact, in '68, what we wanted was to avenge all those whom we
> admired and whom society had despised: to avenge Artaud, Péret,
> Breton, Flora, Tristan. To avenge poetry.[94]

Lebel speaks of the events of May 1968 as a defence of minds like Breton's. Many Surrealists were directly or indirectly involved in the events, but they too seem to have recognized that 1968 brought with it the end of an era, as Surrealism as an avant-garde group became lost in the powerful rush of a much larger group – the activists. As the Surrealist Claude Courtot explained in an interview:

> The events of May 1968 which one could see as Surrealism in the
> streets, by the same token meant that it no longer remained within
> the confines of the group. We were almost ejected from it. We felt we
> had been overtaken.[95]

It is in this way that the events of May 1968 might be viewed as the apotheosis of Surrealism and its politics of Eros.

165 **Jean-Jacques Lebel, with Caroline de Bendern on his shoulders, Latin Quarter, Paris, 8 May 1968. Bendern, a model and actress of the underground film 'Zanzibar' group which was formed in early 1968, was carried by Lebel as she had hurt her foot. The resultant striking image of Bendern, as 'La Marianne de mai '68', soon flooded the front covers of the international press.**

166 **Marianne (Anna Karina), defending herself from hit-men from Algeria in Jean-Luc Godard's *Pierrot le fou*, 1965.**

167 **Students occupying the Odéon, Paris, May 1968. Jean-Jacques Lebel's slogans, proclaiming 'The ex-Odéon is a free forum!' dominate the posters which reclaim the space. Photo by Bruno Barbey.**

168 **Daniel Cohn-Bendit at the Grand Amphithéâtre of the Sorbonne, Paris, 28 May 1968.**

169 **Cover of *L'Archibras*, no.3, March 1968. The Surrealist review makes its affiliations clear – BLACKPOWER is spelt out on the telephone dial.**

The May Contestation: Surrealism in the Streets

In time, the thousand elements will become clear which were fused
together in the May 68 revolution, a revolution without a face because
a revolution of a thousand faces with its open-minded outbursts and
its libertarian eruptions, the multiple revolts of regions, provinces,
peasants, workers, college students, high-school students, intellectuals,
employees, against the authorities and Authority, the autonomist,
decentralizing, co-organizing, self-organizing, revolutionary
endeavours, the great push for a better life for the individual
and the great push to modify the balance of power in the process.
What surging, fabulous wealth in one month, what a rush of liberty-
equality-fraternity, this modern revival of French revolution crossed
with Russian and Spanish soviets, with surrealism, with Castroism,
with spontaneous cultural revolution…

Edgar Morin, 'Une révolution sans visage', 1968[1]

The phenomenon of May 1968 in France was part of a much larger phenomenon of
political youth unrest globally (in Czechoslovakia, Italy, Germany, Holland, the USA,
and elsewhere).[2] In terms of French history, it has been viewed by historians in a
variety of ways: as a utopian rising which was doomed from the start; as a historical

moment of mass youth unrest peculiar to the late 1960s, when the French education system was in crisis; as a moment of a new political consciousness marked by the full-scale emergence of youth as a social and political force; as an ideological spasm that rocked France for a fortnight in preparation for a revolution that never came; and as an intensely creative and transformative moment in cultural, social and political life whose legacy has exerted an influence worldwide for decades since. Whichever position one favours, it is undeniable that inter-generational politics were central to the occurrences of May 1968 and that the events were led by a generation, the class of 1968, for whom they constituted a very special 'coming of age'.

The events of May 1968 were the culmination of a growing dissatisfaction, especially among French youth but also among French workers, with the bourgeois capitalism of the Fifth Republic and its repressive social values. In 1968, Daniel Cohn-Bendit [168] and Jean-Pierre Duteuil – two key figures of the May events, members of the Mouvement du 22 mars and the closely related Noir et Rouge anarchist group – explained the student movement in terms of an economic crisis which was also profoundly social and existential:

> With de Gaulle, capitalism hoped to modernize itself, but it was the working class that was to pay the costs of the operation. Once the economy had reached a certain level of modernization, education had to be modernized too; hence the Fouchet Plan and the Fifth Plan. At a particular moment, the petty and middle bourgeoisie had to pay the costs. Education was rationalized to train technocrats, thus the contradictions of capitalism re-emerged in education.[3]

Jacques Sauvageot, one of the leaders of the Union Nationale des Etudiants de France (UNEF), explained that 'the students' role was that of a detonator, posing the problem of power very early.'[4] Students took stands on the Cuban crisis, the Vietnam War, the Cultural Revolution in China, workers' rights, women's issues, education and a range of other hotly contested subjects. As the decade wore on, more and more students became more and more radical, and the student movement established activist links with like-minded university professors, labour unions and overseas national liberation movements. Many students were involved in such groups as the Fédération des Etudiants Révolutionnaires (FER) and the Jeunesse Communiste Révolutionnaire (JCR).[5]

The Surrealists joined the critique of technocratic society in their 1965 'Absolute Deviation' exhibition, making efforts to welcome and absorb elements of the emerging youth counter-culture and its *engagé* attitudes. In the years after the exhibition, as social and political turmoil in France reached boiling point, the Surrealists came out in support of student activism at home and of other progressive causes abroad. For example, the Surrealists were supportive of student activism at the University of Paris at Nanterre, one of the most important flashpoints of the unrest, where Daniel Cohn-Bendit and others initiated a sit-in in response to the arrest of Xavier Langlade. He was one of six students apprehended after a leftist was reported to have attacked the American Express building in Paris on 21 March 1968 in protest against the Vietnam War. Cohn-Bendit and others took over the Salle de Conseil at Nanterre on 22 March, thus forming the group Le Mouvement du 22 mars.[6] In the March 1968 edition of *L'Archibras*, the Surrealists endorsed the action by printing a photograph of the police breaking up furniture in a classroom at Nanterre above the caption 'Faculté de Nanterre: la culture française sous la Ve République' [170].[7]

170 **Photograph of 'Faculté de Nanterre: la culture française sous la Ve République', dated 26 January 1968, in *L'Archibras*, no.3, March 1968, p.84. This choice of photograph indicated the Surrealists were aware early on of the full significance of student activism in Nanterre. In the texts which surrounded the photograph, Gérard Legrand referred back to his essay in the 1959 EROS exhibition catalogue and to Norman O. Brown on the relationship between Eros and Thanatos, and Georges Sebbag referred to Charles Fourier's *Le Nouveau Monde amoureux*, published by Jean-Jacques Pauvert, Paris, in 1967.**

Pour Cuba

Le mouvement surréaliste :

— souscrit sans réserve aux conclusions du congrès de l'Organisation Latino-Américaine de Solidarité (O.L.A.S.) ;

— salue la mémoire du Commandant Guevara, dont l'exemple continuera d'animer la lutte armée en Amérique latine ; rend hommage à l'admirable combat du peuple vietnamien et à la lutte menée contre l'impérialisme par les Noirs des U.S.A. et d'Afrique sous domination portugaise ;

— dénonce les manœuvres des partis qui, cherchant à faire partout prévaloir les méthodes de la démocratie parlementaire, utilisent la mort de Guevara comme un argument contre la guerilla ;

— considérant la diversité des conditions objectives, estime que l'imagination créatrice est un ressort révolutionnaire essentiel et qu'il lui revient en chaque circonstance de définir les voies originales conduisant à la conquête du pouvoir ; après la prise du pouvoir, reconnaît l'action du même ressort dans la révolution cubaine et accueille avec les plus grands espoirs son refus de toute pétrification dans les domaines politique, économique et culturel ;

— retrouve les principes constants de son activité dans les propositions de Guevara et de Castro quant au rôle des intellectuels dans le processus révolutionnaire et entend, pour ce qui le concerne, contribuer dans tous les domaines de sa compétence à la lutte idéologique du peuple cubain.

Paris, le 14 *novembre* 1967

Philippe Audoin, Jean-Louis Bédouin, Jean Benoit, Vincent Bounoure, Bernard Caburet, Margarita et Jorge Camacho, Agustin Cardenas, Claude Courtot, Adrien Dax, Gabriel der Kevorkian, Aube et Yves Elléouët, Guy Flandre, Henri Ginet, Giovanna, Louis Gleize, Jean-Michel Goutier, Robert Guyon, Radovan Ivsic, Charles Jameux, Alain Joubert, Wifredo Lam, Annie Le Brun, Jean-Pierre Le Goff, Gérard Legrand, Joyce Mansour, Roberto Matta, François Nebout, Mimi Parent, Nicole et José Pierre, Bernard Roger, Huguette et Jean Schuster, Georges Sebbag, Marijo et Jean-Claude Silbermann, François-René Simon, Hervé Télémaque, Jean Terrossian, Maryse et Michel Zimbacca.

3

171 'Pour Cuba' tract printed in *L'Archibras*, no.3, March 1968.

172 *La Beauté est dans la Rue* (Beauty is in the Street), poster from May 1968.

As José Pierre has noted, the photograph indicated that the Surrealists were not just aware of the situation at Nanterre but recognized its full significance early on.[8] Equally significant, was the Surrealists' support of Cuba and of Black Power in the same edition of *L'Archibras*. The cover had a black telephone with 'B-L-A-C-K-P-O-W-E-R' spelt out on the dial in place of numbers [169]; and the contents included an article by Ted Joans entitled 'Black Flower' in which he wrote of the importance of Black Power, Malcolm X and the novelist Richard Wright, drawing out the connections between Black Power, Surrealism and the quest for liberty; a tract 'Pour Cuba', which paid homage to the Cuban revolution, Fidel Castro and the memory of Che Guevara, proclaiming the imagination as 'an essential revolutionary responsibility' [171]; and an article by Jean Schuster, 'Flamboyant de Cuba, arbre de la liberté', in which he writes of Cuba as 'the interior man of humanity, his reserve of dream everywhere else erased or enclosed by walls'.[9]

On 14 May, activists began to paste posters on the walls of the Sorbonne, assaulting commodity culture, bureaucracy, the police, de Gaulle and the Church, and often echoing Surrealist provocations since the 1920s in the choice of words and images [172 & 173]. 'Vive la Révolution Surréaliste!' (Long live the Surrealist revolution!) was painted across the Sorbonne's walls; posters and graffiti quoted Benjamin Péret, 'L'art n'existe pas' (Art does not exist). Other slogans echoed the spirit of Surrealism: 'Vive la révolution passionnée' (Long live the passionate revolution); 'Les beaux arts sont fermés: mais l'art révolutionnaire est né' (The fine arts are shut down: but revolutionary art is born), 'Il est interdit d'interdire' (It is forbidden to forbid); and 'Écrivez partout' (Write everywhere). Antonin Artaud and Michel Leiris's 'Lettre aux Recteurs des Universités Européennes' of 15 April 1925 was reprinted in *Le Pavé*, the widely distributed newspaper of the Mouvement du 22 mars, and then printed as a leaflet which was handed out at demonstrations and pinned to university walls. Tract no.1 of *Le Pavé* (May 1968), the only edition ever

produced, showed a clear indebtedness to Surrealist tradition in tone and citing Georges Bataille on transgression, and Duchamp's *L.H.O.O.Q.* alongside Léon Trotsky and Rosa Luxemburg [174].

The emphasis on mental and bodily liberation from repression in these slogans and literature reiterated the Surrealist movement's faith in the radical power of Eros demonstrated in its exhibitions, art works and writings of over forty years. The Marquis de Sade's presence was also felt in the events of May 1968 as students paid homage to him with such graffiti slogans as 'Pour les nouvelles perversions sexuelles – Sade' (For the new sexual perversions – Sade). In recalling his legacy, activists proclaimed the importance of desire in revolutionary practice and, in alluding to sexual perversion, they implicitly assaulted bourgeois sexual mores and capitalism's regulation of the libido. Indeed, just as Louis Aragon had glorified Sade and the violence of the French Revolution in *Paysan de Paris* (1926), so now did the students recall the 1789 Revolution. Jacques Sauvageot also made the comparison:

> If the movement stops, it is true that the traditional left forces
> may be able to sweep the board and act as an alternative to the
> Gaullist regime. But if it continues to grow, there may be a total
> reorganization of the game, as there was in 1789, when, once the
> traditional representatives had been discredited, entirely new
> modes of representation had to be found.[10]

Some students wore eighteenth-century garb as a symbolic protest; others took titles from the Revolution for their cultural committees. For example, one group, the Enragés, took their name from the proto-anarchists led by Jean Roux during the French Revolution.[11] Their preference for the slogan 'Prenez vos désirs pour la réalité' (Take your desires for reality), and their emphasis on the eradication of all oppression, also echoed the Surrealists:

> Our sole programme is the total destruction of the university, along
> with the destruction of all institutions, of all forms of oppression,
> the only point of departure possible for the realization of art
> and philosophy.[12]

On 5 May 1968, the Surrealists issued a tract entitled 'Pas de pasteurs pour cette rage', where they stated, 'Today it is youth which possesses revolutionary conscience and energy.'[13] The tract denounced Gaullists, right-wing activists and the Communist Party, advising students to retain their spirit of independence and individualism without falling behind any one 'Pastor'. A short, half-page tract, it ended with what José Pierre described as a modest offer of assistance:

> The Surrealist movement is at the disposal of students for all practical
> action destined to create a revolutionary situation in this country.[14]

The tract was not signed by individual members but by 'Le Mouvement Surréaliste', indicating that the Surrealists too saw themselves as a revolutionary collective.

The Surrealists drew up this tract as an immediate response to the activities which had occurred in the first five days of May. By then, the Faculty at Nanterre was closed, an official investigation into Cohn-Bendit was launched, protests and police retaliation in the Sorbonne had occurred, and a number of student demonstrators had been arrested, of whom seven were given suspended prison sentences. Cohn-Bendit and Sauvageot were subjected to over twenty hours of interrogation and all protests were officially prohibited by the Préfecture de Police. The Surrealists distributed their tract on 9 May at 8.30 p.m., during a meeting that

174 *Le Pavé*, May 1968, p.2. Lebel wrote the editorial for this broadsheet and he (alongside the Situationists J.-L. Brau and Jean Franklin, the other two key people involved in its production), drew on Dada and Surrealism in their rally cry for social revolution: excerpts from Bataille, Duchamp, Michel Bakounine, Rosa Luxemburg, Trotsky, R.D. Laing and Antonin Artaud's 1925 'Lettre aux recteurs des universités européennes' dominate its four pages. The last lines of the review read in bold capital letters 'Je jouis dans les pavés' ('I come in the paving stones').

173 The Sorbonne occupied by students, May 1968, their posters attacking de Gaulle as the cause of chaos (La chientlit c'est lui!).

176 **Roberto Matta, *Disciples occupez la discipline pour une discipline révolutionnaire*, black and white lithograph, May 1968.**

was organized by the Trotskyist Jeunesse Communiste Révolutionnaire at the Mutualité concert hall, also attended by the UNEF, the Mouvement du 22 mars, the FER and others.

Occasionally, individual Surrealists also acted independently to demonstrate their support of the students. Jacques Hérold, Roberto Matta and Mimi Parent produced posters. As early as April 1968 Hérold made lithographs with revolutionary procla-mations and put poster-size prints of them on public walls in Aix-en-Provence, Avignon and Lacoste. He made three designs, each an ornate tribute to authors he admired: Susan Wise, Gilbert Lely and the Marquis de Sade, each of whom represented a different generation but the same spirit of revolt, a need Hérold spontaneously decided to act upon.[15] In May, he took more posters to Paris and put them on walls around Saint-Germain-des-Prés and Montparnasse. Matta made four posters and became involved in student discussions, demonstrations and sit-ins [175].[16] A black-and-white lithograph by him exemplifies the anti-authoritarian and utopian tenor of the day, stating, 'disciples occupy the discipline for a revolutionary discipline' [176]. Mimi Parent and Jean Benoît were also involved in demonstrations, Parent producing two posters which were distributed widely, and Benoît making a protest 'mannequin' of a police officer which would become an iconic prop and dramatic photo image distributed widely by the press [177].

In June 1968 the Surrealists published a special edition of *L'Archibras* in response to the May rising. Put together between 28 May and 8 June by Vincent Bounoure, Claude Courtot, Annie le Brun, Legrand, Pierre, Schuster, Georges Sebbag and Jean-Claude Silbermann, it amounted to a number of articles written up as events occurred. The tone of these articles was aggressive, inciting readers to revolt and damning the French state. In 'Portrait of the Enemy' (dated 8 June 1968) de Gaulle was described in uncompromising terms:

> Supreme realist head of the real police, realist organizer of real repression; realist protector of threatened capitalism, through the participatory project that divides profit into two parts: a real one for capitalism, a fictional one for the workers.[17]

Also condemned were the Communist Party, trade unions, the electoral realm, the majority, the culture of 'dead ideas', and 'the realism of authority. Of the father, the head, the boss, the teacher, the priest.'[18] The essay stated that the storming of the

177 Jean Benoît's dummy with engorged baton-
phallus amongst protestors, Paris, May 1968.

Sorbonne on 3 May had been an assault on 'reality'. It ended defiantly: 'On 3 May realism was condemned to death. The objective of the revolution, intact today in its reality, is to send it before the firing squad.'[19]

'Down with France!' was even more outrageous in its assault on the Fifth Republic. The essay described France as 'a model sty' housing pigs: 'the old combatant pig, the sporty pig, the worker pig, the reproductive pig, the literary pig, and so on. When one makes as if to want to clean their troughs, all these pigs cry out "Long Live France!" and, faced with danger, form the sacred union of tricolour snouts.'[20] The essay also attacked French monuments, echoing again the 'Absolute Deviation' exhibition and its *Re-routed Arch*:

> Let's continue to defile all monuments to the dead to turn them into
> monuments of ingratitude. (Let's admit that only a nation of pigs
> could have the idea of honouring the unknown soldier – a German
> deserter, let's hope – by placing his tomb under a grotesque triumphal
> arch which, with its four outstretched hoofs, looks like it's shitting on
> the poor sod who, on a day white with snow, was sent to spill his red
> blood for the thin blue line of Vosges.)[21]

Another untitled note in the special edition echoed Fourier in insisting that passion would lead the revolutionary way. It evoked Rimbaud's 'I is another':

> I Surrealism is another, a free captive of a torrent whose control – by
> itself or by anyone else – it prohibits.
>
> Everything depends from now on the quantity of passion – the
> measure of everything and of which nothing has the measure – cast
> into the street. I Surrealism – dissolved in the anonymous revolution –
> producers of passion.[22]

This edition of *Archibras*, unsurprisingly, was seized by the police for insulting de Gaulle, defaming the police and incitement to crime. Although the charge was later dropped following a presidential amnesty, it indicated that the Surrealists were viewed as part of a movement that needed to be stopped.[23]

The uprising of May 1968 was prompted by a complex range of social and political factors, but the nature of the uprising demonstrated the lasting and deeply embedded influence of Surrealism. Collective actions of creativity and revolt blended politics, philosophy, art and manifestations in a spontaneous demonstration of popular indignation which spilled out onto the streets of the capital. From the point of view of Surrealism, May 1968 was a finale, the apotheosis of a long series of manifestations. Jean Schuster, in his official announcement of the end of historical Surrealism in *Le Monde* on 4 October 1969, portrayed the recent events as the birth of something new, the overtaking of Surrealism by a new radical spirit:

> Cuba, Prague, May 68, it is history itself tracing a path Surrealism
> recognizes as its own and to which it remains committed. The great
> collective festivity…revealed that a superior exigency of the mind –
> poetic necessity – would henceforth condition political reality.[24]

Alain Jouffroy, an ex-Surrealist and poet, saw the events as a rebirth for art. In *Art et confrontation* (1968), he stated that 'we have just discovered – in May 1968 – that an unacknowledged void separates the system that governs us from the life and from the power of each of us.'[25] Jouffroy went on to depict May 1968 in terms that resonated with the anti-bourgeois intentions of Surrealism since its foundation. Everything the Surrealists had striven for in their international exhibitions had now been unleashed in a fundamental transformation of cultural space:

Art and literature no longer needed publishers, museums, galleries, or Houses or Ministries of Culture to 'function'; everyone's thought reverberated on every wall and expressed itself on every tongue; the irrational was no longer the enemy of the rational, disproportion created its own proportion.[26]

Jouffroy's description of May 1968 as a sort of joyous collage lends further credence to this idea of a 'surrealpolitik' on the streets of Paris:

The great joy that we experienced for the first time in the streets of Paris during May 1968, that joy in the eyes and on the lips of all those who for the first time were talking to each other, although complete strangers, this was exactly the joy that the individual lacks most, for he is a prisoner of his 'private life'...the joy of making a collage of disparate situations, the joy of discovering differences, the joy of linking up solitudes, without for an instant losing the subtlest and most abstract movements of thought.[27]

Like the international Surrealist exhibition, the events of May 1968 involved bizarre occurrences, a collective feeling of uncertainty, transgressions of logic, and the dissociation of the senses. Both operated in a hostile mode, seeking to create a new and perturbing reality. For the Surrealists, the most effective route to that reality was through the erotic – the most essential but also the most volatile aspect of human experience. The exhibitions of 1938, 1947, 1959 and 1965 produced heterogeneous erotic spaces which confronted the spectator as he/she moved through a labyrinth in a sometimes exhilarating, sometimes terrifying process of discovery and insight. The continuity and successive elaboration of this process by the Surrealists underpinned their decisive and impassioned contribution to post-war French and international culture. Their avant-garde ideas and iconography helped to fuel the events of 1968.

That the radical movements of 1968 failed to produce a total revolution and that Surrealism disbanded with the recognition that its dream of revolution could no longer be confined to the group is not to say that their resistance was in vain, however. Certainly the utopianism of both gave way to a dystopia with the gradual de-Marxification of France and the proclamation of the death of the avant-garde. Today, in the popular imagination, Surrealism is all too often fetishized and stripped of politics. It is loosely associated with desire, with ironic humour, highjacked by consumer capitalism for advertising and mass-media spectacles. As Fredric Jameson has written, much new art since the 1960s can be described as 'Surrealism without the unconscious', an art 'without the charge and investment either of a personal unconscious or of a group one.'[28] He asks rhetorically whether the notion of the 'unconscious' itself was a historical construct, an illusion which can be left behind by the postmodern age.[29] However, Surrealism without the unconscious is Surrealism without its *raison d'être*. It is Surrealism not just co-opted but censored, neutered and denied its subversive potential. While our understanding and appreciation of the unconscious itself is undoubtedly historically circumscribed, its death knell cannot be sounded nor its power to disturb the conscious world denied. The legacy of Surrealism after 1968 must surely follow artists, writers, thinkers and activists who are committed to the power of the unconscious and to the imagination of other possible worlds.

Notes

Bibliographical references given in abbreviated form in the Notes are given in full in the Bibliography. Translations are by the author unless otherwise indicated.

Introduction The Politics of Eros: Surrealism in France 1938–1968

1   Breton, *L'Amour fou*, 1937; trans. Mary Ann Caws as *Mad Love*, 1987, p.37. This sentence is part of a '2nd P.S. (1936)' which Breton adds to his analysis of the art of Alberto Giacometti.

2   See Jean Schuster, 'The Fourth Canto', *Le Monde*, 4 October 1969; trans. Peter Wood in Richardson and Fijalkowski, *Surrealism Against the Current, Tracts and Declarations*, pp.198–202.

3   Maurice Nadeau, *Histoire du surréalisme*, Paris, Editions du Seuil, 1945 and 2nd edition 1964; trans. Richard Howard as *The History of Surrealism*, with introduction by Roger Shattuck, Harmondsworth, Penguin, 1973. This translation originally published New York, Macmillan, 1965; London, Cape, 1968.

4   Other examples include the Musée National d'Art Moderne's *Paris–New York 1908–1968* exhibition (1977), which depicted post-war Surrealism as the 'vieille garde', and the follow-up exhibition *Paris–Paris 1937–1957* (1981), which emphasized the 1938 Surrealist exhibition as the pinnacle of Surrealism, giving little attention to its war-time or post-war activities. Many books on post-war culture have tended to adopt this position too, including Spector, *Surrealist Art and Writing 1919–1939*, who refers to the role of Surrealism in Paris in May 1968 from the outset but still ends his historical account in 1939.

5   See Guilbaut, *How New York Stole the Idea of Modern Art: Abstract Expressionism, Freedom and the Cold War*, p.5.

6   Huyghe, *Les Contemporains*, p.108.

7   Bazaine, *Notes sur la peinture d'aujourd'hui*. When Bazaine was interviewed by Michèle C. Cone on 5 May 1984 his attitude to Surrealism had not changed: he stated that 'Expressionism and Surrealism are an abomination and further they are totally alien to French sensibility'. See Cone, *Artists under Vichy: A Case of Prejudice and Persecution*, p.210 (footnote 75, p.60).

8   Breton formally applied for membership of the Parti Communiste Français (PCF) in January 1927 but he ceased attending his cell meetings between the end of March and May 1927, as documented by Marguerite Bonnet in André Breton, *Oeuvres Complètes*, vol.I, pp.liii–liv. Breton was expelled from the Party in 1933 according to Nadeau, p.208. His difficulty with the PCF was voiced in the 'Second Manifesto of Surrealism' (1930) where he states that his duties as a cell member of the PCF 'made it clear to me that I was to stick strictly to the statistical facts (steel production, etc.) *and above all not to get involved with ideology*. I couldn't do it'. See Breton, 'Second Manifesto of Surrealism', *Manifestoes of Surrealism*, p.143.

9   André Breton, Diego Rivera and Léon Trotsky 'Manifesto for an Independent Revolutionary Art' (25 July 1938), in Breton, *What is Surrealism? Selected Writings*, p.243 and p.246 respectively. Breton and Rivera signed the tract, though as Breton makes clear in 'Visit with Leon Trotsky', the text of a talk he gave on 1 November 1938 (at a meeting organized by the Parti Ouvrier Internationaliste (Internationalist Workers Party), the French section of the Fourth International, to commemorate the twenty-first anniversary of the Russian October Revolution), it was drawn up by him and Trotsky, and, indeed, that 'one owes more to Trotsky than to Rivera or myself for the total independence which is, from the artistic point of view, demanded [in the manifesto]'. The Cárdenas government had forbidden Trotsky to write on politics and the threat of losing his visa no doubt lay behind his decision not to sign the manifesto. See Breton, 'Visit with Leon Trotsky' in Breton, *What is Surrealism?*, p.240. This text was published in *Quatrième Internationale*, nos 14–15, Nov–Dec 1938 and in Breton, *Free Rein*.

10   Here I refer to Peter Bürger's definition of the 'historical avant-garde', an avant-garde he defines as one that 'intends the abolition of autonomous art by which it means that art is to be integrated into the praxis of life'. See Bürger, *Theory of the Avant-Garde*, p.54.

11   Benjamin, 'Surrealism: The Last Snapshot of the European Intelligentsia' (1929), trans. Edmond Jephcott, *New Left Review*, no.108, March/April 1978, p.49. See also Margaret Cohen's analysis of Benjamin and Surrealism and her suggestion that the Benjaminian concept of 'Gothic Marxism' is the best route to understanding Surrealism's political stance, in Cohen, *Profane Illumination: Walter Benjamin and the Paris of Surrealist Revolution*.

12   Benjamin, 'Surrealism: The Last Snapshot of the European Intelligentsia', p.55.

13   Lionel Trilling, *The Liberal Imagination, Essays on Literature and Society*, Garden City, Doubleday, 1953, p.61, cited in Spector, *The Aesthetics of Freud*, p.191.

14   French publications of writings by Freud in the 1920s included: *Introduction à la psychanalyse* (Paris, Payot, 1922); *Trois essais sur la théorie de la sexualité* (Paris, Editions Nouvelle Revue Française, 1923); *Totem et Tabou* (Paris, Payot, 1924); *La Science des rêves* (Paris, Alcan, 1926); and *Essais de psychanalyse* (Paris, Payot, 1927).

15   Breton, 'Manifesto of Surrealism', *Manifestoes*, pp.1–47.

16   Sigmund Freud defined wit in terms of 'play' but, as Norman O. Brown convincingly argues, his analysis of wit is equally applicable to art. See Freud, 'Wit and the Unconscious' in *The Basic Writings of Sigmund Freud*, and Norman O. Brown, *Life Against Death*, p.66.

17   Freud explained society's need to repress Eros in *Civilization and its Discontents*.

18   Louis Aragon, 'The Challenge to Painting' (1930) in Hulten (ed.), *The Surrealists Look at Art*, p.50.

19   Hal Foster has argued that the pleasure and death principles complicate and permeate Surrealism though he sees this factor as the very point where 'surrealism is at once achieved and undone', drawing on the dispute between Breton and Georges Bataille in 1929–30 over Sade as evidence. See Foster, *Compulsive Beauty*, especially p.11 and p.111. For a succinct synopsis of the Breton-Bataille dispute see Briony Fer, 'Surrealism, Myth and Psychoanalysis', in Fer, Batchelor and Wood, *Realism, Rationalism, Surrealism*, pp.204–6.

20   See Paul Avis's synopsis of Eros in *Eros and the Sacred*.

21   See Breton et al., 'L'Age d'or' in José Pierre (ed.), *Tracts Surréalistes et Déclarations Collectives, Tome I, 1922–1939*, p.440. Pierre notes that the programme for *L'Age d'or* had several aspects to it including Breton on 'L'Instinct sexuel et l'instinct de mort'. See also Breton, *Mad Love*, p.37.

22   André Breton, 'Political Position of Today's Art' (1 April 1935), *Manifestoes*, p.232.

23   Ibid.

24   Breton et al., 'Manifesto for an Independent Revolutionary Art' (25 July 1938), in Breton, *What is Surrealism?*, p.244.

25   Breton and Ford, 'Interview with André Breton'.

26   The classic text of Herbert Marcuse (1898–1979), which informs my understanding of Eros as a defiance of the taboos that sanction libidinal pleasure and, by extension, libidinal revolt, is *Eros and Civilization: A Philosophical Inquiry into Freud*.

27   On this issue, see Spector's succinct reading of Surrealism and Freud in Spector, *The Aesthetics of Freud*, p.191.

28   Freud, 'Wit and the Unconscious' cited in Brown, p.62.

29   Michel Foucault, 'Nietzsche, Genealogy, History', *The Foucault Reader*, p.83.

30   Sigmund Freud, 'Das Unheimliche' (1919), trans. as 'The Uncanny', Penguin Freud Library, vol.14, *Art and Literature*, pp.339–76.

31   Ibid., p.367.

32   See Hélène Cixous, 'Fictions and its Phantoms: A Reading of Freud's Das Unheimliche (The "uncanny")', *New Literary History*, vol.7, no.3, Spring 1976, pp.525–48, esp. pp.530–1.

33   Freud, 'The Uncanny', pp.341–2. Freud acknowledges his debt to Dr Theodor Reik for these definitions.

34   Kristeva, *Strangers to Ourselves*, p.191.

35   Ibid., p.170.

36   Kristeva, *Powers of Horror: An Essay on Abjection*, p.4.

37   Freud, 'The Uncanny', p.345.

38   André Breton, 'Second Manifesto of Surrealism' and 'Prolegomena to a Third Surrealist Manifesto or Not', *Manifestoes*, p.137 and p.292 respectively.

39   Anthony Vidler, *The Architectural Uncanny*; Cohen, *Profane Illumination*; Foster, *Compulsive Beauty*; and Rosalind Krauss, *The Optical Unconscious*. Given that I explore the uncanny in this book in terms of space, the 1978 special edition of *Architectural Design* devoted to Surrealism and architecture must also be acknowledged here, and the essays of Dalibor Veseley, 'Surrealism, Myth and Modernity' and Bernard Tschumi, 'Architecture and its Double'. See *Architectural Design*, vol.48, nos 2–3, 1978, pp.87–95 and pp.111–16 respectively.

40   Sigmund Freud, 'Femininity' (1931), in Freud, *New Introductory Lectures on Psychoanalysis*, vol.2, p.145.

41   Nadeau, p.25.

42   Important contributors to the history of Surrealism who have questioned the role of woman as bearer of the phallus, muse and *femme-enfant* include Whitney Chadwick in 'Eros or Thanatos – the Surrealist Cult of Love Reexamined', *Artforum*, vol.14, no.3, Nov 1975, pp.46–56 and *Women Artists and the Surrealist Movement*. See also Xavière Gauthier's insightful analysis of Eros and its thematic manifestations in *Surréalisme et Sexualité*.

43   André Breton, *Arcane 17*, Paris, Editions Pauvert, 1944, trans. Zack Rogow as *Arcanum 17*, Los Angeles, Sun and Moon Press, 1994, p.61.

44   James Clifford, *The Predicament of Culture*, p.236.

45   Henri Lefebvre, *The Production of Space*, p.18.

Chapter One **Profane Illumination: the 1938 Surrealist Exhibition**

1   André Breton and Diego Rivera, 'Manifesto for an Independent Revolutionary Art' (25 July 1938), in Breton, *What is Surrealism?*, p.242. As explained in the Introduction, fn 9, the Manifesto was actually drawn up by Breton and Trotsky.

2   The Surrealists' politics of display and appreciation of the commodification of fetishism was undoubtedly evident in their involvement in the earlier 'The Truth about the Colonies' (La Vérité sur les colonies) exhibition of 1931 and in their 1936 group show 'Exhibition of Surrealist Objects' (Exposition surréalistes d'objets) at the Galerie Charles Ratton, but neither exhibition was as elaborate or sophisticated in its exploration of the political potential of eroticism as the international Surrealist exhibitions of 1938 and after. For an excellent analysis of these two earlier exhibitions see Janine Mileaf's 'Body to Politics. Surrealist exhibition of the tribal and the modern at the anti-Imperialist exhibition and the Galerie Charles Ratton', *Res*, no.40, Autumn 2001, pp.239–55.

3   This view of the 1938 'International Surrealist Exhibition' as a critical engagement with the 'International Exhibition of Arts and Technology applied to Modern Life' in Paris in 1937 has also been addressed by James Herbert, *Paris 1937: Worlds on Exhibition*, pp.12–160; and more recently by Elena Filipovic, who assesses the 1938 exhibition in terms of the 'International Exhibition' and the 'Degenerate Art' exhibition in 'Surrealism in 1938: The Exhibition at War' in Spiteri and LaCoss (eds), *Surrealism, Politics and Culture*, pp.178–205.

4   'Degenerate' was either an 'insult to German feeling, or [deemed to] destroy or confuse natural form, or simply reveal an absence of adequate manual and artistic skill.' See *Degenerate Art* (exh. cat.), p.19.

5   The exhibition opened on 19 July 1937 and was extended from September to 30 November due to popular demand.

6   Adolf Hitler, 'Address on Art and Politics' at the Nuremberg Parteitag on 11 September 1935, in Baynes, *The Speeches of Adolf Hitler, April 1922 to August 1939*, p.577.

7   Adolf Ziegler, cited in Dunlop, *The Shock of the New*, p.253. Goebbels had issued a decree on 30 June 1937 giving Ziegler and a five-man commission the authority to visit all German museums and select works for the degenerate art exhibition. The other members were Count Klaus von Baudissin, who had worked as Director of the Museum Folkwang in Essen; Wolfgang Willrich, author of a racist pamphlet entitled *Cleansing of the Temple of Art*; Hans Schweitzer, commissioner for artistic design; Robert Scholz, an art theoretician; and Walter Hansen, an art teacher.

8   See Bruce Altshuler, *The Avant-Garde in Exhibition*, pp.143–4.

9   Ibid.

10   It was one of the few works from the exhibition that was probably burnt.

11   Jimmy Ernst, *A Not-So-Still Life*, p.95.

12   Ibid.

13   Ibid.

14   Ibid., p.96.

15   *Beaux-Arts*, 21 Jan 1938, cited in Dunlop, *The Shock of the New*, p.198.

16   The British Surrealists held a counter-exhibition to the 'Degenerate Art' exhibition in London entitled '20th Century German Art', organized by Roland Penrose, Herbert Read and E.L.T. Mesens at the New Burlington Galleries. In addition, Penrose and members of the British Surrealist group formed the Artists' Refugee Committee in November 1938, with representatives of the New English Art Club, the London Group, Artists' International Association and other bodies, to assist such refugees by raising funds, finding them host families and employment so that they could obtain visas. They raised over £4000 and helped between 30 and 40 people. See Penrose, *Roland Penrose*, pp.92–3.

17   The Chief of Police, Monsieur Chiappe, decided to withdraw the film's licence as a result and for fifty years *L'Age d'or* could only be viewed in private screenings and cinemas. It would only go on public release in New York in 1980 and in Paris in 1981. See Luis Buñuel, *My Last Breath*, trans. Abigail Israel, London, Vintage, 1994, p.118. No doubt foreseeing the outcry, the Surrealists issued a declaration in support of the film, praising it for its assault on moral myths and religion. The declaration was included with the film programme given to the audience who came to see the film in Studio 28 in the 18è arrondissement on 28 Nov 1930. See Pierre, *Tracts, Tome I*, pp.155–69.

18   Breton, 'Political Position of Surrealism' (1935), *Manifestoes*, p.211.

19   One of the key topics of discussion for the group was the revolutionary violence of the Marquis de Sade's writings, a topic of particular concern to Pierre Klossowski. See my essay 'Pierre Klossowski, Theo-Pornologer', in Wilson (ed.), *Pierre Klossowski, The Decadence of the Nude/La décadence du Nu*, pp.33–101.

20   In 1933 Bataille wrote an essay on the heterogeneous aspects of Fascism and in *Acéphale*, a small brochure review published four times between June 1936 and June 1939, several essays on Nietzschean thought including 'Nietzsche and the Fascists' (1937). See Bataille 'The Psychological Structure of Fascism' (first pub in *La Critique Sociale* no.10, Nov 1933, pp.159–65 and no.11, March 1934 pp.205–11) trans. Carl R. Lovitt, and 'Nietzsche and the Fascists' (first pub in *Acéphale* 2, Jan 1937 pp.3–13), trans. Allan Stoekl, in Bataille, *Visions of Excess, Selected Writings 1927–1939, Theory and History of Literature*, vol.14, pp.137–60 and pp.182–96 respectively. André Masson was also involved in *Acéphale* and designed the cover for the first edition of the review. On Bataille and Masson, see my essay 'The Poetic Jouissance of André Masson', in Khalfa (ed.), *The Dialogue between Painting and Poetry*, pp.85–104.

21   Georges Bataille, *Oeuvres Complètes*, vol.VII, Paris, Gallimard, 1976, p.461, cited by Stoekl in Bataille, *Visions of Excess*, p.xviii. This division between Breton and Bataille must not be over-exaggerated however, especially as Bataille would be a contributor to the 1947 Surrealist exh. cat. as we shall see in Chapter 3.

22   Paul Eluard and Max Ernst also spoke of going to Spain, but neither they nor Breton did. See Polizzotti, *Revolution of the Mind*, fn p.699 for p.436.

23   Webb and Short, *Hans Bellmer*, p.98.

24   Hans Bellmer's *Die Puppe* had ten photographs of the *Doll* (documenting her gradual construction) and a short introduction by the artist entitled 'Memories of the Doll Theme'. It was printed by a friend of Bellmer's, Thomas Eckstein, and at Bellmer's own expense. It was Bellmer's photographs of the *Doll* which won him a place in the Surrealist group. In 1934 the Surrealists had published eighteen of Bellmer's photographs of the *Puppe* in *Minotaure* (no.6) under the title 'Poupée: Variations sur le Montage d'Une Mineure Articulée'. A French edition of *Die Puppe* was also published as *La Poupée* by Guy Levis Mano in which Bellmer's essay was translated by Robert Valançay. In 1935 Bellmer exhibited with the Surrealists in a group show at the Galerie des Quatre Chemins; in 1936 he participated in the 'Exhibition of Surrealist Objects' at the Galerie Charles Ratton in Paris.

25   Bellmer's photographs of his second *Doll* were published in *Minotaure*, no.10, 1937. *Les Jeux de la poupée* was intended for publication in 1939. However, due to the war, it was not published until 1949 by Editions Premières, Paris.

26   See Foster, *Compulsive Beauty*, Chapter 4, and Therese Lichtenstein, *Behind Closed Doors*.

27   Webb and Short, p.38.

28   Eric Hobsbawm, foreword to Dawn Ades et al., *Art and Power*, p.11.

29   Edmond Labbé, quoted in Warnod, *Exposition 37*, p.ii.

30   Bloch and Delot, *Quand Paris allait à l'Expo*, p.167. Indeed, in their analysis of the exhibition, the authors suggest that the exhibition might best be viewed as a ring within which a sporting match between the Left and the dethroned Right was fought out.

31   Edmond Labbé, *Le Livre d'or officiel de l'exposition internationale des Arts et des Techniques*, Paris, 1937, p.24, quoted in trans. in Dawn Ades, 'Paris 1937, Art and the Power of Nations', in Ades et al., *Art and Power*, p.58.

32   See Marko Daniel, 'Spain: Culture at War', Ades et al., *Art and Power*, pp.63–8.

33   See Herbert, p.53.

34   According to the invitation to these events held in the Getty Research Institute (Jean Brown papers, 'Dada and Surrealist ephemera 1916–1984'), Paul Eluard spoke at 4.15 p.m. on Saturday 2 October (with poetry of Rimbaud, Jarry, Saint-Paul Roux, Breton, Tzara, Michaux, Eluard, Char and others read by Eluard, Itkine and Jean-Louis Barrault) and Breton at the same time the following Saturday, 9 October, at the Comédie des Champs-Elysées.

35   Robert Couturier cited in Dominique Autié, 'Artificial Bodies or the Naturalist's Chamber', in Parrot, *Mannequins*, p.147.

36   *Femina*, cited ibid., p.148.

37   *London Bystander* and *Le Temps*, cited ibid.

38   Jean Zay, Minster of National Education and Fine Arts, on the 'Chefs d'oeuvre' exhibition, quoted in Herbert, p.83.

39   Raymond Escholier, Head of the Municipal Curatorial Staff for the 'Maîtres de l'art indépendant' exhibition in the preface to the exh. cat., quoted in Herbert, p.100. Picasso was accepted as a French artist since he had lived in France for a long time. One work by Max Ernst was also shown.

40   Gibson, *The Shameful Life of Salvador Dalí*, p.377.

41   See 'Lettre ouverte à Monsieur Camille Chautemps, Monsieur Jean Zay, Monsieur Georges Huisman', in Pierre, *Tracts, Tome I*, pp.311–12.

42   André Breton 'Devant le rideau' (1947), trans. Parmentier and d'Amboise as 'Before the Curtain' in Breton, *Free Rein*, pp.80–1.

43   Ibid., p.81.

44   Breton, 'Gradiva' (1937), in *Free Rein*, p.22.

45   Marcel Duchamp, in Cabanne, *Dialogues with Marcel Duchamp*, p.81.

46   This was listed on the cover of the catalogue for the 'International Surrealist Exhibition', Galerie Beaux-Arts, Paris, 1938.

47   Jean, *The History of Surrealist Painting*, pp.281–2.

48   Hugnet, *Pleins et déliés*, p.323.

49   Enigmarelle was an automaton made of 365 different parts and powered by electricity. This androgynous robot was capable of performing basic human tasks; created by the architect 'Ireland' in 1900 and exhibited at the London Hippodrome in 1905.

50   No doubt in homage to the Comte de Lautréamont (1846–70), author of *Les Chants de Maldoror* (1869) and his famous metaphor so loved by the Surrealists, 'As beautiful as the chance encounter of a sewing machine and an umbrella on a dissecting table.'

51   Dalí, *The Unspeakable Confessions of Salvador Dalí*, p.191.

52   The Surrealists first began to play this game in 1925. It involved a few collaborators who would compose a drawing or a sentence on a piece of paper by contributing a word or image in turn, without seeing what the preceding collaborator(s) contributed. Inevitably a bizarre anthropomorphic picture resulted with male and female sexual parts, and multiple limbs (human, animal or inanimate), or a sentence which made little sense but resounded with poetic potential. The name of this game of chance was derived from the first sentence composed in this manner: 'Le cadavre-exquis-boira-le vin nouveau' (The-exquisite-corpse-will-drink-new-wine). This explanation of the game is given in Breton and Eluard (eds), *Dictionnaire abrégé du surréalisme*. See also André Breton's preface to *Le Cadavre exquis son exaltation* (exh. cat.), Paris, Galerie Nina Dausset, 1948, pp.5–11.

53   Breton decided on *Déjeuner en fourrure* as a title. See Robert J. Belton, 'Androgyny: Interview with Meret Oppenheim', in Mary Ann Caws et al., *Surrealism and Women*, p.68.

54   In his 1927 essay on 'Fetishism', Freud writes 'Probably no male human being is spared the fright of castration at the sight of the female genital'. See Freud, *On Sexuality, Three Essays on the Theory of Sexuality, and Other Works*, p.354. Kaja Silverman elaborates on this association between female castration and the uncanny and the fact that the fetish works in this way due to the fact that the male subject *already* has an intimate knowledge of loss in *The Acoustic Mirror*, pp.17–18.

55   Freud, 'The Uncanny', p.248 and p.359 respectively. See E.T.A. Hoffmann 'The Sandman' (1816) in *Tales of Hoffmann*, trans. R.J. Hollingdale, Harmondsworth, Penguin, 1982, pp.85–125.

56   De Beauvoir, *The Prime of Life*, p.259.

57   Hugnet made this installation but writes that the idea was Breton's. See Hugnet, p.330.

58   See Kachur, *Displaying the Marvellous*, pp.43–67.

59   Hugnet, p.329.

60   Walter Benjamin, 'Das Passagen-werk', in *Gesammelte Schriften*, vol.5:1, p.516, cited in trans. in Janet Ward, *Weimar Surfaces: Urban Visual Culture in 1920s Germany*, Berkeley, University of California Press, 2001, p.228.

61   Kachur notes the pipes refer to Man Ray's earlier glass bubble pipes, specifically *Ce que manque à nous tous* (1935) and reads the mannequin as an appropriation of 'the space and format of advertising' perhaps to mockingly reject the merchandise usually put on a mannequin and to say, instead, 'hello to nakedness'. See Kachur, p.61.

62   *Gradiva* has a conch/pomegranate-like sex too, an allusion to Masson's traumatic experience of combat in World War I too when he saw a fellow soldier whose skull had been split open like a ripe pomegranate by a shell. As David Lomas notes, Masson's depictions of wounds are often 'overtly vulvic in shape'. See Lomas, *The Haunted Self*, p.36.

63   Breton singled out Masson's mannequin in his article 'Prestige d'André Massson', in *Minotaure*, nos 11–12, May 1939, p.13.

64   On Bellmer's 'polymorphously perverse' photography, see my essay 'Hans Bellmer's Libidinal Politics', in Spiteri and LaCoss, pp.246–66.

65   See Brassaï, *The Secret Paris of the 30's*. Of course the mannequin was also deemed a vessel for the marvellous in the first Surrealist manifesto of 1924.

66   The 'ville Surréaliste' is mapped out in the dictionary around a drawing by Hans Bellmer entitled *Mains de demi-mijaurées fleurissant des sillons de parterre* (Hands of semi-precious women touching grooves in the floor). See Breton and Eluard (eds), *Dictionnaire abrégé du surréalisme*, p.72.

67   See *The Immaculate Conception* (excerpts), in Breton, *What is Surrealism?*, pp.69–85.

68   Vidler, pp.150–3.

69   Tristan Tzara, 'D'un certain automatimse du Goût', *Minotaure*, nos 3–4, Dec 1933, p.84.

70   Ibid.

71   Matta Echaurren, 'Mathématique sensible – Architecture du temps' (adaption by Georges Hugnet), *Minotaure*, no.11, Spring 1938, p.43.

72   Ibid.

73   Ibid.

74   Jean, p.280.

75   See Cabanne, p.81.

76   The coffee was roasted by Claude Rollin behind a screen, according to Durozoi, *History of the Surrealist Movement*, p.343.

77   Man Ray, *Self Portrait*, p.252.

78   Hugnet, Breton and Eluard auditioned Vanel for the role. See Hugnet, p.342. Note Vanel is included in the *Dictionnaire abrégé du surréalisme* and 'defined' on p.76 as 'L'iris des brumes. Danseuse surréaliste.'

79   Dalí, *The Unspeakable Confessions of Salvador Dalí*, p.192.

80   Showalter, *The Female Malady*, p.150. Freud studied at the Salpêtrière Hospital in Paris from October 1885 to February 1886.

81   See André Breton and Louis Aragon, 'La Cinquantenaire de l'hysterie', *La Révolution surréaliste*, no.11, 15 March 1928.

82   Freud, 'The Uncanny', p.347.

83   See Kristeva on *jouissance* in *Powers of Horror*, pp.9–10.

84   Aristotle's *Politics* is to be thanked for establishing these 'natural', hierarchical differences.

85   Michèle C. Cone has examined the French policy of *rayonnement culturel* further. She argues that the French government's willingness to collaborate with the Germans in the 'French Art of the Present' (Ausstellung Französischer Kunst der Gegenwart) in Berlin in June 1937 presages the state collaboration that would follow. See Cone, 'Collaboration Foretold, French Art of the Present in Hitler's Berlin', *French Modernisms*, pp.11–39.

86   Louis Brunet, 'Du Surréalisme', *La Croix*, 20 Jan 1938, p.1. On the relationship between sex, race and pathology as pertaining to the 'Hottentot Venus' (Sarah Baartmann) see Sander L. Gilman, 'Black Bodies, White Bodies: Toward an Iconography of Female Sexuality in Late Nineteenth Century Art, Medicine and Literature', in Gates (ed.), *Race, Writing and Difference*. On negrophilia and 'The Darker Side of Surrealism' see Chapter 5 of Archer-Straw's *Negrophilia, Avant-Garde Paris and Black Culture in the 1920s*.

87   Maurice Henry, 'Le Surréalisme dans le décor', *Marianne*, 26 Jan 1936, p.11.

88   René Guetta, 'L'Expo du rêve', *Marianne*, 26 Jan 1938, p.13.

89   *Dictionnaire abrégé du surréalisme*, p.11.

90   Ibid., p.18.

91   Breton, 'Before the Curtain', in *Free Rein*, p.81.

92   The International Federation of Independent Revolutionary Art (FIARI) published two editions of *Clé*, the first of which, dated January 1939, published the manifesto.

93   Jean-François Chabrun wrote an article in this edition of *Réverbères* against Nazism – where he attacked the Nazis 'reactionary oppression of art'. He mentioned the FIARI tract in a postscript where he stated that he, Jean-Claude Diamant-Berger, Pierre Minne and Roger Sby believed in the need for FIARI's call for 'independent art' and would support it (although in the next edition of *Réverbères* it was indicated that Sby's name should not have been added to the postscript as he had not read Breton's tract).

Chapter Two **Surrealism and World War II**

1   Breton and Ford, 'Interview with André Breton', p.1.

2   Leonora Carrington, who married Renato Leduc, a Mexican diplomat, in Lisbon in 1941 as a means of getting a visa to travel to the US, would regroup with the Surrealists in New York before also travelling to Mexico in 1942. 'Down Below' was published in *VVV*, no.4, 1944.

3   Robert Rius had been Breton's assistant at the Galerie Gradiva and was one of the founder members of the neo-Surrealist Réverbères group.

4   Benjamin Péret, letter to G. Heinein, 18 April 1942, in Péret, *Oeuvres Complètes*, vol.5, p.57.

5   In interview Dalí explained that politics simply did not interest him: 'Politics-commitment, as the Surrealists called it – came between us. Marxism to me was no more important than a fart, except that a fart relieves me and inspires me. Politics seemed to me a cancer on the body politic.' See Dalí, *The Unspeakable Confessions of Salvador Dalí*, p.117.

6   Sawin, *Surrealism in Exile and the Beginning of the New York School*, p.115.

7   Ballard had published Breton's poem *Pleine Marge* in *Cahiers du sud* in November 1959. On the artistic activity in Marseilles at this time, see Cone, *Artists under Vichy*, p.106; and Guiraud, *Varian Fry à Marseille, 1940–1941* (exh. cat.), pp.9–12.

8   It was a committee of concerned American citizens under the patronage of Eleanor Roosevelt. They drew up a list of endangered persons in New York in response to one of the clauses in the armistice between Germany and France whereby the French were to 'surrender on demand' German refugees, and sponsored the activities of the Committee and the safe travel of those under threat.

9   See Fry, *Surrender on Demand*, pp.xi-xiii. Fry was expelled from France for his rescue work in September 1941 and returned to New York in November 1941. In April 1967, shortly before his death, he was honoured by the French and in February 1996 he was honoured as 'Righteous Among the Nations' at Yad Vashem by the state of Israel.

10   Ibid., p.31. While Fry states that Einstein hung himself, it seems he threw himself in the river Gave d'Oloron with a stone tied to his neck. See Conor Joyce, *Carl Einstein in Documents and his Collaboration with Georges Bataille*, p.210.

11   Fry, *Surrender on Demand*, pp.113–14.

12   Ibid., pp.115–16.

13   Ibid., p.117.

14   Masson, *Anatomie de mon univers*. This work was written and illustrated in 1939, when Masson travelled from Normandy to Marseilles to New Preston, Connecticut, where it was published in French in 1942. It was first published in English in 1943 in New York.

15   Three examples of these communicated drawings were used as illustrations in Maurice Blanchard, *Le Surréalisme encore et toujours, cahiers de poésie*, nos 4–5, Paris, np., 1943, which was published by La Main à Plume.

16   Itkine also set up a co-operative sweetmeat factory in Marseilles at this time, where Brauner, Dominguez, Hérold, Jean Ferry Lély, Péret and Prévert worked. In December 1942, the factory closed down due to fear of the Gestapo. Itkine joined the Resistance and was arrested on 1 August 1944, tortured by the Gestapo and either executed or gassed in a concentration camp. See Alexandrian, *Jacques Hérold*, p.37; and Cone, *Artists under Vichy*, pp.124–5.

17   Masson quoted in Durozoi, p.386.

18   Breton, 'The Marseilles Deck', *Free Rein*, p.49.

19   The deck of cards was subsequently redrawn by Frederick Delanglade and exhibited at the Museum of Modern Art in New York in 1941. A new edition of the deck was issued by André Dimanche in 1983.

20   Breton, 'Interview with André Breton', *View*, p.2 (Breton's emphasis).

21   Breton, 'Le Jeu de Marseille', *VVV*, March 1943, reproduced in Breton, *La Clé des champs* (1953), pp.67–70, and in trans. in *Free Rein*, pp.48–50.

22   Masson, *Vagabond du Surréalisme*, p.35.

23   See Breton and Parinaud, *Entretiens*, p.195.

24   Breton, 'D.A.F. de Sade' in *Anthologie de l'humour noir*, pp.38–42. This re-edition includes a third extract from Sade's work, a letter from Sade to his wife – a new addition to the post-war print of the *Anthologie*. In the re-edition, Breton also thanked Gilbert Lely for the letter and for continuing the cause of Maurice Heine. In the letter Sade satirizes the Academy and nobility, and professes his own 'genius' and the 'richness of his knowledge'. See Sade, 'A Madame de Sade', in *Anthologie de l'humour noir*, p.49.

25   Adorno and Horkheimer, *Dialectic of Enlightenment*, p.94.

26   Wifredo Lam and his partner Helena Holzer left Marseilles at the end of May 1941 for Cuba and arrived in Havana in July. Four years later he would meet up with Breton again, in Haiti.

27   André Breton, cited in Polizzotti, p.491. This remark was omitted from the printed version of the interview to Breton's disgust and he would write to the newspaper to complain.

28   Breton, 'Interview with André Breton', *View*, p.2.

29   Fry, pp.140–1.

30   Alexandrian, *Jacques Hérold*, p.38.

31   Chabrun and Rius only took his 'Surrealist stickers'. Les Réverbères was founded by Jean Marembert and Michel Tapié in April 1938 and disbanded in Spring 1941. Involved in the group were writers, Tapié, Noël Arnaud, Henri Bernard, Louis Cattiaux, Jean-François Chabrun, Jean-Claude Diamant-Berger, Aline Gagnaire, Jean Jausion, Marc Patin, Nadine, Gérard de Sède; and artists, including Simone Bry, Louis Cattiaux, Gio Colucci, Aline Gagnaire, Geneviève la Haye, Pierre Ino, Jean Janin and Jean Lafon. They took their name from the last words of Tristran Tzara's *La Première Aventure céleste de Mr Antipyrine*, which ends: 'Nous sommes devenus des réverbères (le mot est répété dix fois) puis ils s'en allèrent.' See Fauré, *Histoire du surréalisme sous l'occupation*, p.9. Of course the name had other connotations too: the French Revolution a century later was 'the citizen's right to light' and the Directorate extended the maintenance of 'réverbères' – the newly designed fixtures that reflected the light downward – throughout the night and all year round. It must also be noted here that the group would not tolerate Breton's firm control over Surrealism and were keen to bring music (notably, jazz) and theatre into their activities – two aspects of the arts they claimed were neglected by Breton in the first edition of *Les Réverbères*, in an article by Jacques Bureau entitled 'Poisson d'avril'.

32   Breton, *Entretiens*, p.194.

33   Duchamp described the *Boîte-en-valise* as a 'portable museum' and began work on it in 1936. Joseph Cornell assisted him in the project when Duchamp arrived in New York in 1942 and by 1966 Duchamp produced seven versions of the box, each including reproductions of his major works, though all varying in size and scale. For the most extensive account and illustrations of this project see Bonk's excellent study, *Marcel Duchamp: The Portable Museum*.

34   Breton to Bonneaud, 13 Oct 1940, published as AB, *Lettre à Maud, 13 octobre 1940* (Marseille, Villa Air Bel, 1989), p.7, cited in Polizzotti, p.485.

35   Breton, 'Prolegomena to a Third Surrealist Manifesto or Not' (1942), *Manifestoes*, p.284.

36   Ibid., p.282.

37   Breton, 'Situation of Surrealism between the two wars' (1942), in Breton, *What is Surrealism?*, pp.311–25. The essay was also published in *VVV*, nos 2–3, March 1943.

38   Breton, 'Interview with André Breton', *View*, p.2.

39   Abel, 'The Surrealists in New York', *Commentary*, October 1981, p.47.

40   On Surrealism's importance according to these artists (and Matta being torn between his young American friends and Breton's circle) see Sidney Simon, 'Concerning the Beginnings of the New York School: An Interview with Peter Busa and Matta', and 'Concerning the Beginnings of the New York School: Interview with Robert Motherwell', *Art International*, Summer 1967.

41   See Levy, *Memoir of an Art Gallery*, and Schaffner and Jacobs, *Julien Levy: Portrait of an Art Gallery*.

42   On Julien Levy and Dalí's *Dream of Venus* pavilion for New York's World's Fair see Kachur, pp.106–51, and Schaffner's sumptuously illustrated (with photographs by Eric Schaal) *Salvador Dalí's Dream of Venus*.

43   This gallery project would end in the summer of 1938 but lead to a much bigger one – a gallery of modern art at 30 West 57th Street, New York. See Vail, 'Peggy Guggenheim: Life and Art' in *Peggy Guggenheim, A Celebration* (exh. cat.), pp.17–125.

44   Frederick Kiesler, cited in Altshuler, p.151. Kiesler made his reputation for the stage sets he designed for Karel Capek's play, *R.U.R.*, at the Kurfurstendamn Theatre, Berlin in 1923 and then with his three-dimensional wood and canvas 'City in Space' construction (officially a support system for an exhibition of modern Austrian theatre) at the 1925 'Exposition internationale des arts décoratifs et industriels modernes' in Paris. By 1926 he was in New York to organize a major international theatre exhibition and he went on to renovate the Film Guild Cinema in 1929 and to design a utopian 'Space House' which was exhibited in the showrooms of the Modernage Furniture Company in New York in 1933. He also designed window displays for Saks Fifth Avenue and was set designer at the Juilliard School of Music.

45   Letter dated 26 February 1941 from Peggy Guggenheim to Frederick Kiesler, Frederick and Lillian Kiesler Archive Vienna, reproduced in *Friedrich Kiesler, Art of this Century* (exh. cat.), p.17.

46   Weld, *Peggy: The Wayward Guggenheim*, p.288.

47   In this space, Guggenheim held a number of exhibitions of direct relevance to Surrealism, such as *Exhibition by 31 Women* (5 January 1942 – 6 February 1943), where Breton, Ernst and Duchamp helped select the chosen

artists and which included works by Leonora Carrington, Meret Oppenheim, Dorothea Tanning and Kay Sage, and *Natural, Insane, Surrealist Art* (1–31 December 1943), where natural works included found driftwood and skeletons, and Surrealist artists included were from both Europe and America.

48 Charles Selliger, 'Un Portrait de la Galerie Art of this Century' in *Les Surréalistes en exil et les débuts de l'école de New York* (exh. cat.), p.171 (reproduced in trans. p.389).

49 Kiesler 'Manifeste du Corréalisme' in *L'Architecture d'aujourd'hui*, June 1949, reprinted in trans. in *Frederick J. Kiesler: Endless Space* (exh. cat.), p.97.

50 Robert Coates, 'The Art Galleries, Sixteen Miles of String', *New Yorker*, 31 Oct 1942, pp.72–3.

51 John Cage, who stayed with Peggy Guggenheim and Max Ernst in the summer of 1942, quoted in Altshuler, p.154.

52 Kiesler, *Brief Note of Designing the Gallery*, typescript, 1942, cited in Eva Kraus, 'ATC – A Reconstruction', *Friedrich Kiesler, Art of this Century* (exh. cat.), p.21.

53 Cabanne, p.86. That said, it must be pointed out that Kiesler was indebted to Duchamps's anti-retinal art, notably his *Bride Stripped Bare by her Bachelors Even (The Large Glass)* of 1915–23, which Kiesler praised as 'architecture, sculpture and painting in one' in his essay, 'Kiesler on Duchamp', *Architectural Record*, 81, May 1937, p.54.

54 See Josefina Alix, 'Indigenous Art and Nature: The Encounter of the art of the old and New Worlds', in *Les Surréalistes en exil et les débuts de l'école de New York* (exh. cat.), pp.359–70.

55 Polizzotti, p.509.

56 Denis de Rougemont, *Journal de deux mondes*, Paris, Gallimard 1946, p.104 cited in trans. in Sawin, p.222.

57 Rodoti, cited ibid., p.510.

58 Breton, *Entretiens*, p.196.

59 Thirion, *Revolutionaries without a Revolution*, p.469.

60 For an introduction to the history of *View* see Catrina Neiman, 'View Magazine: Transatlantic Pact', in Ford (ed.), *View, Parade of the Avant-Garde 1940–1947*, pp.xi–xvi.

61 Cabanne, p.85.

62 Tomkins, *Duchamp. A Biography*, p.147.

63 Breton's 'Lighthouse of the Bride' essay was first published in *Minotaure* in 1935 and was his longest essay on Duchamp, surveying Duchamp's career from 1915 to 1935. See Breton, 'The Lighthouse of the Bride', in Ford (ed.), pp.123–30.

64 Clive Philpot and Lynne Tillman, 'Interview with Charles Henri Ford: When Art and Literature Come Together', *Franklin Furnace Flu*, Dec 1980, p.1. On the relationship between Duchamp and Kiesler see also Gough-Cooper and Caumont, 'Frederick Kiesler and The Bride Stripped Bare' in Safran (ed.), *Frederick Kiesler 1890–1965*, pp.62–71.

65 Breton hoped Charles Henri Ford would edit *VVV* and abandon *View*, but he declined the offer. From then on, Breton was negative towards the rival publication, describing it to Péret as 'pederasty international'. Breton to Péret, letter 19 April 1943, Doucet archives, cited in Polizzotti, p.508.

66 'Declaration VVV' (trans. unknown), reproduced in Breton, *What is Surrealism?*, pp.337–8. This declaration appeared on the title page of each of the three issues of *VVV*.

67 Breton, 'Prolegomena to a Third Surrealist Manifesto or Not', *Manifestoes*, pp.289–90.

68 Breton, *Entretiens*, p.197.

69 It should be noted that André Masson and Césaire were among the contributors to the same edition of *Hemispheres* (nos 2–3, Fall/Winter 1943–4) and Masson, Césaire and Paul Eluard among the contributors to the same edition of *Fontaine* (no.35, 1944).

70 Péret, *La Parole est à Péret*, New York, Editions Surréalistes, 1943; republished with some changes as introduction to *Anthologie des mythes, légendes et contes populaires d'Amérique*, Paris, Editions Albin Michel, 1960. It was also republished in *Le Déshonneur des poètes, précédé de la Parole est à Péret*, Paris, Editions Pauvert, 1965.

71 Durozoi, p.409. Durozoi also makes the important point here that those names which were not included indicate either a loss of communication with certain members of the group, as with Mesens in London and Bellmer in France, or 'a certain distancing' as in the case of Masson and Wolfgang Paalen in Mexico.

72 See Kachur on the history of the Whitelaw Reid Mansion and the Co-ordinating Council of French Relief Societies in *Displaying the Marvellous*, pp.166–70.

73 Letter from Marcel Duchamp to Man Ray, early Oct 1942 (Getty Research Institute Collection), reproduced in translation in Naumann and Obalk (eds), *Affect/Marcel: The Selected Correspondence of Marcel Duchamp*, p.231.

74 Breton, *Entretiens*, p.196–7.

75 Duchamp fired shots at the stone foundation wall of Kurt and Arlette Seligmann's nineteenth-century barn in Sugar Loaf, New York. He then photographed the section of damaged wall and used this photo for the cover. See Sawin, p.225.

76 Breton, *First Papers of Surrealism* (exh. cat.), New York, 14 Oct – 7 Nov 1942, np.

77 The fifteen myths were: The Age of Gold, Orpheus, Original Sin, Philosopher's Stone, The Grail, The Artificial Man, Interplanatory Communication, Messiah, The Execution of the King, The Androgyne, The Triumphant Science, The Myth of Rimbaud, The Sùrmale, The Great Transparent Ones.

78 See Sawin, p.227.

79 Max Kozloff, 'An interview with Matta', *Art Forum*, vol.4, Sept 1965, pp.24–5.

80 Alain Jouffroy, 'Matta: Ulysse passe-partout', *Matta* (exh. cat.), Paris, 1985, p.58. Of course, *The Vertigo of Eros* also entailed a homage to Duchamp's alter-ego, Rrose Sélavy ('le Vertige de Rrose') and, as William Rubin points out in *Matta* (exh. cat.), New York, 1957, p.4, the title puns on the phrase 'le vert-tige des roses' (the green stem of the roses) which relates to a passage in which Freud located all consciousness as falling between Eros and Thanatos.

81 Matta, cited in *Matta Hom'mere* (exh. cat.), Cambridge, Kettles Yard Gallery, 1978, np.

82 See Anna Balakian, introduction to André Breton, *Arcanum 17*, p.9.

83 *Arcanum 17*, p.63.

84 Anna Balakian, *André Breton: Magus of Surrealism*, 1971, p.204.

85 Breton, *Arcanum 17*, p.29.

86 Ibid., p.96.

87 Balakian, *André Breton*, p.240.

88 Breton, letter of 1 December 1940 to Victor Brauner, cited in Dourthe, *Hans Bellmer, le principe de la perversion*, 1999, p.111.

89 Interview between Webb and Ferdinand Springer, Grasse, 4 August 1984, cited in Webb and Short, p.114.

90 Max Ernst, *Ecritures*, Paris, Gallimard, 1970, p.61, cited ibid., p.113.

91 Dourthe, p.108, also makes this point. Webb and Short, p.123, relate this portrait to Man Ray's portrait of Sade too.

92 Hans Bellmer, *Petite Anatomie de l'inconscient physique ou l'anatomie de l'image*, p.44.

93 Hans Bellmer, letter to Robert Valançay, 21 Nov 1946, cited in Webb and Short, pp.185.

94 Joë Bousquet, preface to *Hans Bellmer: Dessins 1935–1946* (exh. cat.).

95 As Dourthe documents, the Mayor of Castres and 'chef de secteur politique no.8', François Houppe, issued a document on 9 September 1944 in which it was noted that Bellmer had been active in the Resistance. See Dourthe, p.116 and illustration no.169, p.115.

96 The exhibition opened on 30 October and ran until mid-November. Toulouse was liberated on 19 August. See Jean Brun, 'Désir et réalité dans l'oeuvre de Hans Bellmer', *Obliques, numéro spécial Hans Bellmer*, Paris, Borderie, 1975, p.7–12.

97 Victor Brauner, *Archives Victor Brauner* (Carnet 'Alpin'), Musée National d'Art Moderne, Centre Georges Pompidou, Paris.

98 See Semin, *Victor Brauner dans les collections du MNAM-CCI*, p.16.

99 See Fauré, p.166.

100 Brauner also visited Air Bel as Consuelo de Saint-Exupéry, a patron of his, was staying there. In *Oppède*, Paris, Gallimard, 1947, Consuelo de Saint-Exupéry documents her time in Marseilles in fictional terms, combining her memories of Brauner and Hérold in the fictional character Octave (who lost an eye as Brauner did but has the disposition of Hérold).

101 Cone, *Artists under Vichy*, p.106.

102 Alexandrian, *Jacques Hérold*, p.43.

103 As Cone documents, Zehrfuss was one of a number of young demobilized architects who gathered at Oppède in the hope of establishing an art centre there, sponsored by Jeune France. See Cone, *Artists under Vichy*, pp.95–6.

104 As far back as 1930, Hérold had done a drawing entitled 'Hommage à Sade'. In interview, Muguette Hérold described this drawing, which he did when he was only nineteen and had just arrived in Paris for the first time, having fled Romania via Vienna, but acknowledged that it was his friendship with Lely which developed his interest in Sade. The drawing has since been lost. Muguette Hérold, interview with the author, Paris, 2 October 1996.

105 René Char joined the movement on meeting Eluard in Paris in 1928 and severed his relations with the group over internal bickerings in 1935. He met Hérold at Air Bel and befriended the young Romanian but never returned to the Surrealist fold, having emerged from the war as a major Resistance officer and poet whose loyalties were firmly with Stalinism.

106 See Hérold in Butor, *Hérold*, p.18. This experience at Lacoste also heralded the start of a series of 'Sadean' collaborations between Hérold and Surrealist writer Gilbert Lely. In 1949, a vivid print of *The Eagle Reader* would be used for the frontispiece of a publication of Sade's letters, prefaced and edited by Gilbert Lely, and in 1950 he collaborated again with Lely, producing five illustrations for Sade's *La Vanille et la manille*, one of which was a variation on this same 'eagle-woman' in a state of metamorphosis. Indeed, many years later Hérold would buy his own house in Lacoste and invite Lely and others to gather there and discuss Sade among other things. See D.A.F. de Sade, *L'Aigle mademoiselle*, letters, prefaced by Gilbert Lely (the first 104 copies had this *Eagle Reader* on the cover) and D.A.F. de Sade, *La Vanille et la manille*, unedited letter to Madame de Sade (with five illustrations by Hérold).

107 Jacques Hérold, interview by Alain Jouffroy, series of four radio interviews on *France Culture*, June 1986 (Archive Muguette Hérold).

108 Cone points out that the circumstance of war led to new technical innovation, and the use of gouache by a number of artists including Hérold, Sonia Delaunay and André Masson and decalcomania gouaches by Bellmer. See Cone, *Artists under Vichy*, p.97.

109 Hérold, *Maltraité de peinture*, 1957, p.38.

110 Adolphe Acker (1913–76), signed Surrealist tracts since 1932 and was a key figure in FIARI and its mouthpiece, *Clé*. In 1941 he left Paris for Marseilles, before moving to live near Grenoble. He returned to Paris at the end of 1943. He was a regular contributor to La Main à Plume publications, signing his articles Adolphe Champ or Paul Chancel.

111 Alexandrian, *Jacques Hérold*, p.46.

112 With the German invasion of Paris most of the Réverbères group disbanded, leaving only Rius, Chabrun and Acker in Paris, who decided to form La Main à Plume.

113 Gérard de Sède came up with this phrase of Arthur Rimbaud's. See Fauré, pp.65–6, fn 2.

114 Alexandrian, *Jacques Hérold*, p.53.

115 The review was published by Lucien Caro, a key figure in the publishing of underground press during the Occupation.

116 See, for example, the theoretical manifesto of the group, drawn up by Jean-François Chabrun and published in July 1941 and in a second review launched by the group, *Géographie Nocturne*, of September 1941.

117 Fauré, p.58.

118 Paul Eluard's 'Les Vainqueurs d'hier périront' was published in *Commune*, no.57, May 1938.

119 Eluard's poem was published despite an altercation between Eluard and Adolphe Acker over an article by Acker on Gide's opinion of Henri Michaux (as expressed at a conference Gide organized in Nice on 21 May 1941). Eluard found Acker's article offensive, Acker edited his article, and so Eluard's poem was printed.

120 J.-V. Manuel, 'La Conquête du monde par l'image', *La Conquête du monde par l'image*, 1942, p.40. *La Conquête du monde par l'image* was published in June 1942, but backdated to 24 April 1942 to evade the attention of censors.

121 Note that *Poésie et vérité* was backdated to 3 April 1942 to evade attention of censors and was published as a 28-page collection of 5000

editions as well as 75 luxury editions, the most luxurious being one (no.1) on *Japon nacre*.

122 The letter was written by Jacques Bureau and his wife Reine, Noël Arnaud and his wife Cécile, Marc Patin, Charles Delaunay, Jean Remaudière and Jean-François Chabrun (alias Léo Meunier). It is reproduced in Fauré, pp.263–9.

123 Alexandrian, *Jacques Hérold*, p.53.

124 The print run was as follows: 1500 copies at 40F, 50 copies on art paper (paper couché) at 150F, 10 copies on Japanese paper at 500F and 2 copies on chiffon with original drawings by Tanguy, Breton and Péret at 2000F.

125 Alexandrian, *Jacques Hérold*, p.59.

126 Jean-François Chabrun, cited in Fauré, pp.428–9. Eight members were killed: Jean-Claude Diamant Berger, Marc Patin, Hans Schoenhoff, Tita, Jean-Pierre Mulotte, Marco Ménegoz, Robert Rius, Jean Simonpoli.

127 Alexandrian, *Jacques Hérold*, p.59.

128 Equally, it was Eluard (and Aragon) who persuaded Picasso to declare his adherence to the Communist Party in October 1944.

129 Desnos fell out with the Surrealists in 1929, opting to follow Georges Bataille's 'dissident Surrealist' Documents group; he was one of the contributors to the *A Corpse* pamphlet of January 1930 against Breton. This quote is from 'Le Paysage' (The Landscape), in *Contrée*, in Desnos, *The Voice: Selected Poems of Robert Desnos*, p.65. Desnos was arrested by the Gestapo on 22 February 1944 for acts of resistance and he died on 8 June 1945 in the newly liberated camp in Terezin, Czechoslovakia having survived several camps (Royallieu in Compiègne, Auschwitz-Birkenau, Flossenbürg near the Czech border, and Flöha). For an insightful and moving account of Desnos as Surrealist and Resistant poet and his ordeals in these camps, see Conley's critical biography *Robert Desnos, Surrealism and the Marvelous in Everyday Life*.

130 See Pablo Picasso, *Desire Caught by the Tail*.

131 The influence of Alfred Jarry on this play is indicated by the fact that after it was read Picasso brought a group back to his studio where he showed them an original manuscript by Jarry. *Desire Caught by the Tail* was first performed in 1967 when Jean-Jacques Lebel directed it at the 4th Workshop of Free Expression. Produced by Victor Herbert, the actors were Rita Renoir, Jacques Seiler, Jacques Blot, Taylor Mead, Ultra Violet, Laszlo Szabo, Katherine Moreau and Soft Machine.

132 Christian Zervos, letter dated 28 March 1945 cited in Cone, *Artists under Vichy*, pp.233–4. This letter was in response to Alfred H. Barr's Museum of Modern Art Bulletin of January 1945 entitled 'Picasso 1940–1944: A Digest with Notes' where he presented Picasso as a man who fostered the resistance from his studio.

133 Hugnet, p.407 and Thirion, p.468.

134 Nadeau, p.128.

Chapter Three Post-War Paris and 'Surrealism in 1947'

1 Review in *Combat*, Feb 1947, quoted in Sawin, p.391.

2 André Breton, *Ode à Charles Fourier*, p.103 and p.109. The *Ode* was first published in 1947 by Revue Fontaine, Paris, and republished in 1961

with an introduction by Jean Gaulmier. Breton wrote his *Ode* in exile, but Fourier was still at the forefront of his mind on his return to Paris. In a letter from Breton (in Huelgoat) to Enrico Donati (in New York) dated 24 August 1946, Breton asks Donati to buy eight volumes of Fourier for him at a bookshop, run by M. Hoog, on 56th Street as he realized on returning to France that the $100 Hoog was asking for the volumes was a fair price. Donati is asked to bring them to Paris with him, since Donati was scheduled to have an exhibition at the Galerie Drouant-David in Paris in November 1946. Getty Research Institute, Enrico Donati papers.

3 Breton, 'A Tribute to Antonin Artaud' (7 June 1946), *Free Rein*, p.78. The event was organized by Arthur Adamov and Jean Paulhan.

4 Breton, 'Speech to the Congress of Writers' (June 1935) in *Manifestoes*, p.241.

5 Breton and Ford, 'Interview with André Breton', p.1.

6 Charles de Gaulle, *Mémoires de guerre, vol.3, Le Salut (1944–1946)*, p.1, quoted in Rioux, *The Fourth Republic*, p.18.

7 Rousso, *The Vichy Syndrome*, p.10.

8 Judt, *Past Imperfect: French Intellectuals 1944–1956*, p.255.

9 The figures for the *épuration* are still disputed. See Rousso, 'L'Epuration en France, une histoire inachevée'.

10 Albert Camus, speech at La Mutualité, 15 March 1945; reprinted in Camus, *Actuelles*, vol.1, 1950; reprint Paris, 1977, p.116, quoted in Judt, p.35.

11 Brasillach's execution was carried out despite a petition signed by many intellectuals, including Mauriac, Camus and Paulhan (de Beauvoir and Sartre refused to sign it). See Assouline, *L'Epuration des intellectuels, 1944–45*, especially Annexe 3 (Petition to de Gaulle) and Annexe 4 (Brasillach's letter of thanks to the signatories of the petition, dated 5 February 1945, in which he insists that he never wished to harm his country, thanking his fellow intellectuals for their support).

12 The exhibition was held in the Musée prior to its official re-opening in 1947.

13 Utley, *Picasso, the Communist Years*, p.49. Here Utley builds on David Caute's classification of the five principles of the Communist intellectuals' utility to the Party in *Communism and the French Intellectuals 1914–1960*. See also Chapter 4 where Utley addresses *The Charnel House* at length.

14 Although, of course, the Communist Party had deemed *Guernica* to be inappropriate for the mentality of the proletariat.

15 Boris Taslitzky, *Cent onze dessins faits à Buchenwald*, Paris 1946 (reprinted 1989, with a preface by Julien Cain) cited in Sarah Wilson 'Saint-Germain-des-Prés: Anti-fascism, Occupation, and Postwar Paris', in Wilson et al., *Paris: Capital of the Arts 1900–1968* (exh. cat.), p.242.

16 Jean Bazaine, 'La Peinture bleu blanc rouge' (Tricolour painting), *Comoedia*, 30 Jan 1943, pp.1–6. For an analysis of this article and direction in post-war art see Chapter 4 '"Abstract" Art as a Veil. Tricolor Painting in Vichy France', in Cone, *French Modernisms*.

17 On the subject of landscape in inter-war art and its gendered, nostalgic nature see Golan, *Modernity and Nostalgia*, especially pp.17–21.

18 See Jean Dubuffet, 'Anticultural positions', from a lecture delivered at the Arts Club of Chicago, 20 Dec 1951, in *Jean Dubuffet* (exh. cat.).

19 Dubuffet may have been evoking Henri Bergson's ideas of 'matter and memory' as intimated by Francis Ponge in his essay 'Matière et Mémoire' for Dubuffet's exhibition *Les Murs* at the Galerie André in Paris in April 1945. See Wilson, 'Paris Postwar: In Search of the Absolute', in Morris (ed.), *Paris Post War: Art and Existentialism 1945–55* (exh. cat.), p.33.

20 Francis Ponge, 'Notes sur les otages' (Paris, 1946), cited ibid., p.27.

21 Paul Eluard, *Poèmes pour tous*, Paris, 1959, p.204, cited in trans. in Caute, *Communism and the French Intellectuals 1914–1960*, p.163.

22 Breton, *Entretiens*, pp.205.

23 Tristan Tzara, *Le Surréalisme et l'après-guerre*, lecture given in Sorbonne, Paris, on 17 March 1947, republished, Paris, Editions Nagel, 1948, 1966, p.28 (all quotes from 1966 edition).

24 See the tract against Aragon's move away from Surrealism in 'Paillasse! (Fin de "l'Affaire Aragon")', 1932, in Pierre, *Tracts, Tome I*, pp.223–8.

25 Benjamin Péret's pamphlet entitled *Le Déshonneur des poètes* (1945) was a rebuttal to *L'Honneur des poètes*, a clandestine anthology distributed during the Occupation which included the poems of Aragon, Eluard and Hugnet. Péret attacked those who had sacrificed poetry for Stalinism, accusing them of being 'advertising agents'. In many ways it continued the argument of the 1938 FIARI tract.

26 Tzara, p.77.

27 Ibid., p.78.

28 Jean-Paul Sartre, 'Qu'est-ce que la littérature?' *Les Temps modernes*, no.20, 1947; reprinted in book form with extensive footnotes, Paris, Gallimard, 1947; trans. David Caute as *What is Literature?*, p.228.

29 Ibid., p.136.

30 I am indebted to Joseph Mahon for his clarification to me of Sartrean nothingness.

31 For an extensive analysis of this subject see Plank, *Sartre and Surrealism*.

32 Sartre, p.174.

33 'Liberté est un mot vietnamien' was signed by Acker, Yves Bonnefoy, Joë Bousquet, Francis Bouvet, André Breton, Jean Brun, J.-B. Brunius, Eliane Catoni, Jean Ferry, Guy Gillequin, Jacques Halpern, Arthur Harfaux, Maurice Henry, Marcel Jean, Pierre Mabille, Jehan Mayoux, Francis Meunier, Maurice Nadeau, Henri Parisot, Henri Pastoureau, Benjamin Péret, N. and H. Seigle, Iaroslav Serpan, Yves Tanguy. See Pierre, *Tracts, Tome II*, pp.27–8 and notes pp.315–16.

34 The tract was written in June and published on 4 July 1947. See 'Rupture inaugurale, Déclaration adoptée le 21 juin 1947 par le groupe en France pour définir son attitude préjudicielle a l'égard de toute politique partisane' (21 June 1947) and notes, in Pierre, *Tracts, Tome II*, pp.30–6, and pp.316–20, respectively; trans. as 'Inaugural Rupture' in Richardson and Fijalkowski, pp.42–8. The tract was signed by Acker, Sarane Alexandrian, Maurice Baskine, Hans Bellmer, Joë Bousquet, Francis Bouvet, Victor Brauner, André Breton, Serge Bricianer, Roger Brielle, Jean Brun, Gaston Criel, Antonio Dacosta, Pierre Cuvillier, Frédéric Delanglade, Pierre Damarne, Matta

Echaurren, Marcel and Jean Ferry, Guy Gillequin, Hnery Goetz, Arthur Harfaux, Heisler, George Henein, Maurice Henry, Jacques Hérold, Marcel Jean, Nadine Kraïnik, Jerzy Kujawski, Robert Lebel, Pierre Mabille, Jehan Mayoux, Francis Meunier, Robert Michelet, Nora Mitrani, Henri Parisot, Henri Pastoureau, Guy Péchenard, Candido Costa Pinto, Gaston Puel, René Renne, Jean-Paul Riopelle, Stanislas Rodanski, N. and H. Seigle, Claude Tarnaud, Toyen, Isabelle and Patrick Waldberg, Ramsès Younane.

35 Ibid., p.317.

36 Breton, *Entretiens*, pp.271–2.

37 'Rupture inaugurale' led to splintering among the Surrealists too: the Revolutionary Surrealism group issued a tract against it (and the exhibition) in 'La Cause est entendue' (1 July 1947), criticizing Breton and his allies for supposedly abandoning dialectical materialism. It also attracted the attention of Anarchists – the Federation Anarchiste and their weekly *Libertaire*, which would celebrate Surrealism and the 1947 exhibition and in 1951 launched a weekly Surrealist column 'Billets Surréalistes'. Until January 1953 this was where the Surrealists curried even more favour among a growing militant body as they criticized Socialist Realist art, religious, political and philosophical dogma. On the subject of Surrealists and the FA, see Pierre, *Surréalisme et anarchie*, and Paligot, *Parcours politique des surréalistes 1919–1969*, pp.160–76.

38 Jacques Prévert cited in Jean, p.343.

39 Adrian Maeght, interview with the author, Saint-Paul, 4 August 2000. The Galerie Maeght opened in Paris in 1945 with an exhibition of Henri Matisse and from then until the Surrealist exhibition in 1947 showed the art of Bonnard, Braque, Léger, Picasso, Rouault and others. For a history of the Maeghts and the artists they represented see *L'Univers d'Aimé et Marguerite Maeght* (exh. cat.), Saint-Paul, Fondation Maeght, 1982.

40 Letter, Aimé Maeght (Paris) to Enrico Donati (New York), 3 Feb 1947; Getty Research Institute, Donati papers.

41 André Breton, 'Projet Initial' (extract from 'Lettre d'invitation aux participants'), *Le Surréalisme en 1947: Exposition internationale du surréalisme* (exh. cat.), Galerie Maeght, Paris, 1947, p.135–8.

42 Kurt Seligmann, 'Magic and the Arts', *View*, no.7, Fall 1946, pp.15–17.

43 Chadwick, *Myth in Surrealist Painting*, pp.14–15.

44 Freud, 'The Uncanny', Seigle, p.363 and p.372.

45 René Guénon, *Aperçus sur l'initiation*, p.34, cited in Mitchell, '"Secrets de l'art magique surréaliste": Magic and the Myth of the Artist-Magician in Surrealist Aesthetic Theory and Practice', p.339. See also Bataché, *Surréalisme et tradition: La Pensée d'André Breton jugée delon l'oeuvre de René Guénon*.

46 Breton, 'Before the Curtain', p.85.

47 *Arcanum 17*, p.61.

48 Kiesler, 'Brief note on Designing The Gallery', two-page typescript, 1942, reproduced in *Friedrich Kiesler: Art of this Century* (exh. cat.), p.34.

49 Jean, p.342. Jean adds that he was a great asset given the lack of 'material means' in post-war Paris but also that the man lost three fingers to a circular saw on the exhibition site.

50 Frederick J. Kiesler, 'Art and Architecture, Notes on the Spiral-Theme in Recent Architecture' (1946), in Kiesler, *Selected Writings*, p.47.

51 Ibid., pp.49–50. Of course Kiesler's ideas must also be recognized as part of a new shift away from modernism's strict geometry and towards natural, biomorphic and spiral forms, as witnessed in Frank Lloyd Wright's writings and architectural designs at this time too. It was in 1943 that Wright was commissioned to produce a new Guggenheim museum for modern art and when he began his plans for a building that would reflect the plasticity of organic forms. His Guggenheim Museum, an inverted ziggurat, was not only spiral in form, it also insisted that architecture and art flow within a continuous space just as Kiesler did. Kiesler specifically refers to, and quotes from, Wright in this essay, p.52.

52 Alexandrian, *Surrealist Art*, p.190.

53 Charles Estienne, 'Surréalisme 1947, De l'expérience poétique à la magie noire et blanche', *Combat*, 8 July 1942, p.2.

54 See Frederick J. Kiesler, 'L'architecture magique de la salle de superstitions', *Le Surréalisme en 1947* (exh. cat.), p.131.

55 Alexandrian, *Surrealist Art*, p.190.

56 Jean Arp, 'L'Oeuf de Kiesler et la "Salle des Superstitions"', *Cahiers d'art*, no.22, August 1947, p.281.

57 Yehuda Safran, 'In the Shadow of Bucephalus', in Safran (ed.), *Frederick Kiesler 1890–1965*, p.18.

58 Frederick Kiesler, 'Endless House – Space House', *VVV*, no.4, Feb 1944, pp.160–1.

59 Ibid.

60 Alexandrian, *Surrealist Art*, p.190.

61 See Clifford, note 29, p.15. Kiesler was conscious of the importance of the primitive. In his 1942 notes on his conception of Guggenheim's Art of this Century gallery, Kiesler specifically referred to the primitive view of the world. See 'Note brève sur la conception de la Galerie Art of This Century, de Peggy Guggenheim' (1942), reproduced in *Frederick Kiesler, Artiste-architecture* (exh. cat.), p.114.

62 Breton, *Surrealism and Painting*, p.1. First pub. as *Le Surréalisme et la peinture*, Gallimard, Paris, 1965.

63 This was not Duchamp's first recourse to this trick: at the 1942 'First Papers of Surrealism' exhibition in New York, reproductions of Duchamp's works, from his *Valise*, could be looked at only through a peephole in the wall.

64 Duchamp authorized Kiesler to construct this. See *Frederick Kiesler, Artiste-architecture* (exh. cat.), p.125.

65 Breton, *Mad Love*, p.471. Breton wanted to include Giacometti's *Invisible Object* in the room of altars in the exhibition but Giacometti refused to lend it. He would lend it for the 1959 exhibition though, as we shall see in the next chapter.

66 Matta, interview June 1984, cited in *Matta: The Logic of Hallucination* (exh. cat.).

67 Nicolas Calas, 'Magic Icons', *Horizon*, vol.14, no.83, Nov 1946, p.309.

68 Ibid. Ernst's satire of the fig leaf could also be compared to Francis Picabia's 1922 painting *The Fig Leaf* and its attack on Old Masters and the French academic tradition. David Hopkins has read the roses in this painting as a reference to Rosicrucianism in *Marcel*

Duchamp and Max Ernst: the Bride Shared, p.178.
69 Pierre Guerre, 'L'Exposition internationale du surréalisme', *Cahiers du sud*, no.284, second semester 1947, pp.677–81.
70 Alexandrian, *Surrealist Art*, p.191.
71 Jean, p.343.
72 Jacques Hérold, interview by Alain Jouffroy, June 1986: recording of a series of four radio interviews on *France Culture*, June 1986. Muguette Hérold archive.
73 Jacques Hérold, *Le Surréalisme en 1947* (exh. cat.), p.85. Hérold wrote this in 1943 and then repeated it as explanation for his 'L'Oeuf obéissant, L'Oeuf désobéisant' in the 1947 exh. cat. Hérold was introduced to the movement in the mid-1930s by fellow-Romanian Tristan Tzara.
74 Hérold, interview by Michel Butor, in Butor, *Hérold*, pp.18–19.
75 See Alexandrian, *Jacques Hérold*, p.82.
76 Breton, 'Prolegomena to a Third Surrealist Manifesto or Not', *Manifestoes*, p.293.
77 Breton, 'Projet Initial', pp.136–7.
78 See Comte de Lautréamont, *Les Chants de Maldoror*, pp.173–81 and pp.203–7.
79 This was a reference to Sir Walter Scott's romantic novel *Ivanhoe* where battles and sacrifices are made at the town of Ashby.
80 See Breton on Rimbaud and 'La Chasse Spirituelle' in Breton, *Flagrant délit*.
81 See Verena Kuni's notes on the work, in Semin, pp.38–9.
82 Brauner cited ibid., p.38.
83 Ibid., p.39.
84 *Three Standard Stoppages* was based on an experiment which consisted of dropping a one metre-long piece of string from the height of one metre onto a strip of painted canvas. This operation was repeated three times, creating three 'standard stoppages'. Duchamp refered to this process in his writings as 'canned chance'. The string, in the shape it assumed, was then secured to the canvas with drops of varnish. Each of the strips of painted canvas (measuring 47¼" x 5¼") were glued to pieces of glass (49⅜" x 7³⁄₁₆"). Three wooden templates were cut following the shape of each of the lines, and the templates, along with the glass plates, were then placed inside a wooden croquet box.
85 Breton, 'Victor Brauner: Entre Chien et Loup' (14 July 1946), in *Surrealism and Painting*, p.126.
86 Ibid., p.127.
87 Jean, p.342.
88 Martins is also meant to be the inspiration behind Duchamp's last, highly erotic, sculptural installation, *Given* (*Etant Données*) of 1946–66 as he titled a pencil drawing dated 1947 'Etant donnés: Maria, la chute d'eau et le gaz d'éclairage' (Given: Maria, the Waterfall, and the Lighting Gas).
89 Breton, 'Maria' (1947), *Surrealism and Painting*, p.320.
90 André Breton, 'At Night in Haiti' (Jan 1946), trans. in Richardson and Fijalkowski (trans. and eds), *Refusal of the Shadow, Surrealism and the Caribbean*, p.213.
91 Durozoi, p.471. It should be noted here that while the Surrealists had always been loyal to the 'art of the insane', post-war Paris was becoming increasingly interested in such art: in November 1947 a Foyer de l'Art Brut was opened in the Galerie Drouin in Paris and in May 1948 Jean Dubuffet founded the Société de l'Art Brut which Breton joined.
92 Adrian Maeght, interview with the author, Saint-Paul, 4 August 2000.
93 Donati cited in Sawin, p.394.
94 Letter from Jacques Kober to Enrico Donati, 8 May 1947, Getty Research Institute, Donati papers. Kober was associated with La Main à Plume during the war.
95 Breton, 'Prolegomena to a Third Surrealist Manifesto or Not', *Manifestoes*, p.291.
96 Breton, 'Devant le rideau', *Le Surréalisme en 1947* (exh. cat.), pp.13–19; trans. as 'Before the Curtain' in *Free Rein*, pp.80–7.
97 Benjamin Péret, 'Le Sel répandu', *Le Surréalisme en 1947* (exh. cat.), pp.21–4.
98 Ibid.
99 Jules Monnerot, 'Contre la peur d'imaginer', and Arpad Mezei's 'Liberté du Langage', *Le Surréalisme en 1947* (exh. cat.), pp.52–5 and pp.59–61 respectively.
100 Georges Bataille, 'L'absence de Mythe', *Le Surréalisme en 1947* (exh. cat.), in Bataille, *The Absence of Myth*, p.48.
101 Henri Pastoureau, 'Pour une offensive de grand style contre la civilisation chrétienne', *Le Surrealisme en 1947* (exh. cat.), p.83.
102 Henri Lefebvre, *Critique de la vie quotidienne*, vol.I, Paris, Editions Grasset, 1947; rev. ed. Paris, L'Arche, 1958; trans. John Moore as *The Critique of Everyday Life*, London, Verso, 1991; p.211 (all quotes from 1991 edition).
103 Ibid., pp.117–18.
104 Letter from David Hare to Enrico Donati, August 14 1947, Getty Research Institute, Donati papers. The orthography of Hare's letter has not been corrected.
105 Gaëton Picon, 'Le Surréalisme et l'espoir', *Gazette des lettres*, 28 June 1947, p.9.
106 Jean-José Marchand, 'Le Surréalisme de langue française', *Gazette des lettres*, 28 June 1947, p.11.
107 Camille Bourniquel, 'Chroniques: Magie, Surréalisme et Liberté', *Esprit*, Nov 1947, pp.775–6.
108 Ibid., p.778.
109 Albert Palle, 'L'exposition international Surréaliste', *Le Figaro*, 9 July 1947, quoted in Sawin, p.398. Sawin expressed similar distaste, stating that the occult and rain could not hold the public's attention, since it could only associate rain, for example, with 'the millions herded to their death in "the showers"', p.401.
110 Marie Louise Barron, 'Surréalisme en 1947, En retard d'une guerre comme l'État-Major', *Les Lettres françaises*, 18 July 1947, p.2.
111 See Xavier Canone, 'Brouillon Cobra', preface to no.1 of *Le Surréalisme révolutionnaire*, March–April 1948, and a facsimile of no.1, in *Le Surréalisme révolutionnaire*, Brussels, Didier Devillez Éditeur, 1999, pp.3–13. Their voice of dissent continued in the *Bulletin international du surréalisme-révolutionnaire*, a bi-monhtly review launched in 1948 with Noël Arnaud, Asger Jorn, Zdenek Lorenc and Dotremont as editorial board.
112 Letter from Jacques Hérold to Frederick Kiesler, 17 May 1948. Getty Research Institute, Kiesler papers.
113 l Jean, p.344.
114 Alexandrian, *Surrealist Art*, p.194.
115 Sawin, p.401.
116 Marcel Jean, Paris, letter to Frederick Kiesler, New York, 11 November 1947; and 17 January 1948 respectively. Getty Research Institute, Kiesler papers.
117 Breton, 'Prolegomena to a Third Surrealist Manifesto or Not', *Manifestoes*, p.292.
118 Breton, 'Second Arche', 1947, reproduced in trans. in *Free Rein*, p.99.
119 Breton, 'Comète Surréaliste', 1947, reproduced in trans. in *Free Rein*, pp.88–97.
120 Ibid., p.96.
121 Ibid., p.97.
122 In 1959 Breton would decide that the 1959 'International Surrealist Exhibition' at the Galerie Cordier was the eighth international show. He then chose seven past shows (of many more) to precede it, listing the official International shows from 1935, which would continue until the eleventh in 1965. See Gilles Rioux, 'À propos des Expositions internationales du Surréalisme, un document de 1947 et quelques considérations', *Gazette des Beaux-Arts*, no.1311, vol.120, April 1978, pp.163–71.

Chapter Four **Embattled Eros**

1 André Breton, 'Avis aux Exposants/Aux Visiteurs', *Exposition internationale du surréalisme* [EROS] (exh. cat.), Paris, Galerie Daniel Cordier, 1959, p.7. Hereafter referred to as EROS.
2 See John P. Loughlin, 'The Algerian war and the One and Indivisable French Republic', in Hargreaves and Heffernan (eds), *French and Algerian Identities from Colonial Times to the Present*, pp.149–60.
3 See Rioux, p.281.
4 Breton, 'Pour la défense de la liberté', *Le Surréalisme, même*, no.1, 1956, pp.4–5. This was a copy of Breton's speech delivered at the Salle des Horticulteurs on 20 April 1956. Breton edited *Le Surréalisme, même*, Schuster was assistant editor.
5 Durozoi, p.554.
6 'Message des Surréalistes aux intellectuels polonais', Paris, 4 June 1959. Signed by Anne and Jean-Louis Bédouin, Robert Benayoun, Vincent Bounoure, André Breton, Adrien Dax, Yves Elléouët, Elie-Charles Flamand, P. A. Gette, Roger van Hecke, Alain Joubert, Jean-Jacques Lebel, Gérard Legrand, Jehan Mayoux, Nora Mitrani, Benjamin Péret, José Pierre, Jean Schuster, Jean-Claude Silbermann; reproduced in Pierre, *Tracts, Tome II*, p.181. The tract was also published in *Front unique*, no.2, Autumn 1960, with the addition of three names: Edouard Jaguer, Jacques Lacomblez and Tristan Sauvage.
7 See 'Déclaration sur le droit à l'insoumission dans la guerre d'Algérie', reproduced in Pierre, *Tracts, Tome II*, pp.203–8 and commentary, pp.393–4. Non-French Surrealists were advised not to sign, as they could be deported.
8 Simone de Beauvoir, *La Force des Choses*, Paris, Gallimard, 1963; trans. Richard Howard, *Force of Circumstance*, Harmondsworth, Penguin, 1968, p.560.
9 See *Les Temps modernes*, nos 173–174, September 1960, pp.194 and 195; the reason for this blank spread was given on p.193.
10 Breton, letter 22 September 1960, quoted in Polizzotti, p.602.
11 Martin Harrison, 'Government and Press in France during the Algerian War', *The American*

Political Science Review, no.2, vol.LVIII, June 1964, pp.273–85.

12 Ibid., fn 1, p.273.

13 Ibid., p.275.

14 Jean-Paul Sartre, 'La Victoire', preface to Alleg, *La Question*, Paris, Editions de Minuit, 1958 and 1961; trans. John Calder as 'Victory' in *The Question*, p.12.

15 Ibid.

16 De Beauvoir, *Force of Circumstance*, p.397.

17 Ibid., p.514. See Simone de Beauvoir 'Pour Djamila Boupacha' *Le Monde*, 2 June 1960 p.6, reprinted with Gisèle Halimi, Paris, Gallimard, 1962.

18 Ibid., p.517.

19 The collective painting was painted in 1960, after it was first exhibited at the *Anti-Procès* 3 in Milan in 1961 it was seized by the Italian police and impounded until 1988. See Enrico Baj et al., *Grand Tableau antifasciste collectif*.

20 Said, *Orientalism, Western Conceptions of the Orient*, p.187.

21 Nochlin, *The Politics of Vision*, p.41.

22 See Ross, *Fast Cars, Clean Bodies*, p.125, referencing Stora, *La gangrène et l'oubli: La mémoire de la guerre d'Algérie*, p.18.

23 De Gaulle, *Mémoires de Guerre*, vol.3; Jackson, *Charles de Gaulle*.

24 De Gaulle quoted in Rioux, p.305.

25 'Une enquête sur le strip-tease', *Le Surréalisme même*, no.4, Printemps 1958, pp.56–64; questions posed trans. as 'An Inquiry into Striptease (1958–59)', Appendix IV, in Pierre (ed.), *Investigating Sex: Surrealist Discussions 1928–1932*, p.163.

26 Barthes, *Mythologies*, p.84.

27 Ibid.

28 Dean, *The Self and its Pleasures*, p.162.

29 Indeed, it was on seeing photographs of the art of Mimi Parent and Jean Benoît (presented to him by his daughter Aube who had friends in common with the couple) that Breton sent Parent and Benoît a telegraph asking if he could meet them. When he arrived at their apartment he invited them to join the group and to contribute to the exhibition.

30 Cordier, foreword to *Huit ans d'agitation* (exh. cat.). See also Tarenne's history of the gallery in *Donations Daniel Cordier*.

31 Daniel Cordier in interview in 'Daniel Cordier, les arts et les armes', *Le Monde*, Sunday 25 – Monday 26 July 2004, p.19. Cordier would close his gallery in Paris in 1964 and open a new one in New York on 970 Madison Avenue.

32 Breton (ed.), 'Avis aux Exposants/Aux Visiteurs', EROS, p.5.

33 Ibid.

34 The first aspect was Batailléan, Breton directly citing Georges Bataille's book *L'Erotisme* (1957); the latter might be described as more Sadean in its interest in the relationship between Eros and Thanatos or as a reminder to the Batailléan school of thought that desire and joy were not to be overlooked when assessing the darker aspects of man's erotic drive.

35 Matta was expelled on 25 October 1948 for having an affair with Gorky's wife (Gorky would commit suicide as a result of the affair), and Brauner was expelled on 8 November 1948 for refusing to disown Matta. See *Néon*, no.4, Nov 1948, for details.

36 Benoît, interview with the author, Paris, 22 September 1996.

37 Sade's testament was written at Charenton-Saint-Maurice, 30 January 1806.

38 Lever, *Marquis de Sade: A Biography*, p.565.

39 Gilles Ehrmann would photograph Benoît in the costume during and after the performance. Gilles Ehrmann, interview with the author, Paris, 4 May 1996. Some of these photographs were reproduced in the EROS catalogue, and many were exhibited at the Librairie Oterelo in Paris in October 1996.

40 See Artaud's *Theatre and its Double*. On Dada performance see Chapter 3 of Goldberg, *Performance Art from Futurism to the Present*; on the Happening see Michael Kirby, 'Happenings: An Introduction', in Sandford (ed.), *Happenings and Other Acts*, pp.1–28.

41 See Roger Cardinal, 'Les Arts marginaux et l'esthétique Surréaliste', in Thompson (ed.), *L'Autre et le sacré: Surréalisme, cinéma, ethnologie*, p.66.

42 Le Brun (ed.), *Petits et Grands Théâtres du Marquis de Sade* (exh. cat.), pp.248 and 245 respectively.

43 Jean-René Major was also from Québec, he was a writer and friend of Benoît as well as of Jacques Derrida.

44 Benoît, 'Notes concernant l'exécution', EROS, p.64.

45 This was a symbolic reinstatement of the Surrealist equation of Sade with absolute love, and the words of Maurice Heine (*Avant-propos* to *120 Journées de Sodome*) were stated: 'Quoi de surprenant, dès qu'opposant le sexe à l'esprit, le romancier décide de faire abdiquer à l'homme ses énergies spirituelles pour mieux exalter en lui le je de ses fonctions matérielles?.' Benoît, 'Notes concernant l'exécution', EROS, p.66.

46 Breton praised the performance, in particular the impulsive demonstration of Matta which 'le requalifie totalement à nos [Surrealist group] yeux'. See 'Dernière heure', 4 Dec 1959, in Pierre, *Tracts, Tome II*, pp.182–3. Matta's impulsive act resulted in him being carried off to hospital where he spent the next day nursing his burns. Benoît was better prepared for the pain of his branding, having branded himself with the letter M on his buttock, on a previous date ten years earlier, in honour of Mimi Benoît; interview with the author, Paris, 22 September 1996.

47 De Beauvoir, 'Faut-il brûler Sade?', *Les Temps modernes*, Dec 1951, reproduced in *Privilèges*, Paris, Gallimard, 1955; trans. Annette Michelson as 'Must we Burn Sade?' in D.A.F. de Sade, *The 120 Days of Sodom, and Other Writings*, pp.3–64. Sade's union of the sexual with the ethical attracted de Beauvoir and led her to defend his 'human signification' for society as one based on the important realization that sexual practice was socially nurtured. Sade, she argued, posed a difficult problem which was of continued socio- historical concern. De Beauvoir depicted Sade as a historical barometer: measuring the height of individualism and alienation within society.

48 Benoît stated that Breton was particularly impressed by the primitive virility of his costume. Benoît, interview with the author, Paris, 22 September 1996. Of course it must be remembered that Breton had several Oceanic artefacts in his art collection and had written a preface to an exhibition of Oceanic art in Paris

in 1948 where he emphasized the importance of Oceanic art to Surrealism's own iconography and concept of the sacred. See Breton, 'Oceania' (1948), in *Free Rein*, pp.170–4.

49 Benoît, 'Notes concernant l'exécution', EROS, p.68.

50 Breton befriended Pierre Faucheux, a graphic and interior designer, in the post-war years. In 1955 he asked Faucheux to design the cover for a re-edition of the *Manifestes du Surréalisme* to be published by Sagittaire. In the same year that he assisted with the EROS show, Faucheux was also the architect behind the Première Biennale at the Musée d'Art Moderne de Paris. He was the architect of the Biennale up until 1967.

51 One of these images of Unica Zürn adorned the cover of *Le Surréalisme, même*, no.4, Printemps 1958. I have discussed these photographs in detail in 'Twist the Body Red: The Lifewriting of Unica Zürn', *n.paradoxa*, vol.3, Jan 1999, pp.56–65.

52 Benayoun, *Erotique du surréalisme*, p.231.

53 Radovan Ivsic, interview with the author, Paris, 19 July 2000. See also Ivsic's published account of this installation, 'When the Walls sighed in Paris', trans. Roger Cardinal, in my essay 'Staging Desire' in Mundy and Ades (eds), *Surrealism: Desire Unbound*, p.287.

54 Breton specifically requested such paintings of *femme-fatales* in a letter inviting Molinier to exhibit in the EROS show, having appreciated Molinier's cover for the Spring 1957 (no.2) edition of *Le Surréalisme, même*.

55 Later, Molinier would develop this twinning in his portrait of his two muses: Emmanuelle Arsan (author of *Emmanuelle* (1959) whom he began writing to in 1964) and Hanel Koeck (whom he met in Paris in 1967).

56 The Succubus is a demon who takes on the form of a woman and who then has sex with men in their sleep, although Breton defined the 'Succubus' in the 'Lexique succinct de l'érotisme' in EROS in more romantic terms: 'Créature féminine de tentation qui hante l'autre versant de la vie, celui qu'on aborde les yeux fermés. Bien que décrite d'ordinaire comme d'aspect répulsif, elle peut être admirablement belle'. Molinier would portray the Succubus several times during his career but Breton would purchase this first image of the Succubus for his own private collection.

57 Jean-Clarence Lambert, *L'Observateur littéraire*, 17 Dec 1959 (Mimi Parent archive).

58 '8e Exposition Internationale du Surréalisme ou Le Cabinet des Mirages érotiques', *Les Lettres nouvelles*, 16 Dec 1959, p.24 (Mimi Parent archive).

59 Ibid.

60 Freud, 'Fetishism', p.357.

61 Cross-dressing, masquerade and lesbianism had of course been explored by Claude Cahun prior to World War II. Cross-dressing, or transvestism, subverts stereotypes and the traditional polarity of desire itself. See Leperlier, *Claude Cahun: L'écart et la métamorphose*; and on transvestism see Herdt (ed.), *Third Sex, Third Gender*, p.19.

62 Many artists, male and female, have since explored the subject of gender through the cultural symbolism of hair. One might consider Jana Sterbak's *Hairwhip* (1993) and Robert Gober's *Untitled* (1991).

63 As a cultural phenomenon it subverts sexual dimorphism, it insists on transgenderism, while as a sexual phenomenon it embraces the multiple. In her examination of cross-dressing and its 'challenge to easy notions of binarity', Marjorie Garber writes of the 'third' sex: women who impersonate men and men who impersonate women – as opposed to wishing to take it to a surgical conclusion. Significantly, the third sex are dependent on the fetish for their cultural appropriation of their desired sex. Garber defines the fetish, for the transvestite, as follows: 'the fetish is a metonymic structure, but it is also a metaphor, a figure for the undecidability of castration…a figure of nostalgia for originary "wholeness" – in the mother, in the child. Thus the fetish, like the transvestite – or the transvestite like the fetish – is a sign at once of lack and its covering over…' See Garber, *Vested Interests: Cross-dressing and Cultural Anxiety*, pp.10–11 and p.121 respectively.

64 Again, one thinks of Carolee Scheemann's performances, such as her *Meat Joy*, performed at Jean-Jacques Lebel's *Festival of Free Expression*, 25–30 May 1964 at the American Center in Paris.

65 Mikhail Bakhtin, 'Rabelais and His World' (1965), trans. H. Iswolsky, in *The Bakhtin Reader*, p.228.

66 Ibid., p.229.

67 See Belton, p.70. Oppenheim was concerned that 'the original intention was misunderstood. Instead of a simple Spring festival, it was yet another woman taken as a source of male pleasure.'

68 Mimi Parent, interview with the author, Paris, 18 July 2000. Duchamp has frequently been credited with the idea for the *Boîte alerte* but he only added the label. Parent presented the idea in a letter to Breton and he welcomed it, replying 'En ce qui concernes la boîte verte dont Mimi au eu la si heureuse idée et établi la maquette, je suppose qu'aucun obstacle n'a surgi au sujet de sa réalisation'. Letter Breton to Mimi Parent and Jean Benoît, dated 4 Aug 1959, Mimi Parent archive.

69 José Pierre, interview with the author, Paris, 26 October 1996.

70 'Lexique succinct de l'érotisme', EROS, p.126.

71 Ibid., p.134. Obscenity was defined as 'L'obscenité existe seulement dans les cerveaux de ceux qui la découvrent et qui en accusent les autres'. This was a quote from an 'anonymous pastor of the nineteenth century', as cited in Theodore Schröder's *A Challenge to Sex Censors*, New York, privately printed, 1938.

72 Ibid., p.137.

73 Said, pp.54–5 and pp.219–20.

74 Morton, *Hybrid Modernities: Architecture and Representation at the 1931 Colonial Exposition, Paris*, pp.47–8.

75 See 'Ne Visitz pas l'Exposition Coloniale' (May 1931) and 'Premier Bilan de l'Exposition Coloniale' (3 July 1931) in Pierre, *Tracts, Tome I*, pp.194–5 and pp.198–200, respectively.

76 Arsan, *Emmanuelle* (Emmanuelle Arsan admitted to its authorship in 1968).

77 Claude Nicolas Ledoux's plan for an ideal town of Chaux included the 'Oïkéma' or Temple of Love, where sexual instruction was to be taught, and whose plan resembled an erect phallus. This town was Ledoux's last project,

an allegorical city for an ideal society, designed from c.1780 and published 1804.

78 Doumayrou, EROS, p.93.

79 Ibid., p.94.

80 Bedouin, '1+1 = 1', EROS, p.95.

81 The reviews of the EROS exhibition were closely monitored by the Surrealists, who documented them and divided them into six 'schools' of thought: La Lumpenkritik; Trop Cher, Trop de Jeunes Gens; La Foire Surréaliste; Des Bourgeois et des Snobs; Pauvre France! and Un Mort pas comme les autres. These were presented in an article entitled 'Des Biscuits pour la route'; signed by 'Le mouvement Surréaliste' in *Bief, jonction surréaliste* in February 1960.

82 Jean-Jacques Lévêque, review of EROS exhibition, 1 January 1960, p.188.

83 Yvonne Hagen, 'Surrealists' "Eroticism"', *New York Herald Tribune*, Dec 1959, np.

84 This was not a new choice of comparison for it had appeared in reviews during the years 1938–59: 'Cela tenait du Musée Grévin, du Musée Dupuytren et de la boîte de nuit' (*Liberté*, 17 January 1938); 'La mise en scène de la salle des superstitions fait penser invinciblement (!) au Musée Grévin' (*Carrefour*, 16 July 1947); 'Une sorte de Musée Grévin animé' (M.C.L., *Le Monde*, 1959) and 'C'est le décor funèbre et saturnin du Musée Dupuytren et du Musée Grévin' (W. George, *Combat*, 1 February 1960). All quoted in 'Des Biscuits pour la route', reproduced in Pierre, *Tracts, Tome II*, pp.188–9.

85 Ibid., p.186.

86 Jean Bardiot, *Finance*, 31 Dec 1959, quoted ibid., p.262.

87 Guy Dornand, *Libération*, 17 Dec 1959; quoted ibid., p.186.

88 Jean Revol, *La Nouvelle Revue française*, 1 February 1960; quoted ibid., p.190.

89 See Garçon (ed.) *L'Affaire Sade*. Georges Bataille, André Breton, Jean Cocteau and Jean Paulhan gave testimonies in defence of Pauvert.

90 'Des Biscuits pour la route', in Pierre, *Tracts, Tome II*, p.190.

Chapter Five **Absolute Deviation**

1 Audoin, *Les Surréalistes*, p.147, cited in trans. in Durozoi, p.629.

2 *Médium, Informations surréalistes* was published as a newsletter 1952–3 and then as a review *Médium, Communication surréaliste* 1953–5.

3 'L'Exemple de Cuba et la Révolution, Message des Surréalistes aux écrivains et artistes cubains', dated Summer 1964, printed in *La Brèche, action surréaliste*, no.7, Dec 1964 and reproduced in *Tracts, Tome II*, p.232; trans. as 'The Example of Cuba and the Revolution: A Message from the Surrealists to Cuban Writers and Artists' in Richardson and Fijalkowski, p.127. Richardson and Fijalkowski note that while the Surrealists supported the Cuban Revolution, and many members of the French group attended the Cultural Congress in Havana in 1967, they were disillusioned by the Cuban government's refusal to condemn the Soviet invasion of Czechoslovakia in 1968.

4 Ibid., p.128. Block capitals in original.

5 Henri Lefebvre, *Critique de la vie quotidienne II, Fondements d'une sociologie de la quotidienneté*, Paris, L'Arche, 1961; trans. John

Moore, preface by Michel Trebitsch, as *Critique of Everyday Life*, vol.II, London, Verso, 2002. The third volume was published twenty years later: *Critique de la vie quotidienne, III. De la modernité au modernisme (Pour une métaphilosophie du quotidien)* Paris, L'Arche, 1981.

6 Bataille, *Les Larmes d'Eros*.

7 'Cent Morceaux' was a Chinese torture ritual wherein the criminal was doped with opium (to extend his capacity for torture) and then mutilated. Bataille first saw this method of torture in a photograph reproduced in Georges Dumas's *Traité de psychologie* of 1923. He acquired his own copy of the photograph in 1928 from his psychoanalyst Dr Borel, which he printed in *Documents*.

8 Herbert Marcuse, *Eros et civilisation: contribution à Freud*, Paris, Editions de Minuit, 1963.

9 Herbert Marcuse, *Eros and civilization: a philosophical inquiry into Freud* (1955), London, Routledge, 1998. All quotes from this edition.

10 Ibid., p.155.

11 See *One Dimensional Man: Studies in the Ideology of Advanced Industrial Society*, Boston, Beacon Press, 1964, trans. as *L'Homme unidimensionnel: essai sur l'idéologie de la société industrielle avancée*, Paris, Editions de Minuit, 1968.

12 Joubert, *Le Mouvement des surréalistes, ou, Le fin mot de l'histoire*, p.296. Jean Schuster also refers to Marcuse's *Eros and Civilization* in 'A l'ordre de la nuit. Au désordre du jour', Archibras, no.1, April 1967, p.6 and p.9.

13 Marcuse, *Eros and Civilization*, p.217.

14 Patrick Waldberg, 'Le Surréalisme, Sources – Histoire – Affinités', *Le Surréalisme* (exh. cat.), np.

15 André Breton, statement read on French radio on 17 April 1964 and reprinted on 22 April in the review *Arts* and later in a Surrealist tract entitled 'Cramponnez-vous à la Table'. Reproduced in trans. as 'Surrealism Continues' in Breton, *What is Surrealism?*, p.412. Breton was particularly irked that Balthus was portrayed as a Surrealist and Baskine too (Baskine was only a 'Sunday Surrealist' according to Breton).

16 'Tranchons-en', emphasis in original, signed by Pierre Alechinsky, Philippe Audoin, Jean-Louis Bédouin, Robert Benayoun, Jean Benoît, Raymond Borde, Vincent Bounoure, André Breton, Guy Cabanel, Jorge Camacho, Augustín Cárdenas, Adrien Dax, Hervé Delabarre, Gabriel Der Kervorkian, Nicole Espagnol, Calude Féraud, J.-P. Guillon, Marianne Ivsic, Radovan Ivsic, Charles Jameux, Alain Joubert, Robert Lagarde, Annie Le Brun, Gérard Legrand, Joyce Mansour, Jehan Mayoux, Mimi Parent, Nicole Pierre, José Pierre, Georges Sebbag, Jean Schuster, Jean-Claude Silbermann, Jean Terrosian, Toyen, Michel Zimbacca. Dated Paris, Dec 1965, trans. in Richardson and Fijalkowski as 'Let's Get to the Point', p.55. The title, 'Tranchons-en' referred to the phrase in the First Manifesto of 1924, 'Tranchons-en: Le Meveilleux est toujours beau, n'importe quel merveilleux est beau, il n'y a même que le merveilleux qui soit beau'. See Pierre, *Tracts, Tome II*, p.412.

17 Audoin, *Les Surréalistes*, p.152, cited in trans. in Polizzotti, p.616.

18 Ernst, *La Femme 100 têtes*. Phonetically this title can allude to a woman who is 'headless' (sans tête) or 'stubborn' (s'entête).

19 See 'La Femme selon l'optique Surréaliste: un projet d'exposition avorté' in *La Femme et le Surréalisme*, pp.465–81.

20 José Pierre, interview with the author, Paris, 10 October 1996.

21 See Introduction to Beecher and Bienvenu (eds and trans.), *The Utopian Vision of Charles Fourier, Selected Texts on Work, Love, and Passionate Attraction*, pp.1–75.

22 Fourier, *Grand traité* (1822) in *Fourier, Oeuvres Complètes*, vol.I, p.279.

23 Breton, 'Générique', *L'Ecart absolu* (exh. cat.), Galerie de l'Oeil, 1965, np. Hereafter *L'Ecart absolu*.

24 See Beecher and Bienvenu, p.23.

25 Breton, 'As in a Wood', published in *L'Age du cinéma*, nos 4–5, Aug–Nov 1951, pp.26–30, reproduced in trans. in Hammond, *The Shadow and its Shadow: Surrealist Writings on the Cinema*, p.72 and p.76 respectively.

26 Barthes, introduction to *Sade, Fourier, Loyola*, pp.3–5.

27 See Jonathan Beecher 'L'Archibras de Fourier', and Charles Fourier 'L'Archibras', *La Brèche, action surréaliste*, no.7, Dec 1964, pp.66–8 and pp.69–71 respectively. For a very thorough analysis of Surrealism and Fourier see also Donald LaCoss's essay 'Attacks of the Fantastic', in Spiteri and LaCoss, pp.267–99.

28 While citing Charles Fourier's *La Fausse Industrie* (1835–6), he also quoted and footnoted other texts, including Kostas Axelos' *Vers la Pensée planétaire* (1964), Octavio Paz's *L'Arc et la lyre* (1965), Alphonse Toussenel's *Ornithologie passionnelle* (1853–5), and Dr W. Mogenthaler, *Adolf Wölfli* (1964). See Breton, 'Générique', *L'Ecart absolu*.

29 J. F. Revel, 'Jesus Bond contre Docteur Yes', *L'Ecart absolu*, np.

30 Philippe Audoin, 'L'Air de fête', *L'Ecart absolu*, np.

31 The explanations of Alain Joubert, Robert Benayoun, Jean Schuster, Georges Sebbag, Raymond Brode, Philippe Audoin, José Pierre, Robert Lagarde and Radovan Ivsic make up the 'Désordinateur' section of *L'Ecart absolu*, which is unpaginated.

32 A law was passed in 1965 giving equal property rights to husband and wife, and allowing wives to control their own property, open their own bank accounts and organize their own domestic budgets, without needing the permission and signature of their husbands. See Laubier (ed.), *The Condition of Women in France, 1945 to the Present*, p.49.

33 Joyce Mansour, 'L'Ecart absolu', *L'Archibras*, no.1, April 1967, p.60.

34 Jean Benoît, 'Le bouledogue de Maldoror', in *Jean Benoît* (exh. cat.), p.44.

35 Interview with Mimi Parent, 18 July 2000. In a further conversation in July 2004 Parent stated that this annexe-room was locked for most of the duration of the exhibition as Bernier was not prepared to pay someone to staff it, so unfortunately many people did not get to see the art on exhibit there.

36 The gun used in this object was from the Armée des Deux Siciles according to the catalogue. It is also worth noting that the biomorphic form of the armchair is quite reminiscent of Matta's design for furniture from his 1938 article 'Mathématique sensible – Architecture du temps' discussed in Chapter 1.

37 According to Pierre, *Tracts, Tome II*, p.415, 'Bellmer et Masson n'étaient pas représentés ni, il va sans dire, Labisse ou Leonor Fini'. In an interview with the author, 10 October 1996, Pierre stated that, most probably, Bellmer was too ill to attend at the time, Masson had distanced himself, and Labisse and Fini were no longer deemed 'true' Surrealists.

38 De Beauvoir, *Force of Circumstance*, p.94.

39 *Jean Benoît*, p.14.

40 This angel and devil couple was most likely inspired by a South American reliquary, particularly for the Day of the Dead, of which Benoît was familiar from his travels.

41 Letter from Jean Benoît to Gilbert Lely, Tuesday 14 Dec 1965, correspondance Gilbert Lely, Bibl. Jacques Doucet. In this letter Benoît also thanked him for sending him a copy of *La Vie du Marquis de Sade* (Lely's re-edition published by Jean-Jacques Pauvert in 1965).

42 After the opening night his costume was displayed on a mannequin in the gallery.

43 Mansour, p.49.

44 It must not be forgotten that the French only belatedly gave women the right to vote – in 1944.

45 De Gaulle and the Catholic Church were against the use of contraception, but in July 1967 the bill was passed in the Assemblée Nationale. See Laubier (ed.), *The Condition of Women in France*, p.49.

46 De Beauvoir, preface to Weill-Hallé's book *La Grande Peur d'aimer*, quoted in Jean-Marie Brohm, 'La Lutte contre la répression sexuelle', *Partisans*, Oct–Nov 1966, p.45.

47 This article in *Partisans* insisted that social revolution began in the home. Beginning with French materialists (referring to Sade as one who appreciated the need for female sexual pleasure), and referring to the work of Marxist-psychoanalyst Wilhelm Reich, it ended in a list of revolutionary criteria (contraception, abortion and concerted critiques of maternal ideologies). Ibid, p.46.

48 See Laubier, chapters 3 and 4.

49 De Beauvoir, *Les Belles Images*, p.147.

50 Ibid., p.37.

51 Pierre, *Tracts, Tome II*, p.430.

52 See notes on 'A la Presse' in ibid., pp.413–15.

53 Paul Waldo Schwartz, 'Breton & Allies with New Protest', *The New York Times International Edition*, 14 Dec 1965.

54 Frank Elgar 'Nouvelle vague surréaliste', *Carrefour*, Mercredi 22 Dec 1965, p.9.

55 *L'Arche*, no.108, February 1966, p.57.

56 Marc Albert-Levin, 'Le Surréalisme à l'Oeil', *Les Lettres françaises*, 9–15 Dec 1965, p.32.

57 C.C., *New York Herald Tribune*, Paris, 14 Dec 1965, p.5.

58 Otto Hahn, 'Le Surréalisme, à l'heure du musée ou de la jeunesse?', *Arts*, 1–7 Dec 1965, p.20 and p.29.

59 Otto Hahn, 'Le Surréalisme face à la machine à laver', *L'Express*, 13–19 Dec 1965, p.81.

60 Ibid.

61 François Pluchart, 'Le Surréalisme a l'assaut de la société', *Combat*, 13 Dec 1965, p.9.

62 André Ferrier, 'Des pièges à quoi?', *Le Nouvel Observateur*, 12 Jan 1966, p.55.

63 Jean Paulhan, 'Héros du monde occidental', *La Nouvelle Revue française: André Breton, 1896–1966: Hommages, témoignages, l'œuvre*, p.11.

64 Mustapha Khayati, 'De la misère en milieu étudiant, considérée sous ses aspects économiques, politique, psychologique, sexuel et notamment intellectuel et de quelques moyens pour y remédier' (1966), entailed a synopsis of the SI agenda and aesthetic, and demanded the liquidation of all student organizations, including the UNEF, so that energy could be focused on workers' councils. See Feuerstein, *Printemps de révolte à Strasbourg*, and the *SI* journal, no.11, Oct 1967, pp.23–31.

65 See Debord, *La Société du spectacle: La Théorie situationniste* and Vaneigem, *Traité de savoir-vivre à l'usage des jeunes générations*.

66 Gombin, *Origins of Modern Leftism*, p.75.

67 Debord, 'Hurlements en faveur de Sade' (1952), *Les Lèvres Nues*, no.7, Dec 1955, pp.18–23.

68 Mustapha Khayati, 'Captive Words: Preface to a Situationist Dictionary', *Internationale Situationniste*, no.10, 1966, trans. in Knabb, *Situationist International Anthology*, p.171.

69 Guy Debord, 'Theory of the Dérive' (1956), *Internationale Situationniste*, no.2, Dec 1958, reprod in trans. in Knabb, p.51.

70 Ibid., p.53.

71 Guy Debord, 'Report on the Construction of Situations and on the International Situationist Tendency's Conditions of Organization and Action' (excerpts), June 1957, in Knabb, p.24.

72 See Chapter 3 of Sadler, *The Situationist City*, for discussion on Constant's *New Babylon* and p.114 for the visual comparison between Constant and Matta.

73 'The Sound and the Fury', *Internationale Situationiste*, no.1, June 1958, trans. in Knabb, p.42.

74 Wollen, 'The Situationist International: on the passage of a few people through a rather brief period of time', in *Raiding the Icebox*, pp.120–1.

75 The term 'Happening' was often used in Jazz circles in New York in the 1950s, but did not become current in art circles until 1959 when Allan Kaprow entitled one of his public works '18 Happenings in Sixteen Parts'. Others were effectively producing Happenings – such as Claes Oldenburg and his 'Ray Gun Theater' or Ken Dewey and his 'Action Theatre' – but were wary of an indiscriminate generic labelling. The structure of each performance was generally loosely compartmentalized, as opposed to informative and narratological, and evolved, often non-verbally, through chance and disjunction. See introduction by Kirby in Sandford, *Happenings and Other Acts*, pp.1–28.

76 The Dadaists would create a 'found environment', taking advantage of an exhibition opening or some public activity, and disrupting it with nonsensical discourse and actions. John Cage would re-enact this form of disruption with his 'simultaneous lectures' at Black Mountain College in the 1950s. Kurt Schwitters's 1921 'Merz composite work of Art' stated: 'In contrast to the drama of the opera, all parts of the Merz stage work are inseparably bound together; it cannot be written, read or listened to, it can only be produced in the theatre.' Schwitters's essay was reproduced in Motherwell's *The Dada Painters and Poets*, pp.62–3. Artaud's *The Theatre and its Double* had also just been translated into English by Grove Press, New York in 1958.

77 The Grosz-Mehring Berlin Dada Messe action group's activities of 1919, such as their 'Race between a sewing machine and a typewriter' and the Osaka Gutaï Group, founded in Japan in 1954 under Jiro Yosihira, were other influences for Lebel's Happening.

78 Gombin, p.85.

79 Bédouin cited by J.L. Gérard, 'Le surréalisme continue', *Le Monde libertaire*, June 1964, cited in Paligot, p.199.

80 'Tir de Barrage' (1960), in Pierre, *Tracts, Tome II*, pp.202–4. The tract was published in Edouard Jaguer's review *Phases* on 28 May 1960.

81 Lebel, *Poésie directe*, p.56.

82 Lebel, 'Quelques indications supplémentaires sur LA MORT et son incidence sur l'activité artistique dite d'avant-garde', poster for exhibition and series of manifestations – Happenings, lectures, etc., at Galerie Raymond Cordier, Paris. Jean-Jacques Lebel archive, Paris.

83 See Lebel, *Le Happening*.

84 Victor Brauner, preface, in *Jean-Jacques Lebel* (exh. cat.), np.

85 Jean-Jacques Lebel, interview with the author, Normandy, 25 July 2004. Quotes from Sade's *Les 120 Journées* were also read out at the first Happening Lebel organized in Venice in 1960.

86 In *Poésie directe*, p.73, Lebel suggests that this coincidence was in fact orchestrated by him. However, in an interview with the author, May 1996, he admitted it was – ironically – a chance encounter.

87 The other main participants were Frédéric Pardo, Bob and Barbara Benamou, Philippe Hiquily, B. Copley, Shirley Goldfarb and Gérard Rutten. In April 1966, Jacques Rivette's *La Religieuse*, starring Anna Karena, was banned. A theatrical staging of this tale by Denis Diderot was not banned in 1964 (at the Studio des Champs Elysées), and the screening of an extract on television on 11 December 1965 went without scandal. The censorship of 1966 came as a result of Catholic petitions. It would be banned by the Minister of Information Yvon Bourges on 1 April 1966. See Antoine de Baecque (ed.), *Cahiers du cinéma: Histoire d'une revue (Tome II: 1959–81)*, pp.173–5. Baecque also points out that Rivette had voiced his support of the FLN in *Cahiers du cinéma* in December 1962 (which was itself a blatantly left-wing publication). Such liberalism would not have gone unnoticed. See *Cahiers du cinéma*, no.177, April 1966, for controversy over censorship.

88 Jean-Jacques Lebel, interview with the author, Normandy, 25 July 2004.

89 It was Lucien Goldman who fainted: a friend of Lukacs and Marcuse, and author of *Le Dieu caché*, which argued that atheists secretly desired God. Jean-Jacques Lebel, interview with the author, Paris, 15 May 1996.

90 Jean-Jacques Lebel, interview with the author, Paris, 9 October 1996.

91 Jean-Luc Godard, letter in *Le Nouvel Observateur*, 6 April 1966, footnoted in Baecque, pp.175–6.

92 This article was signed by 'Le Groupe Surréaliste Rupture'.

93 Letter to *Rupture*, dated 19 April 1966 and signed by Philippe Audoin, Vincent Bounoure, André Breton, Gérard Legrand, José Pierre and Jean Schuster.

94 Jean-Jacques Lebel, in Dagen, 'Jean-Jacques Lebel, un artiste fulminant', *Le Monde*, 14 June 2003, p.33.

95 Claude Courtot, interview by Polizzotti, Paris, 24 June 1984, quoted in Polizzotti, p.623.

Conclusion **The May Contestation: Surrealism in the Streets**

1 Edgar Morin, 'Une révolution sans visage', in Morin et al., *Mai 68*, p.85.

2 See Fraser, *1968: A Student Generation in Revolt*.

3 Daniel Cohn-Bendit and Jean-Pierre Duteuil, *Mouvement du 22 mars*, interview by Hervé Bourges, 20 May – 1 June 1968, Paris, printed in Sauvageot, *The Student Revolt*, p.68. The Fouchet Plan, was a plan for the university system to rationalize the education system according to the needs of the French economy. The Fifth Plan was an economic scheme to encourage the concentration of industry, allowing capital to control salaried workers, and maintaining a pool of unemployed.

4 Sauvageot, p.34.

5 The *Clarté* club, the UEC travel agency, organized trips to Cuba for students, who would be inspired by the revolutionary action of students there. The UEC posed such a threat to the PCF that it was expelled from the Party in 1965.

6 As Keith Reader has pointed out, this title was also indebted to the anarchy of the day itself and Castro's Cuban 'Movement of 26 July'. See Reader and Wadia, *The May 1968 Events in France, Reproductions and Interpretations*, p.8.

7 The photograph was reproduced in the 'round up', 'Le fond de l'air', section at the end of the review, compiled by Audoin, Courtot, Ivsic, Joubert, Le Brun, Legrand, P. A. de Paranagua, Pierre and Georges Sebbag. See *Archibras*, no.3, March 1968, pp.81–7.

8 Pierre, *Tracts, Tome II*, p.429.

9 See 'Pour Cuba' (dated 14 Nov 1967, signed by forty-three), Ted Joans, 'Black flower' and Jean Schuster, 'Flamboyant de Cuba, arbe de la liberté' (dated Jan 1968), in *Archibras*, no.3, March 1968, p.3, pp.10–11 and p.52 respectively.

10 Sauvageot, pp.34–5.

11 The Estates General of the Cinema (EGC), which was formed by filmmakers and technicians, took its name from the Estates General of 1789. Its title proclaimed a revolutionary, progressive agenda, in referring to the assembly of nobles, clergy and commons who had met in Versailles in May 1789.

12 An Enragé statement of 1968 quoted in Bernard E. Brown, *Protest in Paris*, p.94.

13 'Pas de pasteurs pour cette rage', 5 May 1968, signed by 'Le Mouvement Surréaliste', in Pierre, *Tracts, Tome II*, p.276.

14 Ibid. and Pierre's notes pp.429–30.

15 Hérold chose Susan Wise's 'Tu Sera Délivré'; an untitled poem by Gilbert Lely capturing Sade's chateau at Lacoste; and Sade's letter 'Aux Stupides Scélérats qui me tourmentent.' Muguette Hérold, interview with the author, Paris, 2 October 1996.

16 Bernard Dufour, 'A propos des affiches de peintres de mai 68', *Mai 68, ou l'imagination au pouvoir* (exh. cat.), pp.146–7. Bernard Dufour also produced posters which he sold in La Hune bookshop (the proceeds went to

the Comité du Sorbonne). He then created a collection (text and illustrations) in June 1968 entitled *Insolations*, which was edited and distributed by Fata Morgana, had three editions which involved Hérold, Matta and Wifredo Lam, and again paid homage to the events of May 1968. The three editions were: *Tourmente*, dated 13 June 1968, with texts by Michel Butor and drawings by Jacques Hérold, Bernard Dufour and Pierre Alechinsky (150 exemplaires); *Sorbonne*, dated 22 June 1968, with texts by Jean-Pierre Faye, Claude Ollier and Maurice Roche and drawing by Bernard Dufour and Roberto Matta (200 exemplaires); *Le Seul mot de liberté est tout ce qui, 'exalte encore'*, dated 9 Dec 1968, with texts by Pierre Guyotat, Denis Roche, Roman Weingarten and Kateb Yacine and drawing by Bernard Dufour, Ipoustéguy, Wifredo Lam and François Lunven (200 exemplaires). Note that the third edition was indebted to Breton's expletive of 1924.

17 'Portrait of the enemy', *L'Archibras*, June 1968, no.4, trans. in Richardson and Fijalkowski, *Surrealism Against the Current*, p.133.

18 Ibid.

19 Ibid., p.134.

20 'Down with France!', *L'Archibras*, June 1968, no.4, trans. in Richardson and Fijalkowski, *Surrealism Against the Current*, pp.134–5.

21 Ibid., p.134.

22 Ibid., p.135.

23 See Pierre, *Tracts, Tome II*, p.431.

24 Jean Schuster, 'The Fourth Canto', *Le Monde*, 4 Oct 1969, trans. Peter Wood in Richardson and Fijalkowski, *Surrealism Against the Current*, p.200.

25 Alain Jouffroy 'What's to be done about Art? From the abolition of art to revolutionary individualism', *Art and Confrontation* (1968), trans. Nigel Foxell, London, Studio Vista, 1970, p.175. Jouffroy had made his peace with Breton in 1964. He edited *Nadja, Le Surréalisme et la peinture* and *Les Champs Magnétiques* for Gallimard (where he worked), and he travelled with Breton through Brittany in April 1966.

26 Ibid., p.199.

27 Ibid.

28 Jameson, *Postmodernism or The Cultural Logic of Late Capitalism*, p.174.

29 Ibid., p.175.

Bibliography

Interviews

Sarane Alexandrian, Paris, 28 October 1996, 20 July 2000

Jean Benoît, Paris, 5 May, 22 September 1996, 23 July 2004

Christian Descamps, Paris, 19 October 1996

Gilles Ehrmann, Paris, 4 May 1996

Marcel Fleiss, Paris, 23 March 1996

Ruth Henry, Paris, 24 April 1996

Muguette Hérold, Paris, 2, 22, and 23 October 1996

Radovan Ivsic, Paris, 19 July 2000

Pierre Klossowski, Paris, 18 March, 1 April, 2, 4 and 6 May, 26 September, 10, 20 and 26 October 1996

Jean-Jacques Lebel, Paris, 23 April, 15 May, 9 October, 22 October 1996 and Normandy, 25 July 2004

Annie Le Brun, Paris, 23 October 1996 and 19 July 2000

Adrian Maeght, Saint-Paul, 4 August 2000

Mimi Parent, Paris, 9 October 1996 and 18 July 2000, 23 July 2004

Jean-Jacques Pauvert, Paris, 8 October 1996

José Pierre, Paris, 28 March, 26 April, 10 and 26 October 1996

André Thirion, Paris, 8 May 1996

Archival Sources

Bibliothèque Littéraire Jacques Doucet, Paris (correspondence of Georges Bataille, André Breton, René Char, Gilbert Lely)

Centre Georges Pompidou, Musée National d'Art Moderne archives, Paris (Victor Brauner, René Char, Daniel Cordier archives)

Galerie Dionne, Paris (Roberto Matta)

Getty Research Institute, Los Angeles (Josef Breitenbach, Jean Brown, Enrico Donati, Frederick Kiesler, Man Ray papers)

J. Paul Getty Museum, Los Angeles (Man Ray photograph archive)

Institut Mémoires de L'Edition Contemporaine, Paris (Jean Paulhan, Jean-Jacques Pauvert papers)

Personal archives of Michèle C. Cone (New York), Muguette Hérold (Paris), Jean-Jacques Lebel (Paris), Mimi Parent (Paris), José Pierre (Paris)

Surrealist Reviews/Reviews close to Surrealism published between 1938 and 1968 (dates correspond to print run)

Minotaure (nos 1–12, 1933–9). Republished Paris, Flammarion, 1981

La Main à Plume (collective publications, May 1941–Jan 1945)

VVV (nos 1–4, 1942–4)

Néon (nos 1–5, 1948–9)

Médium, Information surréaliste (nos 1–8, 1952–3)

Médium, Communication surréaliste (nos 1–4, 1953–5)

Le Surréalisme, même (nos 1–5, 1956–9)

Bief, jonction surréaliste (nos 1–12, 1958–60)

Front unique (review) (nos 1–2, 1959–60)

La Brèche, action surréaliste (nos 1–8, 1961–5)

L'Archibras (nos 1–7, 1967–9)

Frequently cited Surrealist Exhibition Catalogues

Exposition des objets surréaliste, Paris, Galerie Charles Ratton, 1936

Exposition internationale du surréalisme, Paris, Galerie Beaux-Arts, 1938.

First Papers of Surrealism, New York, Co-ordinating Council of French Relief Societies, 1942

Le Surréalisme en 1947: Exposition internationale du Surréalisme, Paris, Galerie Maeght, 1947

Exposition internationale du surréalisme [EROS], Paris, Galerie Daniel Cordier, 1959

L'Ecart absolu, Paris, Galerie de l'Oeil, 1965

Books, Essays, Reviews, Exhibition Catalogues

Abel, Lionel, 'The Surrealists in New York', *Commentary*, October 1981, pp.44–54

Ades, Dawn, et al., *Art and Power: Europe under the Dictators 1930–45*, London, Hayward Gallery/Thames & Hudson, 1995

Adorno, Theodor W. and Max Horkheimer, Dialectic of Enlightenment (1944), trans. John Cumming, London, Verso, 1997

Albert-Levin, Marc, 'Le Surréalisme à l'Oeil', *Les Lettres françaises*, 9–15 December 1965, p.32

Alexandrian, Sarane, *Jacques Hérold*, Paris, Fall Editions, 1995

—, *Surrealist Art* (1970), London, Thames & Hudson, 1997

Alleg, Henri, *The Question*, Paris, Editions de Minuit (1958), trans. John Calder, New York, Braziller, 1958

Alquiée, Ferdinand, *Entretiens sur le Surréalisme*, Paris, Mouton, 1968

Altshuler, Bruce, *The Avant-Garde in Exhibition: New Art in the 20th Century*, New York, Abrams, 1994

André Breton: La beauté convulsive, exh. cat., Paris, Musée National d'Art Moderne, 1991

Archer-Straw, Petrine, *Negrophilia, Avant-Garde Paris and Black Culture in the 1920s*, London, Thames & Hudson, 2000

Aron, Raymond, *France, Steadfast and Changing: The Fourth to the Fifth Republic*, Cambridge, MA, Harvard University Press, 1960

—, *Opium of the Intellectuals* (1955), trans. Terence Kilmartin, London, Secker and Warburg, 1986

Arp, Jean, 'L'Oeuf de Kiesler et la "Salle des Superstitions"', *Cahiers d'art*, no.22, August 1947, pp.281–6

Arsan, Emmanuelle, *Emmanuelle*, Paris, Eric Losfeld, 1957

Artaud, Antonin, *The Theatre and its Double* (1938), trans. Victor Corti, New York, Grove Press, 1958; London, Calder, 1993

Assouline, Pierre, *L'Epuration des intellectuels, 1944–45*, Brussels, Editions Complexe, 1990

Audoin, Philippe, *Les Surréalistes*, Paris, Editions de Seuil, 1973

Avis, Paul, *Eros and the Sacred*, London, SPCK, 1989

Baecque, Antoine de (ed.), *Cahiers du cinéma: Histoire d'une revue (Tome II: 1959–81)*, Paris, Editions Cahiers du Cinéma, 1991

Baj, Enrico, Laurence Bertrand-Dorléac, Julien Blaine et al., *Grand Tableau antifasciste collectif*, Paris, Editions Dagorno, 2000

Bakhtin, Mikhail 'Rabelais and His World' (1965), in Pam Morris (ed.) and H. Iswolsky (trans.), *The Bakhtin Reader: Selected Writings of Bakhtin, Medvedev and Voloshinov*, New York and London, Edward Arnold, 1994, pp.227–44

Balakian, Anna, *Surrealism: the Road to the Absolute*, New York, Noonday Press, 1959

—, *André Breton: Magus of Surrealism*, Oxford and New York, Oxford University Press, 1971

Barron, Marie Louise, 'Surréalisme en 1947, En retard d'une guerre comme l'Etat-Major', *Les Lettres françaises*, 18 July 1947, p.2

Barthes, Roland, *Sade, Fourier, Loyola* (1971), trans. Richard Miller, New York, Hill and Wang, 1976; London, Jonathan Cape, 1977.

—, *Mythologies* (1957), trans. Annette Lavers, London, Vintage, 1993

Batache, Eddy, *Surréalisme et tradition: La Pensée d'André Breton jugée delon l'oeuvre de René Guénon*, Paris, Editions Traditionnelles, 1978

Bataille, Georges, *Les Larmes d'Eros*, Paris, Jean-Jacques Pauvert, 1961

—, *Oeuvres Complètes*, vol.VII, Paris, Gallimard, 1976

—, *Eroticism* (1957), London, Boyars, 1987

—, *The Absence of Myth: Writings on Surrealism*, trans. and introduction by Michael Richardson, London and New York, Verso, 1994

—, *Visions of Excess, Selected Writings 1927–1939, Theory and History of Literature*, vol.14, edited and introduction by Allan Stoekl, trans. Allan Stoekl, with Carl R. Lovitt and Donald M. Leslie, Jr, Minneapolis, University of Minnesota Press, 1999

Bauer, George, *Sartre and the Artist*, Chicago and London, University of Chicago Press, 1969

Baynes, Norman H. (ed. and trans.), *The Speeches of Adolf Hitler, April 1922 to August 1939: an English translation of representative passages arranged under subjects*, London, Oxford University Press, 1942

Bazaine, Jean, 'La Peinture bleu blanc rouge', *Comoedia*, 30 January 1943, pp.1–6

Bazaine, Jean, *Notes sur la peinture d'aujourd'hui*, Paris, Editions du Seuil, 1953

Beauvoir, Simone de, 'Must we Burn Sade?' (1951), trans. Annette Michelson in D.A.F. de Sade, *The 120 Days of Sodom, and Other Writings*, pp.3–64

—, 'Pour Djamila Boupacha' *Le Monde*, 2 June 1960 p.6, reprinted, with Gisèle Halimi, Paris, Gallimard, 1962

—, *Force of Circumstance* (1963), trans. Richard Howard, Harmondsworth, Penguin, 1968

—, *The Prime of Life* (1960), trans. Peter Green, Harmondsworth, Penguin, 1984

—, *Les Belles Images* (1966), trans. Patrick O'Brian, London, Flamingo, 1985

Bedouin, Jean-Louis, *Vingts ans de Surréalisme, 1939–59*, Paris, Editions Denoël, 1961

Beecher, Jonathan, 'L'Archibras de Fourier, un manuscrit censuré', *La Brèche, action surréaliste*, no.7, Dec 1964, pp.64–8

—, *Charles Fourier: The Visionary and his World*, Berkeley and London, University of California Press, 1986

Beecher, Jonathan and Richard Bienvenu (eds and trans.), *The Utopian Vision of Charles Fourier, Selected Texts on Work, Love, and Passionate Attraction*, London, Jonathan Cape, 1972

Beevor, Anthony and Artemis Cooper, *Paris after the Liberation 1944–1949*, London, Hamish Hamilton, 1994

Béhar, Henri, *André Breton: Le Grand Indésirable*, Paris, Calmann-Lévy, 1990

— (ed.), *Melusine IV: Le Livre*, Lausanne, L'Age d'Homme, 1982

Bellmer, Hans and Paul Eluard, *Les Jeux de la poupée*, Paris, Editions Premières, 1949

Bellmer, Hans, *Petite Anatomie de l'inconscient physique ou l'anatomie de l'image*, Paris, Terrain Vague, 1957

Benayoun, Robert, *Erotique du surréalisme*, Paris, Jean-Jacques Pauvert, 1965

Benjamin, Walter, 'Surrealism: The Last Snapshot of the European Intelligentsia' (1929), trans. Edmond Jephcott, *New Left Review*, no.108, March/April 1978, pp.47–56

—, 'Das Passagen-Werk', in *Gesammelte Schriften*,

Rolf Tiedmann and Hermann Schweppenhäuser (eds), 7 vols, Frankfurt-am-Main, Suhrkamp, 1972; trans. Howard Eiland and Kevin McLaughlin as *The Arcades Project*, Cambridge, MA, Belknap Press, 1999

Berreby, Gérard (ed.), *Documents rélatifs à la fondation de l'Intérnationale Situationniste*, Paris, Editions Allia, 1985

Bertrand-Dorléac, Laurence, *L'Histoire de l'art: Paris 1940–1944*, Paris, Presses de la Sorbonne, 1986

—, *L'Art en Europe: Les Années Décisives 1945–1953*, exh. cat., Saint Etienne, Musée d'Art Moderne, 1987

Bloch, Jean-Jacques and Marianne Delot, *Quand Paris allait à l'Expo*, Paris, Fayard, 1980

Bonk, Ecke, *Marcel Duchamp: The Portable Museum: The Making of the Boîte-en-Valise de ou par Marcel Duchamp ou Rrose Sélavy*, New York, St Martin's Press; London, Thames & Hudson, 1989

Bonnet, Marguerite, *André Breton, naissance de l'aventure surréaliste*, Paris, José Corti, 1975

Bounoure, Vincent, *Moments du surréalisme*, Paris, L'Harmattan, 1999

Bourdrel, Philippe, *L'Épuration sauvage: 1944–1945*, Paris, Perrin, 1988

Bourniquel, Camille, 'Chroniques: Magie, Surréalisme et Liberté', *Esprit*, November 1947, pp.775–82

Brassaï, *The Secret Paris of the 30's* (1976), trans. Richard Miller, New York, Random House/Pantheon; London, Thames & Hudson, 1977

Breton, André, *Flagrant délit: Rimbaud devant la conjuration de l'importure et du truquage*, Paris, Thésée, 1949

—, *Anthologie de l'humour noir*, Paris, Jean-Jacques Pauvert, 1969

—, *Manifestoes of Surrealism* (1962), trans. Richard Seaver and Helen R. Lane, Ann Arbor, University of Michigan Press, 1969

—, *What is Surrealism? Selected Writings*, edited and introduced by Franklin Rosemont, New York, Pathfinder; London, Pluto Press, 1978, 2001

—, *Mad Love* (1937), trans. Mary Ann Caws, Lincoln and London, University of Nebraska Press, 1987

—, *Oeuvres Complètes*, 2 vols, Marguerite Bonnet, Philippe Bernier, Etienne-Alain Hubert and José Pierre (eds), Paris, Gallimard, 1988–92

—, *Arcanum 17* (1944), trans. Zack Rogow, introduction by Anna Balakian, Los Angeles, Sun and Moon Press, 1994

—, *Ode à Charles Fourier* (1947), Paris, Editions Fata Morgana, 1994

—, *Free Rein* (1953), trans. Michel Parmentier and Jacqueline d'Amboise, Lincoln, Univeristy of Nebraska Press, 1995

—, *Surrealism and Painting* (1965), trans. Simon Watson Taylor, introduction by Mark Polizzotti, Boston, MFA Publications, 2002

Breton, André and Paul Eluard (eds), *Dictionnaire abrégé du surréalisme*, Paris, Galerie Beaux-Arts, 1938

Breton, André and Charles Henri Ford, 'Interview with André Breton', *View*, vol.1, no.7–8, Surrealist Number, Oct–Nov 1941, pp.1–3, reproduced in Breton, *What is Surrealism?*, pp.263–72

Breton, André and André Parinaud, *Entretiens (1913–1952)*, Paris, Gallimard, 1969

Brohm, Jean-Marie, 'La Lutte contre la répression sexuelle', *Partisans*, Oct–Nov 1966, pp.39–46

Brown, Bernard E., *Protest in Paris; Anatomy of a Revolt*, Morristown, NJ, General Learning Press, 1974

Brown, Norman O., *Life Against Death: The Psychoanalytic Meaning of History* (1959), London, Sphere Books, 1970

Brun, Jean, 'Désir et réalité dans l'oeuvre de Hans Bellmer', *Obliques, numéro spécial Hans Bellmer*, Paris, Borderie, 1975, pp.7–12

Brunet, Louis, 'Du surréalisme', *La Croix*, January 20 1938, p.1

Bürger, Peter, *Theory of the Avant-Garde*, Minneapolis, University of Minnesota Press, 1984

Butor, Michel, *Hérold*, Paris, Georges Fall/Le Musée de Poche, 1964

—, *Petites Liturgies intimes pour hâter l'avènement du Grand Transparent*, exh. cat., Paris, Galerie de Seine, 1972

C.C, review of the *Ecart absolu* exhibition, *New York Herald Tribune*, Paris, 14 December 1965, p.5

Cabanne, Pierre, *Dialogues with Marcel Duchamp* (1967), trans. Ron Padgett, New York, Da Capo Press, 1987

Calas, Nicolas, 'Magic Icons', *Horizon*, vol.14, no.83, November 1946, pp.304–15

Carrouges, Michel, 'Surréalisme et occultisme', *Cahiers d'Hermès*, no.2, November 1947 pp.194–218

—, *André Breton et les données fondamentales du Surréalisme*, Paris, Gallimard, 1950

Caute, David, *Communism and the French Intellectuals 1914–1960*, London, André Deutsch; New York, Macmillan, 1964

Caws, Mary Ann, et al., *Surrealism and Women*, Cambridge, MA and London, MIT Press, 1991

Chadwick, Whitney, 'Eros or Thanatos – the Surrealist Cult of Love Reexamined', *Artforum*, vol.14, no.3, November 1975, pp.46–56

—, *Myth in Surrealist Painting*, Ann Arbor, UMI Research Press, 1979

—, *Women Artists and the Surrealist Movement*, London and New York, Thames & Hudson, 1985

Cixous, Hélène, 'Fictions and its Phantoms: A Reading of Freud's Das Unheimliche (The "uncanny")', *New Literary History*, vol.7, no.3, Spring 1976, pp.525–48

Clébert, Jean-Paul (ed.), *Mythologie d'André Masson*, Geneva, Pierre Calder Editeur, 1971

Clifford, James, *The Predicament of Culture: 20th Century Ethnography, Literature and Art*, Cambridge, MA, Harvard University Press, 1988

Coates, Robert, 'The Art Galleries, Sixteen Miles of String', *New Yorker*, 31 October 1942, pp.72–3

Cohen, Margaret, *Profane Illumination: Walter Benjamin and the Paris of Surrealist Revolution*, Berkeley and London, University of California Press, 1993

Cone, Michèle C., *Artists under Vichy: A Case of Prejudice and Persecution*, Princeton University Press, 1992

—, *French Modernisms, Perspectives on Art Before, During and After Vichy*, Cambridge University Press, 2001

Conley, Katharine, *Robert Desnos, Surrealism and the Marvelous in Everyday Life*, Lincoln and London, University of Nebraska Press, 2004

Cordier, Daniel, *Huit ans d'agitation*, exh. cat., Paris, Galerie Cordier, 1964

—, in interview, 'Daniel Cordier, les arts et les armes', *Le Monde*, Sunday 25 – Monday 26 July 2004, p.19

Costich, Julia Field, *The Poetry of Change. A Study of the Surrealist Works of Benjamin Péret*, Chapel

Hill, University of North Carolina Press, 1979

Dagen, Philippe, 'Jean-Jacques Lebel, un artiste fulminant', *Le Monde*, 14 June 2003, p.33

Dalí, Salvador, *La Vie sécrète de Salvador Dalí*, Paris, La Table Ronde, 1960

—, *The Unspeakable Confessions of Salvador Dalí, as told to André Parinaud*, London, Quartet Books, 1977

Dean, Carolyn J., *The Self and its Pleasures. Bataille, Lacan and the History of the Decentered Subject*, Ithaca and London, Cornell University Press, 1992

Debord, Guy, 'Hurlements en faveur de Sade' (1952), *Les Lèvres Nues*, no.7, Dec 1955, pp.18–23

—, *La Société du spectacle: La Théorie situationniste*, Paris, Buchet-Chastel, 1967

Degenerate Art, The Fate of the Avant-Garde in Nazi Germany, exh. cat., Los Angeles, LACMA, 1991

Desnot, Rothert, *The Voice: Selected Poems of Robert Desnos*, trans. William Kulik and Carole Frankel, New York, Grossman, 1972

Dourthe, Pierre, *Hans Bellmer, le principe de la perversion*, Paris, Jean-Pierre Faur, 1999

Dross, Bernard and Evelyne Lever, *Histoire de la guerre d'Algérie 1954–1962*, Paris, Editions du Seuil, 1982

Dubuffet, Jean, 'Anticultural positions' (1951), *Jean Dubuffet*, exh. cat., New York, World House Galleries, 1960

Dufour, Bernard, 'A propos des affiches de peintres de mai 68', *Mai 68, ou l'imagination au pouvoir*, exh. cat., Vence and Paris, Galerie Beaubourg and Editions de la Différence, 1998, pp.146–7

Dunlop, Ian, *The Shock of the New: Seven Historical Exhibitions of Modern Art*, London, Weidenfeld and Nicolson, 1972

Dupin, Jacques, *Miró*, Paris, Flammarion, 2004

Durozoi, Gérard, *History of the Surrealist Movement* (1997), trans. Alison Anderson, University of Chicago Press, 2002

Elgar, Frank, 'Nouvelle vague surréaliste', *Carrefour*, Mercredi 22 December 1965, p.9.

Ernst, Jimmy, *A Not-So-Still Life* (1984), New York, Pushcart Press, 1992

Ernst, Max, *La Femme 100 têtes*, Paris, Editions du Carrefour, 1929

Estienne, Charles, 'Surréalisme 1947, De l'expérience poétique à la magie noire et blanche', *Combat*, 8 July 1942, p.2

Fauré, Michel, *Histoire du surréalisme sous l'occupation*, Paris, La Table Ronde, 1982

Fer, Briony, David Batchelor and Paul Wood, *Realism, Rationalism, Surrealism: Art between the Wars*, New Haven and London, Yale University Press in association with the Open University, 1993

Ferrier, André, 'Des pièges à quoi?', *Le Nouvel Observateur*, 12 Janvier 1966, p.35

Feuerstein, Pierre, *Printemps de révolte à Strasbourg*, Strasbourg, Saisons d'Alsace, 1968

Fletcher, Valerie, *Crosscurrents of Modernism: Four Latin American Pioneers*, Washington, DC, Hirshhorn Museum and Sculpture Park, and Smithsonian Institution Press, 1992

Ford, Charles Henri, (ed.), *View, Parade of the Avant-Garde 1940–1947*, New York, Thunder's Mouth Press, 1991.

Foster, Hal, *Compulsive Beauty*, Cambridge, MA and London, MIT Press, 1993

Foucault, Michel, 'A Preface to Transgression', trans. D. F. Bouchard and S. Simon, in D. F. Bouchard (ed.), *Language, Counter Memory, Practice*, Ithaca, Cornell University Press, 1977, pp.29–52

—, *The Foucault Reader*, ed. Paul Rabinow, Harmondsworth, Penguin, 1991

Fourier, Charles, 'L'Archibras', *La Brèche, action surréaliste*, no.7, Dec 1964, pp.69–71

—, *Grand traité* (1822) in *Fourier, Oeuvres Complètes*, vol.1, Paris, Anthropos, 1966

—, *Le Nouveaux Monde amoureux*, ed. and introduction by Simone Debout-Oleszkiewicz, Paris, Anthropos, 1967

—, *The Theory of the Four Movements*, eds Gareth Stedman Jones and Ian Patterson, Cambridge University Press, 1996

Charles Fourier

Fraser, Ronald, *1968: A Student Generation in Revolt*, London, Chatto and Windus, 1988

Frederick Kiesler, Artiste-architecture, exh. cat., Paris, Musée National d'Art Moderne, 1996

Frederick J. Kiesler: Endless Space, exh. cat., Los Angeles, MAK Center for Art and Architecture, 2001

Freud, Sigmund, *The Basic Writings of Sigmund Freud*, trans. and ed. A.A.Brill, New York, The Modern Library, 1938

—, *Civilization and its Discontents* (1930), trans. Joan Riviere, London, Hogarth Press, 1949

—, Pelican Freud Library, vol.2, *New Introductory Lectures on Psychoanalysis*, Harmondsworth, Penguin, 1973

—, Penguin Freud Library, vol.7, *On Sexuality, Three Essays on the Theory of Sexuality, and Other Works*, Harmondsworth, Penguin, 1991

—, Penguin Freud Library, vol.13, *The Origins of Religion*, London and New York, Penguin, 1990

—, Penguin Freud Library, vol.14: *Art and Literature*, Harmondsworth, Penguin, 1990

Friedrich Kiesler, Art of this Century, exh. cat., Frankfurt-am-Main, Museum für Moderne Kunst, 2002

Fry, Varian, *Surrender on Demand*, Boulder, CO, Johnson Books/United States Holocaust Memorial Museum, 1997

Garber, Marjorie, *Vested Interests: Cross-dressing and Cultural Anxiety*, New York and London, Routledge, 1992

Garçon, Maurice (ed.), *L'Affaire Sade: Compte-rendu exact au procès intenté par le Ministère Public*, Paris, Editions Jean-Jacques Pauvert, 1957

Gates, Jr, Henry Louis (ed.), *Race, Writing and Difference*, University of Chicago Press, 1986

Gaulle, Charles de, *Mémoires de guerre, vol.3, Le Salut (1944–1946)*, Paris, Plon 1959

Gauthier, Xavière, *Surréalisme et Sexualité*, Paris, Gallimard, 1971

Gibson, Ian, *The Shameful Life of Salvador Dalí*, London, Faber and Faber, 1997

Giles, Frank, *The Locust Years, The Story of the Fourth Republic*, London, Secker and Warburg, 1991

Golan, Romy, *Modernity and Nostalgia: Art and Politics in France between the Wars*, New Haven and London, Yale University Press, 1995

Goldberg, RoseLee, *Performance Art from Futurism to the Present*, London, Thames & Hudson, 1988

Gombin, Richard, *Origins of Modern Leftism* (1971), trans. Michael K. Perl, Harmondsworth, Penguin, 1975

Grosshans, Henry, *Hitler and the Artists*, New York, Holmes and Meier Publishers, 1983

Guénon, René, *Aperçus sur l'initiation*, Paris, Edition Traditionnelles, 1946

Guerre, Pierre, 'L'Exposition intérnationale du Surréalisme', *Cahiers du sud*, no.284, second semester 1947, pp.677–81

Guetta, René, 'L'Expo du Rêve', *Marianne*, 26 January 1938, p.13

Guggenheim, Peggy, *Out of This Century: Confessions of an Art Addict* (1946), London, André Deutsch, 1983

Guilbaut, Serge, *How New York Stole the Idea of Modern Art: Abstract Expressionism, Freedom and the Cold War* (1983), trans. Arthur Goldhammer, University of Chicago Press, 1993

Guiraud, Jean-Michel, *Varian Fry à Marseille, 1940–1941: 'Les Artistes et l'Exil'*, exh. cat., Mona Bismark Foundation, Paris, 2000

Hagen, Yvonne, 'Surrealists' "Eroticism"', *New York Herald Tribune*, December 1959, np, Mimi Parent archive, Paris

Hahn, Otto, 'Le Surréalisme, à l'heure du musée ou de la jeunesse?', *Arts*, 1–7 December 1965, pp.20 and 29

—, 'Le Surréalisme face à la machine à laver', *L'Express*, 13–19 December 1965, pp.80–1

Hamon, Hervé and Patrick Rotman (eds), *Génération*, vol.1, *Les Années du rêve*; vol.2, *Les Années de poudre*, Paris, Editions du Seuil, 1987 and 1988

Hammond, Paul (ed., trans. and introduction), *The Shadow and its Shadow: Surrealist Writings on the Cinema*, San Francisco, City Lights, 2000

Hanley, David and A.P. Kerr (eds), *May 68 – Coming of Age*, Basingstoke, Macmillan, 1989

Hans Bellmer: Dessins 1935–1946, exh. cat., Paris, Galerie du Luxembourg, 1947

Hargreaves, Alec G. and Michael J. Heffernan (eds), *French and Algerian Identities from Colonial Times to the Present*, Lewiston, NY and Lampeter, Edwin Mellen Press, 1993

Harrison, Martin, 'Government and Press in France during the Algerian War', *American Political Science Review*, vol.LVIII, no.2, June 1964, pp.273–85

Heine, Maurice, *Le Marquis de Sade*, Paris, Gallimard, 1950

Hénaff, Marcel, *Sade: L'invention du corps libertin*, Paris, Presses Universitaires de France, 1978

Henry, Maurice, 'Le Surréalisme dans le décor', *Marianne*, 26 January 1936, p.11

Herbert, James D., *Paris 1937: Worlds on Exhibition*, Ithaca, Cornell University Press, 1998

Herdt, Gilbert (ed.), *Third Sex, Third Gender: Beyond Sexual Dimorphism in Culture and History*, New York, Zone Books, 1994

Hérold, Jacques, *Maltraité de peinture*, Paris, Falaize, 1957

Hollier, Denis, *Against Architecture: The Writings of Georges Bataille* (1989), trans. Betsy Wing, Cambridge, MA and London, MIT Press, 1992

— (ed.), *The College of Sociology*, Minneapolis, Minnesota University Press, 1988

Hopkins, David, *Marcel Duchamp and Max Ernst: the Bride Shared*, Oxford, Clarendon Press, 1998

Hugnet, Georges, *Pleins et déliés, souvenirs et témoignages 1926–1972*, La Chapelle-sur-Loire, Guy Authier, 1972

Hulten, Pontus, et al., *Paris–Paris, 1937–1957*, exh. cat., Paris, Editions du Centre Pompidou/Gallimard, 1981

—, *Paris–New York, 1908–1968*, exh. cat., Paris, Editions du Centre Pompidou/Gallimard, 1991.

— (ed.), *The Surrealists Look at Art*, trans. Michael Palmer and Norma Cole, Venice, CA, Lapis Press, 1990

Huyghe, René, *Les Contemporains*, Paris, Pierre Tisné, 1949

Huyssen, Andreas, *After the Great Divide: Modernism, Mass Culture, Post Modernism*, Bloomington, Indiana University Press, 1986

Jackson, Julian, *Charles de Gaulle*, London, Sphere Books, 1990

Jameson, Fredric, *Marxism and Form*, Princeton University Press, 1971

—, *Postmodernism or The Cultural Logic of Late Capitalism*, London and New York, Verso, 1991

Jardine, Alice, *Genesis: Configurations of Woman and Modernity*, Ithaca, Cornell University Press, 1985

Jean Benoît, exh. cat., Paris, Galerie 1900–2000, 1996

Jean Dubuffet, exh. cat., New York, World House Galleries, 1960

Jean-Jacques Lebel, exh. cat., Milan, Galleria Schwarz, 16–30 June 1961, preface by Victor Brauner

Jean-Jacques Lebel, Bilder, Skulpturen, Installationen, exh. cat., Vienna, Museum Moderner Kunst Stiftung Ludwig, 1998

Jean, Marcel, *The History of Surrealist Painting* (1959), trans. Simon Watson Taylor, New York, Grove Press; London Weidenfeld & Nicolson, 1960

Johnson, R.W., *The Long March of the French Left*, London, Macmillan, 1981

Joly, Danièle, *The French Communist Party and the Algerian War*, Basingstoke, Macmillan, 1991

Jones, Amelia, *Postmodernism and the Engendering of Marcel Duchamp*, Cambridge University Press, 1994

Joubert, Alain, *Le Mouvement des surréalistes, ou, Le fin mot de l'histoire*, Paris, Editions Maurice Nadeau, 2001

Jouffroy, Alain, *Brauner*, Paris, Georges Fall, 1959

Joyce, Conor, *Carl Einstein in Documents and his Collaboration with Georges Bataille*, Philadelphia, Xlibiris, 2003

Judt, Tony, *Past Imperfect: French Intellectuals 1944–1956* (1992), Berkeley and London, University of California Press, 1994

Kachur, Lewis, *Displaying the Marvellous, Marcel Duchamp, Salvador Dalí and Surrealist Exhibition Installations*, Cambridge, MA and London, MIT Press, 2001

Khalfa, Jean (ed.), *The Dialogue between Painting and Poetry*, Cambridge, Black Apollo Press, 2001

Kiesler, Frederick, 'Kiesler on Duchamp', *Architectural Record*, 81, May 1937, p.54

Kiesler, Frederick, *Selected Writings*, Siegfried Gohr and Gunda Luyken (eds), Ostfildern bei Stuttgart, Verlag Gerd Hatje, 1996

Kirby, Michael, 'Happenings: An Introduction', in Mariellen R. Sandford (ed.), *Happenings and Other Acts*, London, Routledge, 1995, pp.1–28

Klossowski, Pierre, *Sade my Neighbour* (1947) trans. Alphonso Lingis, London, Quartet Books, 1992

Knabb, Ken (ed. and trans.), *Situationist International Anthology*, Berkeley, Bureau of Public Secrets, 1981

Kozloff, Max, 'An interview with Matta', *Art Forum*, vol.4, September 1965, pp.24–5

Krauss, Rosalind, Jane Livingston and Dawn Ades, *L'Amour fou: Photography and Surrealism*, New York, Abbeville Press, 1985

Krauss, Rosalind, *The Optical Unconscious*, Cambridge, MA and London, MIT Press, 1993

Kristeva, Julia, *Powers of Horror: An Essay on Abjection*, trans. Leon S. Roudiez, New York, Columbia University Press, 1982

—, *Strangers to Ourselves* (1988), trans. Leon S. Roudiez, New York, Harvester Wheatsheaf, 1991

La Femme et le Surréalisme, exh. cat., Lausanne, Musée Cantonal des Beaux-Arts, 1987

L'Univers d'Aimé et Marguerite Maeght, exh. cat., Saint-Paul, Fondation Maeght, 1982

La Planète Affolée: Surréalisme, Dispersion et Influences, 1938–1947, Marseilles and Paris, Direction des Musées de Marseille and Flammarion, 1986

Labbé, Edmond, *Le Livre d'or officiel de l'Exposition internationale des Arts et des Techniques*, Paris, 1937

Lambert, Jean-Clarence, *L'Observateur Litteraire*, 17 December 1959

Laubier, Claire (ed.), *The Condition of Women in France, 1945 to the Present*, London and New York, Routledge, 1990

Lautréamont, Comte de (Isidore Ducasse), *Les Chants de Maldoror*, trans. Guy Wernham, New York, New Directions, 1965

Lavine, Steven D. and Ivan Karp (eds), *Exhibiting Cultures: The Poetics and Politics of Museum Display*, Washington, DC, Smithsonian Institution Press, 1991

Le Brun, Annie (ed.), *Petits et Grands Théâtres du Marquis de Sade*, exh. cat., Paris Art Centre, 1989

Lebel, Jean-Jacques, *Le Happening*, Paris, Denoël and Les Lettres Nouvelles, 1966

Lebel, Jean-Jacques and Arnaud Labelle-Rojous, *Poésie directe*, Paris, Opus International Edition, 1994

Lefebvre, Henri, *The Production of Space*, Oxford, Blackwell, 1991

—, *The Critique of Everyday Life* (1947), trans. John Moore, London, Verso, 1991

—, *Critique of Everyday Life*, vol.II (1961), trans. John Moore, London, Verso, 2002

Lely, Gilbert, *La Vie du Marquis de Sade*. Paris, Gallimard, 1952–7; reprinted in Marquis de Sade, *Oeuvres Complètes*, vols I and II, Paris, Cercle du Livre Precieux, 1962–6; partial English trans. by Alec Brown as *The Marquis de Sade*, New York, Grove Press, 1970

Leperlier, François, *Claude Cahun: L'écart et la métamorphose*, Paris, Jean-Michel Place, 1992

—, *Third Sex, Third Gender: Beyond Sexual Dimorphism in Culture and History*, ed. Gilbert Herdt, New York, Zone Books, 1994

Lever, Maurice, *Marquis de Sade: A Biography* (1991), trans. Arthur Goldhammer, New York, Farrar, Strauss and Giroux; London, HarperCollins, 1993

Levy, Julian, *Memoir of an Art Gallery*, New York, Putnam, 1977

Lewis, Helena, *The Politics of Surrealism*, New York, Taplinger Books, 1988

Lichtenstein, Therese, *Behind Closed Doors: The Art of Hans Bellmer*, Berkeley, University of California Press, 2001

Limbour, Georges, *Hérold*, Paris, Les Lettres Nouvelles, 1949

Loeb, Pierre, *Regards sur la peinture*, Paris, Librairie-Galerie La Hune, 1950

Lomas, David, *The Haunted Self: Surrealism, Psychoanalysis, Subjectivity*, New Haven and London, Yale University Press, 2000

McGrath, William J., *Freud's Discovery of Psychoanalysis: The Poetics of Hysteria*, Ithaca, Cornell University Press, 1986

Mahon, Alyce, 'Outrage aux bonnes moeurs: Jean-Jacques Lebel and the Marquis de Sade', in *Jean-Jacques Lebel, Bilder, Skulpturen, Installationen*, exh. cat., pp.93–112

—, 'Twist the Body Red: The Lifewriting of Unica Zürn', *n.paradoxa: international feminist art journal*, vol.3, Jan 1999, pp.56–65

—, 'The Poetic Jouissance of André Masson', in Khalfa (ed.), *The Dialogue between Painting and Poetry*, pp.83–104

—, 'Staging Desire' in Mundy and Ades (eds), *Surrealism: Desire Unbound*, pp.277–91

—, 'Pierre Klossowski, Theo-Pornologer', critical introduction in Wilson (ed.), *Pierre Klossowski, The Decadence of the Nude/La décadence du Nu*, pp.35–101

—, 'Hans Bellmer's Libidinal Politics', in Spiteri and LaCoss, pp.246–66

Maitron, Jean, *Le Mouvement anarchiste en France*, Paris, François Maspero, 1983

Man Ray, *Self Portrait* (1964), Boston, Little, Brown/New York Graphic Society, 1988

Maran, Rita, *Torture: the Role of Ideology in the French-Algerian War*, New York and London, Praeger, 1989

Marchand, Jean-José, 'Le Surréalisme de langue française', *Gazette des lettres*, 28 June 1947, p.11

Marcuse, Herbert, *One Dimensional Man: Studies in the Ideology of Advanced Industrial Society*, Boston, Beacon Press, 1964

—, *Eros and Civilization: A Philosophical Inquiry into Freud* (1955), London, Routledge, 1998

Marks, Elaine and Isabelle de Courtivon (eds), *New French Feminism: an Anthology*, Amherst, MA, University of Massachusetts Press, 1980

Masson, André, *André Masson: Le Rebelle du Surréalisme – Ecrits*, Paris, Collection Savoir, 1972

—, *Vagabond du Surréalisme*, Paris, Editions St Germain-des-Prés, 1975

—, *Anatomie de mon univers*, Marseilles, André Dimanche, 1988

—, *Les années surréaliste: correspondance 1916–42*, Paris, La Manufacture, 1990

Matthews, John Herbert, *Benjamin Péret*, Boston, Twayne Publishers, 1975

—, *Joyce Mansour*, Amsterdam, Rodopi, 1985

Matta, exh. cat., New York, Museum of Modern Art, 1957

Matta Hom'mere, exh. cat., Cambridge, Kettles Yard Gallery, 1978

Matta: The Logic of Hallucination, exh. cat., London, Arts Council of Great Britain, 1984

Matta, exh. cat., Paris, Musée National d'Art Moderne, 1985

Mileaf, Janine, 'Body to Politics. Surrealist Exhibition of the Tribal and the Modern at the anti-Imperialist Exhibition and the Galerie Charles Ratton', *Res*, no.40, Autumn 2001, pp.239–55

Mitchell, Clio, '"Secrets de l'art magique Surréaliste": Magic and the Myth of the Artist-magician in Surrealist Aesthetic Theory and Practice', PhD dissertation, Courtauld Institute of Art, University of London, 1994

Mitrani, Nora, *Rose au Coeur Violet*, Paris, Editeur Terrain Vague/Losfeld, 1988

Monnerot, Jules, *La Poésie Moderne et le sacré*, Paris, Gallimard, 1945

Morin, Edgar, Claude Lefort, Jean-Marc Coudray, *Mai 68: La Brèche: Premières réflexions sur les évènements*, Paris, Fayard, 1968

Morris, Frances (ed.), *Paris Post War: Art and Existentialism 1945–55*, exh. cat., London, Tate Gallery, 1993

Mortimer, Elizabeth, *The Rise and Fall of the French Communist Party, 1920–1947*, London, Faber and Faber, 1984

Morton, Patricia A., *Hybrid Modernities: Architecture and Representation at the 1931 Colonial Exposition, Paris*, Cambridge, MA and London, MIT Press, 2000

Motherwell, Robert, *The Dada Painters and Poets*, New York, George Wittenborn, 1951

Mulvey, Laura, *Fetishisms and Curiosity*, London, BFI, 1996

Mundy, Jennifer and Dawn Ades (eds), *Surrealism: Desire Unbound*, London, Tate Publishing; Princeton University Press, 2001

Nadeau, Maurice, *The History of Surrealism* (1945), trans. Richard Howard, Harmondsworth, Penguin, 1973

Nash, Steven A. (ed.), *Picasso and the War Years*, London and New York, Thames & Hudson/Fine Arts Museum of San Francisco, 1998

Naumann, Francis M. and Hector Obalk (eds), *Affect/Marcel: The Selected Correspondence of Marcel Duchamp*, trans. Jill Taylor, London, Thames & Hudson, 2000

Nochlin, Linda, *The Politics of Vision. Essays on Nineteenth-Century Art and Society* (1989), London, Thames & Hudson, 1991

Noël, Bernard, *André Masson, la Chair de regard*, Paris, Gallimard, 1993

Novick, Peter, *The Resistance versus Vichy: The Purge of the Collaborator in Liberated France*, London, Chatto and Windus, 1968

O'Doherty, Brian, *Inside the White Cube: The Ideology of the Gallery Space* (1976), Santa Monica, Lapis Press, 1986

Paligot, Carole Reynaud, *Parcours politique des surréalistes 1919–1969*, Paris, CNRS Editions, 2001

Parrot, Nicole, *Mannequins*, London, Academy Editions, 1983

Paulhan, Jean, 'Héros du monde occidental' in *La Nouvelle Revue française, April 1967: André Breton, 1896–1966: Hommages, témoignages, l'oeuvre*, Paris, Gallimard, 1990, pp.9–11

Penrose, Antony, *Roland Penrose, The Friendly Surrealist*, London, Prestel, 2001

Péret, Benjamin, *La Parole est à Péret*, New York, Editions Surréalistes, 1943; republished with some changes as introduction to *Anthologie des mythes, légendes et contes populaires d'Amérique*, Paris, Editions Albin Michel, 1960; also republished in *Le Déshonneur des poètes, précédé de la Parole est à Péret*, Paris, Editions Pauvert, 1965

—, *Oeuvres Complètes*, 6 vols, Paris, José Corti, 1969–92

Petit, Pierre, *Molinier, Une Vie d'Enfer*, Paris, Editions Jean-Jacques Pauvert/Editions Ramsay, 1992

Philpot, Clive and Lynne Tillman, 'Interview with Charles Henri Ford: When Art and Literature Come Together', *Franklin Furnace Flu*, December 1980, p.1

Picasso, Pablo, *Desire Caught by the Tail* (1945), trans. Roland Penrose, London, Calder and Boyars, 1970

Picon, Gaëton, 'Le Surréalisme et l'espoir', *Gazette des Lettres*, 28 June 1947, pp.8–9

Pierre, José, *Surréalisme et anarchie*, Paris, Plasma, 1983

— (ed.), *Tracts Surréalistes et Déclarations Collectives, Tome I, 1922–1939*, Paris, Le Terrain Vague, 1980

—, *Tracts Surréalistes et Déclarations Collectives, Tome II, 1940–69*, Paris, Le Terrain Vague, 1982

—, *Investigating Sex: Surrealist Discussions*

1928–1932 (1990), trans. Malcolm Imrie, London and New York, Verso, 1992

Plank, William, *Sartre and Surrealism*, Ann Arbor, MI, UMI Research Press, 1981

Pluchart, François, 'Le Surréalisme a l'assaut de la société', *Combat*, 13 December 1965, p.9

Polizzotti, Mark, *Revolution of the Mind: The Life of André Breton*, London, Bloomsbury, 1995

Poulat, Emile, 'Les Cahiers manuscrits de Fourier, étude historique et inventaire raisonné', Paris, Editions de Minuit, 1957

Reader, Keith A. and Khursheed Wadia, *The May 1968 Events in France: Reproductions and Interpretations*, London, Macmillan, 1993

Restany, Pierre, *The New Realists*, exh. cat., Milan, Galerie Apollinaire, 1960

Richardson, Michael and Krzysztof Fijalkowski (eds and trans.), *Refusal of the Shadow, Surrealism and the Caribbean*, London, Verso, 1996

—, *Surrealism Against the Current: Tracts and Declarations*, London, Pluto Press, 2001

Rioux, Gilles, 'A propos des Expositions internationales du Surréalisme, un document de 1947 et quelques considérations', *Gazette des Beaux-Arts*, vol.120, no.1311, April 1978, pp.163–71

Rioux, Jean-Pierre, *The Fourth Republic, 1944–1958* (1980), trans. Godfrey Rogers, Cambridge University Press, 1987

Rosemont, Penelope (ed.), *Surrealist Women: An International Anthology*, Austin, University of Texas Press, 1998

Ross, Kristin, *Fast Cars, Clean Bodies*, Cambridge, MA and London, MIT Press, 1995

Rousso, Henry, *The Vichy Syndrome: History and Memory in France since 1944*, trans. Arthur Goldhammer, Cambridge, MA, Harvard University Press, 1991

—, 'L'Epuration en France, une histoire inachevée', *Vingtième Siècle: revue d'histoire*, no.33, January–March 1992, pp.78–105

Sade, D.A.F. de, *L'Aigle mademoiselle*, letters, prefaced by Gilbert Lely, Paris, Editions Georges Artigues, June 1949

—, *La Vanille et la manille*, unedited letter to Madame de Sade, Paris, Collection Drosera, I, June 1950 (with five illustrations by Hérold)

—, *The 120 Days of Sodom, and Other Writings*, trans. Austryn Wainhouse and Richard Seaver, New York, Grove Press, 1966

Sadler, Simon, *The Situationist City*, Cambridge, MA and London, MIT Press, 1998

Safran, Yehuda (ed.), *Frederick Kiesler 1890–1965*, London, Architectural Association, 1989

Said, Edward W., *Orientalism, Western Conceptions of the Orient* (1987), London, Penguin, 1995

Sandford, Mariellen R. (ed.), *Happenings and Other Acts*, London, Routledge, 1995

Sartre, Jean-Paul, *Sculptures à n dimensions*, Paris, Editions Pierre à Feu, 1947

—, 'Victory', preface to Henri Alleg, *The Question*, trans. John Calder, New York, Braziller, 1958

—, *Essays in Existentialism* (1963), New York, Citadel Press, 1993

—, *What is Literature?* (1947), trans. David Caute, London, Routledge, 1993

Sauvageot, Jacques, Alain Geismar, Daniel Cohn-Bendit, Jean-Pierre Duteuil, *The Student Revolt: The Activists Speak*, trans. B. R. Brewster, London, Panther Books, 1968

Sawin, Martica, *Surrealism in Exile and the Beginning of the New York School*, Cambridge, MA and London, MIT Press, 1995

Schaffner, Ingrid, *Salvador Dali's Dream of Venus: The Surrealist Funhouse from the 1939 World's Fair*, New York, Princeton Architectural Press, 2002

Schaffner, Ingrid and Lisa Jacobs, *Julien Levy: Portrait of an Art Gallery*, Cambridge, MA and London, MIT Press, 1998

Schnapp, Alain and Pierre Vidal-Naquet, *Journal de la Commune Étudiante, Textes et Documents Novembre 1967–Juin 1968*, Paris, Editions du Seuil, 1969

Schuster, Jean, *Archives 57–68: Bataille pour le Surréalisme*, Paris, Eric Losfeld, 1969

Schwartz, Paul Waldo, 'Breton and Allies with New Protest', *The New York Times International Edition*, 14 December 1965

Schwitters, Kurt, 'Merz composite work of Art' (1921), in Robert Motherwell (ed.), *The Dada Painters and Poets*, New York, George Wittenborn, 1951, pp.62–3

Semin, Didier, *Victor Brauner dans les collections du MNAM-CCI*, Paris, Filipacchi, 1996

Showalter, Elaine, *The Female Malady: Women, Madness and English Culture 1830–1980* (1987), London, Virago, 1991

Silverman, Kaja, *The Acoustic Mirror: The Female Voice in Psychoanalysis and Cinema*, Bloomington, Indiana University Press, 1988

Sims, Lowery Stokes, *Wifredo Lam and the International Avant-Garde, 1923–1982*, Austin, University of Texas Press, 2002

Spector, Jack, *The Aesthetics of Freud: A Study in Psychoanalysis and Art*, London, Allen Lane, 1972

—, *Surrealist Art and Writing 1919–1939, The Gold of Time*, Cambridge University Press, 1997

Spies, Warner, et al., *La Révolution Surréaliste*, exh. cat., Paris, Editions du Centre Pompidou, 2002

Spiteri, Raymond and Donald LaCoss (eds), *Surrealism, Politics and Culture*, Aldershot, Ashgate, 2003

Stallybrass, Peter and Allon White, *The Politics and Poetics of Transgression*, Ithaca, Cornell University Press; London, Methuen, 1986

Staniszewski, Mary Anne, *The Power of Display: A History of Exhibition Installation at the Museum of Modern Art*, Cambridge, MA and London, MIT Press, 1998

Stich, Sidra, et al., *Anxious Visions: Surrealist Art*, Berkeley, University Art Museum, 1990

Stora, Benjamin, *La gangrène et l'oubli: La mémoire de la guerre d'Algérie*, Paris, La Découverte, 1991

Suleiman, Susan Rubin, *Subversive Intent, Gender, Politics and the Avant-Garde*, Cambridge, MA, Harvard University Press, 1990

— (ed.), *The Female Body in Western Culture*, Cambridge, MA, Harvard University Press, 1985

Les Surréalistes en exil et les débuts de l'école de New York, exh. cat., Strasbourg, Musée d'Art Moderne et Contemporain, 2000

Surya, Michel, *Georges Bataille: La Mort à l'oeuvres*, Paris, Gallimard, 1992

Tarenne, Vivianne, *Donations Daniel Cordier: Le Regard d'un Amateur*, Paris, Musée National d'Art Moderne, 1989

Tashjian, Dickran, *A Boatload of Madmen: Surrealism and the American Avant-Garde 1920–50*, London and New York, Thames & Hudson, 1995

Theweleit, Klaus, *Male Fantasies, vol.I: Women, Floods, Bodies, History*, trans. E. Carter and C. Turner, Minneapolis, University of Minnesota Press, 1992

Thirion, André, *Revolutionaries without a Revolution* (1972), trans. Joachim Neugroschel, London, Cassell, 1975

Thompson, C.W. (ed.), *L'Autre et le sacré: Surréalisme, cinéma, ethnologie*, Paris, Editions L'Harmattan

Tomkins, Calvin, *Duchamp. A Biography*, New York, Henry Holt, 1996; London, Chatto and Windus, 1997

Tschumi, Bernard, 'Architecture and its Double', in *Architectural Design*, vol.48, nos 2–3, 1978, pp.87–95

Tzara, Tristan, *Le Surréalisme et l'après-guerre* (1948), Paris, Editions Nagel, 1966

Une nouvelle figuration, exh. cat., Paris, Galerie Matthias Fels, 1961

Utley, Gertje R., *Picasso, the Communist Years*, New Haven and London, Yale University Press, 2000

Vail, Karole P. B., et al., 'Peggy Guggenheim: Life and Art' in *Peggy Guggenheim, A Celebration*, exh. cat., New York, Guggenheim Museum, 1998

Vailland, Roger, *Le Surréalisme contre la Révolution* (1948), Paris, Editions Complexe, 1988

Vaneigem, Raoul, *Traité de savoir-vivre à l'usage des jeunes générations*, Paris, Gallimard, 1967

Veseley, Dalibor, 'Surrealism, Myth and Modernity' in *Architectural Design*, vol.48, nos 2–3, 1978, pp.87–95

Viatte, Germain, *Aftermath: France 1945–1954, New Images of Man*, exh. cat., London, Barbican Art Gallery, 1982

Victor Brauner, exh. cat., Paris, Musée National d'Art Moderne, 1996

Vidler, Anthony, *The Architectural Uncanny, Essays in the Modern Unhomely* (1992), Cambridge, MA and London, MIT Press, 1999

Viénet, René, *Enragés and Situationists in the Occupation Movement, France, May '68* (1968), New York, Autonomedia; London, Rebel Press, 1992

Waldberg, Patrick, 'Le Surréalisme et ses affinités à Paris', *Quadrum*, no.VIII, 1960, pp.135–42

—, 'Le Surréalisme, Sources – Histoire – Affinités', *Le Surréalisme*, exh. cat., Paris, Galerie Charpentier, 1964

Wall, Irwin, *The United States and the Making of Post-War France, 1945–1954*, Cambridge University Press, 1991

Warnod, André, *Exposition 37, La Vie flamboyante des expositions, Renseignements pratiques avec la carte détaillée de l'exposition*, Paris, Les Editions de France, 1937

Webb, Peter, *The Erotic Arts*, London, Secker and Warburg, 1983

Webb, Peter and Robert Short, *Hans Bellmer*, London, Quartet Books, 1985

Weld, Jacqueline Bograd, *Peggy: The Wayward Guggenheim*, New York, E.P. Dutton; London, Bodley Head, 1986

Wilson, Sarah, 'Paris Post War: In Search of the Absolute' in Morris (ed.), *Paris Post War: Art and Existentialism 1945–55*, pp.25–52

Wilson, Sarah (ed.), *Pierre Klossowski, The Decadence of the Nude/La décadence du Nu*, London, Black Dog Publishing, 2002

Wilson, Sarah, et al., *Paris: Capital of the Arts 1900–1968*, exh. cat., London, Royal Academy of Arts, 2002

Wollen, Peter, *Raiding the Icebox: Essays in Twentieth Century Culture*, London, Verso, 1993

List of Illustrations

Measurements are given in centimetres, followed by inches, height before width before depth, unless otherwise stated.

page 1 Jean Benoît in costume for *Execution of the Testament of the Marquis de Sade*, EROS exhibition, Galerie Daniel Cordier, Paris, 1959. Photo Gilles Ehrmann

page 2 The Surrealist artists who organized the 'Surrealism in 1947' exhibition, Galerie Maeght, Paris, 1947. Photo © les films de l'équinoxe–fonds photographique Denise Bellon

page 3 Jacques Hérold, 'Sade' playing card, *Le Jeu de Marseille*/Marseilles Deck of Cards, 1940, published in *VVV*, nos 2–3, March 1943, p.88. © ADAGP, Paris and DACS, London 2005

1 'International Surrealist Exhibition', Galerie Beaux-Arts, Paris, 1938. Photo © les films de l'équinoxe–fonds photographique Denise Bellon

2 Cover of La Main à Plume's *The Conquest of the World by the Image (La Conquête du monde par l'image)*, 24 April 1942, with Pablo Picasso's *Head of a Bull*, 1942. Private Collection. © Succession Picasso/DACS 2005

3 The Surrealists at the Désert de Retz, near Saint-Nom-la-Bretéche, April 1960. Photo © les films de l'équinoxe–fonds photographique Denise Bellon

4 Cover of *Le Pavé*, May 1968

5 Mimi Parent, *Français, Me Voila!*, May 1968. Poster. Collection Mimi Parent, Paris

6 *La Révolution surréaliste*, no.1, 1 December 1924, p.17

7 EROS exhibition, Galerie Daniel Cordier, Paris, 1959. Photo © les films de l'équinoxe–fonds photographique Denise Bellon

8 *La Révolution surréaliste*, no.1, 1 December 1924. Cover with three photographs by Man Ray. © Man Ray Trust/ADAGP, Paris and DACS, London 2005

9 National Institute for Political Sciences, Paris, May 1968. Photo Bruno Barbey/Magnum Photos

10 André Masson, *Mannequin with Bird Cage*, 1938. Photo © les films de l'équinoxe–fonds photographique Denise Bellon. Masson: © ADAGP, Paris and DACS, London 2005

11 Cover for 'Degenerate Art' (Entartete Kunst) exhibition catalogue, Munich 1937

12 View from the Palais de Chaillot, 'International Exhibition of Arts and Technology applied to Modern Life', Paris, 1937. Edmond Labbé, *Rapport général, exposition internationale des arts et techniques dans la vie moderne*, Imprimerie Nationale, Paris, 1938–40. Research Library, Getty Research Institute, Los Angeles

13 Room Three at the 'Degenerate Art' exhibition, Munich, 1937

14 'Degenerate Art' exhibition catalogue, Munich, 1937. Page showing Max Ernst, *The Beautiful Gardener* (also known as *Creation of Eve*), 1923; Willi Baumeister, *Figure with Pink Stripe III*, 1920 and Johannes Molzahn, *Twins*, *c*.1930. Ernst: © ADAGP, Paris and DACS, London 2005. Baumeister: © DACS 2005

15 Hans Bellmer, *The Doll*, 1934, printed 1936. Vintage gelatin silver print, 11.7 × 7.7 (4⅝ × 3). Collection Ubu Gallery, New York and Galerie Berinson, Berlin. © ADAGP, Paris and DACS, London 2005

16 Cover of *Vu et Lu*, no.492, 18 August 1937

17 View of the German and Russian pavilions at the 'International Exhibition of Arts and Technology applied to Modern Life', Paris, 1937

18 Pablo Picasso, *Guernica*, 1937. Oil on canvas, 349 × 777 (137⅜ × 305⅞). Museo Nacional Centro de Arte Reina Sophía, Madrid. On permanent loan from the Museo del Prado, Madrid. © Succession Picasso/DACS 2005

19 Joan Miró, *The Reaper (Catalan Peasant in Revolt)*, 1937 (destroyed). Oil on celotex panels, 550 × 365 (216½ × 143¾). Installation at the Spanish pavilion, 'International Exhibition of Arts and Technology applied to Modern Life', Paris, 1937. © Successio Miró, DACS 2005

20 Robert Couturier mannequins with Lanvin gowns in the Fashion pavilion at the 'International Exhibition of Arts and Technology applied to Modern Life', Paris, 1937. Photo © les films de l'équinoxe–fonds photographique Denise Bellon. Couturier: © ADAGP, Paris and DACS, London 2005

21 Hall 4 at the 'Chefs-d'oeuvre de l'art français' exhibition, Paris, 1937. Edmond Labbé, *Rapport général, exposition internationale des arts et techniques dans la vie moderne*, Imprimerie Nationale, Paris, 1938–40. Research Library, Getty Research Institute, Los Angeles

22 Salvador Dalí, *Rainy Taxi*, 1938. 'International Surrealist Exhibition', Galerie Beaux-Arts, Paris, 1938. Photo © les films de l'équinoxe–fonds photographique Denise Bellon. © Salvador Dalí, Gala-Salvador Dalí Foundation, DACS, London 2005

23 Invitation to the 'International Surrealist Exhibition', Galerie Beaux-Arts, Paris, 1938

24 Salvador Dalí, *Rainy Taxi*, 1938. 'International Surrealist Exhibition', Galerie Beaux-Arts, Paris, 1938. Photo Josef Breitenbach Archive, Center for Creative Photography, University of Arizona. © The Josef Breitenbach Trust, New York. © Salvador Dalí, Gala-Salvador Dalí Foundation, DACS, London 2005

25 Oscar Dominguez, *Never*, 1937. 'International Surrealist Exhibition', Galerie Beaux-Arts, Paris, 1938. Photo © les films de l'équinoxe–fonds photographique Denise Bellon. Dominguez: © ADAGP, Paris and DACS, London 2005

26 André Breton, *Object Chest*, 1938. 'International Surrealist Exhibition', Galerie Beaux-Arts, Paris, 1938. Photo Josef Breitenbach Archive, Center for Creative Photography, University of Arizona. © The Josef Breitenbach Trust, New York. Breton: © ADAGP, Paris and DACS, London 2005

27 Kurt Seligmann, *Ultra Furniture*, 1938. 'International Surrealist Exhibition', Galerie Beaux-Arts, Paris, 1938. Unattributed photograph courtesy of Orange County Citizens Foundation, Sugar Loaf, New York

28 Meret Oppenheim, *Object (Le Déjeuner en fourrure)*, 1936. Fur-covered cup, saucer and spoon, cup diameter 11 (4⅜), saucer diameter 24 (9½), spoon length 20 (7⅞). Museum of Modern Art, New York. © DACS 2005

29 The 'Exhibition of Surrealist Objects', Galerie Charles Ratton, Paris, May 1936. Collection Guy Ladrière, Paris. © Man Ray Trust/ADAGP, Paris and DACS, London 2005

30 The 'Exhibition of Surrealist Objects', Galerie Charles Ratton, Paris, May 1936. Collection Guy Ladrière, Paris. © Man Ray Trust/ADAGP, Paris and DACS, London 2005

31 Wolfgang Paalen, *Articulated Cloud*, 1938. Bath sponge, height 50 (19⅝). Photo Moderna Museet, Stockholm

32 A spectator looking at paintings with a flashlight at the 'International Surrealist Exhibition', Galerie Beaux-Arts, Paris, 1938. Photo Josef Breitenbach Archive, Center for Creative Photography, University of Arizona. © The Josef Breitenbach Trust, New York

33 The 'International Surrealist Exhibition', Galerie Beaux-Arts, Paris, 1938. Max Ernst's *Widow Mannequin* in foreground and a mannequin by Joan Miró behind. Photo Raoul Ubac. Ernst: © ADAGP, Paris and DACS, London 2005. © Successio Miró, DACS 2005

34 Sonia Mossé, *Untitled*, 1938. Mannequin with mixed media. Ubu Gallery, New York and Galerie Berinson, Berlin. Photo Gaston Paris

35 Man Ray, *Rrose Sélavy*, *c*.1921. Gelatin silver print, 21 × 17.3 (8¼ × 6¾). Philadelphia Museum of Art. The Samuel S. White 3rd and Vera White Collection. © Man Ray Trust/ADAGP, Paris and DACS, London 2005. © Succession Marcel Duchamp/ADAGP, Paris and DACS, London 2005

36 Marcel Duchamp, Rrose Sélavy mannequin, 1938. Wax mannequin dressed in Duchamp's clothes, red electric lamp. Photo Raoul Ubac. © Succession Marcel Duchamp/ADAGP, Paris and DACS, London 2005

37 The 'International Surrealist Exhibition', Galerie Beaux-Arts, Paris, 1938. Photo Josef Breitenbach Archive, Center for Creative Photography, University of Arizona. © The Josef Breitenbach Trust, New York

38 André Masson, *Gradiva*, 1939. Oil on canvas, 97 × 130 (38¼ × 51⅛). Private Collection. © ADAGP, Paris and DACS, London 2005

39 Oscar Dominguez, *Mannequin*, 1938. 'International Surrealist Exhibition', Galerie Beaux-Arts, Paris, 1938. Photo Raoul Ubac. Dominguez: © ADAGP, Paris and DACS, London 2005

40 Hans Bellmer, *The Doll* (*La Poupée)*, 1935. Vintage gelatin silver print, 66 × 66 (26 × 26). Ubu Gallery, New York and Galerie Berinson, Berlin. © ADAGP, Paris and DACS, London 2005

41 Roberto Matta, 'Mathématique sensible – Architecture du temps', illustration in *Minotaure*, no.11, Spring 1938, p.43. © ADAGP, Paris and DACS, London 2005

42 Hélène Vanel performing *L'Acte manqué* (Unconsummated Act), at the 'International Surrealist Exhibition', Galerie Beaux-Arts, Paris, 1938. Photo Keystone/Katz

43 Main grotto, 'International Surrealist Exhibition', Galerie Beaux-Arts, Paris, 1938. Photo Josef Breitenbach Archive, Center for Creative Photography, University of Arizona. © The Josef Breitenbach Trust, New York

44 Jean-Martin Charcot's 'Augustine' (one of six), from André Breton and Louis Aragon 'Les Attitudes Passionelles en 1878', *La Révolution surréaliste*, no.11, 15 March 1928

45 Joan Miró, *Le Corps de ma Brune*, 1925. Oil on canvas, 129.8 × 95.8 (51⅛ × 37¾). Private Collection. © Successio Miró, DACS 2005

46 Roland Penrose, *Real Woman*, 1937. Paper, collage, decalcomania, frottage and pencil on

card, 43.3 × 69 (17 × 27⅛). Copyright © The Roland Penrose Estate, England 2005. All rights reserved
47 Salvador Dalí, *Sleep*, 1937. Oil on canvas, 51 × 78 (20⅛ × 30⅝). Private Collection. © Salvador Dalí, Gala-Salvador Dalí Foundation, DACS, London 2005
48 René Magritte, *The Healer*, 1937. Oil on canvas, 92 × 65 (36¼ × 25⅝). Private Collection. © ADAGP, Paris and DACS, London 2005
49 Roland Penrose, *Seeing is Believing (l'Île Invisible)*, 1937. Oil on canvas. Copyright © The Roland Penrose Estate, England 2005. All rights reserved
50 André Breton, Diego Rivera and Léon Trotsky, Mexico, July 1938. *Minotaure*, nos 12–13, May 1939, p.48. Photo Fritz Bach
51 Albert Speer, Adolf Hitler and Arno Breker on the esplanade of the Palais de Chaillot, Paris, 23 June 1940. National Archives and Records Administration, Maryland, USA
52 Lee Miller, photograph of Leonora Carrington and Max Ernst at St Martin d'Ardèche, Summer 1939. Photograph © Lee Miller Archives, England, 2005. All rights reserved
53 Max Ernst, *The Robing of the Bride*, 1940. Oil on canvas, 130 × 96 (51⅛ × 37¾). Peggy Guggenheim Collection, Venice. © ADAGP, Paris and DACS, London 2005
54 Vichy police on patrol in Marseilles, 1940. Hiram Bingham Collection, United States Holocaust Memorial Museum
55 Photograph of Varian Fry, Marseilles, Autumn 1940. Collection Varian Fry Papers, Rare Book & Manuscript Library, Columbia University/Friends of Le Chambon
56 Wifredo Lam, Jacques Hérold, André Breton and Oscar Dominguez in front of Villa Air Bel, Marseilles, 1941. Photo André Gomes
57 Varian Fry (right foreground), André Breton (centre) and friends at Villa Air Bel, Marseilles, Winter 1940–1. Collection Varian Fry Papers, Rare Book & Manuscript Library, Columbia University/Friends of Le Chambon
58 André Masson, *Portrait of André Breton and Jacqueline Lamba*, 1941. Ink drawing, 60 × 47 (23⅝ × 18½). Private Collection. © ADAGP, Paris and DACS, London 2005
59 André Masson. *The Roughneck Soldier*, 1940–1. Pastels, 33 × 25.5 (13 × 10). Private Collection. © ADAGP, Paris and DACS, London 2005
60 Victor Brauner, André Breton, Oscar Dominguez, Jacques Hérold, Wifredo Lam and Jacqueline Lamba, *Collective Drawing*, 1940. Ink, colour pencils and collage on paper, 31 × 48 (12¼ × 18⅞). Private Collection. © ADAGP, Paris and DACS, London 2005
61 Victor Brauner, André Breton, Oscar Dominguez, Max Ernst, Jacques Hérold, Wifredo Lam, Jacqueline Lamba and André Masson, *Le Jeu de Marseille/Marseilles Deck of Cards*, reproduced in *VVV*, New York, nos 2–3, March 1943, p.88. © ADAGP, Paris and DACS, London 2005
62 Wifredo Lam, 'Alice' card, *Le Jeu de Marseille/Marseilles Deck of Cards*, reproduced in *VVV*, New York, nos 2–3, March 1943, p.88. © ADAGP, Paris and DACS, London 2005
63 Wifredo Lam, 1941. Illustration in André Breton's *Fata Morgana*, 1942. Research Library, Getty Research Institute, Los Angeles. © ADAGP, Paris and DACS, London 2005
64 Marcel Duchamp, *La Boîte-en-valise*, c.1935–41 (1941 version). Assemblage, dimensions variable. Philadelphia Museum of Art, Walter and Louise Arensberg Collection. © Succession Marcel Duchamp/ADAGP, Paris and DACS, London 2005
65 André Masson, illustration in André Breton's *Martinique charmeuse de serpents*, Paris, Sagittaire, 1948, p.95. Masson: © ADAGP, Paris and DACS, London 2005
66 Salvador Dalí, *Dream of Venus*, 1939. Pavilion at the New York World's Fair 1939–40. Photo Eric Schaal. Courtesy Jan Van Der Donk Rare Books. © Salvador Dalí, Gala-Salvador Dalí Foundation, DACS, London 2005
67 Frederick Kiesler in the Surrealist Gallery, Art of this Century gallery, New York, 1942. Archive of the Kiesler Foundation Vienna. © Austrian Frederick and Lillian Kiesler Private Foundation. Photo Berenice Abbott
68 Hans Richter and unknown lady in front of Joan Miró's *Seated Woman II* in the Surrealist Gallery, Art of this Century gallery, New York, 1942. Archive of the Kiesler Foundation Vienna. © Austrian Frederick and Lillian Kiesler Private Foundation. Photo Berenice Abbott. © Successio Miró, DACS 2005
69 *Vision Machine* for Marcel Duchamp's *Boîte-en-valise* in the Kinetic Gallery, Art of this Century gallery, New York, 1942. Archive of the Kiesler Foundation Vienna. © Austrian Frederick and Lillian Kiesler Private Foundation. Photo Berenice Abbott. © Succession Marcel Duchamp/ADAGP, Paris and DACS, London 2005
70 Max Ernst and his collection of Hopi and Zuñi Kachina dolls. Published in *View*, Max Ernst special issue, Spring 1942. Photo James Thrall Soby
71 Cover of *View*, Marcel Duchamp special issue, March 1945, series v, no.1. © Succession Marcel Duchamp/ADAGP, Paris and DACS, London 2005
72 Cover of *VVV*, no.1, June 1942, designed by Max Ernst. © ADAGP, Paris and DACS, London 2005
73 Marcel Duchamp and Frederick Kiesler, *Sixteen Miles of String*, 1942. Installation at 'First Papers of Surrealism' exhibition, Co-ordinating Council of French Relief Societies, Whitelaw Reid Mansion, New York, 14 October – 7 November 1942. Vintage gelatin silver print, 19.4 × 25.4 (7⅝ × 10). Philadelphia Museum of Art. © Succession Marcel Duchamp/ADAGP, Paris and DACS, London 2005
74 Marcel Duchamp, cover of exhibition catalogue for 'First Papers of Surrealism', Co-ordinating Council of French Relief Societies, Whitelaw Reid Mansion, 14 October – 7 November 1942. © Succession Marcel Duchamp/ADAGP, Paris and DACS, London 2005
75 Roberto Matta, *The Earth is a Man*, 1942. Oil on canvas, 183 × 239 (72 × 94⅛). Private Collection, Chicago. © ADAGP, Paris and DACS, London 2005
76 Roberto Matta, *The Vertigo of Eros*, 1944. Oil on canvas, 195.7 × 251.6 (77 × 99). Collection Museum of Modern Art, New York. Photo © SCALA, Florence. The Museum of Modern Art, New York 2005. © ADAGP, Paris and DACS, London 2005
77 Hans Bellmer, *Portrait of Max Ernst*, 1941–2. Gouache. © ADAGP, Paris and DACS, London 2005
78 Man Ray, *Imaginary Portrait of the Marquais de Sade*, 1938. Oil on canvas with painted wood panel, 61.7 × 46.6 (24¼ × 18⅜). Menil Collection, Houston, Texas. © Man Ray Trust/ADAGP, Paris and DACS, London 2005
79 Hans Bellmer, *Céphalopode à la rose*, 1946. Crayon on paper, 12.5 × 18.5 (4⅞ × 7¼). Private Collection. © ADAGP, Paris and DACS, London 2005
80 Hans Bellmer, *Subterranean*, 1946. Drawing and gouache, 25 × 21 (10 × 8). Private Collection. © ADAGP, Paris and DACS, London 2005
81 Victor Brauner, *Self Portrait*, 1931. Oil on canvas, 22 × 16.2 (8⅝ × 6⅜). Musée National d'Art Moderne, Centre Georges Pompidou, Paris. © ADAGP, Paris and DACS, London 2005
82 Victor Brauner, *Portrait of Dina Vierny*, 1942. Ink and pastel on cardboard, 27 × 19 (10⅝ × 7½). Collection Dina Vierny. © ADAGP, Paris and DACS, London 2005
83 Victor Brauner, *Object of Counter-Bewitchment*, 1943. Assemblage, wax, clay, paper, wire, in a wooden box, 25 × 13.8 × 5.2 (9⅞ × 5⅜ × 2). Musée National d'Art Moderne, Centre Georges Pompidou, Paris. © ADAGP, Paris and DACS, London 2005
84 Jacques Hérold, *The Eagle Reader*, 1942. Oil on canvas, 63 × 47 (24¾ × 18½). Courtesy Galerie Patrice Trigano, Paris. © ADAGP, Paris and DACS, London 2005
85 Jacques Hérold, *Flayed Figures*, 1943. Gouache, 60 × 45 (23⅝ × 17¾). © ADAGP, Paris and DACS, London 2005
86 Pablo Picasso, *The Charnel House*, 1945. Oil and charcoal on canvas, 199.8 × 250.1 (78⅝ × 98½). Collection Museum of Modern Art, New York. © Succession Picasso/DACS 2005
87 Boris Taslitzky, *The Small Camp at Buchenwald*, 1945. Oil on canvas, 300 × 500 (118⅛ × 196⅞). Musée National d'Art Moderne, Centre Georges Pompidou, Paris. © ADAGP, Paris and DACS, London 2005
88 Jean Fautrier, *Hostage no.22*, 1944. Oil on paper, pasted on canvas, 27 × 22 (10⅝ × 8⅝). Private Collection. © ADAGP, Paris and DACS, London 2005
89 'Liberté est un mot vietnamien', April 1947, a tract written by Yves Bonnefoy, André Breton, Pierre Mabille and signed by twenty-five people
90 Etienne Martin, *Totem of Religions*, executed for the Room of Superstitions, 'Surrealism in 1947' exhibition, Galerie Maeght, Paris, 1947. The model also wears the 'false breast' from Marcel Duchamp and Enrico Donati's *Please Touch* luxury exhibition catalogue. Archive of the Kiesler Foundation Vienna. © Austrian Frederick and Lillian Kiesler Private Foundation. Martin: © ADAGP, Paris and DACS, London 2005. © Succession Marcel Duchamp/ADAGP, Paris and DACS, London 2005
91 Frederick Kiesler, *Anti-Taboo Figure*, Room of Superstitions, 'Surrealism in 1947' exhibition, Galerie Maeght, Paris, 1947. Archive of the Kiesler Foundation Vienna. © Austrian Frederick and Lillian Kiesler Private Foundation. Photo Willy Maywald. © Association Willy Maywald/ADAGP, Paris and DACS, London 2005
92 Installation view of the Room of Superstitions, 'Surrealism in 1947' exhibition, Galerie

Maeght, Paris, 1947. David Hare, *Anguished Man*; Roberto Matta, *The Whist*; Joan Miró, *The Rigid Cascade of Superstitions*; Yves Tanguy, *The Ladder Announcing Death*, all 1947. Archive of the Kiesler Foundation Vienna. © Austrian Frederick and Lillian Kiesler Private Foundation. Matta: © ADAGP, Paris and DACS, London 2005. © Successio Miró, DACS, 2005. Tanguy: © ARS, NY and DACS, London 2005. Photo Willy Maywald. © Association Willy Maywald/ADAGP, Paris and DACS, London 2005

93 Marcel Duchamp and Frederick Kiesler, *The Green Ray*, *c.*1947. 'Surrealism in 1947' exhibition, Galerie Maeght, Paris, 1947. Photo © les films de l'équinoxe-fonds photographique Denise Bellon. © Succession Marcel Duchamp/ ADAGP, Paris and DACS, London 2005

94 Alberto Giacometti, *Invisible Object (Hands Holding the Void)*, 1934–5. Bronze, 153 × 32 × 29 (60¼ × 12⅝ × 11⅜). National Gallery of Art, Washington, DC. © ADAGP, Paris and DACS, London 2005

95 Max Ernst, *Euclid*, 1945. Oil on canvas, 64 × 59 (25¼ × 23¼). Menil Collection, Houston, Texas. © ADAGP, Paris and DACS, London 2005

96 Jacques Hérold, *The Great Transparent One*, 1947. Bronze with patina, 183 × 44.5 × 39 (72 × 17½ × 15⅜). Collection Galerie Patrice Trigano, Paris. © ADAGP, Paris and DACS, London 2005

97 Wifredo Lam, altar to *The Hair of Falmer*, 'Surrealism in 1947' exhibition, Galerie Maeght, Paris, 1947. Photo © les films de l'équinoxe-fonds photographique Denise Bellon. Lam: © ADAGP, Paris and DACS, London 2005

98 André Breton, altar to *Léonie Aubois d'Ashby*, 'Surrealism in 1947' exhibition, Galerie Maeght, Paris, 1947. Photo © les films de l'équinoxe-fonds photographique Denise Bellon. Breton: © ADAGP, Paris and DACS, London 2005

99 Roberto Matta, altar to *Le Soigneur de Gravité*, 'Surrealism in 1947' exhibition, Galerie Maeght, Paris, 1947. Photo © les films de l'équinoxe-fonds photographique Denise Bellon. Matta: © ADAGP, Paris and DACS, London 2005

100 Victor Brauner, *The Lovers*, 1947. Oil on canvas, 92 × 73 (36¼ × 28¾). Musée National d'Art Moderne, Centre Georges Pompidou, Paris. © ADAGP, Paris and DACS, London 2005

101 Victor Brauner, altar to *The Secretary Bird or Serpentine*, 1947. 'Surrealism in 1947' exhibition, Galerie Maeght, Paris, 1947. Musée National d'Art Moderne, Centre Georges Pompidou, Paris. Courtesy Galerie Maeght. Photo Willy Maywald © Association Willy Maywald/ADAGP, Paris and DACS, London 2005. Brauner: © ADAGP, Paris and DACS, London 2005

102 Victor Brauner, *Wolf-table*, 1947. Wood and stuffed fox elements, 54 × 57 × 28.5 (21¼ × 22½ × 11¼). Musée National d'Art Moderne, Centre Georges Pompidou, Paris. © ADAGP, Paris and DACS, London 2005

103 Victor Brauner, *Ceremony*, 1947. Oil on cotton sheet laid down on canvas, 187.5 × 236.5 (73¾ × 93⅛). Private Collection. © ADAGP, Paris and DACS, London 2005

104 Enrico Donati, *Fist*, 1946. Bronze and glass eyes, 68.6 × 30.5 × 30.5 (27 × 12 × 12). Private Collection

105 Enrico Donati, *The Evil Eye*, 1947. Mixed media, 24.7 × 29 × 17.8 (9¾ × 11½ × 7). Private Collection

106 Maria Martins, *The Path, the Shadow, Too Long, Too Narrow*, 1946. Bronze, 143.4 × 179.7 × 59.4 (56½ × 70¾ × 23⅜). Museum of Modern Art, New York

107 Maria Martins, *The Impossible III*, 1946. Bronze, 80 × 82.5 × 53.3 (31½ × 32½ × 21). Museum of Modern Art, New York

108 Marcel Duchamp and Enrico Donati, *Please Touch*, 1947. Collage of foam rubber breast and velvet mounted on board, 25 × 22.8 (10 × 9). Cover of 'Surrealism in 1947' exhibition catalogue. © Succession Marcel Duchamp/ ADAGP, Paris and DACS, London 2005

109 Marianne Van Hirtum, Radovan Ivsic, André Breton, Jean-Jacques Lebel and Elisa Breton at the inauguration of the monument to Guillaume Apollinaire by Pablo Picasso, Paris 1959. Jean-Jacques Lebel Archive. Photo Pablo Volta. © Archives de la Fondation Eric Satie

110 Jean-Jacques Lebel, *André Breton and Guillaume Apollinaire (dream of 30 June 1956)*, 1956. Collage-drawing, 31 × 38 (12¼ × 15). Private Collection. Jean-Jacques Lebel Archive

111 Double page in *Front unique*, no.1, Milan, 1959

112 Déclaration sur le droit à l'insoumission dans la guerre d'Algérie', published in *Front unique*, no.2, Milan, 1960

113 Erró, Enrico Baj, Roberto Crippa, Gianni Dova, Jean-Jacques Lebel and Antonio Recalcati, *Le Grand Tableau antifasciste collectif*, 1960. Oil on canvas, 400 × 500 (157½ × 196⅞). Courtesy Musée d'Art Moderne et Contemporain de Strasbourg. Photo N. Fussler. Recalcati: © ADAGP, Paris and DACS, London 2005

114 Eugène Delacroix, *Death of Sardanapalus*, 1827–8. Oil on canvas, 392 × 496 (154⅜ × 195¼). The Louvre, Paris

115 Pablo Picasso, *Femmes d'Algers*, 1955. Oil on canvas, 114 × 146 (44⅞ × 57½). Mr and Mrs Victor Ganz Collection, New York. © Succession Picasso/DACS 2005

116 Poster for EROS exhibition, Paris, 1959. Private Collection. Courtesy Musée National des Beaux-Arts du Québec

117 Mimi Parent, *Masculine-Féminine*, 1959. Jacket, tie, hair and tie pin, 47.5 × 38 × 12.2 (18¾ × 15 × 4¾). Collection Isidore Ducasse. Courtesy Musée National des Beaux-Arts du Québec. Photo Patrick Altman

118 Photograph of Jean Benoît and Mimi Parent, Montréal 1943. Collection Mimi Parent, Paris

119 Invitation to *Execution of the Testament of the Marquis de Sade*, 2 December 1959. Private Collection. Courtesy Musée National des Beaux-Arts du Québec

120 Jean Benoît in costume for *Execution of the Testament of the Marquis de Sade*, Paris, December 1959

121 Jean Benoît, *Execution of the Testament of the Marquis de Sade*, Paris, December 1959. Photo Gilles Ehrmann

122 Jean Benoît with his costume for *Execution of the Testament of the Marquis de Sade* hanging on the interior wall of the EROS exhibition, Galerie Daniel Cordier, Paris, December 1959. Private Collection. Courtesy Musée National des Beaux-Arts du Québec

123 Hans Bellmer, *The Doll*, 1932–45. Painted wood, hair, shoes, socks, 61 × 170 × 51 (24 × 66⅞ × 20⅛). Musée National d'Art Moderne, Centre Georges Pompidou, Paris. © ADAGP, Paris and DACS, London 2005

124 Hans Bellmer, *Unica Ligotée*, 1958. Collaged photographs and gouache, 23.4 × 23.9 (9¼ × 9⅜). Reproduced as 'Keep Cool' on the cover of *Le Surréalisme, même*, no.4, 1958. Ubu Gallery, New York and Galerie Berinson, Berlin. © ADAGP, Paris and DACS, London 2005

125 Interior of EROS exhibition, Galerie Daniel Cordier, Paris 1959–60. Photo Henri Glaeser

126 Robert Rauschenberg, *Bed*, 1955. Mixed media, oil and graphite on fabric, 191.8 × 80 × 20.3 (75½ × 31½ × 8). © Robert Rauschenberg/VAGA, New York/DACS, London 2005

127 Joan Miró, *Sleeping Object*, 1936. Painted carob tree trunk with metal components, 64 × 44 × 26 (25¼ × 17⅜ × 10¼). © Successio Miró, DACS, 2005

128 René Magritte, *Invisible World*, 1954. Private Collection. © ADAGP, Paris and DACS, London 2005

129 Fetish wall, interior of EROS exhibition, Galerie Daniel Cordier, Paris 1959–60. Photo Roger van Hecke

130 Frida Kahlo, *Self-Portrait in Red and Gold Dress*, 1941. Oil on canvas, 39 × 27.5 (15⅜ × 10⅞). © 2005 Banco de México Diego Rivera & Frida Kahlo Museums Trust. Av. Cinco de Mayo no. 2, Col. Centro, Del. Cuauhtémoc 06059, México, D.F.

131 Meret Oppenheim, *The Couple*, 1956. Pair of brown boots attached at the toes, 20 × 40 × 15 (7⅞ × 15¾ × 5⅞). Private Collection. © DACS 2005

132 Adrien Dax, *Reliquary*. Assemblage. Private Collection. Courtesy Simone Dax

133 Meret Oppenheim, *Cannibal Feast*, 1959. Installation at the EROS exhibition, Galerie Daniel Cordier, Paris, 1959. Collection Centre Pompidou. Bibliothèque Kandinsky. Fonds Breton. Photo Roger van Hecke. Oppenheim: © DACS 2005

134 Mimi Parent, *Boîte alerte*, 1959. Cardboard box and mixed media, 47.5 × 38 × 12.2 (10⅝ × 15 × 4¾). Private Collection. Courtesy Musée National des Beaux-Arts du Québec. Photo Patrick Altman

135–136 The Surrealist 'The Truth About the Colonies' exhibition, Paris, September 1931, published in *Le Surréalisme au service de la révolution*, no.4, December 1931. Designed by Yves Tanguy, André Thirion, Paul Eluard and Louis Aragon. Research Library, Getty Research Institute, Los Angeles. Tanguy: © ARS, New York and DACS, London 2005

137 Jean Tinguely, *Metamatics no.17*, 1959. Mixed media sculpture. Trocadéro Esplanade, Biennale de Paris, October 1959. © ADAGP, Paris and DACS, London 2005

138 Cover of *Bief, jonction surréaliste*, numéro spécial 10–11, 15 February 1960

139 Ben Vautier, *Brushing Teeth after Mystery Food*, Fluxus Festival of Total Art and Comportment, Nice, 1963. Courtesy the Gilbert and Lila Silverman Fluxus Collection, Detroit

140 Pierre Faucheux, cover of 'Absolute Deviation' exhibition catalogue, Galerie de l'Oeil, Paris 1965

141 Jean-Jacques Lebel, *Parfum Grève Générale, Bonne Odeur*, 1960. Collage and paint on

board, 112 × 82.5 (44⅛ × 32½). Private Collection. Jean-Jacques Lebel Archive

142 Max Ernst, 'The Woman with a Hundred Heads Opens her August Sleeve', from *La Femme 100 têtes*, 1929. Collage on paper, 32.7 × 16.9 (12⅞ × 6⅝). Menil Collection, Houston, Texas. © ADAGP, Paris and DACS, London 2005

143 *Does-not-Computer (Le Désordinateur)*, collective work, at the 'Absolute Deviation' exhibition, Galerie de l'Oeil, Paris 1965–6. Photo Suzy Embo

144 Jean Benoît, *Antiquity at the End of the Twentieth Century*, 1965. Exhibited in the *Does-not-Computer* at the 'Absolute Deviation' exhibition, Galerie de l'Oeil, Paris 1965–6. Photo Marcel Lannoy

145 Cover of *L'Archibras*, no.1, April 1967, designed by Pierre Faucheux

146 Jean-Claude Silbermann, *The Consumer*, at the 'Absolute Deviation' exhibition, Galerie de l'Oeil, Paris 1965–6. Mattress, washing machine, television, refrigerator, taxi radio, sirens, number plate, wedding dress, veil and shoes, height 364.8 (144). Photo Marcel Lannoy. © the artist

147 Jean-Claude Silbermann, *The Consumer*, at the 'Absolute Deviation' exhibition, Galerie de l'Oeil, Paris 1965–6. Mattress, washing machine, television, refrigerator, taxi radio, sirens, number plate, wedding dress, veil and shoes, height 364.8 (144). Photo Marcel Lannoy. © the artist

148 Jean Benoît, *Bulldog of Maldoror*, 1959, at the 'Absolute Deviation' exhibition, Galerie de l'Oeil, Paris 1965–6. Photo Marcel Lannoy

149 Pierre Alechinsky, *Central Park*, 1965. Acrylic and india ink on paper mounted on canvas, 162 × 193 (64⅘ × 77⅕). Private Collection. © ADAGP, Paris and DACS, London 2005

150 Collaboration of artists, *Re-routed Arch*, 1965. 'Absolute Deviation' exhibition, Galerie de l'Oeil, Paris 1965–6. Photo Marcel Lannoy

151 Max Walter Svanberg, *Portrait of a Star*, 1965. Mixed media, 187 × 82 (73⅝ × 32¼)

152 Jean-Claude Silbermann, *Au Plaisir des demoiselles*, 1963–4. Oil on wood, 85 × 68 (33½ × 26¾). Private Collection. © the artist

153 Ugo Sterpini, *Armchair with Armed Hand*, 1965. Sculpted and silvered wood, revolver of an officer of the Deux-Siciles, 130 × 200 × 140 (52 × 80 × 56). Photo Marcel Lannoy

154 Robert Lagarde, *Brothel Towards the Courtyard: One Visits the Garden*, 1965. Mixed media, 100 × 43 × 17(39⅜ × 16⅞ × 6¾). Photo Marcel Lannoy

155 Jean Benoît as the *Necrophiliac*, at the opening night of the 'Absolute Deviation' exhibition, Galerie de l'Oeil, Paris, 1965. Photo Marcel Lannoy

156 Jean Benoît as the *Necrophiliac*, at the opening night of the 'Absolute Deviation' exhibition, Galerie de l'Oeil, Paris, 1965. Photo Marcel Lannoy

157 Jean Benoît as the *Necrophiliac*, at the opening night of the 'Absolute Deviation' exhibition, Galerie de l'Oeil, Paris, 1965

158 Demonstration of some 25,000–50,000 people from Place Denfert-Rochereau to the Tomb of the Unknown Soldier at L'Etoile, Paris, 7 May 1968. Photo Getty Images

159 Jean-Luc Godard, *Weekend*, 1967. Courtesy British Film Institute

160 Constant Nieuwenhuys, *New Babylon*, 1958. Ink on map, 200 × 300 (78¾ × 118⅛). Installation at Amsterdam Historical Museum. Photo Richard Kasiewicz. © documenta Archiv. © DACS 2005

161 Jean-Jacques Lebel, performance of *120 Minutes dedicated to the Divine Marquis*, 3rd Festival of Free Expression, Théâtre de la Chimère, Paris, April 1966. Jean-Jacques Lebel Archive. Photo François Massal

162 Jean-Jacques Lebel, performance of *120 Minutes dedicated to the Divine Marquis*, 3rd Festival of Free Expression, Théâtre de la Chimère, Paris, April 1966. Jean-Jacques Lebel Archive. Photo François Massal

163 Jean-Jacques Lebel, performance of *120 Minutes dedicated to the Divine Marquis*, 3rd Festival of Free Expression, Théâtre de la Chimère, Paris, April 1966. Jean-Jacques Lebel Archive. Photo François Massal

164 Jean-Jacques Lebel, performance of *120 Minutes dedicated to the Divine Marquis*, 3rd Festival of Free Expression, Théâtre de la Chimère, Paris, April 1966. Jean-Jacques Lebel Archive. Photo François Massal

165 Jean-Jacques Lebel at a demonstration in the Latin Quarter, Paris, 8 May 1968. Jean-Jacques Lebel Archive. Photo J.P. Rey

166 Jean-Luc Godard, *Pierrot le fou*, 1965. Courtesy British Film Institute

167 Students occupying the Odéon, Paris, May 1968. Photo Bruno Barbey/Magnum Photos

168 Daniel Cohn-Bendit in the Grand Amphithéâtre of the Sorbonne, 28 May 1968. Photo Bruno Barbey/Magnum Photos

169 Cover of *L'Archibras*, no.3, March 1968

170 'Faculté de Nanterre: la culture française sous la Ve République', dated 26 January 1968, in *L'Archibras*, no.3, March 1968, p.84

171 'Pour Cuba', tract printed in *L'Archibras*, no.3, March 1968

172 *La Beauté est dans la Rue (Beauty is in the Street)*, poster from May 1968. Courtesy Galerie Beaubourg, Paris

173 The Sorbonne occupied by students, May 1968. Photo Bruno Barbey/Magnum Photos

174 *Le Pavé*, May 1968, p.2

175 Roberto Matta, Paris, May 1968. Photo André Morain

176 Roberto Matta, *Disciples occupez la discipline pour une discipline révolutionnaire*, May, 1968. Black and white lithograph, 58 × 38 (22⅞ × 15). © ADAGP, Paris and DACS, London 2005

177 Protesters, Paris, May 1968. Photo Bruno Barbey/Magnum Photos

Every effort has been made to trace the copyright holders of the images contained in this book, and we apologise in advance for any unintentional omissions. We would be pleased to insert the appropriate acknowledgment in any subsequent edition of this publication.

Index

Page numbers in *italic* refer to illustrations